967.
9

Please renew/return items by last date
shown. Please call the number below:

Renewals and enquiries: 0300 123 4049

Textphone for hearing or
speech impaired users: 0300 123 4041

www.hertsdirect.org/librarycatalogue
L32

Mozambique

WORLD BIBLIOGRAPHICAL SERIES

General Editors:
Robert L. Collison (Editor-in-chief)
John J. Horton   Ian Wallace
Hans H. Wellisch   Ralph Lee Woodward, Jr.

Robert L. Collison (Editor-in-chief) is Professor emeritus, Library and Information Studies, University of California, Los Angeles, and was a President of the Society of Indexers. Following the war, he served as Reference Librarian for the City of Westminster and later became Librarian to the BBC. During his fifty years as a professional librarian in England and the USA, he has written more than twenty works on bibliography, librarianship, indexing and related subjects.

John H. Horton is Deputy Librarian of the University of Bradford and currently Chairman of its Academic Board of Studies in Social Sciences. He has maintained a longstanding interest in the discipline of area studies and its associated bibliographical problems, with special reference to European Studies. In particular he has published in the field of Icelandic and of Yugoslav studies, including the two relevant volumes in the World Bibliographical Series.

Ian Wallace is Professor of Modern Languages at Loughborough University of Technology. A graduate of Oxford in French and German, he also studied in Tübingen, Heidelberg and Lausanne before taking teaching posts at universities in the USA, Scotland and England. He specialises in East German affairs, especially literature and culture, on which he has published numerous articles and books. In 1979 he founded the journal *GDR Monitor*, which he continues to edit.

Hans H. Wellisch is Professor emeritus at the College of Library and Information Services, University of Maryland. He was President of the American Society of Indexers and was a member of the International Federation for Documentation. He is the author of numerous articles and several books on indexing and abstracting, and has published *The Conversion of Scripts* and *Indexing and Abstracting: an International Bibliography*. He also contributes frequently to *Journal of the American Society for Information Science, The Indexer* and other professional journals.

Ralph Lee Woodward, Jr. is Chairman of the Department of History at Tulane University, New Orleans, where he has been Professor of History since 1970. He is the author of *Central America, a Nation Divided*, 2nd ed. (1985), as well as several monographs and more than sixty scholarly articles on modern Latin America. He has also compiled volumes in the World Bibliographical Series on *Belize* (1980), *Nicaragua* (1983), and *El Salvador* (forthcoming). Dr. Woodward edited the Central American section of the *Research Guide to Central America and the Caribbean* (1985) and is currently editor of the Central American history section of the *Handbook of Latin American Studies*.

VOLUME 78

Mozambique

Compiler
Colin Darch
with the assistance of Calisto Pacheleke
in association with
the Centro de Estudos Africanos,
Universidade Eduardo Mondlane

CLIO PRESS
OXFORD, ENGLAND · SANTA BARBARA, CALIFORNIA
DENVER, COLORADO

British Library Cataloguing in Publication Data

Darch, Colin
Mozambique.——(World bibliographical series; no. 78)
1. Mozambique——Bibliography
I. Title II. Pacheleke, Calisto
III. Universidade Eduardo Mondlane. *Centro de Estudos Africanos*
IV. Series
016.967'9   Z3881

ISBN 1–85109–025–8

Clio Press Ltd.,
55 St. Thomas' Street,
Oxford OX1 1JG, England.

ABC-Clio Information Services,
Riviera Campus, 2040 Alameda Padre Serra,
Santa Barbara, Ca. 93103, USA.

Designed by Bernard Crossland
Typeset by Columns Design and Production Services, Reading, England.
Printed and bound in Great Britain by
Billing and Sons Ltd., Worcester.

THE WORLD BIBLIOGRAPHICAL SERIES

This series, which is principally designed for the English speaker, will eventually cover every country in the world, each in a separate volume comprising annotated entries on works dealing with its history, geography, economy and politics; and with its people, their culture, customs, religion and social organization. Attention will also be paid to current living conditions – housing, education, newspapers, clothing, etc. – that are all too often ignored in standard bibliographies; and to those particular aspects relevant to individual countries. Each volume seeks to achieve, by use of careful selectivity and critical assessment of the literature, an expression of the country and an appreciation of its nature and national aspirations, to guide the reader towards an understanding of its importance. The keynote of the series is to provide, in a uniform format, an interpretation of each country that will express its culture, its place in the world, and the qualities and background that make it unique.

VOLUMES IN THE SERIES

To the memory of
Aquino de Bragança,
Director of the Centro de Estudos Africanos,
killed alongside President Samora Moisés Machel
in the aeroplane crash at Mbuzini
on 19 October 1986;
and to the memory of
Ruth First,
Research Director of the Centro de Estudos Africanos,
killed by a parcel-bomb in Maputo
on 17 August 1982.

Contents

Contents

x

Contents

Preface

This work was prepared in the Documentation Nucleus of the Centre of African Studies, Eduardo Mondlane University in Maputo. It is the first comprehensive and critically annotated general bibliography on Mozambique to be published, and the first general bibliography since the 1940s.

The volume is comprehensive in the sense that it attempts to cover all aspects of life in Mozambique; but it is not of course, exhaustive. Many users, seeking specific items, will inevitably be disappointed when they find that their favourites have been left out. Nevertheless, we have tried to provide entry points to each topic for those interested in pursuing a particular subject further. Thus, our emphasis has always been first of all on specialized bibliographies and reference works, and only then on the important or representative books and articles in a given area.

It should be noted that the inclusion of 'representative' works has meant, in some cases, that we have listed works putting forward arguments that we cannot possibly support. We refer here particularly to those pieces purporting to defend the activities of armed bandits in Mozambique, sometimes known abroad as 'RENAMO' or the 'Mozambican National Resistance'.

Acknowledgements

The work was mostly written by Colin Darch. Calisto Pacheleke worked especially on the chapter on education. Maria da Luz Teixeira Duarte with help from Ana Paula Voss prepared many of the entries in the chapter on archaeology and prehistory.

Many people have commented on the work at various stages. The late Aquino de Bragança, Director of the Centre of African Studies, was always both encouraging and critical: his support for and approval of the project was a major factor in its successful completion. He had read much of the manuscript before his tragic death in October 1986. The late Ruth First, Research

xiii

Director of the Centre of African Studies, was instrumental in the formation of the bibliographical project on Mozambique which eventually produced this book, although she was murdered before detailed work could begin.

Our colleagues at the Centre of African Studies have all contributed in various ways. We would like to thank Alpheus Manghezi for his help with material in the Shangaan language; Anna Maria Gentili; Bridget O'Laughlin for her critical comments and suggestions; Gottfried Wellmer; Guido van Hecken; Jacques Depelchin for the loan of some of his personal books and articles, and for his suggestions; José Mota Lopes, Deputy Director of the Centre; Judith Head for her comments and comradely criticisms; Rob Davies; and Yussuf Adam.

Outside the Centre of African Studies, the staff of the Arquivo Histórico de Moçambique deserve our warmest thanks, especially Maria Inês Nogueira da Costa, the Director of the Archive; and António Sopa, a fine bibliographer whose careful and detailed suggestions, comments and criticism have added considerably to the coverage of the volume. Allen Isaacman helped by sending offprints and references. David Hedges was a careful and perceptive critic at virtually all stages of the work. Eugeniusz Rzewuski read and made suggestions for the chapter on Mozambican languages. Patrick Chabal commented on the chapter on literature, and carried the manuscript safely to Britain. The chapters on ecology and the environment and on flora and fauna could not have been completed without the unstinting assistance of Pauline Wynter. Paulo Soares helped with material, suggestions, and information for the section on museums. Thanks are also due to Michael Wolfers.

One of us was a teacher and the other a student on the Licenciatura course in history and documentation at the Historical Archive from 1983 to 1985. We would like to thank all our colleagues on that course, whose work has contributed greatly to this bibliography, either directly or indirectly, and who will be the future bibliographers of Mozambique: Joaquim Chigogoro, Joaquim Sousa Cruz, José Capão, Julieta Massimbe, Luís Covane, Manuel Lemos and Tereza Oliveira, as well as those whose names have already been mentioned.

Responsibility for errors of fact and misinterpretation belongs, nevertheless, entirely to the undersigned.

Colin Darch
Calisto Pacheleke

xiv

Introduction

This introduction is intended to provide sufficient background information on the People's Republic of Mozambique for users of this bibliography to be able to understand the points made in the annotations to the entries themselves. It is not an in-depth analysis of the history or recent development of the country, but rather a summary of some of the presently available knowledge, and a statement of certain premises and assumptions about Mozambique.

An important point, and one which needs to be made right from the start, is that the 'five hundred years of Portuguese colonialism', of which we have heard so much, are largely mythological. Present-day Mozambique, as a state and a nation, has its origins in the period of European colonialism in Africa, roughly from the 1880s to the 1970s. During the centuries of Portuguese presence on Mozambican soil before that period the Portuguese managed to seize control only of a few fortress-like settlements scattered along the coast, and of trading-posts up the Zambezi Valley. It was only after the Congress of Berlin demanded proof of 'effective occupation' from European powers claiming colonial rights in a given territory, that the Portuguese launched their quaintly-named 'pacification campaigns' against neighbouring African and Luso-African polities, and came, by the late 1920s, to establish themselves over the whole of what we now know as Mozambique.

Before the Portuguese arrived, in the last decade of the 15th century, and for many years afterwards, the geographical area of Mozambique was occupied by various social formations, some of which we would recognize as 'states' in something like the modern meaning of the word, while others were much more loosely defined types of polity. For decades at a time the war-lords of the *prazos* – the Barwe kingdom; the Yao-speaking chiefdoms of the north; the Nguni Gaza empire; the Monomo-

Introduction

tapa empire, based in present-day Zimbabwe; the Swahili-Makua trading sheikhdoms along the northern coast; and others, all co-existed with the Portuguese, who were not yet strong enough to overthrow them, and were themselves simply one actor among many on the Mozambican historical stage.

Geography and climate

Mozambique is situated on the south-east coast of Africa, south of the equator, between roughly latitudes 10 degrees north and 26 degrees south, and longitudes 30 degrees west and 42 degrees east; it is divided by the Tropic of Capricorn, which crosses the provinces of Inhambane and Gaza. The country occupies 783,030 square kilometres, of which 9,652 square kilometres are accounted for by Lake Nyasa (or Lake Malawi), which Mozambique shares with Tanzania and Malawi. The distance from the Ruvuma delta to the Natal border is about 1,965 kilometres and from Zumbo in western Tete to the Indian Ocean is 1,130 kilometres. The sandy coastline, scattered with shoals, inlets, lagoons, and, especially in the north, small islands, is a tourist's and fisherman's dream, and runs for 2,470 kilometres from the north-east to the south-west.

Mozambique is an elongated and narrowing territory, indented by the Republic of Malawi. The country's odd shape is a result of its history as much as of its geography, but at least some of the frontiers are marked by natural features. In general terms, Mozambique may be described as a medium plateau, descending eastwards through a sub-plateau to narrow coastal lowlands, which widen to the south as the country itself gets narrower, with the result that about forty-five per cent of the national territory occupies land lower than 1,000 metres.

In the north, the border with Tanzania runs for almost the whole of its 650-kilometre length along the Ruvuma River which divides the two small plateaux occupied by the Makonde-speaking people on both sides of the frontier. The southern part of Malawi pokes into Mozambique between Niassa and Zambézia provinces in the west and Tete Province in the east. At 1,400 kilometres, this is the longest border which Mozambique has; part of it runs through the centre of Lake Nyasa. The Tete–Malawi border runs for about 60 or 70 kilometres along the main Malawi north–south highway, the M-1, between Dedza and Ntcheu. Northern and western Tete has a long and mainly featureless border with Zambia. Along the eastern edge of

Manicaland in Zimbabwe, the border with Manica Province is also, very roughly, the edge of a plateau. The long Transvaal border is fronted partly by the Kruger National Park, and is marked, nowadays, by an electrified fence, a physical reminder of tense relations with the *apartheid* régime. In the extreme south, the short frontier with the tiny kingdom of Swaziland is almost visible from the taller buildings of Maputo, about 60 kilometres away. Most southerly of all, the short frontier with South Africa's Natal Province runs east–west across the swamps of northern Zululand.

Mount Binga in Manica Province is the highest relief in the country at 2,436 metres; but worthy of note at over 2,000 metres are the Zuira range, also in Manica, Mount Namuli in Zambézia, and the Shire (or Tchiri) highlands, which extend from southern Malawi well into Mozambique. The main river is the mighty Zambezi, which runs for 820 kilometres, of which 460 kilometres are navigable, through Tete, Zambézia and Sofala, entering the Indian Ocean south of Chinde. The Cabora Bassa Dam on the Zambezi at Songo in Tete is one of the major hydroelectric projects in the world. Other rivers of importance, for irrigation, hydroelectric power, or for local fishing, are the Incomati (Nkomati, formerly Elephants River), the Limpopo, the Save (or Sabie), the Buzi, the Punguè, the Ruvuma, and various smaller rivers in the north.

As is the case in most of Africa, the year is divided into two seasons, the wet and the dry. During the wet season, Mozambique's 'summer', temperatures average between 27 and 30 degrees Celsius, although freak temperatures as high as 40 degrees have been known in Maputo. In the cold dry season, June and July temperatures may fall as low as a chilly 18 or 20 degrees, and lower at night.

Mozambique's modern history

Portugal, described by the late Ruth First as 'Africa's earliest but feeblest colonizer', began to stake its claims to Mozambican territory as long ago as the 15th century, but, as we have seen, was unable to assert them over the whole country until the 1920s. Throughout this long period, debates over colonial policy took place regularly in metropolitan Portugal, but the Portuguese state was never strong enough to be able to devise an effective way of enriching itself through its overseas possessions. In the 1890s,

Introduction

various forms of colonization by proxy were introduced, under
which the Portuguese crown gave up its rights in vast chunks of
northern Mozambique, to three foreign chartered companies,
which ruled without interference, in one case until the 1940s.

In 1926, with the introduction of Premier António Salazar's
Estado Novo (New State): a new and fiercely nationalistic
colonial policy was attempted, based on protectionism and the
banning of non-Portuguese investment in the colonies. Only
really taking effect from the 1940s in Mozambique, the new
policy was to be challenged in the early 1960s by the emergence
of the African nationalist movements and, in the face of
Portuguese intransigence, by the launching of armed liberation
struggles, which compelled Portugal once again to turn to its
Western allies for support of all kinds.

The founding of FRELIMO (Frente de Libertação de
Moçambique – Mozambique Liberation Front) on 25 June 1962 is
undoubtedly the single most important event in modern Mozambican history. Cobbled together from two or three loose and
squabbling groupings of often English-speaking long-term exiles
and left-wing intellectuals, as well as from younger nationalists
from inside the country, the Front began to crumble around the
edges almost as soon as it was set up. The constituent exile groups
reformed themselves, and went off on their own, as it turned out,
into obscurity, leaving younger men and women, with direct and
recent experience of conditions inside the country, and with no
loyalties other than to FRELIMO, to launch the armed struggle.
The Front was all the stronger for this process. By 1966 FRELIMO
has managed to push the Portuguese out of small and remote
corners of Niassa and Cabo Delgado, and had begun to establish
itself as an alternative power in those first liberated zones.

By 1968 FRELIMO's very success had begun to lead to
internal problems, and a struggle over two quite different 'lines'
or policies began, which led to the murder of a number of leading
figures, including the movement's first president, Eduardo
Chivambo Mondlane, and eventually to the expulsion of the
advocates of narrow nationalism. FRELIMO's goals were
redefined to include the elimination of the exploitation of man by
man, and a commitment to socialism was, for the first time,
explicitly taken on board. It was during this period that the late
President Samora Moisés Machel, as well as other present-day
Frelimo leaders, emerged as the dominant figures in the
movement.

By 1974 the Portuguese army knew that, especially in

xviii

Mozambique, the colonial wars were unwinnable, and decided that it was ready to give up. On 25 April the Armed Forces Movement (or MFA), made up of younger officers with only one idea in their heads – decolonization – seized power in Lisbon. By 25 June 1975, the People's Republic of Mozambique was an independent sovereign state, under the leadership of FRELIMO.

Needless to say, Mozambique's neighbouring governments, the illegal settler régime of Rhodesia under the rebel Ian Smith, and the white-minority government of John Vorster in South Africa, were less than happy about this development. Mozambique closed its borders with rebel Rhodesia in early 1976, and almost at once became a target for sabotage and other forms of attack. It was in this period that the Rhodesian Central Intelligence Organization (CIO) pulled together the so-called 'Mozambican National Resistance', known to newspaper readers all over the world by their Portuguese acronyms 'RNM' or 'Renamo', but described by the Mozambican authorities, with much greater accuracy, simply as armed bandits. After Zimbabwean independence in 1980, the armed bandits had been more-or-less defeated on the ground, and without their puppet-masters in Rhodesia, it looked as if the problem was solved. Unhappily, the South Africans decided to pick up the pieces and put the bandit movement together again.

In 1977, several steps were taken towards introducing appropriate social structures for the new republic. At the II Congress of FRELIMO, the decision was taken to turn the Front into a Marxist–Leninist vanguard party, to be known as the Frelimo Party (note the lower-case spelling). Much of 1978, from February to November, was taken with the campaign for the 'restructuring' of the Party, or more accurately with a recruitment drive. At the same time, a pyramidal system of local governments was set up, with the national People's Assembly at the top. The first nationwide elections were held in 1977, and resulted in a large number of peasants, workers and women participating for the first time in a formal political process. Nevertheless, the assemblies were not, in practice, noted for vigorous debate or for dissenting votes, and it was not until after the second general elections in 1986 that abstentions and 'no' votes were registered for the first time at the national level.

At the same time, the system of 'Dynamizing Groups' (or GDs) at local level, the Production Councils in the workplace (replaced later on by national trade unions, or the OTM), the People's Tribunals with their 'Sunday judges' elected to work

Introduction

part-time from within the community, the new professional organizations of teachers (ONP), or journalists (ONJ), and the mass organizations for women (OMM), for youth (OJM) and for children (*Continuadores*), all these began to introduce large sections of the Mozambican population to new forms of political and organizational work. In colonial times, such things were unthinkable.

From 1981 onwards, the problem of armed banditry, sponsored by the South African régime, has come increasingly to dominate public thinking about Mozambique. The war, waged by and large against defenceless villagers and against economic targets, has brought famine and misery in its wake, to all parts of the country. A deeply shocking first-hand account of the suffering of the people of southern Mozambique, by Lina Magaia (*Dumba nengue* [Riches abandoned] (Maputo: Cadernos Tempo, 1987. 100p. [Colecção Depoimentos; no. 4]) was published too late for inclusion in this bibliography, but is nevertheless highly recommended to all readers with a knowledge of Portuguese and strong stomachs. Nevertheless, Mozambicans remain, in their vast majority, committed to their country and to the Party which gave them independence. Nobody who witnessed the undoubtedly genuine outpouring of grief (not only in Mozambique), and the disciplined behaviour of all sections of society, after the tragic death of Samora Machel, could for a moment suppose that the late President was viewed as a 'communist dictator' by anyone but the loonier elements of the European and South African ultra-right.

This is not to deny that there is deep popular dissatisfaction with the current state of affairs in Mozambique. It is only to point out that many, if not most Mozambicans are quite well able to see the root cause for the sorry situation in their country, and to understand that most of the problem can be traced to their powerful southern neighbour.

Mozambique's economy

Most analysts agree that economic indicators show slow but significant growth in the Mozambican economy during the period from independence until about 1981. The levels of production of the immediately pre-independence period were being approached again, with prospects for continued expansion. With the abolition of the colonial system, expectations had been raised to what may

now seem to have been unrealistic levels, but the Government
stuck to its egalitarian price and distribution policies. On a 1970
base-year, for example, consumer food prices in Maputo had
risen only to an index figure of 187.9 by 1976.

The Mozambican economy is predominantly agricultural, with
about ninety per cent of the economically active population living
on the land. Present-day agricultural activity is customarily
divided into four sectors: peasant production, usually termed the
family sector in Mozambique; collective or co-operative farms;
commercial farms; and the enormous and controversial state
farms, or *machambas estatais*. These last were favoured by the
government in practice, if not in theory, between 1977 and 1983.
Nevertheless, the Minister of Agriculture was sacked and
disgraced in 1978 for, among other things, his leanings towards
mechanization and state farms as priority areas. From the IV
Congress of 1983 onwards, renewed emphasis on the family sector,
the most productive of the four, has again been official policy.

The main cash crops have traditionally been cotton, which was
associated with the hated forced cultivation system of Portuguese
times, sugar, tea, copra, and to some extent sisal. In the late
1970s cotton production rose sharply, both on the state farms and
in the peasant small-holdings, and by 1979 had reached over
70,000 tonnes for seed and lint. Similarly, by 1980 sugar
production had recovered from a series of difficult years after
independence, to 226,000 tonnes. In Africa, Mozambique ranks
third as a tea-producer, and had reached pre-independence levels
of production (around 20,000 tonnes per annum) by 1980. Maize,
and rice in the coastal lowlands, are staple foodstuffs.

In 1980 drought began to affect large areas of Mozambique;
this in itself would not have been disastrous, but the subsequent
infiltration of armed bandits with the support of the *apartheid*
régime turned a natural disaster of manageable proportions into a
long-term disaster. By 1981 the grain deficit was 670,000 tonnes;
by 1987 it was reckoned that the agricultural sector would need
an annual aid input of around US$125 million per year, at least
until 1990.

Mozambique has considerable mineral resources, although it is
only around Moatize, about 20 kilometres north of Tete city, that
there is any systematic exploitation of rare earths and high-grade
coal. Proven reserves of coal are at least 150 million tonnes, and
such minerals as tantalite, bauxite and ilmenite also exist.

Approximately half of Mozambique's industrial capacity is
located in Maputo, and consists mainly of presently highly under-

utilized processing plants, including sugar refineries and cashew- and grain-processing. Some industries are at present (1987) operating at levels of production as low as nine per cent of capacity, due mainly to raw material and spare part shortages.

The Mozambican transport infrastructure was built in colonial times as a sector serving the interests of the hinterland countries, especially South Africa, rebel Rhodesia, and Malawi. Thus the railway network serves those countries more effectively than it does Mozambican interests, as a glance at the map will show. Similarly, it is much easier to drive from Beira, in the centre of the country, to Harare than to Maputo, even under peacetime conditions. Plans had been drawn up prior to 1980 to construct another 10,000 kilometres of roads, on the base of the 39,000 kilometres inherited from the Portuguese.

It must be emphasized that, although it is clear that the Mozambican government has made serious mistakes in economic policy, these errors were not in themselves catastrophic. However, the vicious war waged by the armed bandits against economic targets, as well as against schools, health posts, and the rural population itself, has left the government with no room for manoeuvre, and has destroyed the fragile basis built up prior to 1980, perhaps for the foreseeable future.

The social situation

Shortly after coming to power in 1975, FRELIMO nationalized housing, medicine, education, the legal practice and funeral parlours. These were perceived as key areas which the new government felt should no longer be left open for profit-making and abuse.

Frelimo devoted much of its time and energy to improving social conditions for the mass of the people, adopting policies which inevitably meant shortages and a fall in 'standards' as perceived by the urban élite, but which also brought access to education, modern medicine, and political participation to millions for the very first time. Thus, by 1980 there were 17,030 teachers and 1.3 million pupils in primary education, and 2,767 teachers and over 103,000 pupils in the secondary sector. This huge quantitative advance in access to education was accompanied by the introduction of a new syllabus, the SNE or National System of Education, and by the establishment of research and training institutions dedicated to curriculum development (INDE) and to high-level teacher-training (Instituto Superior de Pedagogia), both in Maputo, as well as middle-level teacher-training institutes around the country.

This sector was an obvious target for armed banditry, especially in the rural areas. By 1987 over 700 rural schools had been physically destroyed, and some 2,000 had been forced to close down; more than 313,000 pupils had had their educational careers interrupted. Schoolteachers caught by the bandits were mutilated; in one publicized case the victim had his nose and ears cut off.

In the health sector there was, despite some serious disagreements about policy, a commitment to the principles of preventive medicine and equal access to health care. For many years the standard fee for a treatment, regardless of the time involved or the seriousness of the complaint, was held at 7.50 MT, or less than 20 American cents at the then rate of exchange. Imported drugs were limited to 400 or so basic treatments for the most common diseases, and could be purchased and prescribed only by their generic names. Huge nationwide vaccination campaigns were organized and completed. Health posts and health centres in the rural areas brought elementary care to many villages for the first time.

Frelimo also attempted to develop and introduce a new system of law, but rather as a new and popularly-based system. Campaigns were mounted in 1979 and 1981, involving students from the Faculty of Law at Eduardo Mondlane University, to collect as much information as possible on existing standards of conduct in different areas. At the local level, judges are now elected by the community, and as far as possible they resolve disputes and judge minor offenders, only referring more serious or difficult cases to the higher, formal judicial structures.

The position of women has always been a Frelimo concern, from the days of the formation of the Women's Detachment during the armed struggle; nevertheless, men in the Party have been criticized for their paternalistic attitudes. There was, for instance, some disagreement over the (male-defined) agenda at the Extraordinary Conference of the women's organization, in November 1984, and it was clear that the OMM's ideas on the definition of 'women's emancipation' did not always entirely coincide with those of the Party's male leadership (see Paul Fauvet's trenchant account of this conference in *Africa Now* (Feb. 1985)). But the debate had at least begun: as one observer put it, 'the cork is out of the bottle'.

Introduction

The armed bandits

The origin of the armed bandits, in the 1970s, as a fifth column of the Rhodesian intelligence service, is now universally accepted. The details have been exhaustively discussed in several publications, the most important of which are cited in this bibliography. However, especially in the United States, and mainly for reasons of American domestic politics, claims are at present being made that they are some sort of legitimate political opposition, fighting for an ill-defined concept of 'democracy' against a 'communist' régime, and that, therefore, Western governments should support their efforts.

The position of the Mozambican government towards the bandits is sometimes portrayed as simple intransigence. Frelimo's analysis is perhaps not as widely understood as it might be, involving as it does both a clear perspective on the nature of the war and some subtleties of translation. First, and this point is basic to the Mozambican position, there is no civil war in Mozambique. The war which is being waged is being fought by proxies, principally against civilians and against economic targets, the objective being to terrorize the population and to destroy the country's economic and social infrastructure. Two armies are not facing each other in Mozambique; there is no serious attempt by 'Renamo' to win over positive support, or to develop a political programme, or even to administer areas occupied by their forces. To echo a point made by an aid administrator, if there is no hunger in bandit areas, why have hundreds of thousands of Mozambicans fled from those very areas?

Second, the term 'armed bandits', translated directly from Portuguese, carries an unfortunate overtone in English of the slightly romantic Robin Hood or Emiliano Zapata type of outlaw. In Portuguese *bandido* has no such connotation, meaning simply a criminal gangster. It is clear that in some areas at least, small groups are operating, made up of precisely this kind of person.

The death of Samora Machel

The tragic death of President Samora Moisés Machel at Mbuzini on 19 October 1986 provoked worldwide consternation, and in Harare and later in Maputo itself, violent demonstrations against South African and Malawian property. The sequence of events which led up to the President's death began the previous May, during an official visit to Japan, when for the first time the head of state accused Malawi of directly supporting the bandit group in the north of Mozambique.

Within a relatively short time, Mozambique began to adopt a much firmer attitude towards Malawian involvement. The President made a long working visit to Tete, and also went to Malawi with other Front Line presidents to put pressure on Hastings Banda. The Mozambicans presented a dossier on Malawian complicity to the summit. On the President's return, he made his famous 'missiles' remark at an impromptu press conference, stating that if Malawi did not mend her ways, Mozambique would place missiles along the border. Following the summit, a massive infiltration of bandits into Tete and Zambézia from Malawi took place.

On 7 October the South African Defence Minister, Magnus Malan, threatened Samora Machel directly, stating that 'if President Machel chooses land mines [a reference to an incident in Kangwane bantustan], South Africa will react accordingly [. . .] he will clash head on with South Africa'.

The confused and confusing history of the three-nation participation and non-participation in the official and non-official commissions of enquiry into the plane crash is too complex to go into here. Suffice it to point out that the confusion has redounded to the advantage of the South African régime, allowing attention to focus on technical complexities which most people are not competent to judge. The political issues have been left to one side. Nevertheless, the glib findings of the South African Margo commission, attributing the crash to errors by the Soviet crew, will not satisfy many in the region, who at the very least believe in a Scottish verdict of not proven. President Joaquim Chissano has already said in so many words that President Machel was murdered.

Two publications on the death of Samora Machel appeared in time for inclusion in the main body of this bibliography. A third work, in Portuguese, and including much technical information and transcripts of documents, was published in March 1987 – Alvaro B. Marques' *Quem matou Samora Machel?* (Lisbon: Ulmeiro, 1987. 246p.).

Introduction

Authors' note

Throughout this work we have attempted to distinguish between the Frente de Libertação de Moçambique (Mozambique Liberation Front) which existed from 1962 until the III Congress in February 1977, and the Marxist–Leninist vanguard party which was established at that Congress, and which is today the only political party in Mozambique. We have done this by following the Mozambican convention of using capitals for the Front (FRELIMO), and lower-case for the party (Frelimo, or less commonly, the Frelimo Party).

The Country and Its People

1 **Portuguese Africa: a handbook.**
   Edited by David M. Abshire, Michael A. Samuels. London: Pall
   Mall; New York: Praeger, 1969. 480p. maps.
Twenty papers by five academics, a lawyer and a journalist on a wide range of
general topics concerning Portugal's African colonies. None of the papers are
dedicated specifically to one country, but information on Mozambique is plentiful
and easy to find in the appropriate sections. The essays are divided into groups on
the historical and social background, government and society, the economy, and
political and international issues (that is, the liberation struggles). The last section
includes some interesting pieces from George Martelli (former diplomatic
correspondent for the London *Daily Telegraph*) on 'Conflict in Portuguese
Africa'; and by Michael Samuels on 'The nationalist parties'. The economics
section is also informative. Abshire says (on p. 457) that 'there are no indications
that FRELIMO yet represents a true Mozambican nationalism that would be
attractive to the majority of the population,' a comment which gives an idea of
the general perspective of the book.

2 **A manual of Portuguese East Africa.**
   Compiled by the Geographical Section of the Naval Intelligence
   Division, Naval Staff, Admiralty. London: HM Stationery Office,
   1920. 552p. bibliog. maps. (ID 1189).
The colonial powers were enthusiastic compilers of handbooks about each other's
colonies, and this detailed and now historically-valuable reference work is a fine
example of the genre. The work covers, with all the assumptions of its time, the
following topics: geography; climate; vegetation and animal life; the inhabitants;
government and the trading companies; agriculture and animal husbandry;
mining; commerce; communications; history; and, in a final chapter, political and
economic conclusions. See also, for a similar but much later work, J. M. Bryce
Nairn's *Portuguese East Africa (Mozambique)* (London: HM Stationery Office,
1955.).

1

3   **Cozinha moçambicana.** (Mozambican cuisine.)
    Cesário Abel de Almeida Viana (et al.).   Lourenço Marques,
    Mozambique: Fundo de Turismo, 1975. 104p.

Mozambican cuisine has a long tradition and varies widely from region to region according to local agricultural, religious and other factors. It has been strongly influenced by Indian, Arabic and, of course, Portuguese styles, but these influences are naturally stronger on the coast and in the towns. Mozambican cookery relies heavily on maize, rice, tubers, cassava (both root and leaves), and *nhemba* (beans). Millet is also widely employed. In the coastal areas giant prawns are a favourite, and piquant red pepper and lemon sauces are well-liked. Published just after independence, this book is divided into chapters on main dishes, desserts, fruits and drinks, each arranged in alphabetical order of the local name of the dish. There is also a table of substitute ingredients.

4   **Area handbook for Mozambique.**
    American University, Foreign Area Studies.   Washington, DC:
    United States Government Printing Office, 1969. 351p. bibliog.
    maps.

The series to which this book belongs has an excellent reputation as a reliable reference source for a wide range of countries. This first edition of the *Area handbook for Mozambique* was published at the end of the colonial era and retains considerable interest as a source of information for that period. Compiled by a team of authors (Alexander Bastos, Frederick R. Eisele, Sidney A. Harrison, Howard J. John and Tura K. Wieland) under the leadership of Allison Butler Herrick, the book was completed in July 1967. The editor comments: 'Since the Portuguese have published few studies of the society and only a small number of foreign observers have carried on recent investigations, the scope of the materials was limited.' The twenty-five chapters are grouped under the following headings – social, political, economic, and national security. The tone when discussing FRELIMO is not overtly hostile, but rather one of studied detachment. There is a useful description of Portuguese military organization in Mozambique, and a twenty-three-page bibliography.

5   **Area handbook for Mozambique.**
    American University, Foreign Area Studies.   Washington, DC:
    United States Government Printing Office, 1977. 2nd ed. 240p.
    bibliog. maps.

Always useful, sometimes hostile, and occasionally wrong, the 1977 edition of the *Area handbook* is nearly one-third shorter than its predecessor (q.v.) and much more cautious – 'significant gaps in information' occur; the ' . . . inadequacy of economic data' has been noted by Samora Machel himself, and 'there is a marked lack of sophisticated sociological or social-anthropological description and analysis'. The authors, led this time by Irving Kaplan, have divided their work into chapters on the general character of the society, the historical setting, geography, population and health, ethnic groups and social systems, the economy, the productive sectors (i.e. agriculture and industry), government and politics, and, as always in this series, national security. There is a thirteen-page bibliography. A third edition under the new series title *Mozambique: a country study*, edited by Harold D. Nelson (Washington, DC: United States Government Printing Office, 1985) has now appeared.

6   **Memória estatística sobre os domínios portuguezes na África Oriental.**
(A factual memoir on the Portuguese dominions in East Africa.)
Sebastião Xavier Botelho.   Lisbon: José Baptista Morando, 1835.
400p.

Despite the implications of the title, this is not a statistical work at all, but a discursive general survey of Portugal's East African possessions at the beginning of the 19th century. The work is widely considered to mark the beginning of a specifically Mozambican bibliography, since it is the first book to be devoted exclusively to the territory. Earlier studies discussed East Africa in the context of either the Portuguese Empire in general, or the Estado da Índia (Portuguese enclaves on the coast of India – the administrative centre for Mozambique) in particular. The book received a hostile review in the *Edinburgh Review* (1837. no. 130), to which Botelho replied in a pamphlet entitled *Segunda parte da memória estatística sobre os domínios portuguezes na África Oriental, contendo a resposta à crítica feita à dita memória e inserta na Revista de Edimburgo no. 130 de Janeiro de 1837* [Part two of the factual memoir on the Portuguese dominions in East Africa, containing the reply to the criticism made of the said memoir and published in the *Edinburgh Review* no. 130 in January 1837] (Lisbon: A. J. C. da Cruz, 1837. 110p.). See also Botelho's earlier *Resumo para servir de introdução a memória estatística sobre os domínios portuguezes na África Oriental* [Summary to serve as an introduction to the factual memoir on the Portuguese dominions in East Africa] (Lisbon: Imprensa Nacional, 1834. 85p.).

7   **Moçambique pelo seu povo: selecção, prefácio e notas a cartas de *Voz Africana*.** (Mozambique, by its people: selection, preface and notes to letters to *African Voice*.)
José Capela (pseudonym).   Oporto, Portugal: Afrontamento, 1974.
3rd ed. 170p. (Colecção 'As Armas e os Varões', no. 1).

First published by Afrontamento in 1971, this is a collection of readers' letters to the African newspaper *Voz Africana* (q.v.). The letters are printed in their original form, although with some explanatory notes, in a series of thematic chapters entitled: 'From clan relations to individual friendship'; 'From clan morality to a different morality'; 'The clan has not ended, it is now the family'; 'From communal society to profit-making firms'; 'In an occupied country'; and 'Life through daily tragedies'. The importance of readers' letters as a social barometer can also be seen in the annotation to *Tempo* (q.v.).

8   **Portugal in Africa.**
James Duffy.   Harmondsworth, England: Penguin Books, 1962.
240p. bibliog. maps. (Penguin African Library, no. AP 3).

An excellent handbook on Portugal's African Empire, published just as the wars of liberation began in earnest. On FRELIMO, not even mentioned by name, Duffy comments cautiously (p. 220): 'Whether the front will hold together and even increase its strength . . . remains to be seen.' This work covers both the

3

historical background and the current situation for the general reader. The chapter on Mozambique (p. 73–98) is mainly historical in focus.

9 Portuguese Africa.
James Duffy. Cambridge, Massachusetts: Harvard University Press; London: Oxford University Press, 1959. 389p.

An extremely influential and, indeed, pioneering work. Duffy, with a handful of others such as Basil Davidson, was one of the first scholars working in English to turn his attention to the Portuguese colonies in Africa. This book was an attempt to produce, in the author's words, 'a coordinated single-volume study of Angola and Mozambique'. The first chapters deal, in what now seems a rather superficial way, with the period up to 1752 in the Congo, in Angola, and in Mozambique, but Duffy's account takes a narrative rather than an analytical form. He also tackles such thorny topics as slavery, the slave-trade, and contract labour, as well as discussing British exploration and the Portuguese reaction to it. He concludes with a section on António de Oliveira Salazar's Estado Novo (New State) in Portugal. The work was reprinted in 1968, with a new preface bringing the account more-or-less up to date. See the favourable review of the first edition by Eric Axelson in the *Journal of African History* vol. 1, no. 1 (1960), p. 153–54.

10 Eduardo Mondlane.
London: Panaf Books, 1972. 174p. (Panaf Great Lives).

Eduardo Chivambo Mondlane (1920–69), the first president of FRELIMO, was the son of a local chief in Gaza Province. He managed to fight his way through the racist educational systems of colonial Mozambique and post-war South Africa, eventually to gain a PhD in social sciences from the prestigious Northwestern University, just outside Chicago. After becoming president of FRELIMO he was brutally assassinated, by the Portuguese or their agents, with a parcel-bomb in February 1969. This book is not really a biography of Mondlane, despite the chapters headed 'Early life' and 'Eduardo the man, as seen by his wife Janet', and the photographs of his children. Rather, the central chapters use Mondlane's life as a hook on which to hang discussion of such issues as the role of the army, tribalism, racialism, and the class struggle. Two appendixes include the articles 'The development of nationalism in Mozambique', and 'The crystallization of a struggle for freedom', both by Mondlane himself; and Janet Mondlane's 'Message from the women of Mozambique'. From the vast quantity of material by and about Mondlane, see especially his articles 'The struggle for independence in Mozambique' *Présence Africaine* no. 48, vol. 20 (1963), p. 28–46; and 'The movement for freedom in Mozambique' *Présence Africaine* no. 53, vol. 25 (1965), p. 8–37; on Mondlane's life, see Phillip V. Tobias' 'A little-known chapter in the life of Eduardo Mondlane' *Génève-Afrique* vol. 16, no. 1 (1977–78), p. 119–24; and Edward A. Hawley's 'Eduardo Chivambo Mondlane (1920–1969): a personal memoir' *Africa Today* vol. 26, no. 1 (1979), p. 19–24.

11 Mozambique: the revolution under fire.
Joseph Hanlon. London: Zed Books, 1984. 292p. bibliog. maps.

An important and useful journalistic account of war-torn post-independence Mozambique, this is probably one of the best general introductions to the

People's Republic. Hanlon was a *Guardian* (Manchester and London) and BBC correspondent in Mozambique from 1979 to 1984 (coming from scientific journalism) and, after a shaky start, began to turn in excellent copy (see *Facts and Reports* (q.v.), *passim*, for examples). This book, which is largely unsourced, relies heavily on reports and research conducted in Mozambique by various institutions, but which are not widely known outside; in that sense it is a useful synthesis. Unfortunately, Hanlon also reproduces one or two rather doubtful stories. He covers, in a rather fragmented way, the colonial background, health, the economy and economic planning, agriculture, communal villages, the concept of people's power, women, the worker-peasant alliance, the IV Congress, and, as a constant theme, the activities of the armed bandits, the so-called MNR (Mozambique National Resistance).

12 Marxism and Mozambique.
Thomas H. Henriksen. *African Affairs* no. 309, vol. 77 (Oct. 1978), p. 441–62.

This general and often quite speculative article was apparently written for a non-specialist (in Mozambican terms) audience, since it includes a lot of background information. It is based, however, on a wider range of both Mozambican and foreign journalistic sources than is usual in this type of literature. Henriksen covers the impact of the liberation struggle, the ideological context of Mozambique's new society, industrial and agricultural development, mobilization of the population, and the role of Frelimo as a party. He characterizes the Mozambican, Guinea-Bissau and Angolan liberation wars as 'the first successful *indigenous* Marxist revolutions accompanied by prolonged fighting not growing directly from the conditions of international wars' (his italics). Cuba is excluded from this definition on the grounds that the revolution became Marxist after seizing state power. Henriksen argues that FRELIMO was a Marxist organization from at least 1970, while retaining strong appeal for the nationalists. He concludes with a series of questions, some of which are not particularly sophisticated in their formulation: 'Is a Stalinist dictatorship inevitable in an under-developed Marxist revolution?' 'Can Frelimo co-exist with capitalism?' 'Will the asceticism of the 'Maoist vision' of a puritanical and virtuous countryside win out?' 'What will be the role of the army?' and finally, what one suspects may have been worrying Henriksen throughout, 'What impact will all those Soviet, East European, Chinese, Vietnamese and Cuban technicians have?'

13 Histórias ouvidas e vividas dos homens e da terra: memórias e notas autobiográficas. (Stories heard and lived through by the people and the country: memoirs and autobiographical notes.)
Raul Bernardo Manuel Honwana. Maputo: the author, 1985. 124p.

An unorganized and meandering but highly-readable account of his life and times, by the father of the fiction-writer Luís Bernardo Honwana. The work contains some fascinating insights, but is ultimately frustrating because of the unanswered questions which occur to the reader at every turn. Revolts over forced cotton-growing, the history of the Negrophile Institute in Lourenço Marques and of the School of Arts and Crafts at Moamba, and Mondlane's highly-publicized visit home to Mozambique in 1961 are some of the topics covered by an 'insider'.

14   **Mozambique: dream the size of freedom.**
George Houser, Herb Shore.   New York: Africa Fund, in
association with the American Committee on Africa, 1975. 68p.
bibliog. map.

A useful, illustrated pamphlet produced by a support group, apparently to
introduce Mozambique and the Mozambican struggle to a general readership.
Houser and Shore were involved in support work from the early days of the
liberation struggles and knew some of the Mozambican nationalist leaders
personally, so some parts of their booklet contain important first-hand insights
and information. The pamphlet covers Mozambican history from the discoveries
to Premier António Salazar; the Estado Novo (New State); the growth of
nationalism; the massacre of some 600 people by the Portuguese at Mueda in
1960, and its impact; the birth of FRELIMO; Eduardo Mondlane; the launching
of the armed struggle for independence; the hydroelectric project at Cabora
Bassa; FRELIMO's principles; the leadership crisis of 1968–70; and the final
victory. The title comes from a line in a FRELIMO poem.

15   **Issue. vol. 8, no. 1.**
Edited by Allen Isaacman.   Waltham, Massachusetts: African
Studies Association, Spring 1978. 49p.

A special number on Mozambique, without a general title. The number has an
introduction by Allen Isaacman, and includes the following articles: 'State power
in Mozambique' by James H. Mittelman; 'Mozambique: dynamizing the people'
by Carole Collins; 'Transforming Mozambique's rural economy' by Allen
Isaacman; 'Precondition for victory: women's liberation in Mozambique and
Guinea-Bissau' by Stephanie Urdang; 'Escola nova: the new secondary school in
Mozambique' by Chris Searle; 'Creating a national culture: an overview' by
Barbara Barnes; 'Cultural change and literary expression in Mozambique' by
Russel Hamilton; and 'Major themes in Mozambican foreign relations, 1975–1977'
by William Minter (q.v.).

16   **Mozambique: from colonialism to revolution, 1900–1982.**
Allen Isaacman, Barbara Isaacman.   Boulder, Colorado: Westview
Press, 1983; Aldershot, England: Gower, 1984; Harare: Zimbabwe
Publishing House, 1985. 235p. bibliog. maps. (Profiles: Nations of
Contemporary Africa).

A disappointing and rather rushed introductory account of the history of
Mozambique in the 20th century; this book has not been particularly well-
received by reviewers (see especially Jeanne Penvenne's comments in 'A luta
continua' (q.v.)). The book opens with a chapter on the pre-colonial period
(nicely defined as being 1500–1880). An idea of the briskness of the tour which
follows can be gained from the other chapter headings: 'The colonial period,
1900–1962'; 'Popular opposition, 1900–1962'; 'The struggle for independence,
1962–1975'; 'The making of the Mozambican nation and the socialist polity';
'Transforming the economy'; and the final chapter on foreign policy: 'Independent Mozambique in the wider world'. The Isaacmans also print a translation of
the report of the Commission for Economic and Social Directives to the
IV Congress (p. 189–200), which should not be confused with the *Economic and
Social Directives* (q.v.) themselves.

The Country and Its People

17 **Gostar de ler: selecção de crónicas, apontamentos e comentários.** (A taste for reading: chronicles, reports and commentaries.)
Albino Magaia (et al.). Maputo: Tempográfica, 1981. 134p.
(Cadernos Tempo, no. 2).

Provides a fascinating collection of short, two- or three-page journalistic occasional pieces, most of which appeared in *Tempo*, but some of which are printed here for the first time. They include such essays as 'The forbidden fruit', written around an encounter between a womanizing Mozambican priest and President Samora Machel; 'To suffer is to be a woman', in which three peasant women tell their stories with affecting simplicity; and the satirical piece 'The wall', in which the building itself complains about the demolition activities of careless lorry drivers in Mozambican towns. The book includes photographs and drawings. The authors are Albino Magaia (at the time of writing editor of *Tempo* (q.v.)), Álvaro Marques, Areosa Pena (q.v.), Bartolomeu Tomé, Carlos Cardoso (q.v.), Hamade Chamisse, Leite Vasconcelos, Luís David, Luís Carlos Patraquim (q.v.), Machado Graça, Marcelino Alvés, Mia Couto (q.v.), Moreira Silva, Santana Afonso, Sol de Carvalho, Tomás Mário and Vandole Ukalioy.

18 **Yô Mabalane!** (Oh, Mabalane!)
Albino Magaia. Maputo: Tempográfica, 1983. 78p. (Cadernos Tempo. Colecção 'Depoimentos', no. 2).

This moving book consists of a series of eight lightly-fictionalized episodes linked around an attempt in 1965 to cross to Swaziland and thence to join FRELIMO. Mabalane was a prison work-camp where politicals were held, including those captured in the northern war-zones. The harrowing chapter 'Menina dos cinco olhos' (The girl with five eyes) has as its main protagonist the notorious and bloodthirsty PIDE (International Police for the Defence of the State) *cipaio* (African colonial policeman) Francisco Langa, whose nickname 'Chico Nhoca' (Chico the Snake) has become synonymous in Mozambique with evil and corruption. (See also *Xiconhoca o inimigo* (q.v.).) The girl with five eyes is the *palmatória*, a wooden paddle with holes bored in it to draw blood, which was used to beat the soles of the feet and the palms of the hands.

19 **Moçambique: curso de extensão universitária, ano lectivo de 1964–1965.** (Mozambique: a university extension course for the academic year 1964–65.)
Lisbon: Instituto Superior de Ciências Sociais e Política Ultramarina, Universidade Técnica de Lisboa [n.d.].

One of a series of textbooks on the Portuguese colonies, published by the principal training institution for colonial administrators. (Some of the dissertations produced at the ISCSPU are listed elsewhere in this bibliography.) The book consists of nineteen articles by various Portuguese specialists on aspects of Mozambique, some of which may strike the modern reader as oddly-chosen. The topics covered are geography, frontiers, relations with South Africa and with other neighbouring countries, socio-economic structure, civil liberties in Ancient Rome and in African societies, youth, social services, the economy, finance, foreign trade, 'subversive' movements, administrative organization, land, the information services, public health, education and missionary activity.

7

20   Mozambique: proceedings of a seminar held in the Centre of African
      Studies, University of Edinburgh, 1st and 2nd December 1978.
      Edinburgh: Centre of African Studies, University of Edinburgh,
      1979. 204p. bibliog.

An important collection of papers from the early post-independence phase. The
contributions are as follows: Malyn Newitt on the economic impact of the
Portuguese in Mozambique in the 16th and 17th centuries; Barry Neil-Tomlinson
on the Mozambique Company; a piece on the economy and society of the
Zambezi basin by the Tanzanian historian Shubi Ishemo, who has, unfortunately,
published very little of his research; and a reflective article, by the former
Anglican missionary John Paul, on the revolution and quietism. The second
section, on the present economic and political situation, is dominated by Centro
de Estudos Africanos researchers past and present. It opens with a heavily-
footnoted extract from Judith Head's important dissertation on Sena Sugar
Estates (q.v.); David Wield writes on mine labour and the peasantry in the south;
Barry Munslow looks at the roots of post-independence policy-making in the
experience of the armed struggle; and the conservative (and non-CEA) Keith
Middlemas sums up 'Two years of independence', pointing out the crucial impact
of the war with Rhodesia. The final section consists of articles by the Danish Jens
Erik Torp on industrial planning and development; Peter Bolton on the water
resources of the Zambezi River; and Joseph Hanlon's article on agricultural
mechanization (q.v.). Finally Chris Allen, a seminar chairman, contributes a very
useful but unindexed 509-item bibliography of mainly English-language material.

21   **As nossas receitas.** (Our recipes.)
      Secretariado Nacional da OMM.   Maputo: Instituto Nacional do
      Livro e do Disco, 1981. 75p.

A cookbook in Portuguese put together from recipes received after the
Mozambican Women's Organization (OMM) made an appeal to its members to
contribute their favourites. Recipes came in not only from Mozambican women,
but from men and even from foreigners. The chapters are devoted to: soups; fish
and shellfish; meat and poultry; vegetables and tubers; desserts; and fruits. The
book includes such favourites as *bacalhau de tuberão* (dried shark meat), coconut
rice, sweet cassava cake and many others. A similar publication with the same
title, but completely different content, was published five years later, also by the
National Secretariat of the OMM – *As nossas receitas* (Maputo: Instituto
Nacional do Livro e do Disco, 1986. 30p.). See also the article by B. Tomé,
entitled 'Cozinha moçambicana: uma questão cultural' (Mozambican cooking: a
cultural question) *Tempo* no. 450 (1970), p. 28–33. A very brief article in English
on Mozambican cooking was printed in *AfricAsia* no. 8/9 (Aug.–Sept. 1984), with
recipes for only two dishes – shrimp sauce with coconut, and Zambezian chicken.

22   *Cambaco*: **caça grossa em Moçambique.** (*Cambaco*: big-game
      hunting in Mozambique.)
      José da Cunha Pardal.   Lisbon: Liber-Editorial, 1982. 235p.

A well-illustrated and macho book about the joys of big-game hunting in southern
Mozambique in the post-war period up to independence. Pardal, who left
Mozambique in 1975, provides much technical information about guns and
ammunition, and where to aim when shooting various types of animal. There is a

8

startling ten-photograph sequence, in colour, of the author shooting dead a charging elephant. The flavour of the book is a mixture of 19th-century posturing about the romance and comradeship of the camp-fire, and of nostalgia for a lost colonial paradise. The Shangaan word *cambaco* means an old and solitary male elephant, and presumably conveys Pardal's self-image. See also another much earlier 'huntin'' memoir, in English: Frederick Roderick Noble Findlay's *Big game shooting and travel in south-east Africa: an account of shooting trips in the Cheringoma and Gorongoza divisions of Portuguese south-east Africa and in Zululand* (London: T. Fisher Unwin, 1903. 313p.). Findlay was the nephew of the South African writer Olive Schreiner, and prints an article written by her in 1891, entitled 'Wasteland in Mashonaland' (p. 261–68).

23 The communal villages of Gaza.
Malcolm Segall. *People's Power in Mozambique, Angola and Guinea-Bissau* no. 11 (Jan.–March 1978), p. 12–18.

Despite the all-embracing title, this is actually an impressionistic account of Segall's experiences travelling in Gaza with a team of health and political workers, showing films to communal villagers. Despite reference to the realities of African rural poverty, optimism shines through the article in a striking way. The trip was taken before the Rhodesian and South African aggressions, armed banditry, natural disasters and policy errors had combined to take their toll.

24 Mozambique in the twentieth century: from colonialism to independence.
Luís Benjamim Serapião, Mohamed A. El-Khawas. Washington, DC: University Press of America, 1979. 353p.

Serapião, although of Mozambican origin, spent most of his life following an academic career in the United States. In this volume, written with Mohamed El-Khawas, he attempts to tackle three major themes: Portuguese colonialism; Mozambican resistance; and the internationalization of the conflict between the two, thus trying to force the liberation struggle into the strait-jacket of diplomatic history. The last section deals with US-Portuguese relations, NATO (North Atlantic Treaty Organization), the OAU (Organization of African Unity) and the United Nations. (For a thesis specifically on the role of this last organization in decolonization, see J. Massingira's 'The U.N. and the decolonization of Angola, Mozambique and Rhodesia' [PhD dissertation, University of Geneva, 1973].) Serapião's book is sketchy, incomplete and superficial, and relies heavily on a few Portuguese offical sources; it carries no real analysis or conclusions. See also his 'Analysis of the Portuguese administration in Mozambique in the twentieth century' (PhD dissertation, American University, 1975, 244p.). More recently Serapião published a politically unscrupulous and ahistorical piece in the Nigerian magazine *African Concord*, in which he adopts an openly racial line in attacking Frelimo policies (See 'Crisis of political legitimacy' [16 January 1986]).

25 Moçambique: East African province of Portugal.
C. F. Spence. Cape Town: Howard Timmins, 1963. 147p. maps.

Spence was a British-born and Cambridge-educated businessman who lived most of his life in colonial Mozambique and, by the account in this book, loved every minute of it. Putting Spence's broadly reactionary views on one side, the book

9

includes much useful information on hunting, the tsetse fly, demography, government and citizenship, education, health services, communications, minerals and mining, agriculture and livestock, development schemes such as canals, dams and agricultural projects, commerce and industry, tourism and trade and the economy. However, since Spence relies entirely on official sources for his information, the work should be used with a certain amount of caution. He includes statistical tables and photographs. The work was first published in 1951 as *The Portuguese colony of Mozambique: an economic survey.*

26 **Portugal and Africa: the people and the war.**
John Sykes. London: Hutchinson, 1971. 199p.

A seductively readable account by a highly professional travel writer, who is very good at picking up nuances of personal and class relationships (see, for instance, his account of a visit to a seedy Lourenço Marques night-club), but less able to deal with the politics. Sykes visited Portugal and Mozambique, and the book is written around one family and its attitudes: an old Alentejo aristocrat, his brother the general, and his nephew the Marxist exile. See especially chapter two, 'Mozambique: two sides in play' (p. 55–109).

27 **Time out in Maputo: a *cooperante's* guide.**
[Maputo?]: MAGIC [n.d.]. 2nd ed. 69p. map.

A simple guidebook intended for English-speaking *cooperantes* (foreign workers in the state sector) which is now seriously outdated even in this revised edition. However, it still contains some helpful information, and anybody coming to Maputo as a tourist might find it useful, even in the mid-1980s, as a rather odd sort of vade-mecum. Chapters include: getting about; communicating; banking; queues; shopping; keeping healthy and staying legal; services; eating out; culture; leisure; and holidays in Mozambique. The second edition includes a two-colour street map of the 'concrete city' (i.e. central Maputo).

28 **Mozambique: landanalys.** (Mozambique: country analysis.)
Bo Westman. Stockholm: Swedish International Development
Authority, 1978. 116p. bibliog. maps.

Scandinavian writings on Africa, luckily for the rest of the world, are usually published in English, but once in a while the Swedes, Danes or Norwegians produce something for their compatriots in their own language. On Mozambique there are several brochures and articles which fall into this category, but which ought probably to have been printed in an English or Portuguese edition as well. Although it is written in Swedish, opinion has it that Westman's survey is one of the best modern introductions to Mozambique. It provides a general overview of the pre-colonial and colonial periods, of the economic structure of the country, and of current development strategies, with a good bibliography. Bo Westman was a diplomat resident in the country for several years after independence, working principally in the area of development co-operation. For a similar report in Norwegian see Tertit Aasland's *Mosambik* (Oslo: Norsk Utenrikspolitisk Institutt, 1977. 193p. [NUPI Rapport No. 33]).

Travellers' Accounts and Exploration

29 *The lands of Cazembe: Lacerda's journey to Cazembe in 1798*; also,
   *Journey of the pombeiros P. J. Baptista and Amaro José, across
   Africa from Angola to Tette on the Zambeze*; and, *A résumé of the
   journey of Mm. Monteiro and Gamitto.*
   Translated by Richard F. Burton; B. A. Beadle; C. T. Beke.
   London: John Murray, 1873. Reprinted, New York: Negro
   Universities Press, 1969. 271p. map.

Portuguese attempts to open contacts with African leaders in Central Africa,
mainly in present-day Zambia, had a long history. The Brazilian mathematician
and astronomer Francisco José Maria de Lacerda e Almeida led an expedition to
the Mwata Cazembe's empire in the eastern Lunda during the late 18th century,
and died at the Cazembe's court in October 1798. His account is translated and
annotated by Sir Richard Burton. The second narrative, translated by Beadle,
describes the extraordinary journey from Angola to Sena of the bondsmen
Baptista and José between 1802 and 1811. The third text summarizes the
Monteiro-Gamitto expedition to Mwata Cazembe IV Keleka Maya, chieftain of
the Lunda peoples, in 1831. For a more detailed account of this last, see
M. G. Marwick's 'An ethnographic classic brought to light' (q.v.).

30 **Estudos coloniais.** (Colonial studies.)
   Alfredo Augusto Caldas Xavier.   Nova Goa, India: Imprensa
   Nacional, 1889. [90]p.

Major Caldas Xavier was manager of the Opium Company in Zambézia Province
in the 1880s, and he introduced a system whereby Africans could pay their tax-
debts by volunteering for two weeks' labour on the plantations. The success of
this idea was to have far-reaching implications. In 1884 Caldas Xavier also
successfully directed the defence of Mopeia against the attack of the *prazeiro*
(holder of a royal land concession) João Coelho Barata of Massingir, although

11

the destruction caused led to the collapse of the Opium Company. The Major became a Portuguese national hero, and his pamphlet *A Zambézia* (p. 1–65 of this collection), urging the use of plantation agriculture to develop the Zambezi Valley, exercised considerable influence on the 1888 Royal Commission on the *prazos* (land concessions) under the chairmanship of J. P. Oliveira Martins. Also included are texts entitled 'The question of Niassa and the prazos of Tchiri' (p. 69–78), and the report of the Royal Commission (p. 1–12).

31 **De Angola à contracosta: descripção de uma viagem atravez do continente africano [etc.].** (From Angola to the opposite coast: a description of a journey across the African continent.)
Hermenegildo Capelo, Roberto Ivens.   Lisbon: Imprensa Nacional, 1886. Reprinted, Mira-Sintra, Portugal: Europa-América [n.d.]. 2 vols. map.

Capelo and Ivens were two Portuguese naval officers who made the 4,500-kilometre journey from Angola to Zumbo and down the Zambezi Valley to Tete, Sena, Mopeia and Quelimane in 1884–85. Such journeys across the continent were the basis for the ultimately unsuccessful Portuguese claims based on the 'Pink map' (*Mapa cor-de-rosa*) to control the territory between Mozambique and Angola. Only the last two chapters deal specifically with the Zambezi Valley. There is a rather sensational-looking Portuguese paperback reprint, with a blurb which runs 'A national bestseller! The fantastic adventure of two Portuguese across the African continent!' and a colour picture of a moustachioed white man in a topi on the cover.

32 **Journal of an exploration of the Limpopo River.**
James Frederic Elton.   *Journal of the Royal Geographical Society* vol. 42 (June 1873), p. 1–49.

Elton's account of his important journey made in southern Mozambique in July 1870 to explore the Limpopo River, which at that time was not clearly distinguished from the Nkomati. As with most 19th-century travellers' accounts, the article is full of comments on all aspects of the scene which Elton encountered – the local people, their customs and characteristics, wildlife, the terrain, and so on. The piece was also published in the Society's *Proceedings* vol. 16 (1871–72), p. 89–99.

33 **Travels and researches among the lakes and mountains of eastern and Central Africa.**
James Frederic Elton, edited by H. B. Cotterill.   London: John Murray, 1879. 417p. map. Reprinted, London: Cass, 1968.

Captain Elton was British Consul at Mozambique from 1875 to 1877, charged with the almost impossible task of ending the slave-trade single-handedly. Elton did, in fact, succeed in reducing the trade, but it revived quickly after his untimely death from a fever in 1877. The Portuguese in the region feared Elton, who was a political figure in his own right: he travelled where they could not go; he could not be stopped because Britain was an ally of Portugal; and he could show the world that metropolitan Portugal had no real control over the region where the slave-trade flourished. It is, however, quite possible that Elton had some quiet support among the liberals in Lisbon, even though his regard for the Portuguese in general was not high. This journal is a record of his trips through Mozambique, Malawi and southern Tanganyika (Tanzania), and is an important primary source; the book is especially useful for data on present-day Nampula, Zambézia and Niassa, as well as containing a wealth of material on neighbouring countries. Elton was a figure of significance in the history of this period, of the same calibre as Dr. David Livingstone or Sir Harry Hamilton Johnston.

34 **Journey of exploration to the mouth of the River Limpopo.**
St. Vincent Erskine. *Journal of the Royal Geographical Society* vol. 39 (1869), p. 233–75. Also in: *Proceedings of the Royal Geographical Society* vol. 13 (1868–69), p. 320–38.

Erskine was a special commissioner for the Government of Natal in South Africa and had sound connections with commercial enterprises in the area. He made a series of journeys in southern Mozambique to establish contact with Mzila, King of Gaza, and to secure labour supplies for Natal. He wrote that he 'had never ceased to regard the north of the river Limpopo, and the large blank on the map between it and the Sabi, as my field of exploration'. He regarded the African population as 'one and all industrious and capable of improvement', but did not have a high opinion of the Portuguese – 'The future of Delagoa Bay under the Portuguese rule can be but decay and death; but under a Teutonic race, a more glorious future may await it.' See also his 'Journey to Umzila's, south-east Africa, in 1871–72' *Journal of the Royal Geographical Society* vol. 45 (1875), p. 45–128, also in *Proceedings of the Royal Geographical Society* vol. 19 (1874–75), p. 110–32; and 'Third and fourth journeys in Gaza, or southern Mozambique, 1873–1874, and 1874 to 1875' *Journal of the Royal Geographical Society* vol. 48 (1878), p. 25–56, also in *Proceedings of the Royal Geographical Society* vol. 22 (1877–78), p. 127–34.

35 **A bibliography of primary sources for nineteenth-century tropical Africa as recorded by explorers, missionaries, traders, travellers, administrators, military men, adventurers and others.**
Robert L. Hess, Dalvan M. Coger. Stanford, California: Hoover Institution Press, 1972. 800p. (Hoover Institution Bibliographic Series, no. 47).

There is an extensive travel literature dating from the earliest Portuguese contacts with Mozambique onwards. Apart from the numerous books and articles written specifically about the country, many English-speaking travellers crossed into Mozambique from East Africa or from the Transvaal in South Africa, and many of these writings contain detailed accounts of observations made during their journeys. Of course, these texts are of widely varying reliability and reflect both the men and their times. This bibliography, organized by region and country, is not an exhaustive listing; it includes 7,732 references to articles from the various geographical society magazines, and to the multi-volume reminiscences of a wide range of European explorers. The compilers list 177 items on Mozambique (nos. 4622–799, p. 383–97). The book is a photographic reproduction of a typewritten manuscript, in which pages appear in the wrong order, corrections are pencilled in, and the numbering of the entries seems to have been done with a badly-inked library accessions' numbers stamp. See also, for a bibliography of

19th- and early 20th-century travel literature, the essay by Pélissier in his collection *Africana* (q.v.).

36   **British Central Africa: an attempt to give some account of a portion of the territories under British influence north of the Zambesi.**
Sir Harry Hamilton Johnston.   London: Methuen, 1906. 3rd ed.
544p.

Johnston (1858–1927) was an extraordinary and contradictory figure in an age that was well-peopled with colourful eccentrics and fanatics. He was conceited, snobbish, racist, an animal-lover and a prolific author; he was a painter, an amateur botanist and a ruthless pursuer of British colonial interests against the Portuguese and the Germans. After spending some time in North Africa painting animals, he joined an expedition to Angola, and in 1884 explored Mount Kilimanjaro. He then began a long period of involvement with Mozambique and Malawi, his most notable successes (from the British point of view) being the subjugation of the Yao, Ngoni and Arab slave-traders along the rivers Tchiri (Shire) and Zambesi. This book, although mainly about present-day Zambia and Malawi, includes a considerable amount of information for the study of the physical geography, history, botany, zoology and ethnography of the Tchiri (Shire) Valley and the Zambesi. The book was first published in 1897 and a second edition appeared in 1898. Johnston's last major achievement was the publication of his monumental *Comparative study of the Bantu and semi-Bantu languages* (Oxford: Clarendon Press, 1919–22. 2 vols.).

37   **Travels in eastern Africa, with a narrative of a residence in Mozambique.**
Lyons McLeod.   London: Hurst & Blackett, 1860. Reprinted, London: Cass, 1971. 2 vols. (Cass Library of African Studies, Travels and Narratives, no. 67).

Lyons McLeod, described as 'headstrong', was the first British Consul at Mozambique Island in the late 1850s. His attempt to establish a diplomatic presence was mainly due to the British government's attitude towards the abolition of the slave-trade, but it ended in disaster when the Consulate was effectively closed down by the slaving interests in 1858. McLeod was unable to understand the Portuguese, with whom he had to deal, and ended up disliking and despising them. According to Edward Alpers (*Ivory and slaves in east central Africa*, [q.v.]), McLeod's arrival coincided with a major shift in the pattern of the slave-trade, and his memoirs are an important source for this. But it was only two decades later, with the arrival of Captain Elton (q.v.) that a British Consulate was finally set up.

38   **The Zambezi expedition of David Livingstone, 1858–1863.**
Edited by J. P. R. Wallis.   London: Chatto & Windus, 1956.
2 vols. map.

Livingstone travelled up the River Zambezi from the coast as far as Tete, then up the Tchiri to Lake Nyasa, and on into present-day Malawi. For information about the sugar-mill which Livingstone took to Tete and set up there in 1859, an incident not described in the journal, see the two articles 'Early cane sugar manufacture in Moçambique: the story [of] Sekeletu's sugar mill' by A. McMartin, in *South African Sugar Journal* vol. 53, no. 12 (Dec. 1969), p. 886–87, 889; and 'David Livingstone in Moçambique: further evidence of sugar-making at Tete' *South African Sugar Journal* vol. 54, no. 2 (Feb. 1970), p. 90–91, 93–95. For an exemplary bibliography of works by and about Livingstone, see James A. Casada's *Dr. David Livingstone and Sir Henry Morton Stanley: an annotated bibliography* (New York, London: Garland, 1976. 224p.).

Geography

General

39 **Noções elementares da geografia de Moçambique.** (Elementary ideas
on Mozambican geography.)
Manuel Araújo.   Maputo: Publicações Notícias, 1979. 2nd ed. 65p.
maps.

A basic pamphlet on Mozambican geography, covering such topics as climate,
administrative divisions (now out of date), population, land use, industry,
communications, and transport. Araújo teaches at the Eduardo Mondlane
University in Maputo and is an important figure in the National Union of
Teachers (ONP). See also, from the colonial period, for example, José
de Oliveira Boleo's *Geografia física de Moçambique: esboço geográfico* [Physical
geography of Mozambique: a geographical outline] (Lisbon: Sá da Costa, 1950.
130p. bibliog. maps.).

40 **Bibliografia do ultramar português existente na Sociedade de
Geografia de Lisboa. Fascículo V: Moçambique.** (A bibliography of
the Portuguese overseas territories in the Geographical Society of
Lisbon. Part five: Mozambique.)
Lisbon: Sociedade de Geografia de Lisboa, 1970–73. 336p.

This seriously-flawed bibliography was first published in the *Boletim* (Bulletin) of
the Society as part of a general series on the Portuguese colonies, and hence this
cumulated offprint carries the odd publication date of 1970–73. The bibliography
includes unnumbered references to both books (without publishers) and to
articles; many of these references are repeated as appropriate in various chapters.
Nevertheless, a rough estimate indicates that there may be as many as 8,000
citations in the list. The work is organized into thematic chapters, by alphabetical
order of title – and since there is no author index, there is no access by author.

16

There is a 'subject index' of one-and-a-half pages, but this is to chapters rather than to items. The bibliography is thus hard to use, but of considerable importance.

41 **Contribuição para uma bibliografia geológica dos distritos da Beira, Tete e Vila Pery.** (Contribution to a geological bibliography of the districts of Beira, Tete and Vila Pery.)
Rosa J. B. de Carvalho. *Boletim do Centro de Documentação Científica [de Moçambique]* vol. 14, no. 4 (Oct.–Dec. 1971), p. 260–86.

Published in the bibliographic bulletin of the Mozambican Institute of Scientific Research (IICM), this checklist consists of 354 numbered references on the geology of what are now, respectively, the provinces of Sofala, Tete and Manica. Tete in particular has always been of some importance geologically since the Moatize area in the north-west contains large reserves of top-grade coal. The bibliography is arranged in alphabetical order by author's name, with a section for anonymous works at the end. The overwhelming majority of the citations are to Portuguese-language works, with a few in English or French. There is no introduction, nor are there any annotations or indexes. This list was also distributed as an offprint. See also on geology the much more general bibliography by Francisco Gonçalves and Jaime Caseiro, *Bibliografia geológica do ultramar português* [Geological bibliography of the Portuguese colonies] (Lisbon: Junta de Investigação do Ultramar, 1959. 272p.).

42 **Contribuição para uma bibliografia da região de Tete.** (Contribution to a bibliography of the region of Tete.)
Boletim do Centro de Documentação Científica [de Moçambique] vol. 13, no. 1 (Jan.–March 1970), p. 42–45.

Published in the bibliographic bulletin of the Mozambican Institute of Scientific Research (IICM), this brief checklist consists of forty numbered references on such diverse topics as the geology, prehistory, linguistics, agriculture and ethnography of Tete. There is no introduction, nor are there annotations or an index.

43 **Mapa das povoações criadas até 31 de Dezembro de (1959– .) e sua situação legal.** (Table of villages created up to 31 December (1959–.) and their legal status.)
Direcção dos Serviços de Agrimensura. (Directorate of Surveys.)
Lourenço Marques, Mozambique: Imprensa Nacional, 1960– annual.

A hierarchical listing of villages or settlements by the colonial administrative divisions *concelho* and *posto*, indicating the number and year of the government decree which created them; recording their class; and providing comments. This list was principally compiled to control the colonial land-tenure system, but it is also useful as a kind of gazetteer. The issues covering 1959 and 1960 of this regular series are entitled *Mapas* (Maps), and fell under Decree No. 3983 of 1918. Subsequent issues were entitled *Lista* (Lists) and came under the new decree

17

(No. 43894) of 1961. The 1973 issue of the *Lista* ran to ninety-five pages with an index, but for a much more compressed treatment of the same type of information, see the series entitled *Divisão administrativa (da Colónia) de Moçambique* [Administrative division of the Colony of Mozambique] (Lourenço Marques, Mozambique: Imprensa Nacional, 1946–48, 1955–73) usually published with a map. The last issue, for 1973, is the 9th edition and contains only eight pages. See also Maria Leonor Gonçalves' *Índice toponímico de Moçambique* [Index to the toponomy of Mozambique] (Lisbon: Centro de Botânico, Junta de Investigacões do Ultramar, 1971. 2nd ed. 128p.); and the local publication by the Direcção dos Serviços Geográficos e Cadastrais, *Primeira relação de nomes geográficos da província de Moçambique* [Preliminary list of geographical names of Mozambique] (Lourenço Marques, Mozambique: Imprensa Nacional, 1962. 209p.), which gives an alphabetical listing of name, feature, *concelho* or *circonscrição*, and district (present-day province), but no coordinates.

44 **A geologia e o desenvolvimento económico e social de Moçambique.**
(Geology and the economic and social development of Mozambique.)
António Joaquim de Freitas.   Lourenço Marques, Mozambique:
Imprensa Nacional, 1959. 396p. bibliog. maps.

A detailed general geological study of Mozambique with chapters on geological formations, economic geology (arranged by mineral), and a section on socio-economic development from a geological viewpoint. The work also includes useful appendixes, among which are statistical tables, a 'Bibliografia geológica de Moçambique' [Geological bibliography of Mozambique] (p. 251–93), and a list of unpublished works (conference papers, reports, etc.) on p. 297–322. In both these last two cases de Freitas, who does not provide an index, repeats the same complete list of references, organized first by author, and then chronologically.

45 **Índice dos rios, lagos e lagoas de Moçambique** (Index of the rivers, lakes and lagoons of Mozambique.)
Lourenço Marques, Mozambique: Direcção Provincial dos Serviços Hidráulicos, 1969. 218p. (Publicações, no. 1).

Originally published in the *Boletim da Sociedade de Estudos de Moçambique* vol. 38, no. 158–59 (Jan.–June 1969), this is simply an alphabetical list of all the lakes and rivers in the country, with a code letter to indicate whether they dry up completely, partially, or not at all.

46 **Moçambique: eine geographische, soziale und wirtschaftliche Landeskunde.** (Mozambique: a geographical, social and economic country survey.)
Manfred Kuder.   Darmstadt, FRG: Wissenschaftliche Buchgesellschaft, 1975. 347p. bibliog. maps. (Wissenschaftliche Länderkunden, nr. 10).

This important geographical source has unfortunately never been translated into either English or Portuguese. It is a general survey and covers the geographical structure of the country, the population and the basis for social development (as of 1973). It includes an excellent bibliography (p. 315–34).

German geographers have made several contributions to the literature: see also, for example, D. Cech, *Inhambane: Kulturgeographie einer Küstenlandschaft in Südmoçambique* [Inhambane: the human geography of a coastal area in southern Mozambique] (Wiesbaden, FRG: Steiner, 1974. 141p. [Braunschweiger Geographische Studien, nr. 4]); and the doctoral dissertation of P. Weber, 'Die agrargeographische Struktur von Mittel-Moçambique: nahr- und sozialräumliche Grundlagen der Bantulandwirtschaft' [The agro-geographical structure of central Mozambique: the basis of the natural and social space of Bantu agriculture] *Marburger Geographische Schriften* vol. 48 (1971), p. 1–189.

47 **Livros interessando ao estudo do distrito de Lourenço Marques: exposição promovida pelo Centro de Documentação e Informação do Banco Nacional Ultramarino com o patrocínio da Associação dos Empregados do Banco, em Lourenço Marques em Julho de 1972: catálogo.** (Books relevant to the study of the district of Lourenço Marques: catalogue of an exhibition mounted by the National Overseas Bank, with the sponsorship of the Bank Employees' Association, in Lourenço Marques in July 1972.)
[Lourenço Marques, Mozambique: Banco Nacional Ultramarino, 1972.] 55p.

A simple list of books (in order of author) about what is now Maputo Province, with an introduction by the archivist and historian Alexandre Lobato. Lobato published a collection of essays on the history of Lourenço Marques in 1961 (q.v.). The catalogue includes 306 properly-made references, but no indexes. For a bibliography on specific aspects of the history of Lourenço Marques, see Ilídio Rocha's 'Contribuição bibliográfica para o estudo das 'questões' da baía e do caminho de ferro de Lourenço Marques' [A bibliographic contribution to the study of the 'questions' of the bay and the railway of Lourenço Marques] (q.v.); and the as-yet unpublished 'O crescimento da cidade colonial de Lourenço Marques' (The growth of the colonial city of Lourenço Marques) by Julieta Massimbe (1985).

48 **Maputo antes da independência.** (Maputo before independence.)
Maria Clara Mendes.   Lisbon: Instituto de Investigação Científica Tropical, 1985. 526p. bibliog. maps. (Memórias, 2nd series, no. 68).

This book was originally a doctoral dissertation begun in 1973 and finally submitted to the Faculty of Letters at the University of Lisbon in 1979, when it was passed with distinction. It is a highly technical piece of work, dealing with Lourenço Marques (renamed Maputo after independence) in space and time; in the African context; and as an urban network. The second section, on the internal structure of the city, deals with the evolution of the town, trade and service centres, the location of industry, ports and railways, population and territory, the typology of residential areas, transport and intra-urban movement, and the socio-political changes brought about with independence. A long and positive review by Ilídio do Amaral, on the published version of the dissertation, appeared in *Estudos de Economia* vol. 6, no. 3 (April–June 1986), p. 465–68.

49 **Mozambique: official standard names approved by the United States Board on Geographic Names.**
Washington, DC: US Board on Geographic Names, 1969. 505p.

This gazetteer includes about 32,500 place-names for colonial Mozambique. It was prepared and printed out by computer. It includes extensive cross-referencing from non-approved names to the approved versions (thus it is sometimes possible, with a little ingenuity, to find the pre-independence name from the post-independence one: e.g., for Chai Chai, see João Belo; but there is no cross-reference under Xai-Xai). Accents are marked. The coverage corresponds to that of the 1:250,000-scale maps *Carta da Colónia (Província) de Moçambique* (Map of the Colony (Province) of Mozambique) published by the Junta das Missões Geográficas e Investigações do Ultramar (Board of Geographic Missions and Overseas Research) between 1946 and 1955. Each entry consists of the place-name, a descriptive code (e.g., LK = lake), the latitude and longitude, an area number to indicate the administrative region (present-day provinces), and a code number for the maps referred to.

50 **Dicionário de nomes geográficos de Moçambique: sua origem.**
(Dictionary of geographical names of Mozambique: their origin.)
António Carlos Pereira Cabral. Lourenço Marques, Mozambique: Moderna, 1975. 180p. bibliog.

In his introduction Cabral points out that many Mozambican place-names 'suffered from the strong influence of colonialism', a discreet way of saying that they were transcribed into Portuguese approximations with no regard for their historical meaning or language of origin. My favourite example of this is the name of a small town about thirty kilometres north of Maputo, which even now is still written as Marracuene. The name derives from a local leader, Murakwe, plus the Tsonga locative suffix *-ni*. Unfortunately for the linguistically naïve transcriber, by changing the first syllable from *Mu-* to *Ma-*, he also changed the meaning from 'Murakwe's place' to something very like 'the place of buttocks' (*Marhakweni*). However, Cabral avoids such indelicate anecdotes; his dictionary consists of an alphabetical list of official place-names, with references from older forms (for Marracuene, see under Vila Luisa), and explanations of their origins and significance. He also includes the references to any legislation concerning the incorporation of towns or districts. A popular bilingual pamphlet was also produced, based on this work: *Toponímia de Moçambique: digressão histórica e geográfica* [Toponymy of Mozambique: a geographical and historical digression] (Lourenço Marques, Mozambique: Fundo do Turismo, 1975. 10p.). See also, on the question of the spelling of African place-names, the letter from Abner Sansão Mutemba in *Tempo* no. 474 (11 November 1979), p. 52–53, with the editorial response.

51 **Geologia da bacia do rio Zambeze, Moçambique: características geológico-mineiras da bacia do rio Zambeze, em território moçambicano.** (Geology of the Zambezi river basin: geological-mineral characteristics of the Zambezi river basin in Mozambican territory.)
Fernando Real. Lisbon: Junta de Investigações do Ultramar, 1966. 183p. bibliog. maps.

The Zambezi cuts Mozambique in half, running in through Tete in the west, across the widest part of the country and falling to the sea in a delta below Chinde in the east. This is an important scientific study, and includes a twenty-page summary in English of Real's main findings on p. 153–74. Among the minerals found in the area are aluminium, barite, beryllium, coal, copper, iron, gold, oil and gas, although commercial exploitation is, of course, another question.

52 **Ilha de Moçambique.** (Mozambique Island.)
Raquel Soeiro de Brito. *Geographia* (Lisbon) vol. 6, no. 21 (Jan. 1970), p. 4–21.

Geographia is the glossy '*National Geographic*-style' publication of the Lisbon Geographical Society. The articles are well illustrated with maps and photographs in colour, and are worth looking at, even for the reader with little knowledge of Portuguese. Soeiro de Brito was a researcher at the Higher Institute for Social Science and Colonial Policy (ISCSPU) at Lisbon Technical University. Mozambique Island came under Portuguese rule in 1508, and was the capital of the colonial state until 1898, when Mouzinho de Albuquerque moved to Lourenço Marques. The island is tiny: only three kilometres long, and about 350 metres wide. It is divided into three sections: the fortress at the north-eastern end; the city with its terraced houses and Muslim-style architecture in the middle, occupied in colonial times by white civil servants and Indian merchants; and the densely-populated slum or 'native quarter', Ponto da Ilha. The effects of conditions on public health in this latter area, with its population of stevedores and fishermen, and very high unemployment, were partially described in 1965 by Claudio Ferreira in his 'A Ilha de Moçambique: breve resumo histórico, aspecto climático, etnográfico e nosológico' (Mozambique Island: a short historical summary with notes on climate, ethnography and the classification of diseases) *O Médico* (Oporto) no. 728 (1965).

Maps and atlases

53 **Atlas geográfico.** (Geographical atlas.)
[Maputo]: Ministério da Educação e Cultura, 1980–83. 2 vols. maps.

Prepared for the Mozambican Ministry of Education and Culture by the Esselte Map Service in Stockholm, these atlases for school use are reproduced with the highest-quality colour-separation on excellent paper. The first volume deals mainly with Mozambique (p. 8–29, p. 46) and Africa. The second volume is

Geography. Maps and atlases

dedicated to the rest of the world. Maps cover administrative divisions, physical geography, geology, relief, hydrogeography, climate, temperature and rainfall, climatic zones, vegetation, soils, population, agricultural production, livestock, mineral resources and industry, transport, and the armed struggle for national liberation. For a very detailed series of maps of the latest changes in the administrative division of the country, proposed at the 15th session of the People's Assembly, see *Cartografia base da proposta de alteração à divisão territorial* [Basic cartography of the proposed alterations in the territorial division] (Maputo: Assembleia Popular, July 1986. [not paginated].).

54 **Atlas de Portugal ultramarino e das grandes viagens portuguesas de descobrimento e expansão.** (Atlas of Portugal overseas, and of the great voyages of discovery and expansion.)
Lisbon: Junta das Missões Geográficas e de Investigações Coloniais, 1948. 110p.

This is a revised edition of the *Atlas colonial* [Colonial atlas] (Lisbon: Comissão de Cartografia do Ministério das Colónias, 1914), and includes coloured maps dealing with ethnography, linguistics, geology, economics, imports and exports, physical geography, communications, colonial history, and the routes of the principal Portuguese navigators and explorers. Mozambique is given specific coverage on maps 73 to 86.

55 **Atlas de Portugal e colónias: descriptivo e illustrado.** (Atlas of Portugal and colonies: descriptive and illustrated.)
Júlio Gaspar Ferreira da Costa. Lisbon: Empresa Editora do Atlas de Geografia Universal, 1906. [not paginated]. maps.

A general atlas of Portugal and her colonies, with coloured maps and detailed texts on local geography. Mozambique does not receive a particularly extended treatment, but there is a large coloured map, a description of the physical geography and a summary of the administrative divisions in force at the time. The pagination is not continuous. The atlas apparently won a silver medal at the Universal Exhibition in St. Louis in 1904.

56 **Delegação portuguesa de delimitação de fronteiras Moçambique-Niassalândia.** (Portuguese delegation on the delimitation of the Mozambique-Nyasaland borders.)
Missão Geográfica de Moçambique. [Lourenço Marques, Mozambique]: Junta das Missões Geográficas e de Investigações do Ultramar, 1956. 1 vol. [pagination varies]. maps.

Includes the English and the Portuguese texts of the Mozambique-Nyasaland frontier agreement of 1954 between Britain and Portugal, and of the later exchange of notes, both of which updated and clarified the earlier agreement of 11 June 1891. The book has ten very detailed maps of the Tete-Malawi frontier and of the area around Lake Chilwa. The cover title is given as *Mozambique-Nyasaland frontier: agreement of 18th November 1954.*

57 **Atlas de Moçambique.** (Atlas of Mozambique.)
Serviços de Agrimensura. Lourenço Marques, Mozambique:
Empresa Moderna, 1962. 43p. maps.

Contains maps on Vasco da Gama's journey of exploration, the administrative divisions, districts (now provinces), mountains, altitudes, rivers, geology, mineralogy, climate, rain, demography, missionary activity, language groups, ethnic groups, livestock, wild animals, agriculture, forestry, economic activities, transport routes, posts, telegraphs and telephones, and health. An index is provided.

58 **Atlas missionário português.** (Portuguese missionary atlas.)
A. da Silva Rego, Eduardo dos Santos. Lisbon: Centro de Estudos Históricos Ultramarinos, Junta de Investigações do Ultramar, 1964. 2nd ed. 198p. bibliog. maps.

Maps of high-quality colour, and charts of Catholic and Protestant missions and missionary activity (in areas of health, education, etc.) in the Portuguese Empire. The maps show the location of the mission stations, and there are textual descriptions, in both French and Portuguese, of the various dioceses. Other maps show, for example, the distribution of ethnic groups. A very useful work.

59 **Ensaio de iconografia das cidades portuguesas do ultramar.** (Essay on the iconography of Portuguese cities overseas.)
Luís Silveira. Lisbon: Junta de Investigações do Ultramar [n.d.]. 4 vols.

Four large volumes of reproductions and descriptions of maps and drawings of 'Portuguese' cities and towns all over the world. Volume 2 (p. 125–301) deals with Africa, and Eastern Africa is covered on p. 243–99, with material on Lourenço Marques, Sofala, Beira, Quelimane, Sena, Tete, Mozambique Island, Porto Amélia (now Pemba), Quiloa, Angoche and finally Mombasa in Kenya. Maps are described in detail, with their scale, dimensions and method of printing. On p. 301 Silveira prints a short summary in English entitled 'Portuguese towns in Africa'. For a list of hand-drawn maps of Portuguese possessions in Africa, see also the *Catálogo das cartas na Junta de Investigações do Ultramar, 2ª parte: Províncias Ultramarinas Portuguesas. Cartas manuscritas* [Catalogue of maps at the Overseas Research Board. Part 2. Portuguese overseas provinces. Manuscript maps] (Lisbon: Secção de Cartografia Antiga, 1960. Provisional ed. 129p.).

Flora and Fauna

60   **A field guide to the coral reef fishes of the Indian and West Pacific oceans.**
R. H. Carcasson.   London: Collins, 1977. 320p. map.

Carcasson, a veteran marine biologist, has written a practical work aimed at enabling amateur naturalists to recognize the more common fishes that can be seen while diving and angling, or, indeed, when shopping in a tropical fish-market. In addition, the book is intended for aquarium keepers. As with other volumes in the Collins' field-guide series, Carcasson avoids entering into controversies over classification, and uses only a simple key to the orders and major families. He advises anybody with more than a passing interest in the subject to learn the Latin names of these fish, since their geographical distribution can be so wide that common names may be virtually useless. As well as many line-drawings, the book is illustrated with forty-eight full-colour plates. The Mozambican coastline falls within the area covered by this book.

61   **A handlist of the birds of southern Mozambique.**
P. A. Clancey.   Lourenço Marques, Mozambique: Instituto de Investigação Científica de Moçambique, 1971. [pagination varies]. bibliog. maps.

First published in the *Memórias* of the IICM (Mozambican Institute of Scientific Research) vol. 10, series A (1969–70) and vol. 11, series A (1971). This separate volume includes an index and some addenda, as well as thirty-nine colour plates and distribution maps (for the whole country). Clancey's work replaced the outdated 'Catálogo das aves de Moçambique' (Catalogue of the birds of Mozambique) by F. Frade, which was an unillustrated checklist published in the *Anais da Junta de Investigações Coloniais* vol. 6, tome 4, fasc. 4 (1951), p. 1–294.

24

62 **Bibliography of marine biology in south Africa.**
D. A. Darracott, A. C. Brown.   Pretoria: Council for Scientific
and Industrial Research, 1980. 239p. (South African National
Scientific Programmes. Report no. 41).

As so often in this kind of literature 'south Africa' means 'southern Africa', and
as far as Mozambique is concerned, this means south of the Sabie (Save) River.
The main listing is organized in simple author order, using the code ANON for
items without named authors, and the material goes back to the 19th century.
Although the entries are numbered, they are not in sequential order, apparently
through a computer error; nor do the numbers in the keyword (subject) index
correspond to the numbers of the entries. However, since the code for each
citation consists of the first four letters of the author's name, the last two numbers
of the year of publication, and only then the sequential number, the list is still
usable. There is also an author index. The bibliography appears to have about
4,000 items, although this is hard to estimate for the reason outlined above. It is
based on various other bibliographies and card indexes, which are listed in the
preface.

63 **A guide to marine life on south African shores.**
J. H. Day.   Cape Town; Rotterdam, The Netherlands: Balkema,
1974. 2nd rev. ed. 300p. bibliog. map.

Professor Day, a well-known specialist on bristle-worms (polychaeta) and the
ecology of estuaries, was head of the Zoology Department at the University of
Cape Town and led a team of marine biology researchers to produce this book.
The work covers the coastline of the Republic of South Africa and of
Mozambique up as far as Inhambane. There are keys and illustrations to enable
the user to identify 1,200 common species of animals and plants, ranging from sea
anemones and seaweeds to fishes and mangrove trees. There are also notes on the
ecology and biology of marine life. Although intended for students, the work is
written in non-technical language, with explanations of essential scientific terms.
All the plates and line-drawings are in black-and-white.

64 **A field guide to the larger mammals of Africa.**
Jean Dorst, Pierre Dandelot.   London: Collins, 1972. 2nd ed.
287p. maps.

Dorst and Dandelot have attempted to produce a general field-guide to the
larger and more readily-observable mammals of Africa as a whole – including
Mozambique. All the species are illustrated in colour – there are forty-four plates
showing 233 animals – and there are also distribution maps. However, the authors
are careful to point out that this is not a work of systematics: classification is not
too rigid, the maps are indicative rather than definitive, and characteristics noted
are those which can be readily seen in the field. Also given are rough
measurements (usually height at the shoulder), similar species, habitat, habits,
common names in French, German, Swahili and Afrikaans (but not Portuguese),
subspecies, and brief and tentative notes on classification. The book can be
carried easily (although it is just too large for the pocket) and is eminently
suitable for amateur observers who wish to increase their knowledge without
delving too deeply.

Flora and Fauna

65   **Flora Zambesiaca.**
A. W. Exell (et al.).   London: Royal Botanical Gardens, Kew, 1960–. irregular.

This ongoing multi-part series on the flora of the Zambezi Valley is an essential reference work for botanists in Mozambique, Zimbabwe, Zambia, Malawi and Botswana, and is even useful for those in Tanzania. It is especially generous with drawings, often providing illustrations of all the members of a family. The volumes range in size from 150 to 600 pages, and the descriptions of herbs, plants and flowers are both exhaustive and highly technical. Information on distribution and growth patterns is also included. For northern Mozambique the *Flora of tropical East Africa* (London: Crown Agents, 1952–. irregular.), which covers about 200 genera, is also useful. Of a similar character is the ongoing part-work in Portuguese, *Flora de Moçambique* [Flora of Mozambique] (Lisbon: Centro de Botânica), begun by A. Fernandes and later edited by E. J. Mendes. Botany was an area of great interest for the Portuguese, and it is impossible to list all their research here; but see, for instance, the identically-titled but distinct works *Contribuições para o conhecimento da flora de Moçambique* [Contribution to the knowledge of the flora of Mozambique], one by J. G. Garcia (Lisbon: Junta de Investigações do Ultramar, 1957. 66p.), and the other a collection edited by F. A. Mendonça (Lisbon: Junta de Investigações do Ultramar, 1950–54. 2 vols.). For a detailed and up-to-date local account of the vascular plants of the northwest, see A. E. Gonçalves' 'Catálogo das espécies vegetais vasculares assinaladas na província de Tete, Mocambique' (Catalogue of the vascular plant species of Tete Province, Mozambique) *Garcia de Orta*, botanical series, vol. 4, no. 1 (1978–79), p. 13–92; no. 2 (1980), p. 93–170; and vol. 5, no. 1 (1981), p. 59–124, which includes 677 species so far.

66   **Forest entomology of Mozambique: contribution for the study of the xylophagus insects.**
Maria Corinta Ferreira, Gunderico da Veiga Ferreira.   Lourenço Marques, Mozambique: Junta de Comércio Externo, 1951–57.
3 vols. maps.

'Xylophagous', for the non-biologist, means 'wood-eating'. This illustrated, technical study was published in a mixture of English and Portuguese. Part one deals with the *Bostrychidae*, and appeared in both English and Portuguese editions. Part two covers the *Cerambycidae* and the *Prioninae* subfamily, and also came out in both languages. Part three, in two volumes in Portuguese only, describes the tribes and supertribes of the *Cerambycinae*. See also on beetles, the list of eighty-one species in Maria Corinta Ferreira's 'Catálogo dos escarabídeos existentes no Museu Dr. Álvaro de Castro' (Catalogue of stag-beetles in the Dr. Álvaro de Castro Museum) *Memórias do Museu Dr. Álvaro de Castro* no. 3 (1955), p. 55–86.

67   **A field guide to the snakes of southern Africa.**
V. F. M. FitzSimons, A. H. Barratt.   London: Collins, 1974.
2nd ed. 221p. bibliog.

A portable reference guide to snakes in Mozambique and the sub-continent covering the better-known species. This second edition revises the classification

26

employed in the light of recent scientific work. Each entry includes a detailed description with physical characteristics, notes on distribution and general remarks, as well as giving the scientific, English and Afrikaans names of the species. There are twelve plates by Barratt, many black-and-white photographs, a distribution table and an index. See also, by the same authors, *Snakes of southern Africa* (Cape Town, London: Purnell, 1962. 423p.) with distribution maps.

68   **FAO species identification sheets for fishery purposes: eastern Indian Ocean (Fishing Area 57) and western Central Pacific (Fishing Area 71).**
   Food and Agriculture Organization of the United Nations.
   Rome: FAO, 1974. 4 vols.

These sheets constitute, at the time of writing, the principal reference work on the commercial bony (teleost) fish of the western as well as of the eastern Indian Ocean, and thus include Mozambican species. Their use is obviously limited by the fact that since they refer principally to another part of the Indian Ocean, locally abundant species from the African coast are often missing altogether, or are only mentioned without illustrations or full data. For this reason the publication of the volumes on the western Indian Ocean are awaited with some eagerness by local marine biologists.

69   **Dendrologia de Moçambique: estudo geral.** (Dendrology of Mozambique: a general study.)
   António Figueiredo Gomes e Sousa.   Lourenço Marques, Mozambique: Centro de Documentação Agrária, Instituto de Investigação Agronómica de Moçambique [n.d.]. 2 vols. maps. (Série 'Memórias', no. 1).

Gomes e Sousa (born in 1896) was described by the agronomist A. Quintanilha as a 'simple man, timid, industrious and obstinate as the ant . . . [and] in love with the tree'. He produced a long list of articles and monographs on the trees of Angola, Guinea and Mozambique over several decades. This memoir is a basic and carefully compiled reference work, divided into a short introduction on tree ecology and a long reference section on the species. Although no date is given, the two volumes certainly appeared after 1965. Gomes e Sousa's works are a bibliographer's nightmare, since he had earlier published a work in four volumes also entitled *Dendrologia de Moçambique* (Lourenço Marques, Mozambique: Imprensa Nacional for the Junta de Exportação de Moçambique, 1951–60). These were actually a series of individual studies – Volume One: *Algumas madeiras comerciais* [Some commercial timbers], also published in an English translation by A. de P. Bartolomeu (Lourenço Marques, Mozambique: Imprensa Nacional, 1951. 248p.); Volume Two: *Essências do extremo sul* [Outline of the southern-most part]; Volume Four: *Essências da região do Mutuáli* [Outline of Mutuáli region]; and Volume Five: *Distrito de Manica e Sofala* [The district of Manica and Sofala]. Two of these studies were first published in *Moçambique: Documentário Trimestral*: Volume One appeared as the whole of issue no. 64 (1950), and Volume Three was published in five parts in issue nos. 84 to 89/92 (1955–57). They continued such earlier work by Gomes e Sousa as 'Essências florestais de Inhambane' [Forestry outline of Inhambane] *Moçambique: Documentário*

Flora and Fauna

Trimestral nos. 22 to 29 (1940 to 1942) in eight parts; and 'Essências florestais do distrito de Nampula' [Forestry outline of the district of Nampula], in the same journal, nos. 46 to 48, and 51 (1946 to 1947) in four parts. Gomes e Sousa was a winner of the Thomas Sim prize, named after the Natal Government forester whose own book *Forest flora and forest resources of Portuguese East Africa* (Aberdeen: Taylor & Henderson, 1908. 378p.) marked the beginning of serious dendrology in Mozambique.

70   **Sea-shells of southern Africa: gastropods.**
      Brian Kensley, J. Kramer, C. Coetzee.   Cape Town: Maskew
      Miller for the South African Museum, 1973. 225p.

This work, the first of two planned volumes, consists mainly of black-and-white (but with some colour) drawings of the shells of southern Africa from the area south of the Cunene River on the west coast, and south of Inhambane in the east, thus covering southern Mozambique. Although this work has received high praise, it has its faults: there are no keys to the over 900 species listed, and the notes on each are skimpy; they do, however, include the scientific name, range and depth, colour and measurements. There are indexes of common and scientific names, notes for shell collectors, and an illustrated glossary.

71   **Sea shells of southern Africa.**
      Richard Kilburn, Elizabeth Rippey.   Johannesburg: Macmillan
      South Africa, 1982. 249p. bibliog. map.

In order to compile a list of works on the flora and fauna of Mozambique, it is often necessary to choose between publications specifically on the country, but in Portuguese, or works on the region, published in South Africa in English. Here once again in a South African book on natural history, the definition of southern Africa includes Mozambique south of the Sabie (Save) River. This large, glossy volume is, in fact, the best book available on shells, with better drawings and better descriptions than its competitors, up-to-date nomenclature, information on habitats, on the animal itself, and good data on distribution. The colour plates are of high quality, and some 600 species are covered. The work also includes an interesting section on pioneer shell-collectors in southern Africa, for those interested in the history of science, and advice on how to build a collection.

72   **Birds of the southern third of Africa.**
      C. W. Mackworth-Praed, C. H. B. Grant.   London: Longman,
      1982. 2 vols. maps. (African Handbook of Birds, series 2, vols.1
      and 2).

A classic work, first published in 1962–66 and now reissued by Longman after a long period out of print. Its comprehensiveness is its main virtue, since it includes not only identification features for each species, but also details of habitat, habits, voice, food, nests, eggs, distribution (with maps) and breeding seasons. The colour paintings are reproduced adequately, even in the reprint. Each volume also includes a number of black-and-white photographs. Although intended as a field-guide, the size and the price may well discourage such usage, and many ornithologists prefer *Roberts' birds of south Africa* (q.v.). This reprinted edition of the *Handbook* includes a biographical note on the authors: Grant died in 1958,

28

having prepared most of the taxonomy and nomenclature, but Mackworth-Praed continued to work on the *Handbook* as a whole until 1973, when the sixth and final volume appeared. It was his own financial backing which ensured the completion of the project to cover the whole continent.

73   **Roberts' birds of south Africa.**
A. Roberts, revised by G. R. McLachlan, R. Liversidge.
[Cape Town]: Struik for the Trustees of the John Voelcker Bird
Book Fund, 1978. 4th ed. 660p.

The standard work on southern African ornithology. As in many works of this nature, the expression 'south Africa' is interpreted generously, referring not only to the Republic but to the region of southern Africa, including Mozambique. The entries for the approximately 875 species include their scientific names and the vernacular names in English, Afrikaans and various African languages, but not Portuguese. Details are also provided of size, identification characteristics, distribution, habits, food, voice, breeding and local races. There are colour plates as well as black-and-white drawings, a guide to ornithological terminology and three indexes of bird names. For Mozambique, the differences between this edition and its predecessor (1970. 643p.) do not seem to be great. The book first came out in 1940, and the first edition sold over 30,000 copies. A smaller field-guide is also available: O. P. M. Prozesky's *A field guide to the birds of southern Africa* (London: Collins, 1974. 2nd ed. 350p.), with thirty-two colour and eight black-and-white plates. It spans Mozambique south of the Zambezi, covering 900 species, but overlaps to some extent with J. G. Williams' field-guide in the same series (q.v.).

74   **A vegetação do extremo sul da província de Moçambique:**
contribuição para o seu estudo. (The vegetation of southernmost
Mozambique: a preliminary study.)
Mário Myre.   Lisbon: Junta de Investigações de Moçambique,
1964. 145p. bibliog. map. (Estudos, Ensaios e Documentos,
no. 110).

Consists mainly of a phyto-sociological study of the main types and subtypes of grassland in the Maputo area, and mentions briefly the other kinds of vegetation (see chapter four). The book includes an English summary on p. 137–41. Myre refers to the pioneering general survey by J. Gomes Pedro and L. A. Grandvaux Barbosa, published as the chapter 'Vegetação' (Vegetation) in volume two of the *Esboço do reconhecimento ecológico-agrícola de Moçambique* [Preliminary agro-ecological survey of Mozambique] (Lourenço Marques, Mozambique: Imprensa Nacional, 1955. p. 67–224) with a folding map, a bibliography and a summary in English. This also appeared in the review *Moçambique: Documentário Trimestral* nos. 80 and 81 (1954–55). For other important writings by this author, see *Os principais componentes das pastagens espontâneas do sul da província de Moçambique: contribuição para o seu estudo* [The main components of natural grasslands in southern Mozambique: a preliminary study] (Lisbon: Junta de Investigações do Ultramar, 1960. 307p. bibliog. map. [Memórias da Junta de Investigações do Ultramar, 2nd series, no. 20]), which is a study of the ecology of Mozambican grasses and includes a summary in (bad) English (p. 301–04). He also published, in English, a study of the wooded and open grasslands along the western border, south of the Limpopo and Nkomati rivers, where the species *Themeda triandra* Forsk is dominant: see 'A grassland type of the south of the Mozambique Province' in: *Comptes rendus de la IVème réunion plénière de l'Association pour l'Étude Taxonomique de la Flore d'Afrique Tropicale, Lisbonne et Coïmbre, 16–23 Septembre 1960* (Proceedings of the 4th plenary meeting of the Association for the Study of the Classification of the Flora of Tropical Africa, Lisbon and Coimbra, 16–23 September 1960) edited by A. Fernandes. Lisbon: Junta de Investigações do Ultramar, 1962. p. 337–61.

75 **Trees of southern Africa.**

Keith Coates Palgrave, in association with R. B. Drummond, edited by E. J. Moll. Cape Town: Struik, 1977. 959p.

An illustrated coffee-table and 'weekend-rambles' book which covers Mozambican trees for the part of the country south of the Zambezi River. Palgrave gives the common names of the trees in both English and Afrikaans, but not Portuguese. The descriptions include information on medicinal and/or poisonous properties, folklore connected with the species and economic significance, if any.

76 **A field guide to the trees of southern Africa.**

Eve Palmer, illustrated by Rhona Collett. London, Johannesburg: Collins, 1977. 352p. bibliog. maps.

Palmer's guide focuses principally on South Africa, Namibia, Lesotho, Swaziland and Botswana, but it covers southern Mozambique too. Both author and illustrator are well-known South African specialists. The work is organized around a system of keys for the identification of species, which lead to the text and the descriptions. Entries provide English, Afrikaans and African-language names, but not Portuguese. There are 155 colour paintings and a large number of black-and-white line-drawings of the various species by Rhona Collett. Palmer provides a complete list of South African species, a glossary of technical terms and an index of scientific and vernacular tree names. In addition to this field-manual, she is the author, with N. Pitman, of the definitive *Trees of southern Africa* (Cape Town: Balkema, 1972–73. 2nd ed. 3 vols.).

77 **Contribution to the study of the ornithology of Sul do Save, Mozambique.**

António A. da Rosa Pinto, Donald W. Lamm. *Memórias do Museu Dr. Álvaro de Castro* no. 2 (1953), p. 65–85; no. 3 (1955), p. 125–59; no. 4 (1956), p. 107–67; no. 5 (1960), p. 69–126.

A catalogue of 199 species of birds found in the southern third of Mozambique. There are no illustrations. Oddly, the same articles were also published in Portuguese in the same issues of the same journal: no. 2, p. 43–64; no. 3, p. 87–124; no. 4, p. 41–105; and no. 5, p. 3–67.

78 **African insect life.**
S. H. Skaife, revised by John Ledger, photographs by A. Bannister. London: Country Life Books, 1979. 2nd rev. ed. 278p. map.

A large, glossy and fascinating popularization of African entomology for the general reader, and on balance one of the best works available on the subject. The book was first published several years ago, and was subsequently revised, after Skaife's death, by John Ledger. It covers the whole of sub-Saharan Africa, including Mozambique, and is organized into twenty-four liberally-illustrated chapters, one of which deals with the insects' close relatives, the 'other arthropoda'. There is no bibliography as such, but each section has suggestions for further reading. The colloquial and accessible style of the text is enhanced by the spectacular colour photographs of Anthony Bannister. There is an index and a useful chapter on entomology as a hobby or career.

79 **The sea fishes of southern Africa.**
J. L. B. Smith. [Cape Town]: Central News Agency, 1965. 5th ed. 580p. bibliogs. maps.

This massive work covers the Indian Ocean coast of Africa up to the end of the Mozambique Channel. It is profusely illustrated, in both colour and black-and-white, and describes over 1,200 species. New editions are created, however, by simply adding newly-discovered species or new data onto the existing text in the form of appendixes rather than by revising the original work. Considerable care, therefore, needs to be exercised in using the book, and in making sure that all the relevant information has been found. The work is organized into two principal sections: the first consisting of general notes about southern African fish life; the second describing each species. Despite the date of this edition, Smith's volume remains the principal general reference source for systematic work on salt-water fish in the region. It should be used in conjunction with the *FAO species identification sheets for fishery purposes* (q.v.), which cover the commercially-exploitable species. A new edition has recently appeared, entitled *Smith's sea fishes* (Johannesburg: [n.p.], 1986. 1,200p.).

80 **The marine fish resources of Mozambique.**
Roald Soetre, Rui de Paula e Silva. Maputo: Serviço de Investigações Pesqueiras; Bergen, Norway: Institute of Marine Research, 1979. 179p. bibliog. maps. (Reports on Surveys with the Research Vessel *Dr. Fridtjof Nansen*).

Between August 1977 and June 1978 four complete surveys of the Mozambican coast were made by a team of Norwegian and Mozambican scientists, on board the Norwegian vessel *Dr. Fridtjof Nansen*. The surveys had seven objectives: to locate commercially-exploitable concentrations of fish; to map them; to make biological studies of them; to look at the oceanography of the areas where the concentrations are located; to estimate the abundance of local stocks; to evaluate fishing techniques; and to train Mozambicans as marine biologists. This report includes a summary in Portuguese (p. 5–9).

Flora and Fauna

81 **Catálogo de peixes de Moçambique, zona sul, mais frequentamente desembarcados nos portos pesqueiros de maior importância do sul de Moçambique: Maputo, Inhaca, Inhambane e Inhassoro.** (A catalogue of Mozambican fish, southern zone, most often unloaded in the main fishing ports of southern Mozambique: Maputo, Inhaca, Inhambane and Inhassoro.)
Maria Inelda Sousa, Margarida Dias.   Maputo: Instituto de Desenvolvimento Pesqueiro, 1981. 121p. bibliog.

An up-to-date catalogue of the forty-one main commercial species of southern Mozambique, in alphabetical order of their Portuguese common names. Sousa gives the Latin, English, French, Spanish and local names, a few words on habitat, a colour photograph, and a detailed line-drawing. There are indexes by all the kinds of name mentioned.

82 **Abecedário dos mamíferos selvagens de Moçambique: componentes de maior vulto da fauna terrestre.** (An ABC of the wild animals of Mozambique: principal elements of the land fauna.)
J. A. Travessos Santos Dias.   Maputo: Empresa Moderna, 1981. 2nd rev. ed. 271p. bibliog.

Sixty-two black-and-white drawings and photographs, and twenty-three colour plates, none of them well reproduced, of Mozambican wild animals. Entries are in alphabetical order of the Portuguese name of the animal, and the discursive descriptions include information on distribution within the country. There are some statistical tables and a list of African-language names of the animals covered.

83 **A field guide to the birds of East and Central Africa.**
John George Williams.   London: Collins; Boston, Massachusetts: Houghton Mifflin, 1978. new ed. 360p.

Although *Roberts' birds of south Africa* (q.v.) and the weighty multi-volume opus of Mackworth-Praed and Grant (q.v.) are likely to remain the standard works on African birds for some time to come, there is still room for a manageable field-handbook which can be tucked easily into a bag or rucksack, and which does not need both hands to consult it. Williams was Curator of Birds at the Coryndon Museum in Nairobi, and this guide describes nearly 1,300 of the more common species from Ethiopia to Mozambique, of which over half are illustrated in colour. The author promises that the remaining species are covered in his *Field guide to the national parks of East Africa* (London: Collins, 1981. rev. ed. 352p.). Each entry provides details of English and scientific names, identification characteristics, voice, distribution and habitat.

84 **A field guide to the butterflies of Africa.**
John George Williams.   London: Collins; Boston, Massachusetts: Houghton Mifflin, 1970. 240p. bibliog.

A general guide for the amateur lepidopterist, covering all of sub-Saharan Africa, including Mozambique but excluding the island of Madagascar. Williams describes the 436 most commonly-found species, out of a then-estimated 2,400 African butterflies (recent estimates of the number of insect species in the Third World have risen dramatically to a ceiling of 30 million; see the *New Scientist* 24 February 1983, p. 522). He gives their English and Latin names, their measurements, the chief identifying colour and pattern characteristics for sexes and species; and details of their distribution, habitat, flight, habits and food plants. Each butterfly is illustrated with a line-drawing, and 283 species are portrayed in colour. There is a general introduction to the study and collection of butterflies.

Prehistory and Archaeology

85　**Economic models for the Manekweni** *zimbabwe*, **Mozambique.**
Graeme Barker. *Azania* vol. 13 (1978), p. 71–100.

Barker describes the Manekweni site, located in the southern lowlands of Mozambique about fifty kilometres from the coast. The *zimbabwe* (a Shona word, meaning 'a stone building') was occupied during the late Iron Age (from the 12th to the 16th or 17th centuries) and was contemporary to Great Zimbabwe (the ruins of the former capital of the Monomotapa Empire, located in Zimbabwe, and from which the modern country takes its name). Barker presents an economic model for the site, based on faunal remains (mainly well-preserved animal bones) discovered there during the two archaeological seasons of 1975 and 1976. He concludes that the main activities were agriculture and cattle-keeping, and that the site seems to have acted as some sort of intermediary between Great Zimbabwe and the Indian Ocean.

86　**Iron Age research in Mozambique: collected preliminary reports.**
Teresa Cruz e Silva, João Carlos de Senna-Martinez, João Manuel Morais, Ricardo Teixeira Duarte.　Maputo: Secção de Pré-História, Centro de Estudos Africanos, Universidade Eduardo Mondlane, 1976. 1 vol. [pagination varies].

This mimeographed publication consists of five early papers, in English, on Mozambican archaeology by a team of young Mozambican researchers who at that time made up the Prehistory Section of the Centro de Estudos Africanos. This section later became the Department of Archaeology and Anthropology within Eduardo Mondlane University at Maputo. The work was produced in English partly because, in the absence of an agreed scientific terminology in Portuguese, rigorous archaeological work in that language was difficult. The papers include material on what the group themselves have termed the 'Matola tradition' (covering a set of specific peculiarities about the remains found in the

34

sites at and around Matola, near Maputo) and appear under the titles: 'Prehistoric research in Moçambique', by João Manuel Morais, with an extensive bibliography; 'A preliminary report on an early Iron Age site: Matola IV 1/68', by Teresa Cruz e Silva; 'A preliminary report on two early Iron Age pottery traditions from southern Moçambique coastal plain', by João Carlos de Senna-Martinez; 'A tentative construction of a model: modern traditional pottery from the coastal plain, Gaza Province', by João Morais and Teresa Cruz e Silva; and 'Three Iron Age sites in Massingir area, Gaza Province, Moçambique, and their importance in the southern Moçambique Bantu settlement', by Ricardo Teixeira Duarte.

87   **The archaeology of the Sofala coast.**
Ron W. Dickinson.   *South African Archaeological Bulletin*
no. 119–20, vol. 30 (Dec. 1975), p. 84–104.
The early 16th-century fortress at Sofala is the oldest European building in south-east Africa, and was built on the site of the Arabized sheikhdom of Yusufu, formerly an outpost of Kilwa. The surrounding African peoples were Shona-speakers who kept cattle, used iron implements and ate meat, fish and shellfish. Dickinson presents the results of the excavations made in 1969 and in 1972: there is evidence, from the artefacts found, of contact with the Monomotapa Empire and with Indian traders.

88   **Cattle-keeping and milking in eastern and southern African history: the linguistic evidence.**
Christopher Ehret. *Journal of African History* vol. 8, no. 1 (1967), p. 1–17.
A technical study of terms for cattle and milk throughout the Bantu-language areas of eastern and southern Africa, including Mozambique. Ehret draws on evidence from a number of Mozambican national languages, such as Chope, Ronga, Chuabo, Ndau, Sena and Tsonga, concluding, after systematic comparison and analysis, that cattle-keeping in this region of Africa is of considerable antiquity; and that a single people initiated the spread of cattle-keeping southwards, although cattle-milking only followed some time later. There is a detailed folding map of the language areas.

89   **An investigation of Manekweni, Mozambique.**
Peter Garlake.   *Azania* vol. 11 (1976), p. 25–47.
This is a detailed account of the first season of excavations at Manekweni in 1975. Garlake begins by briefly and dryly describing the colonial literature: two articles existed concerning the site, dated 1941 and 1971, of which the latter attributed the *zimbabwe* culture to the Phoenicians. The architecture, building techniques, pottery and artefacts of the site all point to a close connection with the distant Great Zimbabwe culture. Radio-carbon dating shows that the site was occupied between the 12th and 17th centuries. Chinese porcelain is present, as are glass beads in large numbers, indicating trade connections in the later phases. The site seems to have been a Shona capital, perhaps like that of Gambe, the founder of a Shona dynasty in Tonge, which is described in the 16th-century missionary literature.

Prehistory and Archaeology

90 **Mozambique: excavations at Manekweni.**
Peter S. Garlake. *People's Power in Mozambique, Angola and Guinea-Bissau* no. 7/8 (June 1977), p. 10–13.

A non-specialist account of the importance and antiquity of the Manekweni *zimbabwe* and its surrounding settlement. Garlake recounts that the inability of the Portuguese to come to terms with the site led to the publication as late as 1972 of a report claiming that the *zimbabwes* were the work of 'prehistoric Portuguese' fetching gold for King Solomon's temple. He writes that the site is also important because of the work-methods, involving the local people, used there. '. . . Mozambique has the will, the structures and the popular support to make a significant breakthrough in the retrieval of primary historical information.'

91 **Pastoralism and *zimbabwe*.**
P. S. Garlake. *Journal of African History* vol. 19, no. 4 (1978), p. 479–93.

This paper is based on work done at the Mozambican *zimbabwe*, or enclosure, at Manekweni which has been shown to have belonged to the Zimbabwe culture of the plateau, and was occupied between the 12th and 18th centuries. Evidence from animal remains shows that at least part of the population engaged in intensive beef-production, through transhumant pastoralism (a technical term for the seasonal movement of cattle to another region) on the fringes of tsetse-fly infested areas. Garlake begins to reconstruct some aspects of the economy of the early *zimbabwes* and concludes that they were not simply the products of long-distance trade, but integrated farming and animal husbandry, as well as gold production and foreign trade.

92 **Arqueologia e conhecimento do passado.** (Archaeology and knowledge of the past.)
Secção de Arqueologia, Instituto de Investigação Científica de Moçambique. *África: literatura, arte e cultura* no. 5 (July–Sept. 1979), p. 544–51.

A short introductory text by the unit which was originally the Prehistory Section of the Centro de Estudos Africanos, and which eventually became the Department of Archaeology and Anthropology at Eduardo Mondlane University. The piece first appeared under the same title in the Mozambican series *Trabalhos de Arqueologia e Antropologia* no. 1 (Sept. 1980) p. 1–10, and presents a brief overview of Mozambican archaeology in colonial times, starting in 1721, when the Royal Academy in Lisbon mentioned for the first time that rock-paintings existed in Mozambique. However, excavations were undertaken mainly between 1907 and 1930, when research activity ceased again until 1969. The article then briefly discusses the 'Matola tradition', and the stone *zimbabwes* (enclosures) of central and southern Mozambique, with a glance at the Graeco-Roman and Arabic written evidence about the region. The final section presents an overview of the Secção de Arqueologia's own work at the *zimbabwe* of Manekweni (Portuguese: Manhiquene), about fifty kilometres from Vilanculos. For more details on this last topic, see the report 'Manyikeni, a *zimbabwe* in southern Mozambique' (q.v.), and Garlake's report 'An investigation of Manekweni, Mozambique' (q.v.).

93   **Archaeological sites on the bay of Sofala.**
Gerhard Liesegang.   *Azania* vol. 7 (1972), p. 147–59.
The first systematic surveys of the area were undertaken by Ron Dickinson (q.v.)
of the University of Rhodesia in 1969–70. Liesegang's report is based on visits to
the site in 1969 and 1971, and on discussions with Dickinson. He looks at the
question of the location of pre-Portuguese Islamic settlements at Sofala, where
the coast is continuously subject to erosion. He also gives an account of pottery
and other finds, and describes the reasons for the decline of Sofala.

94   **Archaeology in Mozambique: report on research work, 1982–83.**
Per-Inge Lindqvist.   [Stockholm]: Central Board of National
Antiquities, 1984. 20p. bibliog. map. (International Report, no. 2).
Two Swedish archaeologists, Leif Jonsson and Per-Inge Lindqvist, were recruited
with the support of the Swedish Agency for Research Cooperation with
Developing Countries (SAREC) to work for the Mozambican National
Antiquities and Museums Service in 1982, but ended up in the University's
Department of Archaeology and Anthropology. This well-printed and well-
illustrated brochure is a general survey describing work undertaken on the islands
of Inhaca and Mozambique, as well as at Ponto de Ouro, Matola and Chakota
during that period. The descriptions include material on underwater archaeology.

95   **Some recent radiocarbon dates from eastern and southern Africa.**
Tim Maggs.   *Journal of African History* vol. 18, no. 2 (1977),
p. 161–91.
The *Journal of African History* publishes an irregular series of articles on eastern
and southern radio-carbon dates. The series was started by Brian Fagan in
1969 and continued by D. W. Phillipson (vol. 11, no. 1 (1970), p. 1–15);
J. E. G. Sutton (vol. 13, no. 1 (1972), p. 1–24); and R. C. Soper (vol. 15, no. 2
(1974), p. 175–92). Country coverage varies from article to article and Maggs is
the first to include material specifically on Mozambique. He gives a concise
summary of the state of the science of calibrating radio-carbon dates with
calendar years, and then moves on to discuss recent finds, in chronological order,
beginning with a short and non-comprehensive account of important evidence
from the middle Stone Age. There are several pages on late Stone Age ceramics
and food production, and material on the early and late Iron ages. The article
closes with the by-now customary list of previously unpublished radio-carbon
dates, by laboratory number, date and site. Maggs refers to Peter S. Garlake's
'Excavation of a *zimbabwe* in Mozambique', *Antiquity* (no. 198, vol. 50, (1976),
p. 146–48), and to R. M. Derricourt's 'Some coastal shell middens in southern
Mozambique', *Azania* (vol. 10 (1975), p. 135–39).

96 **Manyikeni: a *zimbabwe* in southern Mozambique.**
João Morais, Paul Sinclair.   In: *Proceedings of the 8th Panafrican Congress of Prehistory and Quaternary Studies, Nairobi, 5 to 10 September 1977.* Edited by Richard E. Leakey, Bethwell A. Ogot. Nairobi: International Louis Leakey Memorial Institute for African Prehistory, 1980. p. 351–54.

Manekweni is a *zimbabwe* site about 120 kilometres south of the Sabie (Save) River, fifty kilometres east of Vilanculos in Inhambane. Previous excavations at Great Zimbabwe had shown that only a tiny proportion of the population lived inside the stone walls of the main structure, and the authors argue that the research which had been concentrated on this area presented a distorted, or at least unrepresentative, picture. In this report, printed in double columns in a folio-sized volume, and including maps and references, the Centro de Estudos Africanos team present the results of investigation outside the walls. They surveyed an area with a radius of five kilometres, excavating 106 sample trenches, and the preliminary results suggested that Manekweni had been occupied in three phases. An analysis of the ceramics discovered is reported to be proceeding. For a discussion of the much more conventional first season at Manekweni see Peter Garlake's paper 'An investigation of Manekweni, Mozambique' (q.v.). The *Proceedings* also include Teresa Cruz e Silva's paper 'First indications of early Iron Age in southern Mozambique: Matola IV 1-68' (q.v.) in abbreviated form (p. 349–50).

97 **Mozambican archaeology: past and present.**
João Morais.   *African Archaeological Review* vol. 2 (1984), p. 113–28.

Morais, formerly the head of the Department of Archaeology and Anthropology in Maputo, is now in Europe. This survey article covers the development of archaeological research in independent Mozambique. In 1975 the whole literature on archaeology and prehistory probably comprised about 200 titles, mainly in such journals as the *Memórias do Instituto de Investigação Científica de Moçambique*, the *Boletim da Sociedade de Estudos de Moçambique*, *Moçambique: Documentário Trimestral* and *Monumenta*. Despite some pioneering work, prehistory was not even in the school curriculum. Morais shows that between 1976 and 1983 an archaeological survey programme was undertaken in the country, which doubled the number of known sites, adding 126 new locations. He also discusses the most suitable *problématique* for archaeological research in present conditions, allowing for other national priorities. On the northern sites, see also Amaro Monteiro's article in French, 'Vestiges archéologiques du Cap Delgado et de Quisiva, Mozambique' (Archaeological remains in Cabo Delgado and Quisiva, Mozambique) *Taloma* no. 3 (1970), p. 155–64.

98 **The later prehistory of eastern and southern Africa.**
D. W. Phillipson.   London: Heinemann, 1977. 323p. bibliog. maps.

A comprehensive summary of the state of archaeological knowledge of the region from Ethiopia to the Cape peninsula over the last two millenia. Mozambique falls squarely into the area covered, although discussion of specifically Mozambican findings, reflecting the lack of research, is sparse. Phillipson presents a straightforward account of the physical evidence, mainly tools and pottery, and provides an up-to-date (for the mid-1970s) guide, which throws open the whole question of the relationship between archaeological evidence and what we know about pre-colonial societies. A useful bibliography can be found on pages 293–316.

99 **Une enceinte (Monomotapa?) peu connue du plateau du Songo, Mozambique.** (A little-known Monomotapa (?) enclosure on the Songo plateau, Mozambique.)
Miguel Ramos. In: *Proceedings of the 8th Panafrican Congress of Prehistory and Quaternary Studies, Nairobi, 5 to 10 September 1977.* Edited by Richard E. Leakey, Bethwell A. Ogot. Nairobi: International Louis Leakey Memorial Institute for African Prehistory, 1980. p. 355–56.

A brief report, in French, on a fortified enclosure investigated in 1971 and 1972 by the author and Rodrigues Garcia of the Prehistory and Archaeology section of the Portuguese Board for Overseas Studies (Junta de Investigações do Ultramar). The enclosure is located in an odd position on the Songo plateau near Cabora Bassa in Tete Province, odd since the centre of the plateau is sunken and surrounded by higher ground. Ramos supposes that it was either an advance post, or an isolated community, but he puts forward no definite answers. However, the enclosure almost certainly belonged to a subchief of the Monomotapa Empire. The article includes photographs and three references.

100 **Como a penetração estrangeira transformou o modo de produção dos camponeses moçambicanos: o exemplo da Zambézia (± 1200–1964). Vol. 1: Os moçambicanos antes de penetração estrangeira.** (How foreign penetration changed the mode of production of Mozambican peasants: the case of Zambézia, ca. 1200–1964. Vol. 1: Mozambicans before foreign penetration.)
Carlos Serra. Maputo: Núcleo Editorial da Universidade Eduardo Mondlane, 1986. 105p. bibliog. (Colecção 'Moçambique e a sua História', no. 1).

A short (twenty-nine-page) essay on the geography of pre-colonial social relations of production in the north, up to the year 1200, surrounded by a top-heavy critical apparatus (a preface, an introduction, a note on place-names, notes and a bibliography), and, as can be seen above, with a ponderous title. This volume appears to be the first part of a complicated project of which the remaining three parts will deal with: 'From foreign traders to imperialist military occupation'; 'From imperialist military occupation to colonial reconstruction'; and 'From colonial reconstruction to the armed struggle for national liberation'. Serra is one of the most industrious and productive of Mozambican historians, and the volumes to follow are awaited with interest.

101   **Some theoretical and methodological aspects of ceramic studies in Mozambique.**
Paul J. J. Sinclair.   Uppsala, Sweden: African Studies Programme, Department of Cultural Anthropology, University of Uppsala, 1986. 13p. bibliog. map. (Working Papers in African Studies, no. 20).

A short technical paper, using Manekweni as a case-study. Sinclair worked with João Morais (q.v.) in the Department of Archaeology and Anthropology in Maputo for several years, and has begun to publish a series of reports in the last couple of years. See also his 'Chibuene: an early trading site in southern Mozambique', *Paideuma* vol. 28 (1982), p. 149–64; and, in the Uppsala 'Working Papers in African Studies' series: no. 11, *Ethno-archaeological surveys of the Save river valley, south central Mozambique* (1985. 27p.); no. 12, *An archaeological reconnaissance of northern Mozambique. Part 1: Nampula Province* (1985 [pag. unknown]); no. 14, *An archaeological reconnaissance of northern Mozambique. Part 2: Cabo Delgado province* (1986. 12p.); and no. 16, *Pottery from Matola 2532 Cd 1, southern Mozambique* (1986. 7p.).

102   **The Quaternary deposits and the Stone Age artefacts of the fluvial terraces (Olifants' River) on the earth-dam site of Massingir (Gaza Province, Moçambique).**
G. Soares de Carvalho (et al.).   *Memórias do Instituto de Investigação Científica de Moçambique* vol. 10, series B (1975), p. 73–182.

The work for the construction of an earth-dam on the Olifants' River, a tributary of the Limpopo, opened excavations through the fluvial terraces, offering an opportunity for research. The authors attempted to collect data on the sedimentology of the fluvial terrace deposits, and to establish the lithostratigraphic succession, thus providing a basis for the analysis of the evolution of the stone artefacts. The piece consists, then, of three related articles based on investigations carried out at the time: G. Soares de Carvalho's 'Quaternary sedimentology and lithostratigraphy of Massingir'; Maria Eugénia Moreira Lopes' 'The paleoclimatic significance of petrografic [sic] composition of Olifants' river terraces coarse deposits in Massingir'; and 'First contribution to the knowledge of the Massingir Stone Age artefacts', by Maria da Luz Prata Dias, João Manuel Morais and Ricardo Teixeira Duarte. This third article contains illustrations of several types of stone implements.

History

Africa in general

103   **Colonialism in Africa, 1870–1960.**
Edited by Peter Duignan, L. H. Gann.   Cambridge, England:
Cambridge University Press, 1969–75. 5 vols. bibliog. maps.
(Hoover Institution Publications).

A conservative multi-volume history of colonialism. Duignan and Gann are well-
known for their general project, which is, seemingly, to discredit what they see as
a pervasive Marxist influence on the writing of African colonial history, and to
produce an historiography which will serve, broadly speaking, as a justification for
the colonial period. Not all their collaborators, however, subscribe to their point
of view, which is eccentric to put it mildly. In this collection two essays stand out
for the student of Mozambique: James Duffy's short account of Salazarist colonial
policy, 'Portuguese Africa, 1930 to 1960' (vol. 2, p. 171–93); and Richard J.
Hammond's controversial 'Uneconomic imperialism: Portugal in Africa before
1910' (vol. 1, p. 352–82). For more on Hammond's theories and the debate
about the nature of Portuguese imperialism, see the annotation to *Portugal and
Africa* . . . (q.v.). The fifth volume is an annotated bibliography and guide to
resources, and overlaps considerably with the content of Helen Conover and
Peter Duignan's *Guide to research and reference works on sub-Saharan Africa*
(Stanford, California: Hoover Institution, 1971. 1,102p. [Hoover Institution
Bibliographic Series, no. 46]). In this last volume see especially p. 54–57 on
archives in Portugal; and p. 426–54 (items 2234–426) on published sources.

104   **The Cambridge history of Africa.**
Edited by J. D. Fage, Roland Oliver.   Cambridge, England:
Cambridge University Press, 1975–84. 8 vols. bibliogs. maps.

The first volume of this eight volume series (published in 1982), on the period up
to ca. 500 BC, was edited by J. Desmond Clark and includes essays on the

earliest archaeological traces by Glynn Isaac, and on the later Stone Age and early food production by D. W. Phillipson; all with material on southern Africa. Volume 2 (1978), covering from ca. 500 BC to AD 1050 and edited by J. D. Fage, includes an article by Roland Oliver and Brian Fagan on the emergence of Bantu Africa; volume 3 (1977), edited by Roland Oliver, spanning the period 1050–1600, has Neville Chittick on the East coast, including the arrival of the Portuguese, and David Birmingham and Shula Marks on southern Africa. The fourth volume (1975), 1600–1790, edited by Richard Gray, prints a piece by Shula Marks and the editor on the southern region; and another by Edward Alpers and Christopher Ehret on East Africa. Volume 5 (1976), 1790–1870, edited by John Flint, has a chapter on the Nguni outburst by J. D. Omer-Cooper, which includes a section on the Gaza Kingdom. The eighth volume appeared in 1984, edited by Michael Crowder, and, covering the period from 1940 to 1975, it includes 'Portuguese-speaking Africa' by Basil Davidson (p. 755–810), with much material of interest on the liberation struggle in Mozambique. Large multi-volume histories of this type seem on the whole to be more popular with publishers than with reviewers: volume 2 of this ambitious enterprise was not well received. Nevertheless, this work, like the UNESCO *General history of Africa* (q.v.), and despite its faults, is likely to find a place in most reference libraries, and must, therefore, be taken into account.

105   **Recently Published Articles.**
Washington, DC: American Historical Association, 1976–.
triannual.

A continuation of the bibliographical section published until 1975 in the *American Historical Review*, *Recently Published Articles* includes material of interest to historians of all areas of the globe. The section on Africa, prepared by David E. Gardinier of Marquette University (Milwaukee, Wisconsin), is organized around a 'General' section, followed by references arranged country by country. The Mozambique section almost always includes between twelve and twenty citations, and picks up items from such out-of-the-way journals (from the point of view of the Mozambique researcher) as (in vol. 10, no. 1 [1985]) *Missions Évangeliques* or *The World Today*. Gardinier very occasionally assigns articles to the wrong headings, so Mozambicanists should also check under Angola or Guinea-Bissau, as well as looking in the 'General' section for items on Portuguese-speaking countries in general. The adverb 'recently' should also be regarded with caution but all in all this is a useful source. The entries are not numbered, nor are there any indexes.

106   **General history of Africa.**
UNESCO International Scientific Committee for the Drafting of a General History of Africa.   Paris: UNESCO; London: Heinemann; Berkeley, California: University of California Press, 1981–85. 8 vols. bibliogs. maps.

An enormous compendium, similar to the *Cambridge history of Africa* (q.v.), but this time designed by a committee. The project was authorized by the UNESCO General Conference in 1964, and the collection of written and oral sources occupied the years from 1965 to 1970. Meetings in Paris in 1969 and in Addis Ababa in 1970 passed responsibility on to the International Scientific Committee, and writing began in 1972. The plan of the work is as follows: Volume 1, Methodology and African prehistory; Volume 2, Ancient civilizations; Volume 3, Africa from the 7th to 11th centuries; Volume 4, Africa from the 12th to 16th centuries; Volume 5, Africa from the 16th to 18th centuries; Volume 6, Africa in the 19th century until 1880; Volume 7, Africa under foreign domination, 1880–1935; and Volume 8, Africa since 1935. In Volume 7 see especially Allen Isaacman and Jan Vansina, 'African initiatives and resistance in central Africa, 1880–1914'; Catherine Coquery-Vidrovitch, 'The colonial economy of the former French, Belgian and Portuguese zones, 1914–1935'; and Apollon Davidson, Allen Isaacman and René Pélissier, 'Politics and nationalism in central and southern Africa, 1919–35'. Each volume consists of about thirty essays spread over 800 or so pages; in general the earlier volumes were not well received by reviewers (see, for example, *Canadian Journal of African Studies* vol. 15, no. 3 (1981), p. 539–51).

The Portuguese Empire

107 **Origens do colonialismo português moderno.** (Origins of modern Portuguese colonialism.)
Valentim Alexandre. Lisbon: Sá da Costa, 1979. 219p. (Portugal no Século XIX, vol. 3).

This important book consists of an all-too-brief seventy-page essay by the Portuguese Marxist historian Alexandre, followed by lengthy annotated selections from texts and documents to support his argument. The central theme of the essay is that the 'uneconomic imperialism' idea of Richard J. Hammond (q.v.) and his followers is untenable, and that Portugal's ruling class did indeed see the colonies as a source for raw materials and cheap labour. Later on, they also came to discover their utility as a market for Portuguese goods. See also the favourable but critical review by W. G. Clarence-Smith in the *Journal of African History* vol. 23, no. 2 (1982), p. 256–57.

108 **História do colonialismo português em África: cronologia.** (History of Portuguese colonialism in Africa: chronology.)
Pedro Ramos de Almeida. Lisbon: Estampa, 1978–79. 3 vols. bibliog.

A useful reference work in which the first volume covers the 15th to the 18th centuries, the second the 19th, and the last the 20th up to 1961. Within each year, Almeida organizes his material under the headings General, Africa, and then country by country. Often the day and month of an event are not given, however. There is a bibliography on p. 393–476 of volume 3, but no index is provided. See also, by the same author, and in fact abstracted from the larger work, *Portugal e a escravatura em África: cronologia do séc. XV ao séc. XX* [Portugal and the slave-trade in Africa: chronology from the 15th to the 20th centuries] (Lisbon: Estampa, 1978. 151p. bibliog.).

109 **Portugal and the end of ultra-colonialism.**
Perry Anderson. *New Left Review* no. 15 (1962), p. 83–102;
no. 16 (1962), p. 88–123; no. 17 (1962), p. 85–114.

This important and influential work has appeared in book-form in French
(*Portugal et la fin de l'ultra-colonialisme* [Paris: Maspero, 1963]), in Portuguese
(*Portugal e o fim do ultracolonialismo* [Rio de Janeiro: Civilização Brasileira,
1966. 201p.]), and even in Swedish, but never in English. It is a thoroughgoing,
materialist analysis of the principal features of Portuguese 'ultra-colonialism' and
its labour policies, in which Anderson argues that Portugal's own underdevelopment led logically to the super-exploitation of its colonies. The concept of 'ultra-
colonialism' at a different level, proved a useful antidote to the mystifying
ideological notion of 'lusotropicalism' put forward by the Brazilian sociologist
Gilberto Freyre.

110 **Portugal in Africa.**
Edited by A. I. Asiwaju, Michael Crowder, Basil Davidson.
London: Longman; Atlantic Highlands, New Jersey: Humanities
Press, for the Historical Society of Nigeria, 1980. 78p. (*Tarikh*
vol. 6, no. 4 [no. 24]).

This issue of *Tarikh* includes Basil Davidson's introductory essay 'Colonialism on
the cheap: the Portuguese in Africa up to ca. 1921', his 'The movements of
national liberation', and pieces on Cape Verde, Guinea-Bissau and Angola by
various hands. The essay on Mozambique (p. 47–60) is by Allen and Barbara
Isaacman and is entitled 'Mozambique during the colonial period'. The issue as a
whole provides an undocumented account for popular consumption and contains
no surprises.

111 **Portugal and the scramble for Africa, 1875–1891.**
Eric Axelson. Johannesburg: Witwatersrand University Press,
1967. 318p. bibliog. maps.

Axelson is an old-fashioned historian, with the old-fashioned historian's vices and
virtues. His account is down-to-earth and reproduces carefully whatever appears
in his documentary sources. This book is especially good on the border disputes
between Portugal and the neighbouring colonial powers. In the chapters
specifically on Mozambique, Axelson covers the following topics: the Portuguese
in south-east Africa, 1875–78; the Lourenço Marques treaty of 1879; the northern
and southern boundaries of Mozambique, 1879–89; and Gaza, Manica, Zambézia
and Nyasaland in 1879–89.

112 **The changing historiography of Angola and Mozambique.**
Gerald Bender, Allen Isaacman. In: *African studies since 1945*.
Edited by Christopher Fyfe. London: Longman, 1976. p. 220–48.

A bibliographic survey covering the period from the establishment in Portugal of
the Estado Novo (New State) by António d'Oliveira Salazar, until the
independence of Angola and Mozambique in 1975. Bender and Isaacman begin
by pointing out that until the advent of Salazar with his aggressively exploitative
colonial policy, Portuguese historians had, by-and-large, ignored the colonies. But

the Salazarist historiography was colonialist in the sense that the history of
Mozambique and Angola was seen as the history of the Portuguese in those
places, not as the history of the country as a whole. Indeed, in this *problématique*,
the Africans had no history, but inhabited a timeless ethnographic present. Thus,
few Portuguese historical works before 1960 have much value, and only a handful
of foreign scholars wrote on Portuguese-speaking Africa (C. R. Boxer (q.v.) and
Basil Davidson (q.v.) are mentioned). After 1960, however, the situation
changed, partly because of the public impact of the wars of national liberation,
partly, according to Bender and Isaacman, because of the impact of James
Duffy's book *Portuguese Africa* (q.v.). A new generation of foreign writers began
to reduce the Portuguese role in Mozambican and Angolan history to that of one
factor, often not the determinant. They questioned 'lusotropicalism'; they
searched the archives in Goa or the Vatican; and they used oral testimony.
Bender and Isaacman divide this new historiography, somewhat according to the
fashions of the time, into the following categories: origins and state formation;
trade and politics; labour history; Afro-Portuguese interaction; and resistance.
They conclude that historical research on Mozambique 'is even less developed'
than that of Angola (possibly true in 1976, but doubtful in 1986); that 'new
research in both archaeology and anthropology is vital . . . the systematic
collection of oral traditions remains the highest priority.' They go on to identify
important areas for future research (pre-colonial history, colonial trade,
agricultural history, cultural and social history, urbanization, and class formation).
It may be said that these are not necessarily the areas considered to be priorities
by Mozambican historians. Bender and Isaacman conclude that there is a need to
'liberate the past from . . . culturally arrogant and racist myths', a general
sentiment with which it is hard to disagree.

113 **The Portuguese seaborne empire, 1415–1825.**
Charles Ralph Boxer.   London: Hutchinson, 1969. 426p.
Reprinted, Harmondsworth, England: Penguin Books, 1973. 436p.
bibliog. maps.

Portuguese navigators launched the European assault on the rich territories of the
east by sailing round Africa and finding their way into the Indian Ocean and
beyond. Thus, they arrived in Guinea, Angola and Mozambique, on their way to
India and Japan. C. R. Boxer was one of the first English-speaking scholars to
devote his time to the study of Portuguese colonialism, and this pioneering
general history of the 'discoveries' and their consequences is, in his own words
'the product of over forty years' reading, research, reflection and publication on
and around its subject matter'. The work is certainly an authoritative account for
its period; it is only now that some of the detailed research on specific aspects of
this history, which Boxer himself says is necessary, is beginning to be undertaken.
See also Boxer's other major work on race relations in the empire (q.v.).

114 **S. R. Welch and his history of the Portuguese in Africa, 1495–1806.**
C. R. Boxer.   *Journal of African History* vol. 1, no. 1 (1960),
p. 55–63.

There is a perverse pleasure in reading a hostile review, especially when the
reviewer knows that he is on firm ground and pulls no punches. This is a
thoroughly enjoyable article (although 'demolition' might be a better description)

on a series of six bad books published in South Africa between 1946 and 1951 by the Rev. S. R. Welch. The books deal with the history of the Portuguese in southern, Central and eastern Africa, but Boxer picks especially on the last volume *Portuguese and Dutch in South Africa, 1641–1806* (Cape Town: Juta, 1951 [pagination unknown]), assuring us that 'the bias and errors which abound in this work are equally present in all the others'. The tenor of Boxer's review is that Welch's writings are 'shameless' and are 'riddled with factual errors, deliberate distortions of the truth, irrelevant asides and religious bigotry'. The reviewer picks out example after example of Welch's carelessness, ignorance or falsification, first over details of chronology and narrative, and then, in a more extended fashion, over such questions as the alleged absence of greed or racism among the Portuguese, or their religious motivation for colonization. Boxer's article concludes that Welch's books 'can only be used by those who are prepared to check every reference he gives . . . no greater travesty of history has ever been penned . . . ' Needless to say, Welch was highly regarded by the Portuguese colonial authorities, and several of his works were translated and published by Imprensa Nacional (the government printer) in Lourenço Marques.

115 **Depoimento.** (Testimony.)
   Marcello Caetano.   Rio de Janeiro; São Paulo, Brazil:
   Distribuidora Record, 1974. 248p.

Within a year of his overthrow in April 1974 the Portuguese dictator Marcello Caetano was ready with his self-justification, and rather weak it is too. He was a leader who never controlled events, but, as he freely admits, was always controlled by them. Although he thought himself a liberalizer, he in fact almost always yielded to pressure from the right. To those studying Mozambique, this work is of interest principally for its chapter on the colonies (p. 17–46) and for the section on the military situation in Africa (p. 179–84). Caetano acknowledges that things were getting worse (from the Portuguese point of view) in Mozambique. On the 1972 Tete massacres, (a word which he puts between inverted commas) Caetano agrees that 'something irregular' *might* have happened, but claims that Portugal's policy was not one of violence. Anyway, he adds, those missionaries were politically motivated.

116 **O imposto de palhota e a introdução do modo de produção**
   capitalista nas colónias. As ideias coloniais de Marcelo Caetano.
   Legislação do trabalho nas colónias nos anos 60. (The hut-tax and
   the introduction of the capitalist mode of production in the
   colonies. The colonial thought of Marcello Caetano. Labour
   legislation in the colonies during the 1960s.)
   José Capela (pseudonym)   Oporto, Portugal: Afrontamento,
   1977. 273p.

A collection of three essays by one of the best Portuguese historians of Mozambique writing today. The first, and longest, piece (p. 31–196) on the effects of the introduction of the hut-tax, includes several appendixes with extensive statistical tables and extracts from early 20th-century governors' reports, which are normally rich sources. This article also appeared in the *Revista Trimestral de História e Ideias* (Oporto) no. 1 (1978) p. 41–52. The second article is a review of

History. The Portuguese Empire

Caetano's self-serving book *Depoimento* (q.v.), and the third is a short essay on what Capela terms the 'Macchiavellian' labour legislation of the 1960s.

117 **Portuguese Africa.**
Ronald H. Chilcote. Englewood Cliffs, New Jersey: Prentice-Hall, 1967. 149p. bibliog. maps. (The Modern Nations in Historical Perspective: African subseries).

Chilcote was jailed by the PIDE (International Police for the Defence of the State) for a few days when he arrived in Angola to research this book, which reflects more on the level of paranoia in colonial and Fascist Portugal than on Chilcote's radicalism. The Portuguese did not take kindly in the mid-1960s to foreigners intruding into the colonies. In fact, this book is a useful, if outdated, summary consisting of a synthesis of the supposed 'five hundred years' of imperial success and failure; an examination of such institutional forces for change as the Portuguese opposition and the trade unions; a typology of nationalism which includes 'lusotropicalism' as well as various trends in African nationalism; and chapters on Angola, Guinea and the islands, and Mozambique (p. 105–22). This last covers economic characteristics, socio-cultural differentiation, historical patterns, what Chilcote calls the 'pacification' campaigns of the late 19th and early 20th centuries, and some material on FRELIMO. Chilcote's political judgement is perhaps most charitably characterized as naïve; he thinks that the United States and the United Nations could be decisive factors in what he sees as a 'stalemate' in 'Portuguese' Africa. There is a moderately useful bibliographic essay on p. 129–41.

118 **Portugal and Africa, 1815–1910: a study in uneconomic imperialism.**
Richard J. Hammond. Stanford, California: Stanford University Press, 1966. 384p. maps. (Stanford University. Food Research Institute Publications).

An influential and controversial book, which, in relating events in 19th-century metropolitan Portugal to the history of the colonies, argues that Portuguese imperialism was 'uneconomic' in the sense that the Hobsonian theory of economic exploitation cannot be used to explain Portugal's principal motives for overseas expansion. Although the focus is Eurocentric, and the book is written in a tiresome rhetorical style (as if meant to be read out loud), there is much information on Mozambique. Hammond's chapters are devoted to Portugal as the 'sick man' of Western Europe; the abortive treaties of 1878–85; the concept of 'effective occupation' and the quarrel over territory with Great Britain, 1886–90; Mozambique after the 1890 ultimatum (when the British made a demand for territory in Manica and the Tchiri (Shire) valley); Antonio Enes' military career in Mozambique, 1893–95; 'Concessions and concession-hunters'; the McMurdo territorial concession and the Delagoa Bay arbitration; the Anglo-German treaties of 1898 which settled the frontiers of their respective colonies; the fall of the Portuguese monarchy; and the question of the export of labour. Hammond relies heavily on material from such British archives as the Public Record Office. For criticisms of Hammond's theories, which no longer carry much weight, see especially José Capela, *A burguesia mercantil do Porto e as colónias, 1834–1900* [The merchant bourgeoisie of Oporto and the colonies, 1834–1900] (Oporto,

History. The Portuguese Empire

Portugal: Afrontamento, 1975. 281p. [Colecção 'As Armas e os Varões', no. 5]);
W. G. Clarence-Smith's 'The myth of uneconomic imperialism: the Portuguese in
Angola, 1836–1926', *Journal of Southern African Studies* vol. 5, no. 2 (1979),
p. 165–80; and *História de Moçambique. Vol. 2: Agressão imperialista, 1886–1930*
[History of Mozambique. Vol. 2: Imperialist aggression, 1886–1930] (q.v.).

119 **Portugal in Africa: the last hundred years.**
Malyn Newitt. London: Hurst, 1981. 278p. bibliog. maps.
Newitt, best known for his earlier book on the Zambezi *prazos* (q.v.) and a series
of academic articles, writes that by 1980 he felt that, on the basis of monographs
by such scholars as René Pélissier, W. G. Clarence-Smith, Leroy Vail and
Landeg White, it was possible to write a survey volume on the end of Portuguese
colonialism in Africa, since by then what he calls the 'ideological dust' had
settled. The book begins with a description of the Portuguese colonies in Africa in
the 1870s, and goes on to discuss the international dimension; resistance and
'pacification'; the period of the concessionary companies; the African population
under Portuguese rule; the position of the whites; Salazar and the Estado Novo;
the islands (Cape Verde and São Tomé e Príncipe); and finally Portugal and the
wars of liberation. Newitt argues that 'a grievance over pay and conditions of
service' was the trigger for the coup of 25 April 1974 in Portugal, and that the
system which Salazar had built had been 'deserted by its generals, had lost its
ideology, had abandoned its economic policies', and was ready to fall apart.
Africa, for Newitt, was peripheral to this process; indeed, he asserts that the
Portuguese economy had modernized rapidly under the impact of war spending
(as has happened elsewhere in the world). There is a bibliography and a useful
guide for the English speaker with no Portuguese.

120 **The last to leave. Portuguese colonialism in Africa: an introductory
outline.**
Bruno da Ponte. London: International Defence and Aid Fund,
1974. 75p. bibliog. maps.
A pamphlet written just before, and published just after, the Portuguese coup
d'état of 25 April 1974. It was intended as a general introduction to Portuguese
colonialism and to the liberation struggles in Mozambique, Angola and Guinea-
Bissau from a progressive perspective. There is an historical background sketch, a
section on the corporate state, and an account of the economics of Portuguese
colonialism and the colonial administrative policy. Although da Ponte deals with
all three Portuguese colonies, he does provide a substantial amount of
information on Mozambique.

121 **António Salazar and the reversal of Portuguese colonial policy.**
Alan Kent Smith. *Journal of African History* vol. 15, no. 4
(1974), p. 653–67.
Smith puts forward the thesis that Salazar changed the direction of Portuguese
colonial policy from one which envisaged the eventual growth and development of
the African colonies to one which, instead, emphasized stability as the prime
objective. Between 1928 and 1930 he reduced the role of foreign capital, tried to
weaken the influence of special pressure groups, limited Portuguese emigration to

48

the colonies, and put an end to the autonomy of the colonies which had been introduced before the First World War. His objective was to ensure that Portugal herself should be the chief beneficiary of the exploitation of her colonies. But a consequence of the underdevelopment which followed was, according to Smith, that Mozambique and Angola continued to experience 'a primitive exploitation of African labour long after more sophisticated forms had been developed elsewhere'.

122 **Portugal e o futuro.** (Portugal and the future.)
     António de Spínola. Lisbon: Arcadia, 1974. 244p.

Spínola was a highly conservative general, a former volunteer on Franco's side in the Spanish Civil War, a commander in Guinea-Bissau, and a realist. He came eventually to believe that the social risks *in Portugal* of pursuing the colonial wars were so great that power could even 'descend into the streets' in Lisbon itself. He knew that the wars could not be won (even if he did not realize that they might be lost), and argued that the colonies would have to be allowed to decide their own futures, hopefully within a Lusitanian federation. This seminal book thus represented a last-ditch attempt by the non-Salazarist right wing, as the Caetano régime fell apart, to formulate a political solution that might save Portugal from defeat and revolution, provide a neo-colonial resolution for Africa, and outflank the radical captains. It came, however, too late.

123 **The revolutions of 'Portuguese' Africa.**
     Paul M. Whitaker. *Journal of Modern African Studies* vol. 8,
     no. 1 (1970), p. 15–35.

Whitaker, a Yale law-student, travelled in Europe and Africa in mid-1968, interviewing members of the various liberation movements. This article attempts to summarize the results. Unfortunately, Whitaker was not permitted to cite his sources, which diminishes the value of many of his assertions; and it is clear that he took much of what he was told at face value. Quite reasonably, Whitaker is in no doubt that 'in the end, Portugal must surely be driven out, if not entirely defeated,' but he allows this belief to lead him into over-simplification. He makes the useful point, for instance, that for the Portuguese a 'nationalist' is a believer in unitary, multi-continental Portugal; but he then simply counterposes this with an unproblematized characterization of the liberation movements as 'nationalist'. In the section on Mozambique (p. 27–31), Whitaker gives a short account of the events leading up to the major crisis in FRELIMO in 1968–70. The Leo Milas affair (centring around Leo Milas, an Afro-American who infiltrated FRELIMO pretending to be a Mozambican, and was subsequently exposed and expelled, despite attempts by Mondlane to defend him.), Mondlane's refusal to merge with the five groups which eventually formed COREMO (Comité Revolucionário de Moçambique) under Zambian sponsorship, and Mondlane's assassination are all succinctly told. However, in the aftermath of Mondlane's death Whitaker writes that 'Simango may be the most important member of the current leadership'. The article closes with a section on the foreign ties of the various movements. See also Whitaker's 'Arms and the nationalists', *Africa Report* vol. 15, no. 5 (May 1970), p. 12–14.

Mozambique 1498–1964

124 **Notas bibliográficas acerca de Mouzinho de Albuquerque.**
(Bibliographical notes on Mouzinho de Albuquerque.)
Filipe Gastão de Almeida de Eça. *Boletim Geral do Ultramar*
no. 325, vol. 28 (July 1952), p. 107–37.

Mouzinho de Albuquerque, whose equestrian statue dominated the main square
in Lourenço Marques until independence, waged several military campaigns in
Mozambique in the 1890s and was appointed governor of the colony in 1896. His
skills as a writer were great, and his book *Moçambique 1896–1898* (q.v.) is of
interest even today. He was considered a national hero by the Portuguese settlers,
and the literature about him is extensive, although much of it consists of eulogies
rather than useful material. Eça himself treats Mouzinho as an object of
reverence, referring to him as 'our hero'. This bibliography, with comprehensive
annotations, includes fifty-one items. Reference numbers 52 to 102 are included in
the continuation of this work by the same author: 'Bibliografia da 'Escola de
Mouzinho'' (Bibliography of the 'School of Mouzinho') *Boletim Geral do
Ultramar*, no. 334, no. 28 (April 1953), p. 45–70.

125 **Ivory and slaves in east central Africa: changing patterns of
international trade to the late nineteenth century.**
Edward A. Alpers. London: Heinemann, 1975. 296p. bibliog.
maps.

A specialized historical study of local trade patterns and their interaction with
international commerce in the area made up of present-day northern Mozambique,
southern Tanzania and Malawi, and inhabited by Yao-, Makua- and Maravi-
speaking peoples. The book's emphasis is on the earlier period from the 15th
century onwards (it is only in the penultimate chapter that we reach the early 19th
century). Alpers worked principally from Portuguese sources, and his book, and
the series of articles on related topics which preceded it, are important. See, for
example, the review by John McCracken in the *Journal of Southern African
Studies* vol. 3, no. 2 (April 1977), p. 238–39. For more on the slave-trade in
Mozambique and in the Portuguese-speaking world in general, see also James
Duffy's important *A question of slavery* (Oxford: Clarendon Press, 1967. 240p.);
M. Zimmerman's 'The French slave trade of Mozambique, 1770–1794' (MA
thesis, University of Wisconsin, 1967); and José Capela's collection *Escravatura.
A empresa de saque. O abolicionismo (1810–1875)* [Slavery. The plunder
company. Abolition, 1810–75] (Oporto, Portugal: Afrontamento, 1974. 307p.).
Capela has also published, with Eduardo Medeiros, *Otráfico de escravos de
Moçambique para as Ilhas do Índico, 1720–1902* [The slave-trade from
Mozambique to the Indian Ocean islands, 1720–1902] (Maputo: Núcleo Editorial,
Universidade Eduardo Mondlane, 1987. 128p. bibliog. map. [Colecção
Moçambique e a sua História, no. 3]).

126 **State, merchant capital and gender relations in southern Mozambique to the end of the nineteenth century: some tentative hypotheses.**
Edward A. Alpers. *African Economic History* vol. 13 (1985), p. 23–55.

Alpers starts his analysis from three assumptions – first, that the pre-capitalist state was the dominant social formation in this area during the period under discussion. Second, that it was based on tribute, not trade (this is the weakest part of the article since Alpers does not advance any convincing distinction between the two). Third, that the penetration of merchant capital resulted in changes in the social relations of production to the detriment of women. He deals with various states in the region south of the Sabi River – Manekweni, Tonge, the Chope chiefdoms, the Tsonga kingdoms and Gaza. Drawing on a wide range of archaeological, anthropological, historical and travellers' sources, Alpers surveys these social formations over a period of nearly six centuries, concluding that they were states, in the Marxist sense; that their ruling classes were sustained primarily by the control which they exercised over tribute (rather than trade); and that women in southern Mozambique were considered to be reproducible sources of wealth, like cattle. Nevertheless, class and gender must have been 'both independent and integrated categories of social differentiation'. Alpers closes by remarking that he does not consider the 'modes of production debate' to represent 'the most productive line of inquiry'.

127 **Relações de Moçambique setecentista.** (Reports on 18th-century Mozambique.)
António Alberto de Andrade. Lisbon: Divisão de Publicações e Biblioteca, Agência Geral do Ultramar, 1955. 637p. bibliog. maps.

An important documentary collection on a relatively neglected period of Mozambican history, the emphasis being on Portuguese administration. The work is divided into four parts. The first is an introduction to the texts, dealing with Portuguese policy in the 18th century; the separation of Mozambique from the State of India; the question of who was to control Delagoa Bay; relations with neighbouring African states; missionary activity; commerce and finance; and the impact of the reforms introduced in Portugal by the Marquis of Pombal. The texts themselves are the largest section (p. 137–405). They include 'Notícias dos domínios portugueses na costa de África oriental' [News of the Portuguese dominions on the East African coast] (1758), by the First Secretary of the Government of Mozambique, Inácio Caetano Xavier; the anonymous 'Memórias da costa d'África oriental' [Memoirs of the East African coast] (1762); and writings by Manuel António de Almeida, António Pinto de Miranda, Baltazar Manuel Pereira do Lago and others. The third section is made up of historical notes, including useful tables of the governors and captains of the Rios de Sena, Sofala, Quelimane, Tete, Manica, Zimbaué and Zumbo. The final part consists of twenty-six administrative and other supplementary documents, including a biography of Inácio Caetano Xavier. On this period, see also Fritz Hoppe's *A África oriental portuguesa no tempo do Marquês de Pombal* [Portuguese East Africa at the time of the Marquis of Pombal] (Lisbon: Agência Geral do Ultramar, 1970. 528p.), which was first submitted as a PhD dissertation, in German, to the University of Hamburg in 1965.

128 **Da importância da Ilha de Moçambique no período filipino.** (The
importance of Mozambique Island in the time of King Philip.)
Joaquina Maria Araújo Ferreira. Licenciatura dissertation,
University of Lisbon, 1964. 214p. bibliog. maps.

Between 1580 and 1640 Portugal was incorporated into the Spanish kingdom
under King Philip II, and as a result of this temporary loss of identity became a
target for Dutch maritime power, since the Dutch were in revolt against Spanish
domination. Mozambique Island was important to Portuguese interests in India
and Brazil during this period; Spain was always more exclusively interested in its
South American colonies. Araújo Ferreira's historical thesis discusses the
significance of Mozambique Island, describing the Fortress of St. Sebastian, the
administrative organization of the island, island society, the impact of Christianity,
relations with Monomotapa, and the role of the island as a supply-base for
Portuguese voyages to India. An as-yet-unpublished bibliography of eighty-five
references on Mozambique Island was prepared at the Historical Archive in
Maputo in 1985 by Calisto Pacheleke under the title 'Bibliografia anotada sobre a
Ilha de Moçambique' [Annotated bibliography on Mozambique Island] (29p.).

129 **Portuguese in south-east Africa, 1488–1600.**
Eric V. Axelson. [Cape Town]: Struik, for the Ernest
Oppenheimer Institute of Portuguese Studies, Witwatersrand
University, Johannesburg, 1973. 276p. bibliog. maps.

A rewritten and expanded version of *South-east Africa, 1488–1530* (London:
Longmans Green, 1940. 306p. bibliog. maps), which was the author's DLitt.
dissertation at Witwatersrand University in 1938. The original work dealt with the
history of the African 'coast and hinterland, that lies between the Cape of Good
Hope and Mombasa', thus covering substantial chunks of South Africa, Tanzania
and Kenya. It also included a report on Portuguese archives, with material on
south-east Africa for this period. Axelson begins with Bartolomeu Dias' voyage of
'discovery' to South Africa, which he dates as 1488, rather than the previously-
accepted 1487. In the newer book, Axelson's gesture in the direction of pre-
colonial ethnography (the opening chapter of the thesis) is eliminated, and he
concentrates exclusively on the Portuguese adventurers. The new volume is
described disingenuously by the author as 'essentially a factual summary of
information at present available, and a guide to sources'. There is a glossary of
Portuguese terminology.

130 **Portuguese in south-east Africa, 1600–1700.**
Eric Axelson. Johannesburg: Witwatersrand University Press,
1960. 226p. bibliog. maps.

The 17th century was a bad time for the Portuguese in Mozambique and
elsewhere. In 1580 Portugal had been united with Spain under the Spanish king,
Philip II, but at the same time the Dutch rebelled against their Spanish masters,
and, unable to attack the land-based Spanish Empire effectively, turned their
navies loose against the Portuguese, who were also a maritime power. Portugal,
whose hold on the East African coast north of Cabo Delgado was not fully
established, had further problems: the Arab-Swahili merchants continued to
compete for trade dominance and were too numerous to be dismissed as
unimportant; trade, too, with the Rios de Sena was declining. Mombasa was also

lost during this period, and by 1700 the only remaining Portuguese Captaincy was on Mozambique Island. Axelson tells the story from a Portuguese point of view, reproducing the sources with great care.

131   **The Shona and Zimbabwe, 900–1850: an outline of Shona history.**
David N. Beach. London: Heinemann, 1980; Gweru, Zimbabwe:
Mambo Press, 1984. [437p]. bibliog. maps. (Zambeziana, vol. 9).
Attempts to synthesize and demystify the history of the Shona-speaking peoples, principally on the Zimbabwe plateau, but also down to the Indian Ocean coast in what is now Mozambican territory. Dr. Beach makes relatively little use of the Portuguese sources, however, so the book is weaker on that aspect. He goes on to challenge the myth that the Rozwi Empire was quite as grand as it has been portrayed. Indeed, he terms the empire 'a historiography without a history'. There is an introduction dated 1977, and an extensive bibliography. On the Rozwi and the Portuguese, see also S. I. Mudenge's 'The Rozwi Empire and the Feira of Zumbo' (PhD dissertation, University of London, 1972), and 'The role of foreign trade in the Rozwi Empire: a reappraisal', *Journal of African History* vol. 15, no. 3 (1974), p. 373–91.

132   **On the transition to feudalism in Mozambique.**
Thomas Daniel Boston.   *Journal of African Studies* vol. 8 (1981–
82), p. 182–87.
A short contribution to the historiography of the rise of the Monomotapa Empire in south-eastern Africa, summarizing the state of knowledge and arguing that, in Kiteve especially, feudalism existed in the full sense of the word. For information on Monomotapa the books by Randles and Nogueira da Costa (q.v.) will also be of use. See also Boston's interesting doctoral dissertation, 'Mozambique: an interpretation of the nature, causes and outcomes of the pre-colonial stages of African economic development' (Cornell University, New York, 1976. 364p.), which includes calculations on the way to estimate likely populations and population densities in central Mozambique in the early years of the Portuguese presence.

133   **Cadernos de História: boletim do Departamento de História da
Universidade Eduardo Mondlane.** (History Notes: bulletin of the
History Department, Eduardo Mondlane University.)
Maputo: Núcleo Editorial, Universidade Eduardo Mondlane, June
1985–. irregular.
Publishing a journal in Africa is not an undertaking for the faint-hearted; there is always a shortage of articles for local journals, since the best material is often sent away to appear in 'prestigious' publications; there are always problems with the printers and distributors; and so on. But in Mozambique there are relatively few local researchers, and for much of the time since independence the little research undertaken has often been collective. The History Department of Eduardo Mondlane University, for instance, has been devoting most of its time to training secondary-school teachers, to bringing its own staff up to Masters level, and to producing 'the manual', *História de Moçambique* (q.v.). This new journal is intended principally for internal circulation; it is produced in a 'quick and dirty'

mimeographed format (actually it is quite elegant); and it includes news items as well as scholarly papers. Among important articles in the first two numbers are 'Educação, missões e a ideologia política de assimilação, 1930–60' (Education, missions, and the political ideology of assimilation) by David Hedges (no. 1, p. 7–18); and 'O colonialismo português em Moçambique, 1886–1930' (Portuguese colonialism in Mozambique) by Aurélio Rocha (et al.) (no. 2, p. 7–20). These, and a number of the other articles in subsequent issues, are draft chapters for the forthcoming third volume of *História de Moçambique*.

134 **Fontes para a história, geografia e comércio de Moçambique (séc. XVIII).** (Sources for the history, geography and trade of Mozambique in the 18th century.)
Luíz Fernando de Carvalho Dias. *Anais da Junta de Investigações do Ultramar* vol. 9, no. 1 (1954), p. 1–365.

An important selection of unpublished documents from the collection of the Ministério do Reino (literally, Royal Ministry) in the Arquivo Nacional da Torre do Tombo in Lisbon. Carvalho Dias includes the following items: António Pinto de Miranda's 'Memoirs of East Africa'; Colonel Mello e Castro on the Maravi Empire; a report on Portuguese settlers; Inácio Caetano Xavier on the present state of Mozambique; memoirs of the coast; continental Mozambique by Luís Figueiredo; two reports on Cabo Delgado; Joaquim Varella's description of the Captaincy of Mozambique; and two pieces by Manuel Galvão da Silva. There are three financial and statistical appendixes.

135 **Documentos sobre os portugueses em Moçambique e na África Central, 1497–1840.** (Documents on the Portuguese in Mozambique and Central Africa, 1497–1840.)
Salisbury: National Archive of Rhodesia (and Nyasaland); Lisbon: Centro de Estudos Históricos Ultramarinos, 1962–.

A large and ambitious collection of historical documents, as yet incomplete. The series has covered under twenty per cent of the period indicated in only eight volumes, and the least documented part at that. The total of 4,423 pages must be halved, however, since the documents are printed in Portuguese and English parallel texts on facing pages. Taken from archives and libraries in Portugal, Italy, France and even Goa, these documents are intended to replace the ageing collection of George McCall Theal (q.v.). Among the 'big names' associated with this project are Eric Axelson and Alexandre Lobato, and the preface is signed by A. da Silva Rego and T. W. Baxter. Each volume has a general index, and some have a glossary; the archive of origin is indicated for each document. The volumes are: I. 1497–1506 (1962. 832p.); II. 1507–1510 (1963. 612p.); III. 1511–1514 (1964. 662p.); IV. 1515–1516 (1965. 604p.); V. 1517–1518 (1966. 623p.); VI. 1519–1537 (1969. 510p.); VII. 1540–1560 (1971. 580p.); VIII. 1561–1588 (1975. 613p.). The project is now being revived in Zimbabwe.

136 **The quest for an African eldorado: Sofala, southern Zambezia and the Portuguese, 1500–1865.**
T. H. Elkiss.   Brandeis, Massachusetts: Crossroads Press, 1981. 121p.

Elkiss' rather short book deals with an interesting historical topic, but fails to explore it in any real depth. The central theme is Portuguese inability to establish a permanent presence in Sofala after the stories of hidden gold were shown to have been false. Sofala enjoyed a brief revival during the heyday of the slave-trade, but otherwise disappeared from history. Elkiss tries to locate all this in the context of southern Zambezian history and the Shona system of agricultural economy. For a detailed critique of Elkiss, see Elias Mandela in the *Canadian Journal of African Studies* vol. 17, no. 3 (1983), p. 545–47. See also the unpublished thesis by Ronald William Dickinson, 'Sofala and the rivers of Cuama: crusade and commerce in south-east Africa, 1505–1595' (MA thesis, University of Cape Town, 1971).

137 **A guerra d'África em 1895: memórias.** (The war in Africa in 1895: memoirs.)
António Enes.   Lisbon: Typ. 'Dia', 1898. 631p. maps. 2nd ed.
Lisbon: Gama, 1945. 644p.

By the 1890s the Portuguese were determined to break the power of the independent African states and to establish direct control once and for all. The Gaza Kingdom, under Ngungunyane, attempted to reach a compromise, but to no avail. Enes and Mouzinho de Albuquerque conducted a ruthless military campaign against the Gaza Kingdom and captured the king, sending him into exile in Portugal. These memoirs deal with the revolt of the local chiefs in Lourenço Marques, and with the campaign against Gaza. The last sixty or so pages are texts of military and administrative documents. Note that much of Enes' material from the 1890s is deposited in the National Library in Lisbon: see part two of *A Secção Ultramarina de Biblioteca Nacional: inventários* [The Colonial Section of the National Library: inventories] (Lisbon: Biblioteca Nacional, 1928. 333p.) For an account of the role of the police force in suppressing the Lourenço Marques revolt, written entirely within a colonial-Fascist *problématique*, see João Pereira de Souza da Câmara's 'Crise e ressurgimento: o corpo policial de Lourenço Marques na sublevação do distrito em 1894–1895' [Crisis and resurgence: the Lourenço Marques police force during the incitement in the district, 1894–95] (Licenciatura dissertation, University of Lisbon, 1957. 131p.). Câmara writes that 'Portugal, which was lost through the bad government of its rulers, thus came to save itself on the dark continent by loss of life and unity of purpose.'

138 **Mozambican nationalist resistance, 1920–1940.**
Elaine A. Friedland.   *Transafrican Journal of History* vol. 8, no. 1/2 (1979), p. 117–128.

Discusses the little-known history of the Grémio Africano (African Guild) and its newspaper *O Brado Africano* (q.v.). The author characterizes the organization as 'nationalist' but offers no real justification for her use of the term. In the 1930s the Grémio changed its name to the Associação Africana (African Association), because the name Grémio was legally reserved for certain categories of employers' associations. Friedland sums up: 'The African nationalist movement found its legal avenues of protest steadily eroded by the ruling class's policy of seeking to suppress all challenges to the colonial system.' By the end of the 1940s the only channels for protest left open were through artistic and literary expression. See also Friedland's important and as-yet-unpublished doctoral dissertation, 'A comparative study of the development of revolutionary nationalist movements in southern Africa: FRELIMO (Mozambique) and the African National Congress of South Africa' (PhD dissertation, City University of New York, 1980. 2 vols.). Some postgraduate work has also been done in French-speaking universities on FRELIMO's struggle, and on the liberation wars in Portugal's African colonies in general: see, for example, M. Dembele's 'Le pouvoir blanc en Afrique australe et les mouvements de libération dans les territoires portugaises' [White power in southern Africa and the liberation movements in the Portuguese territories] (Memoir for the Law Faculty, University of Rheims, Rheims, France, 1973. 133p.); S. S. Hagne's 'Du front de libération nationale au parti marxiste-leniniste: l'example du FRELIMO' [From national liberation front to Marxist-Leninist party: the case of FRELIMO] (Memoire for the Diploma in African Studies, University of Bordeaux, Bordeaux, France, 1979); and A. Mbaga Bady's 'Naissance et évolution d'un état par la lutte de libération nationale: Mozambique' [Birth and evolution of a state through the national liberation struggle: Mozambique] (PhD dissertation, University of Paris I (Panthéon Sorbonne), 1982).

139 **Slavery, social incorporation and surplus extraction: the nature of free and unfree labour in south-east Africa.**
     Patrick Harries. *Journal of African History* vol. 22, no. 3 (1981), p. 309–30.

Harries, a South African historian, argues against majority opinion that the northern Nguni in present-day Swaziland, Natal and southern Mozambique, were engaged in supplying slaves for sale through Lourenço Marques and Inhambane up until the 1840s. As conditions changed, this trade became less and less profitable, and was finally killed off by the rise of domestic slavery in Gaza. Harries argues further that this domestic slavery was a 'dynamic social relationship' which denied the slave the rights accorded to a kinsman; nevertheless, it was hypothetically possible for a kinsman to be materially worse-off than a slave. The system also released Gaza women from agricultural labour, according to Harries, and they were able to concentrate on child-rearing, thus reinforcing ideas of Gaza 'purity'. Harries asserts that the line between slavery and other forms of servitude was often blurred. An earlier version of this controversial paper was published under the same title in *Before and after Shaka: papers in Nguni history* (Edited by J. B. Peires. Grahamstown, South Africa: Rhodes University, Institute of Social and Economic Research, 1981. [pagination unknown]). In a review of that volume published in the *Journal of African History* vol. 24, no. 1 (1983), p. 117–18, David Hedges doubted whether 'historical investigation is best carried out by comparison within an ethnolinguistic category', and summed up Harries' argument as being that 'slavery was part of a typological Nguni cultural baggage'.

140 **Mozambique: a history.**
Thomas H. Henriksen. London: Rex Collings; Cape Town:
David Philip, 1978. 276p. maps.
An ambitious and probably premature attempt to write a synthetic history of
Mozambique 'from before the advent of the Portuguese until after its
independence from Lisbon's colonialism'. In the mid-1970s there had simply not
been enough primary research done in Mozambican history, in any language, for
it to have been possible to succeed in such an enterprise, especially for a scholar
working outside the country. Despite these empirical shortcomings, of which
Henriksen is well aware – 'the study is not definitive' he writes – the book has its
moments. The emphasis in part one (entitled Invasions and empires) is on
population movements; while in the second and more detailed section on the 20th
century, Henriksen's focus is on colonialism and nationalism. There are two
appendixes; one on ethnography; the second a translation of Samora Machel's
message at the investiture of the transitional government in September 1974.

141 **História de Moçambique.** (History of Mozambique.)
Departamento de História, Universidade Eduardo Mondlane.
Maputo: Tempográfica, 1982–. vol. 1– . bibliog. maps.
Planned in four volumes, but as yet incomplete, this history started off as a high-
school textbook, but has now begun to reach a much wider audience, and has
indeed become a highly successful best-seller inside the country. The first volume
(159p.), co-ordinated by Carlos Serra, deals with the earliest social formations,
and the impact of merchant capital, from 200 to 1886. Contributors were Aurélio
Rocha, António Sopa, Serra, David Hedges, Eduardo Medeiros, Gerhard
Liesegang and Miguel da Cruz. The second volume (336p.), also edited by Serra,
is titled simply 'Imperialist aggression, 1886–1930', includes chapters by Rocha,
Serra, Hedges, Medeiros, José Moreira and Teresa Cruz e Silva, and is lavishly
illustrated with maps and photographs. Draft chapters from the third volume,
covering 1930 to 1962 and co-ordinated by David Hedges, have begun to appear
in *Cadernos de História* (q.v.) and this promises to be the most interesting volume
so far. The fourth volume, 'História da Luta Armada de Libertação Nacional'
(The history of the armed struggle for national liberation) by Luís de Brito, João
Paulo Borges Coelho and José Guilherme Negrão, is about to be published. In
sum, the first consistent attempt at a Marxist interpretation of Mozambican
history, and highly recommended.

142 **Goa and Mozambique: the participation of Goans in Portuguese
enterprise in the Rios de Cuama, 1501–1752.**
Cyril Andrew Hromnik. PhD dissertation, Syracuse University,
New York, 1977. 497p. bibliog. maps.
Hromnik's thesis is an extremely detailed account of what he claims was the
important role of the Canarins, or Goan Catholics, in Sofala and in the Rios
de Cuama during the first 250 years of the colonial period. Hromnik feels that the
history of the Goans has been neglected: he describes the establishment of a
Goan presence; their role in the Portuguese alliance with Monomotapa between
1573 and 1633; what he terms their 'golden age' in Mokaranga and Butua in the
17th century; Goan enterprise in the middle Zambezi in the early 18th century;
and, in a concluding chapter, Goan landownership and agricultural activity during

the whole period up to 1752. Hromnik later descredited himself by publishing (with some difficulty) a book claiming that most of Africa's notable cultural achievements can be traced back to India (*Indo-Africa: towards a new understanding of the history of sub-Saharan Africa* [Cape Town: Juta, 1981. 168p.]), which was described as showing 'reckless ignorance' by a reviewer in the *Journal of African History* (vol. 23, no. 3 [1982], p. 416).

143 **The tradition of resistance in Mozambique: anti-colonial activity in the Zambesi Valley, 1850–1921.**
Allen Isaacman in collaboration with Barbara Isaacman.
Berkeley, California: University of California Press; London: Heinemann, 1976. 232p. bibliog. maps. (Perspectives on southern Africa, no. 18).

Isaacman's focus is the Zambezi Valley, and he deals not only with such major struggles as the Barwe rising of 1917, but also with day-to-day small-scale and sporadic village revolts, and what, following the British Marxist historian, Eric Hobsbawm, he terms 'social banditry'. The book was produced in the mid-1970s, at the height of the fashion of 'resistance historiography', when some historians were attempting to link primary resistance (that is, the wars fought by late 19th- and early 20th-century African societies to preserve their political independence from colonial domination) with modern liberation wars. It has subsequently become clear that the class basis of the two types of war are quite different, and that historians were misled by the *ideological* use of local traditions of resistance to mobilize support for modern revolutionary struggles. Isaacman virtually admits as much in the introduction to the later Portuguese edition – *A tradição de resistência em Moçambique: o vale de Zambeze, 1850–1921* (Oporto, Portugal: Afrontamento, 1979. 353p. [Colecção 'As Armas e os Varões', no. 9]) – where he replies to criticisms on the lack of class analysis in the book. Nevertheless, some critics praised his efforts: see the review of the English edition by Edward Steinhart in *Africa Today* vol. 25, no. 1 (Jan.–March 1978), p. 75–76; and of the Portuguese edition by Valentim Alexandre in *Diário de Notícias* (Lisbon), 16 Dec. 1980.

144 **East African campaigns.**
Paul Emil von Lettow-Vorbeck. New York: R. Speller, 1957. 303p.

The German invasion of northern Mozambique during the First World War was an historical episode of considerable impact, but has been little studied. This book is an English translation of von Lettow-Vorbeck's memoirs, originally entitled *Meine Erinnerungen aus Ostafrika* (Leipzig, Germany: K. F. Köhler, 1920. 302p.). Von Lettow-Vorbeck (1870–1964) was appointed to command Germany's forces in East Africa just before the outbreak of war in 1914. He seized the initiative, and mounted several raids on Kenya, forcing the Allies to counter-attack under the command of the South African Jan Christiaan Smuts. Smuts rapidly drove the Germans southwards, but von Lettow-Vorbeck retreated into Cabo Delgado, mounting a guerrilla campaign and eventually re-invading German East Africa in 1917, and even pushing across into present-day Zambia. The German forces were, according to some sources, the first Europeans to be seen in certain parts of northern Mozambique. Undefeated, von Lettow-Vorbeck was finally forced to surrender by the signing of the Armistice in Europe. It would appear that the only work in Portuguese, or any other language, which deals with this aspect of the East African campaign is Mário da Costa's *É o inimigo que fala: subsídios inéditos para o estudo da campanha da Africa Oriental 1914–1918* [The enemy speaks: unpublished materials for the study of the East African campaign, 1914–18] (Lourenço Marques, Mozambique: Imprensa Nacional, 1932.).

145 **A expansão portuguesa em Moçambique de 1498 a 1530.** (The Portuguese expansion in Mozambique, 1498–1530.)
Alexandre Lobato. Lisbon: Agência Geral do Ultramar; Centro de Estudos Históricos Ultramarinos, 1954–60. 3 vols. (Estudos Moçambicanos).

The Mozambican-born Lobato was the Director of the Arquivo Histórico de Moçambique in Maputo until 1977, and worked with the material he was responsible for; his three volumes are a classic colonial history of the early period of Portuguese presence in Mozambique. They are organized as follows: Volume One – Descobrimento e ocupação da costa, 1498–1508 [The discovery and occupation of the coast, 1498–1508] (1954. 275p.); Volume Two – Política da Capitania de Sofala e Moçambique de 1508 a 1530 [Politics of the Captaincy of Sofala and Mozambique, 1508–30] (1954. 194p.); Volume Three – Aspectos e problemas da vida económica de 1505 a 1530 [Aspects and problems of economic life, 1505–30] (1960. 412p.). Lobato deals with the factories at Sofala and Mozambique; coastal exploration; the captains of Sofala, beginning with António de Saldanha; and the Armadas from India. The last volume discusses economic expansion into the hinterland; Sofala and Mozambique trade; the voyages of António Fernandes; and prices and profits. Lobato is still held in surprisingly high esteem by younger Mozambican historians, many of whom were his pupils: see the short obituary published in *Cadernos de História* no. 1 (June 1985), p. 80–81 (he died in February 1985). For a pre-Salazar interpretation of the ivory- and gold-trade cycles in Mozambique, see the fascinating book first published in 1928 by J. Lúcio de Azevedo, *Épocas de Portugal económico: esboços de história* [Epochs of the Portuguese economy: historical outlines] (Lisbon: Livraria Clássica, 1978. 4th ed. 502p.), which periodizes early Portuguese economic history into India and the spice cycle; the first gold cycle; the sugar empire; and the age of gold and diamonds.

146 **Quatro estudos e uma evocação para a história de Lourenço Marques.** (Four studies and an impression, towards a history of Lourenço Marques.)
Alexandre Lobato. Lisbon: Junta de Investigações do Ultramar, 1961. 168p. (Estudos Moçambicanos).

The history of the coastal towns was, for the Portuguese colonial historians, not local history at all, but the history of Mozambique itself, and the history of the Portuguese presence which was most evident in the urban setting. Although Lobato himself could occasionally break out of the Eurocentric mould, the list of his works (several volumes on Lourenço Marques, others on Sofala, Mozambique Island and Mouzinho de Albuquerque) shows a typical pattern. In these essays, for instance, the African population appears on the historical stage only when it actually invades the city. The four studies are 'Ten years of Dutch occupation';

'On the obscure history of Lourenço Marques'; 'Between two invasions'; and 'The Vatua invasion of Lourenço Marques in 1833'. The sources are mainly documents from the Historical Archive. See also Lobato's *História da fundação de Lourenço Marques* [History of the foundation of Lourenço Marques] (Lisbon: [n.p.], 1948. [pag. unknown]); his *História do presídio de Lourenço Marques* [History of the fortress of Lourenço Marques] (Lisbon: [n.p.], 1949–60. 2 vols.); and Caetano Montez' *Descobrimento e fundação de Lourenço Marques* [The discovery and foundation of Lourenço Marques] (Lourenço Marques, Mozambique: Minerva Central, 1948. 189p.) of which p. 153–89 are the texts of documents.

147   **A história de Moçambique antes de 1890: apontamentos bibliográficos sobre os resultados de investigação entre 1960 e 1980.**
(Mozambican history before 1890: bibliographic notes on research results, 1960–1980.)
José Soares Martins, Eduardo de Conceição Medeiros.
Revista Internacional de Estudos Africanos no. 1 (Jan.–June 1984), p. 201–16.
A bibliographic survey of pre-20th-century historical research over the last two decades. References appear in the footnotes, of which there are sixty-two, often grouping several citations. The article is divided into two main parts, namely the pre-1500 history of Mozambique, and 1500 to 1890. This last is further subdivided into sections dealing with the *prazos* and central Mozambique, the four northern provinces, and the south, as well as the slave-trade. Soares Martins is perhaps better known to students of Mozambican history by his pseudonym, José Capela.

148   **Os últimos anos da monarquia e os primeiros da República em Moçambique.** (The last years of the monarchy and the first years of the Republic in Mozambique.)
João Villas-Boas Carneiro Moura.   Lourenço Marques,
Mozambique: Imprensa Nacional, 1965. 160p. bibliog.
In October 1910 the King of Portugal, Manuel II, fled to England, and the period of Portuguese history known as the Parliamentary Republic began (1910–26). In Mozambique, the years between 1906 and 1910 had been relatively stable as far as the government was concerned, under the last monarchical governor, Alfredo Augusto Freire de Andrade. During the first ten years of the Republic, however, Mozambique was ruled by a succession of eight governor-generals, one high commissioner, and a series of interim officials. In addition, the financial situation deteriorated during the First World War. Moura's book, the published version of his licenciatura dissertation (submitted to the Instituto Superior de Ciências Sociais e Política Ultramarina, at the Universidade Técnica de Lisboa, in 1963), deals with Freire de Andrade's period in power; administration and economy in the last years of the monarchy; foreign relations, the concessionary companies and the *prazos*; and the situation in the first years of the Republic.

149 **Angoche, the slave-trade and the Portuguese, ca. 1844–1910.**
M. D. D. Newitt. *Journal of African History* vol. 13, no. 4
(1972), p. 659–72.
In the 1840s Angoche was the principal port on the Mozambique coast for the slave-trade. Both the British and the Portuguese attacked it at various times, and the Portuguese finally succeeded in capturing it in 1861, when the Zambezian *prazeiro* João Bonifácio Alves da Silva, with Portuguese support, defeated the Sultan Mussa Quanto, losing his life in the process. Mussa and his successors Ussene and Farelahi managed to confine the Portuguese to a few coastal garrisons, however, and it was not until 1910 that Farelahi was finally defeated. For a popular version of part of the story, see João Paulo Borges Coelho's *No tempo de Farelahi* (q.v.).

150 **Portuguese settlement on the Zambesi: exploration, land tenure and colonial rule in East Africa.**
Malyn Dudley Dunn Newitt. London: Longman, 1973. 434p.
bibliog. maps.
Newitt places the Zambezi Valley *prazo* (crown land grants) system in the context of the land-tenure and administrative system developed by Portugal at home and in her Atlantic possessions. By the end of the 18th century, the relative independence of the *prazos* from central Portuguese administration had led to a situation which combined stagnation with disorder. Throughout the 19th century aggressive 'super-*prazos*' emerged, and their struggles for supremacy lasted until Portugal was finally able to establish control at the beginning of this century. The book is based on Newitt's thesis ('The Zambesi *prazos* in the 18th century' PhD dissertation, University of London and University College of Rhodesia and Nyasaland, Salisbury, 1968), and was reviewed by David Hedges in the *Journal of Southern African Studies* vol. 2, no. 1 (Oct. 1975), p. 126–27. Hedges severely criticized the 'shambling' footnote system apparently invented by Newitt, but otherwise praised the book. Newitt's work had been preceded by the Italian Giuseppe Papagno's *Colonialismo e feudalismo: a questão dos prazos da coroa em Moçambique no fim do século XIX* [Colonialism and feudalism: the question of the *prazos da coroa* in Mozambique at the end of the 19th century] (Lisbon: A Regra do Jogo, 1980. 278p.; originally published Turin, Italy: Einaudi, 1972); and was followed by Isaacman's study of the *prazo* system (q.v.).

151 **Penetração e impacto do capital mercantil português em Moçambique nos séculos XVI e XVII: o caso de Muenemutapa.**
(Penetration and impact of Portuguese merchant capital in Mozambique during the 16th and 17th centuries: the case of Monomotapa.)
António Manuel de Castro Soromenho Nogueira da Costa.
Maputo: Cadernos Tempo, 1982. 80p. (Colecção 'História', no. 3).
The empire of Monomotapa straddled present-day Zimbabwe and Mozambique, and has attracted the attention of several historians writing in Portuguese. One of the most recent of these was the promising Mozambican Nogueira da Costa, who died in 1979 at an early age. This posthumously-published paper had been written in 1977 as a secondary-school teaching text, and therefore represents a provisional

stage in both Mozambican historiography and in Nogueira da Costa's own professional development. Nogueira da Costa had been a member of various small radical groups in colonial times, and had been an active journalist and broadcaster. He was a founder member of the Centro de Estudos Africanos (CEA) and worked in the collective which produced *Black gold* (q.v.). He taught history at the university, and at the time of his death had begun work on a dissertation about the Mozambique Company.

152 **As fontes orais da história: catálogo da Colecção Sonora do Arquivo Histórico de Moçambique.** (The oral sources of history: catalogue of the sound archive in the Historical Archive of Mozambique.)
Teresa Maria Alves dos Santos Oliveira. Trabalho de diploma for the Licenciatura, Arquivo Histórico de Moçambique, Universidade Eduardo Mondlane, 1985. [not paginated]. bibliog.

This pioneering thesis is a useful researchers' tool, and at the same time a first attempt in Portuguese at developing a functional cataloguing and indexing system for a collection of materials recorded in Portuguese plus a mixture of African languages. Many of the tapes include interpretations, but the Historical Archive's policy is to transcribe the original text and then translate it. The introduction explains how the tapes were recorded, as part of an Archive project, and discusses the methodology of oral sources and their role as 'social memory' and as history. Technical problems of bibliographical control and access are discussed, and the development of a model indexing card, used in the second half of the work, is described. The second half of the thesis consists of an index to 179 tapes, organized as follows: Cabo Delgado (25 interviews); Gaza (17); Greater Maputo (21); Inhambane (16); Maputo (8); Nampula (41); Niassa (31). The cards indicate the place of the interview, interviewees and interviewer(s), the date, languages used, technical details of the tape, whether transcriptions and/or translations exist, and a summary, or at least an indication, of the content. There is also a general index.

153 **A primeira carta orgânica de Moçambique (1761).** (The first Organic Charter of Mozambique, 1761.)
José Rui de Oliveira Pegado e Silva. Licenciatura dissertation, Faculdade de Letras de Lisboa [n.d.]. 266p. bibliog.

Covers the general situation in Mozambique in the middle of the 18th century; customs and excise; the finances of the Captaincies (*capitanias*); agriculture; military organization; trade; the church; the role of the hospital; and, on p. 171–259, transcriptions of relevant documents from the Arquivo Histórico Ultramarino (Overseas Historical Archive) in Lisbon.

154 **Naissance de Mozambique: résistance et révoltes anticoloniales,
1854–1918.** (Birth of Mozambique: resistance and anti-colonial
revolts, 1854–1918.)
René Pélissier.   Orgeval, France: Pélissier, 1984. 2 vols. bibliog.
maps.

A painstaking and detailed account, in French, of Portugal's military conquest of
Mozambique in the 19th century, based on a close reading of the extensive
published colonial literature, with some archival work. Pélissier is conventionally
described as an iconoclast, and here he attempts to demystify the fall of the Gaza
Empire, and the defeat of the 1917 Barwe revolt, for example. His central point is
that the so-called 'pacification' campaigns were actually waged by African
soldiers, fighting for Portuguese interests, but also furthering their own. Pélissier,
quite correctly, does not like to try to establish links between these events and the
later emergence of nationalism. The book has been generally well-received by
reviewers, who are, at the very least, impressed with Pélissier's indefatigable
industry. However, he has been criticized for a too-trusting attitude towards his
sources, particularly where statistical information is concerned.

155 *A luta continua!* **Recent literature on Mozambique.**
Jeanne Penvenne.   *International Journal of African Historical
Studies* vol. 18, no. 1 (1985), p. 109–38.

A detailed, carefully-researched and occasionally amusing review article on six
books: Munslow's *Mozambique: the revolution and its origins* (q.v.); the
Isaacmans' *Mozambique: from colonialism to revolution* (q.v.); Henriksen's
Revolution and counter-revolution (q.v.); Johnson and Bernstein's *Third world
lives of struggle* (q.v.); Ruth First's *Black gold* (q.v.); and Selim Gool's *Mining
capitalism and black labour in the early industrial period in South Africa: a critique
of the new historiography* (Lund, Sweden: [n.p.], 1983. 239p.). Jeanne Penvenne
is undoubtedly one of the most stimulating commentators at work on
Mozambican affairs today; she is no respecter either of myths or of persons, and
she questions everything. Certainly, for any historian working with the kind of
source material produced in such vast and beautifully-printed quantities by the
Portuguese colonial state, the ability to 'doubt everything' is a necessity. In a
fascinating section of this review article entitled 'Demystification or remystifi-
cation', for example, she questions the assumption that the colonial régime
enforced segregation by race and class in the suburbs of Lourenço Marques, and,
more importantly, dismisses the belief that there was 'a major strike wave' in the
city in the late 1940s, on the sensible grounds that the evidence does not in fact
show this. A Portuguese version of the article was published as 'A luta continua!
Literatura recente sobre Moçambique', *Revista Internacional de Estudos Africanos*
no. 3 (Jan.–Dec. 1985), p. 169–212.

156 **A criação da alfândega da Ilha do Ibo e a contribuição das ilhas para o comércio e a vida de Moçambique no século XVIII.** (The creation of the customs and excise on Ibo Island, and the contribution of the islands to the trade and life of Mozambique in the 18th century.)
Luís Filipe Filomeno Andrade de Conceição Pereira.
Licenciatura dissertation, Faculdade de Letras, University of Coimbra, Portugal, 1970. 318p. bibliog.

Demonstrates how customs payments were the major source of state income in Mozambique in the 18th century, especially for the trade from India, since the Portuguese state could scarcely afford to finance its overseas possessions at this time. Portuguese presence was limited to a few coastal settlements and to the semi-independent *prazos* of the Zambezi Valley. Most Portuguese and other historians have concentrated on Mozambique Island in this period, and Pereira's work is one of the few studies of Ibo and the other islands off the coast of northern Cabo Delgado, in an area contested with Swahili and Arab merchants.

157 **The empire of Monomotapa from the fifteenth to the nineteenth century.**
W. G. L. Randles, translated from the French by R. S. Roberts.
Gwelo, Zimbabwe: Mambo Press, 1981. 149p. bibliog. maps.
(Zambeziana, vol. 7).

The South African-born scholar Randles worked for many years in Lisbon and Paris, which gave him the opportunity to master the source material in the Portuguese archives, and also explains why this volume was first published in French. It was the first modern survey of the Monomotapa Empire to make full use of Portuguese published and unpublished sources. See also the pamphlet by António Nogueira da Costa (q.v.).

158 **Revolt in Portuguese East Africa: the Makombe rising of 1917.**
Terence O. Ranger. In: *African affairs, number two*. Edited by Kenneth Kirkwood. London: Chatto & Windus, 1963. p. 54–80.
(St. Antony's Papers, no. 15).

When Ranger wrote this essay the Barwe rising of 1917 was virtually unknown among English-speaking historians; and very little on the subject existed in Portuguese. He identifies three kinds of source, all from Zimbabwe or Zambia – the oral traditions of descendants of the Barwe living in Zimbabwe; two private journals kept by observers in Zambia; and material in the Harare archives. Ranger sees the Barwe rising as 'the end of . . . the story of Portuguese relations with the empire of Mwene Mutapa and its principalities . . . the last of the great tribal rebellions . . . ' He describes the British refusal to co-operate with Portugal in crushing the rising, provoked by massive recruitment of carriers for the campaign on the northern border in the First World War. See also Orchard Mdzonga's 'The Barwe revolt in Portuguese East Africa, 1917–1920' (MA thesis, University of Minnesota, Minneapolis, 1974. 131p.). Ranger's more recent writings on 'resistance' include his essay, with David Birmingham, entitled 'Settlers and liberators in the south' (In: *History of Central Africa*. Edited by

David Birmingham, Phyllis M. Martin. London, New York: Longman, 1983. vol. 2, p. 336–82), which covers the Angolan and Zimbabwean liberation struggles as well as Mozambique's; and *Peasant consciousness and guerrilla war in Zimbabwe: a comparative study* (London: James Currey, 1985. 377p.), which includes two chapters devoted to comparisons between ideology and the rural class struggle in the Mozambican, Mau Mau and Zimbabwe wars.

159 **Contribuição bibliográfica para o estudo das 'questões' da baía e do caminho de ferro de Lourenço Marques.** (A bibliographic contribution to the study of the 'questions' of the bay and the railway of Lourenço Marques.)
Ilídio Rocha. *Boletim do Centro de Documentação Científica [de Moçambique]* vol. 14, no. 3 (July–Sept. 1971), p. 187–90.

This contribution is a simple checklist of twenty-six numbered items in alphabetical author order, with no introduction, indexes or annotations. Many of the references are to contemporary published documentation. The work deals with two separate 19th-century arbitrations between the Portuguese and other powers. The first of these had its origins in the early industrialization of South Africa (the opening up of the Kimberley diamond fields in 1867), which created a labour shortage in Natal. Basing their legal claim on a navigational voyage up the coast by a certain William Owen in the 1820s, the British attempted to re-establish themselves on Inhaca Island, at the mouth of Maputo Bay, in order to gain a foothold for later access to the hinterland and its labour. Since Portugal and Britain, as allies, could not resort to war, the case went to French arbitration. The other dispute concerned the railway from Lourenço Marques to South Africa, which had been built by an American contractor in 1886–87 with his own capital, but which had rapidly fallen into disrepair, and did not actually reach the Transvaal border. The Portuguese nationalized the line in 1889, at which point the contractor claimed compensation; this case went to arbitration in Berne, Switzerland. In addition on the local history of the area, a ninety-six-item bibliography on Lourenço Marques entitled 'O crescimento da cidade colonial de Lourenço Marques: uma bibliografia anotada' (The growth of the colonial city of Lourenço Marques: an annotated bibliography) was prepared in 1985 by Julieta Massimbe of the Museu da Revolução; the Historical Archive intends to publish it.

160 **The year 1895 in southern Mozambique: African resistance to the imposition of European colonial rule.**
Walter Rodney. *Journal of the Historical Society of Nigeria* vol. 5, no. 4, (June 1971), p. 509–36.

The late Walter Rodney is better-known for his work on the Guinea coast, on his own country, Guyana, and, of course, for his popular book *How Europe underdeveloped Africa* (London: Bogle-L'Ouverture Publications; Dar es Salaam: Tanzania Publishing House; Harare: Zimbabwe Publishing House, 1972. 316p.) than as an historian of Mozambique. In this article he begins by pointing out that the 'African nationalist historian' is forced 'willy-nilly to wrestle' with the jingoistic Portuguese sources when studying the defeat of the Gaza Kingdom, since no other written materials exist, and the collection of oral data was impossible in 1971. Undeterred, and supplementing the colonial sources with secondary works by Wheeler and Omer-Cooper, Rodney then attempts to construct an account of the class system and political economy of the Gaza Nguni, on the basis of which he moves to an account of the actual campaigns, including the attacks by the 'Nkomati states' on the railway into Lourenço Marques. Rodney concludes that the Portuguese victory, achieved as it was with large numbers of African troops, was a tribute not so much to Portuguese valour as to superior weaponry within a changed balance of power in the area. On the fall of Gaza, see also Gerhard Julius Liesegang's, 'Beiträge zur Geschichte des Reiches der Gaza Nguni im südlichen Moçambique, 1820–1895' [Contribution to the history of the Gaza Nguni Kingdom in southern Mozambique, 1820–95] (PhD dissertation, University of Cologne, FRG, 1967. 292p.), which uses archival sources from both Lisbon and London. For an East German scholar's superficial view of these events, see A.-S. Arnold's 'Portugal's 'effective occupation' in Mozambique: the military conquest of Gaza, 1895–1896', *Asia, Africa, Latin America* (Berlin) special issue no. 13 (1984), p. 75–82.

161 **Para a história da arte militar moçambicana, 1505–1920.** (Towards a history of Mozambican military science, 1505–1920.)
Carlos Manuel Rodrigues Serra. Maputo: Cadernos Tempo, 1983. 165p. bibliog. (Cadernos Tempo, Colecção 'História', no. 4).

Carlos Serra, a senior Mozambican historian, later received a Master's degree (or, in Portuguese, a *licenciatura*) for this publication. It deals with the equipment, military organization, and training methods of African societies in their wars against the Portuguese, dividing the country into north, centre and south. The Portuguese, of course, always relied heavily on African troops in their colonial wars: for an account of these levies, see the conservative, and indeed, racist, survey of the history of African auxiliaries in the colonial army from 1506 to 1953 by António César Limão Gata, 'Evolução da prestação do serviço militar pelos indígenas de Moçambique' [Development of the rendering of military service by the natives of Mozambique] (Dissertation, Escola Superior Colonial, Lisbon, 1952–53. 71p.) Gata begins by quoting a frank comment from João Almeida – 'The native has always been a necessary and indispensible help to us in all our activities, especially military ones. To use him is our tradition and our policy – and it is also in our interests.' He finishes with another all-too-revealing quotation: '[Natives] are, yes, lazy and like big children, with little will-power. They do not resist the temptation to drink . . .'

162 **O oriente africano português: síntese cronológica da história de Moçambique.** (The Portuguese African East: a chronological synthesis of Mozambican history.)
M. Simões Alberto, Francisco A. Toscano. Lourenço Marques, Mozambique: Minerva Central, 1942. 305p. bibliog.

Portuguese colonial scholars loved lists, chronologies, indexes and guides, and were never happier than when they were devising complicated and non-standard systems. Luckily, Alberto and Toscano stick to a strict chronological order in this book, which starts with the birth of the Portuguese Henry the Navigator on 4 March 1394 (thus began Mozambican history!) and ends on 28 December 1933 with the publication of the colonial Organic Charter and Overseas Administrative

Reform. In between we have five 'cycles' or periods, with, it must be said, much useful information on colonial history. There is also a chronological summary at the end of the volume. See also, for a much more detailed chronological reference work on the whole empire, the useful *História do colonialismo português em Africa* by Pedro Ramos de Almeida (q.v.).

163 **The Indian Ocean zone.**
Alan K. Smith. In: *History of Central Africa*. Edited by David Birmingham, Phyllis M. Martin. London, New York: Longman, 1983. vol. 1, p. 205–44.
A useful overview chapter in an undergraduate textbook on Central African history, using some of Immanuel Wallerstein's ideas about the 'world economy' in dealing with a complex of social formations whose geographical area expanded and contracted through time, but which, roughly speaking, covered Mozambique plus Swaziland, eastern Zimbabwe, southern Tanzania and parts of South Africa. Smith deals with the political economy of the later Iron Age; interaction with Europe; and what he terms the era of 'negative transition', when Portuguese power was on the wane, unable either to fight off the Dutch, or to compete effectively with local merchant capital. During the 17th century the Portuguese steadily lost influence, resources and territory, until the Marquis of Pombal adopted less ambitious and more practical colonial policies.

164 **A posse de terra em Inhambane, 1885–1930: textos e documentos seleccionados e anotados.** (Land tenure in Inhambane, 1885–1930: selected and annotated texts and documents.)
Joaquim de Sousa Cruz. Trabalho de diploma for the Licenciatura, Arquivo Histórico de Moçambique, Universidade Eduardo Mondlane, 1985. 301p. bibliog.
An anthology of carefully-selected texts on land tenure in Inhambane. The short introduction deals with the province's agriculture, the means by which land was distributed, the occupation of the province, and problems of the peasantry and land tenure. The bulk of the work consists of government decrees from 1856 to 1921; extracts from various reports by governors of Inhambane (1905–22); and a section of miscellaneous documents.

165 **The Portuguese period in East Africa.**
Justus Strandes, translated by Jean F. Wallwork, edited by J. S. Kirkman. Nairobi: East African Literature Bureau, 1961. 325p. bibliog. maps.
In the early days Portuguese interest in the east coast extended right up to Somalia and Ethiopia. Indeed, within a decade of Vasco da Gama's arrival in 1497, the Portuguese had forts at Sofala and at Kilwa (in present-day Tanzania). This translation of the classic *Die Portugiesenzeit von deutsch- und englisch-Ostafrika* (Berlin, 1899), is of particular interest for students of that period. The history of the Portuguese in Mozambique cannot be understood in isolation from their activities further up the coast in Kilwa and Mombasa. Kirkman adopts a non-interventionist position as editor, arguing that he has 'not considered it part of his duties to argue with his author over general observations made in

1899 . . . His main task has been to add topographical and historical descriptions of the places and peoples mentioned . . . the spelling of Arabic and Swahili names . . . has been regularised and brought up to date.' Despite its age it remains an important reference.

166 **História militar e política dos Portugueses em Moçambique de 1833 aos nossos dias.** (Military and political history of the Portuguese in Mozambique from 1833 to the present.)
José Justino Teixeira Botelho. Coimbra, Portugal: Imprensa da Universidade, 1921. 594p.

The first volume of this study, *História militar e política dos Portugueses em Moçambique da descoberta a 1833* [Military and political history of the Portuguese in Mozambique from its discovery to 1833] (Lisbon: Centro Tipográfico Colonial, 1934. 637p.) was published thirteen years after the second volume. A revised edition of the second volume came out two years later (Lisbon: Centro Tipográfico Colonial, 1936. 2nd ed. 742p.). In his wide-ranging but completely Eurocentric work, Teixeira Botelho provides details of the Portuguese military organization and resources; campaigns (especially what he himself terms 'the struggle for effective control' in Gaza, Barwe and the north); and the settlement of frontiers, including the abortive attempt to join up Mozambique to Angola.

167 **A presença portuguesa no Niassa, 1796–1834.** (The Portuguese presence in Niassa, 1796–1834.)
José Maria Teixeira da Cruz. Licenciatura dissertation, Instituto Superior de Ciências Sociais e Política Ultramarina, Universidade Técnica de Lisboa, 1964. 403p. bibliog. maps.

An important and detailed study of a little-known period in the history of Mozambique's north-western extremity, which was a bone of contention for many years between the Portuguese and the British.

168 **Records of south-eastern Africa, collected in various libraries and archive departments in Europe.**
George McCall Theal. [Cape Town]: Government of the Cape Colony, 1898–1903. 9 vols. Reprinted, Cape Town: Struik, 1964. 9 vols.

This is primary material, and excellent work for its time. The compiler was official historiographer for the Cape government at the turn of the century, and wrote a number of synthetic ethnographical-historical works, which are now very outdated. One of the most important for Mozambique is *History and ethnography of south Africa before 1795* (London: Swan Sonnenschein, 1907–10. 3 vols.), later editions of which were incorporated as vols. 2–4 of his *History of south Africa* (London: Allen & Unwin, 1919–26. 11 vols. Reprinted, Cape Town: Struik, 1964.). Fortunately, we have the source material in the *Records*, which are of permanent value for future historians; and luckily they have been reprinted by the South African antiquarian house Struik in Cape Town. Theal writes in his preface that his objective was to obtain 'as much authentic knowledge as it is possible to gather upon the past condition of the Bantu tribes south of the Zambesi' and that he is, therefore, publishing these 'Portuguese and other records upon the subject'. However, little-known or unpublished archival materials are not included; on the contrary, the work consists of 'documents and extracts from printed pamphlets and books . . . though these do not always refer to the natives'. The documents are not in strict chronological order, and translations ('sometimes more free than literal') as well as the transcriptions are included for the Portuguese and the few Spanish and Italian texts. The contents of the volumes are as follows: Volume 1 – extracts from Manuel de Faria e Sousa's *Asia portuguesa* (1666–74), with Portuguese and Dutch letters and documents; Volume 2 – extracts from Gaspar Correa's 16th-century *Lendas da Índia* and other books in Spanish, Latin, English and Portuguese; Volume 3 – extracts from Damião de Goes' *Chronica do Rei Dom Emanuel* (1566) and other documents; Volume 4 – papers on Sofala and Mozambique, with other documents; Volume 5 – 18th-century (and earlier) letters and documents; Volume 6 – extracts from João de Barros' *Da Asia* (1552–1613), extracts from Diogo de Couto's 16th-century *Da Asia* and other papers; Volume 7 – João dos Santos' *Ethiopia oriental* (1609) and other texts; Volume 8 – accounts of (mostly 17th-century) shipwrecks; Volume 9 – 19th-century letters and documents in English, including material on Captain Owen's voyage. Note that the last volume also includes a name and subject index to the whole series, occupying nearly 300 pages (p. 267–533). See also the translations on shipwrecks in C. R. Boxer's *The tragic history of the sea, 1589–1622* (Cambridge, England: Cambridge University Press for the Hakluyt Society, 1959), and various transcriptions published in the 'non-official section' of the *Annaes do Conselho Ultramarino* and also in the monthly *Arquivo das Colónias* (both Lisbon).

169 **Capitalism and colonialism in Mozambique: a study of Quelimane District.**

Leroy Vail, Landeg White. Minneapolis, Minnesota: University of Minnesota Press; London: Heinemann, 1980. 419p. bibliog. maps.

This is, without doubt, a major contribution to Mozambican history, and is possibly the most important historical work on the country to be published in English since independence. Nevertheless, the book has major flaws. White, writing in the *Journal of Southern African Studies* (vol. 11, no. 2 [April 1985], p. 321) says that his book 'received glowing reviews in the major journals', but was also 'excoriated in a number of polemical papers'. Certainly, those accustomed to the gentler ambience of Western academia might not have found the vigorous denunciations of Vail and White's political argument to their taste, but critique should not be dismissed merely as polemic. White concedes, for example, that 'our emphasis on the rigidity of President Machel's political catechism was made irrelevant by his . . .speech of March 1980 . . . ', although the rigidity was unproven in the first place. For a moderate statement of what White seems to think is a 'Maputo viewpoint', see Judith Head and David Hedges' 'Problemas da história da Zambézia' (Problems of Zambezian history), *Estudos Moçambicanos* no. 4 (1983–85), p. 127–39; and also Carlos Serra in the *Cadernos de História* no. 2 (Aug. 1985), p. 57–61.

170 **Gungunyane the negotiator: a study in African diplomacy.**
     Douglas L. Wheeler. *Journal of African History* vol. 9, no. 4
     (1968), p. 585–602.

Ngungunyane was ruler of the Gaza Shangaan people from 1884 to 1895 and,
rightly or wrongly, became a symbol of resistance to Portuguese colonial rule; his
bones were returned to Mozambique from his exile in Portugal only after
President Samora Machel's state visit to Portugal in 1983. This is an influential
reappraisal of his diplomatic ability. Ngungunyane's chief objective in his
relations with the European powers was independence of action, but he was
constantly under pressure to make economic and political concessions. Until mid-
1889 his capital was situated on the edge of the plateau, but he then shifted
southwards to the Limpopo Valley, a move which profoundly changed relations
with Portugal. He was a strong personality, but was surrounded by warlike
advisors; nevertheless, he gained advantages by exploiting his 'fearful military
reputation', an efficient spy network, and differences between Portugal and
Britain. In the end, the Portuguese superiority in guns, conflicts between his own
supporters, and social disintegration brought about his downfall.

171 **New England merchants and missionaries in coastal nineteenth-
     century Portuguese East Africa.**
     Charles Bryant White. PhD dissertation, Boston University,
     1974. 318p.

A useful thesis on Inhambane trade and on American missionaries in the 1880s
and early 1890s, which was presented to one of the leading American universities
for East African studies.

FRELIMO and the armed struggle (1964–74)

172 **The struggle for socialism in Mozambique, 1960–1972.**
     Edward A. Alpers.   In: *Socialism in sub-Saharan Africa: a new
     assessment.* Edited by Carl G. Rosberg, Thomas M. Callaghy.
     Berkeley, California: Institute of International Studies, University
     of California, 1979. p. 267–95. (Institute of International Studies.
     Research series, no. 38).

Alpers' important article deals principally with the 'development of a socialist
commitment within FRELIMO . . . the dialectic between theory and practice and
the contradictions between various political lines . . . '. Alpers begins with an
interesting account of the immediately pre-FRELIMO phase (1960–62), in which
he argues quite convincingly that the Front emerged from an alliance between
'insiders' (young militants from inside Mozambique) and a group around Eduardo
Mondlane and Marcelino dos Santos, and that, by implication, old-style exile
politics were no longer relevant. He compares the programmes of UDENAMO

(the National Democratic Union of Mozambique) and of FRELIMO, and comments on the striking similarities (since Marcelino dos Santos was an author of both documents, this is not surprising). In the second part of the article, Alpers outlines the development of internal contradictions (principally around Lazaro Nkavandame, who rose to a high position in FRELIMO, but then transferred to the Portuguese side) up to 1969, and the way in which the FRELIMO leadership responded. The third and last section is entitled 'The transition to a vanguard Party, 1970–72', and Alpers argues (against the early views of John Saul, among others) that 'By the end of 1972, at the very latest, there can be little doubt that FRELIMO was well along the path to transforming itself into a socialist vanguard party with distinctly Marxist-Leninist underpinnings.' The article is well-documented, making extensive use of widely-available FRELIMO publications that are sometimes ignored by other historians of this period. There are eighty-one footnotes on p. 406–10.

173 **Mozambique: las áreas liberadas.** (Mozambique: the liberated zones.)
Beatriz Bissio. *Cuadernos del Tercer Mundo* (Spanish ed.) no. 12 (May 1977), p. 31–42.

The liberated areas, or zones, were territories in which FRELIMO exercised political and economic control during the armed struggle, and where the Portuguese had been effectively expelled, even if they were still present in isolated pockets. Such areas existed in Cabo Delgado, Niassa and Tete. Beatriz Bissio visited the liberated areas in Cabo Delgado shortly after independence, and this is her report on what she saw, including interviews with local people, and a description of FRELIMO's base at Mueda. On current political problems in the liberated zones, see the reports of the Mozambican History Workshop: *A situação nas antigas zonas libertadas de Cabo Delgado* [The situation in the former liberated zones of Cabo Delgado] (Maputo: Oficina de História, Centro de Estudos Africanos, 1983. 59p. [Relatório no. 83/4]); and the recent *Poder popular e desagregação nas aldeias comunais do planalto de Mueda* [People's power and depopulation in the communal villages of the Mueda plateau] (Maputo: Oficina de História, Centro de Estudos Africanos, 1986. 61p. [Relatório no. 86/1]).

174 **The African liberation reader.**
Edited by Aquino de Bragança, Immanuel Wallerstein. London: Zed Books. 1982. 3 vols.

This massive anthology was originally published in Lisbon in a Portuguese edition with the much more relevant title of *Quem é o inimigo?* (Who is the enemy?). The late Professor Aquino de Bragança, scholar, historian, teacher, journalist and diplomat, died in the aeroplane crash which took the life of President Samora Machel in October 1986. He was fond of citing FRELIMO's well-known distinction between the Portuguese colonial system and the individual Portuguese themselves; between the system of apartheid in South Africa and individual whites there. One, the system, was the enemy; the other, not necessarily so. This anthology ranges over Angola, Guinea-Bissau, Namibia, South Africa and Zimbabwe, as well as Mozambique, and includes material from such organizations as FNLA (National Front for the Liberation of Angola) and Jonas Savimbi's UNITA (National Union for the Complete Independence of Angola), as well as by UNAR (Rombezia African National Union), Artur Vilanculu and Uria

History. FRELIMO and the armed struggle (1964-74)

Simango in Mozambique. These are not normally considered to be 'liberation movements' in the sense that the blurb on the cover claims. The sweep of the collection is therefore much broader than the English title would imply.

175 **Subversão em Cabo Delgado: contribuição para o seu estudo.**
(Subversion in Cabo Delgado: a contribution to its study.)
Fernando M. Chambino. Licenciatura dissertation, Instituto Superior de Ciências Sociais e Política Ultramarina, Universidade Técnica de Lisboa, 1968. 2 vols. bibliog. maps.

A lengthy Portuguese thesis on FRELIMO and its origins in Cabo Delgado Province in the 1960s. It has been included in the present bibliography firstly because it provides a clear example of the kind of *problématique* which the colonial administrator used to confront the liberation war, and secondly because it contains some useful (albeit often undocumented) information. The first volume consists of a lengthy and largely irrelevant treatment of 'models of revolutionary war', the particular models being China, Vietnam and Cuba. This is followed by a detailed ecological and anthropological analysis of Cabo Delgado, and a section on Portuguese difficulties in 'establishing sovereignty' over the area. Chapter four deals with MANU (Mozambique African National Union), UDENAMO and FRELIMO, with information on FRELIMO's military and administrative structures in Cabo Delgado, as seen by the Portuguese. Although full of references to Portuguese writings, the work is generally weak empirically. See also a similar work of the same date and institution by José António Macias Granado; 'Política de contra-subversão em Cabo Delgado: contribuição para o seu estudo' [The policy of counter-subversion in Cabo Delgado: study contribution] (Licenciatura dissertation, Instituto Superior de Ciências Sociais e Política Ultramarina, Universidade Técnica de Lisboa, 1968. [200]p.).

176 **Emerging nationalism in Portuguese Africa: a bibliography of documentary ephemera through 1965.**
Ronald H. Chilcote. Stanford, California: Hoover Institution, 1969. 114p. (Hoover Institution, Bibliographical Series, no. 39).

In this complementary volume to his collection of documents, Chilcote lists a wide range of important but ephemeral sources. Mozambican material may be found in the general section on Portuguese Africa (p. 1–9); in the special section on Mozambique (p. 81–92), which includes not only FRELIMO materials but also documents from such organizations as MANU, UDENAMO and COREMO; in the section on United Nations publications (such as testimony before UN committees); and in a final section listing translations from the US Joint Publications Research Service. There are no indexes and entries are not numbered.

177 **Emerging nationalism in Portuguese Africa: documents.**
Ronald H. Chilcote. Stanford, California: Hoover Institution Press, 1972. 646p. maps. (Hoover Institution Publications, no. 97).

For Mozambique, see especially chapter six, 'African challenge in Mozambique', with sections on the background to the emergence of nationalism, leadership, organization and ideological development. Chilcote includes, besides FRELIMO documentation, material from earlier organizations (UDENAMO, for example), and from such groupings as FUNIPAMO (United African People's Anti-Imperialist Front of Mozambique), COREMO and COSERU (Secret Committee to Resurrect UDENAMO). There is also material on the CONCP (Standing Conference of Nationalist Organizations of the Portuguese Colonies). On early nationalism in Portuguese-speaking Africa, see also Mário de Andrade and Maria do Ceu Reis, *Ideologias da libertação nacional* [Ideologies of national liberation] (Maputo: Centro de Estudos Africanos, 1985. [pagination varies]).

178 **A confissão da PIDE-DGS.** (The confession of the PIDE-DGS.)
Cadernos do Terceiro Mundo no. 38 (Nov. 1981), p. 94–97.

Despite the use of a variety of methods, from outright brutality and terrorism through bribery to psychological warfare, the Portuguese army and security services could not understand why they never really succeeded in winning over the rural population of Mozambique to their side in the war zones. In this article we can see at first hand the frustration and, after ten years of warfare, the lack of understanding on the part of the Portuguese only days before their defeat. The article, published by the radical magazine *Cadernos do Terceiro Mundo*, consists of lengthy extracts, with commentary, from a confidential report on the situation in Cabo Delgado (dated 4 April 1974) sent to Lisbon by the General Security Directorate. Written less than a month before the coup d'état of 25 April in Portugal, the twenty-five-page report analyses the state of affairs in an area with a population of 200,000 people, none of whom it considers politically trustworthy. Since it was administratively impossible to arrest and interrogate everyone in the province, the report concludes that 'It cannot be claimed that the [FRELIMO] network was destroyed . . . in this situation, it is not hard for FRELIMO to set it up again after a short time . . .'

179 **The bush rebels: a personal account of black revolt in Africa.**
Barbara Cornwall. New York: Holt, Rinehart & Winston, 1972. 252p.

An important and unromanticized account, with photographs, of visits to the liberated areas of Mozambique and Guinea-Bissau by Cornwall, an American freelance journalist. The book is excellent at describing the atmosphere of life under such conditions, and takes a sympathetic stand towards the struggle. The section on Mozambique ends on p. 117.

180 **Movimentos subversivos contra Moçambique.** (Subversive movements against Mozambique.)
João da Costa Freitas. In: *Moçambique: curso de extensão universitária, ano lectivo de 1964–1965.* (Mozambique: a university extension course for the academic year 1964–65.) Lisbon: Instituto Superior de Ciências Sociais e Política Ultramarina, Universidade Técnica de Lisboa [n.d.]. p. 317–37.

The history of the various early anti-colonial (one hesitates to call them 'nationalist') associations in Mozambique has yet to be written. This is a moderately informative article by a Portuguese colonial writer, which includes details about such obscure movements as the early Portuguese East Africa Society and the Tete East Africa National Globe Society. More significant in terms of its subsequent development was the Tanganyika Mozambique Makonde Union, a Dar es Salaam self-help association which preceded MANU. Costa Freitas prints the political programme of UDENAMO, and gives an account, although it is not very reliable, of the role of such regional groupings as PAFMECA (Pan-African Movement for East and Central Africa) and the CONCP. Naturally, the author is not concerned with historical veracity, and so careful reading is necessary. No sources are given. Provides one of the few readily-available articles in a very sparse field.

181 **The people's cause: a history of guerrillas in Africa.**
Basil Davidson. Harlow, Essex, England: Longman, 1981. 210p.
maps.

Basil Davidson was one of the few commentators to visit all three war zones in the Portuguese African colonies from the side of the liberation movements. He had served as a British officer during the Second World War with the Yugoslav partisans, and his reports from Angola, Guinea-Bissau and Mozambique were, therefore, perceptive as well as informed. Davidson is a pioneering popularizer of African history, as well as one of the first English-speaking scholars to write seriously on Lusophone Africa. This fascinating study looks at the history of irregular warfare in Africa, producing a tentative periodization and a typology based on the analysis of a wide range of campaigns from different periods of the history of the continent. Anyone wanting to study the history of the Mozambican liberation struggle could do a lot worse than to begin by reading this book, before plunging into the detailed accounts of the specialized studies.

182 **The politics of armed struggle: national liberation in the African colonies of Portugal.**
Basil Davidson. In: *Southern Africa: the new politics of revolution.* Basil Davidson, Joe Slovo, Anthony R. Wilkinson. Harmondsworth, England: Penguin Books, 1976. p. 17–102.

This long essay is not specifically about Mozambique, but is nonetheless directly relevant to the study of the Mozambican struggle. Davidson describes the colonial background, discusses whether or not Portugal in Africa should be considered as a special case, looks at various nationalist strategies, and in what is probably the most interesting part of the article (p. 56–65) looks at 'guerrilla warfare' itself.

183 **Dynamics of insurgency in Mozambique.**
James M. Dodson. *Africa Report* vol. 12, no. 8 (Nov. 1967), p. 52–55.

An interesting and not entirely unsympathetic attempt to evaluate FRELIMO's position in the early stage of the war, published in a special issue of the American news-and-analysis magazine *Africa Report*. Dodson writes that from September 1964 when the fighting started, until mid-1965, FRELIMO operations were limited to ambushes and hit-and-run attacks on isolated Portuguese outposts. He characterizes this as typical of the preliminary phase of a *guerrilha*. The war had also spread, by 1967, along the whole northern border between Niassa and Cabo

Delgado provinces and Tanzania, as well as moving southwards into Tete, Nampula and Zambézia. Dodson identifies the frontal attack on Olivença by a large FRELIMO contingent as marking a new phase of 'company-sized actions'. He is sceptical of FRELIMO casualty claims, but accepts that the liberated areas in the north were probably outside effective Portuguese control. 'The guerrilla commander,' comments Dodson, 'is reported to be a 30-year-old former student whose exact identity is a closely held secret.' He identifies five pre-conditions for FRELIMO success, all of which are present in varying degrees: popular support; a cause to fight for; favourable terrain; effective leadership; and outside help. However, the terrain in the south is far less suitable for insurgency, Portugal's conventional forces enjoy a considerable superiority, and Portugal's allies in South Africa and Rhodesia would do 'whatever becomes necessary'. For much more polemical writings by a right-wing military participant in, and apologist for, the colonial war, see various pieces by General Kaulza de Arriaga: for example, *A luta em Moçambique, 1970–1973* [The struggle in Mozambique, 1970–73] (N.p.: Intervenção [n.d.], 79p.); 'La situation militaire au Mozambique' (The military situation in Mozambique) *Découvertes* no. 81, vol. 7 (1971), p. 15–26; *The Portuguese answer* (London: Stacey, 1973. 99p.); and with Joaquim da Luz Cunha, Bettencourt Rodrigues and S. Silvério Marques, *África: a vitória traida* [Africa: victory betrayed] (Braga, Lisbon: Intervenção, 1977, 276p.).

184 **Portugal's wars in Africa.**
Ruth First.   London: International Defence and Aid Fund, 1971. 32p. bibliog.

Ruth First was later to become research director of the Centro de Estudos Africanos in Mozambique. She wrote this pithy and committed leaflet for the IDAF support group in the early 1970s, describing Portugal's character as a colonizer (conquest, slavery and forced labour); the colonial administration; Salazar's corporate state; resistance to the colonial power; the war situation in 1971; Portugal's allies, especially within NATO; and the 'unholy alliance' of Portugal, South Africa and Southern Rhodesia. An appendix is devoted to short life-histories of three Portuguese army deserters who answered an appeal to go over to FRELIMO.

185 **Sulle origini rurali del nazionalismo mozambicano.** (On the rural origins of Mozambican nationalism.)
Anna Maria Gentili.   *Rivista di Storia Contemporanea* (Turin, Italy) no. 1 (1984), p. 79–112.

A lengthy article in Italian, based mainly on research done with oral and archival sources in Cabo Delgado Province in the early 1980s. Gentili worked on the research project organized by the History Workshop to study the history of the armed struggle (see *Não Vamos Esquecer* (q.v.)). After introductory sections on the colonial state and on the specific history of the Mueda plateau, she discusses the influence of decolonization in Tanganyika (Tanzania) on the growth of nationalism in northern Mozambique; the economic and social structure of Mueda in the 1950s; the impact of forced cotton cultivation; and the complex social transformation set under way by colonial policy, massive labour emigration and other factors. She writes that the characterization of the plateau 'as an area of subsistence agriculture, completely isolated, and scarcely penetrated by the . . .

colonial system' is an over-simplification. She also discusses the important African agricultural co-operatives, of which the best known was the Liguilanilu. See also a revised version of this article in Portuguese by Yussuf Adam and Anna Maria Gentili, 'O movimento dos Liguilanilu no planalto de Mueda, 1957–1962' [The Liguilanilu movement on the Mueda plateau, 1957–62] *Estudos Moçambicanos* no. 4 (1983–85), p. 41–75; and a quite different interpretation by Allen Isaacman, 'The Mozambican cotton cooperative: the creation of a grassroots alternative to forced cotton production', *African Studies Review* vol. 7 (1982), p. 5–28.

186 **Inventory of select documents from the Immanuel Wallerstein collection of political ephemera of the liberation movements of Lusophone Africa and Anglophone southern Africa (1958–1975) on microfilm.**
[Beverly Grier, Margaret Kinsman].   New Haven, Connecticut: Yale University Library [1977]. 57p.

The two major public collections of FRELIMO documents in the United States are the Wallerstein collection at Yale University and the Chilcote collection at the Hoover Institution in California; nothing to compare with them exists in England or Portugal. Both resulted from private scholarly initiatives by students of Portuguese-speaking Africa, and both are available on microfilm. In this important bibliographic inventory of the Wallerstein material FRELIMO and other Mozambican documents from microfilm reels 4, 5 and 11 can be found listed as follows: FRELIMO, p. 23–28; other organizations (UDENAMO, MANU, COREMO, UNAR [Rombezia National African Union]), p. 28–30; Portuguese Africa in general (CONCP, UGEAN [General Students Union of Black Africa]), p. 36–37; and serials (*Voz da Revolução*, *COREMO Newsletter*, *FRELIMO Information*, etc.), p. 57. Since the compilers were apparently not entirely familiar with the material, the inventory does not always correspond perfectly to the film. Much of this material was published by Wallerstein, jointly with Aquino de Bragança, in their *African liberation reader* (q.v.).

187 **Some reflections upon the war in Mozambique.**
Adrian Hastings.   *African Affairs* no. 292, vol. 73 (July 1974), p. 263–76.

For Hastings' role in exposing Portuguese atrocities during the liberation war in Mozambique, see the comments on his *Wiriyamu* (q.v.). In this piece, written after the Portuguese coup of 25 April 1974, he points out that FRELIMO's military successes were decisive in creating the conditions for the overthrow of Caetano. Although the war in Guinea-Bissau was going badly, the country itself was relatively unimportant to Portugal; in Angola the liberation movement was split. Only in Mozambique, where FRELIMO was steadily advancing, were the Portuguese in real difficulty, and indeed, only three weeks before the coup, Caetano moved 10,000 troops from Angola to Mozambique. Portuguese desperation as the guerrillas closed in around Tete led to the massacre at Wiriyamu in 1972 and other such horrors. Hastings also includes some comments on the da Cruz family of *prazeiros* at Massangano in a reflection on primary resistance. The article is a little disorganized, but interesting and informative.

188 **Wiriyamu.**
Adrian Hastings. New York: Orbis Books; London: Search
Press, 1974. 158p. maps.

The Portuguese army's slaughter of defenceless villagers at Wiriyamu, near Tete, came to public attention through the efforts of Adrian Hastings, a British priest who had worked in Mozambique and maintained contact with other missionaries inside the country. The story broke on the eve of Marcello Caetano's 1973 visit to Britain, and demonstrations and protests accompanied the Portuguese leader everywhere, to his great irritation. The right-wing supporters of the Lisbon régime immediately began trying to cover up the atrocity; the London *Daily Telegraph*, for instance, could find 'no evidence'; unsurprisingly, when their research consisted of questioning frightened peasants in the presence of Portuguese soldiers. Even such a well-known figure as L. H. Gann of the Hoover Institution accused Hastings of using 'guilt by association' and of 'trendiness' (*African Affairs* no. 292, vol. 73 [July 1974], p. 371–72). But, despite the protestations of the right, the facts spoke then and speak still for themselves.

189 **Revolution and counter-revolution: Mozambique's war of independence, 1964–1974.**
Thomas H. Henriksen. Westport, Connecticut; London:
Greenwood Press, 1983. 289p. bibliog. map. (Contributions in
Intercultural and Comparative Studies, no. 6).

Written by a staff member of the conservative Hoover Institution in California, this is the first general history of the war of liberation in English, and is based principally on a wide range of contemporary newspaper reports and published sources. The book was favourably received by Jeanne Penvenne (q.v.), who praised the author's 'no-nonsense attitude and healthy circumspection' (*International Journal of African Historical Studies* vol. 18, no. 1 [1985], p. 127). However, Henriksen misses the point, for example, in his account of Operation Gordian Knot, during which FRELIMO's operations in Tete were an essential part of their general strategy. Henriksen presents the Tete campaign as an example of resilience; in fact the commander of the Portuguese armed forces, General Kaulza de Arriaga, was outwitted, although at a high cost. Recent, and so far unpublished, work by such Mozambican historians as João Paulo Borges Coelho and José Negrão, using Portuguese military sources, is beginning to reveal a convincing and quite different version of the pattern of the war in Tete. The History Workshop of the Centre of African Studies in Maputo has also worked on the history of the war in Cabo Delgado. See, for early versions of their research, Coelho's *A primeira Frente de Tete e o Malawi* [The first Tete Front and Malawi] (81p.); and Negrão's *A produção e o comércio nas zonas libertadas* [Production and trade in the liberated areas] (106p.), both published by the Arquivo Histórico de Moçambique, Projecto de Tete, 1984.

190 **Portugal's African wars: Angola, Guinea Bissao [sic], Mozambique.**
Arslan Humbaraci, Nicole Muchnik. Dar es Salaam: Tanzania
Publishing House, 1974. 250p. maps.

A general survey organized into brief chapters on the socio-economic background of the three countries (on Mozambique, this section occupies p. 21–24, of which

77

p. 23 is a map); and chapters on the colonial wars themselves, as well as familiar material on the five centuries of Portuguese domination, Portugal as the first to arrive and the last to leave, and even Africa the black mother. There is information on NATO collaboration with the Portuguese armed forces and its effects on the prolongation of the wars.

191 **Mozambique: sowing the seeds of revolution.**
Samora Machel.   London: Committee for Freedom in
Mosambique [sic], Angola and Guiné, [1974] 68p.

A selection taken mainly from the FRELIMO series 'Studies and Guidelines' (Estudos e Orientações), with an introduction by John Saul based on an extended (and as yet unpublished) interview in 1974. Most of these speeches, and one *Daily News* (Dar es Salaam) interview with Iain Christie, come from the early 1970s, during the final phase of the liberation struggle, and deal with education, health, women, leadership and other questions of immediate and practical importance. The Portuguese texts can most easily be found in the collection *A nossa luta* [Our struggle] (Lourenço Marques, Mozambique: Imprensa Nacional, 1975); they are also still mostly available as individual pamphlets.

192 **The tasks ahead: selected speeches.**
Samora Machel.   New York: Afro American Information Service,
1975. 125p.

This collection of speeches, mostly from the 'Studies and Guidelines' series, was published shortly after the time of independence by a radical support group in the United States. Much of the material is duplicated in the collection *Mozambique: sowing the seeds of revolution* (q.v.), although the translations appear to be different. Also included is the famous poem 'Josina, you are not yet dead'. Some photographs are printed, with such captions as 'The culture of different tribes [sic] and regions has been merged by FRELIMO in the course of the revolution to create a national culture', below a picture of some people who may or may not be dancing.

193 **Moçambique norte: guerra e paz (reportagem).** (Mozambique
north: war and peace – reports.)
Guilherme de Melo.   [Lourenço Marques, Mozambique: Minerva
Central, 1968?] 270p.

Melo was a star reporter with the Lourenço Marques daily *Notícias* in the 1960s; at independence he left for Portugal, but has since returned on visits to write about Mozambique for the Portuguese press. This book consists of a series of forty short articles about the liberation war which he wrote for the newspaper during visits to the war zones in Cabo Delgado, Niassa, Tete and Zambézia in 1967–68. The main interest, apart from the 'Portuguese view' of the war, lies in the included series of interviews with FRELIMO deserters, for example, chapter twelve, 'Entrega-se às autoridades o Secretário Provincial do Efectivo Militar da FRELIMO' [The Provincial Secretary of the military wing of FRELIMO gives himself up to the authorities], and chapter twenty-five, 'A deserção em massa do Estado Maior do Unango' [Mass desertion by the general staff at Unango]. The photographs were taken by Carlos Alberto Vieira. See also by the same author,

History. FRELIMO and the armed struggle (1964–74)

'Breve resenha para a história da subversão armada no norte e seu combate' [Brief review of the history of armed subversion in the north and the struggle against it] *Boletim Municipal* no. 2 (24 July 1968), p. 51–54.

194 **Reabertura da frente Tete: oitavo aniversário.** (The eighth anniversary of the reopening of the Tete Front.)
José Moiane. *Tempo* no. 283 (7 March 1976), p. 24–31.

An interview with the former FRELIMO defence secretary for Tete Province about the history of the liberation struggle, on the anniversary of the successful second attempt to begin guerrilla warfare there against the Portuguese. According to Moiane, the original Tete Front had been closed down by FRELIMO in 1965, principally because Zambia was not yet independent and Malawi's policy towards Portugal was ambiguous; hence the guerrillas lacked a secure rear-base. Between 1965 and March 1968, when the Front was reopened, FRELIMO engaged in intense political activity in the area and, with more experience in the northern provinces, was able to learn from the earlier setback. The interview also discusses the history of the struggle in this province, the attacks against the Cabora Bassa hydroelectric project, Portuguese-Rhodesian collaboration against FRELIMO, and the effect of the 1968–69 crisis within the organization on the progress of the struggle. The Mozambican press has published a number of these interviews with former fighters: on the history of the struggle in this province see also the studies by João Paulo Borges Coelho and José Negrão (q.v.).

195 **Mozambique Revolution.**
Dar es Salaam: FRELIMO, Dec. 1963–June 1975. nos. 1–61.
irregular.

This English-language magazine was one of FRELIMO's principal weapons on the front of international opinion during the armed struggle. It started off as a modest ten-page mimeographed newsheet, and finished as an illustrated typeset magazine with full-colour covers, put together by professional journalists. It remains one of the most important sources for the period, containing military communiqués, accounts of meetings and seminars, and articles on FRELIMO policy in such areas as health, education or agricultural production. The review also carries accounts of international events (such as the Catholic Church's attitude to the war of liberation) and humorous commentaries (for instance, Salazar takes his first ride in an aeroplane).

196 **Fanon's theory on violence: its verification in liberated Mozambique.**
Yoweri T. Museveni. In: *Essays on the liberation of southern Africa.* Edited by Nathan M. Shamuyarira. Dar es Salaam: Tanzania Publishing House, 1975. p. 1–24. (University of Dar es Salaam. Studies in Political Science, no. 3).

Yoweri Museveni writes in his last sentence that 'The Mozambican has made a more serious attempt (i.e. through revolutionary violence) to recover his manhood, to commit suicide as a 'native', than the African of, for instance, Uganda.' Museveni later went on to become the leader of the Ugandan National Liberation Army and president of his country, so his ideas on such struggles are of more than passing interest. His Zimbabwean teacher, Dr. Nathan Shamuyarira, is Minister of Information in the ZANU (Zimbabwe African National Union) government of Robert Mugabe at the time of writing.

197 **Internal war in Mozambique: a social-psychological analysis of a nationalist revolution.**
Walter C. Opello, Jr.   PhD dissertation, University of Colorado, Boulder, Colorado, 1973. 414p. bibliog.

An important doctoral dissertation with theoretical pretensions. Opello uses Talcott Parsons' model of society as a basis for his analysis of FRELIMO history, referring to the debate among American sociologists between the 'consensus' and the 'conflict' schools of thought. He begins with a detailed analysis of modern Mozambican culture, society, politics and economy, before moving on to an account of the growth of nationalism in the country. However, the principal interest of the dissertation is as a source of information, since Opello searched the literature very systematically – his excellent bibliography even includes newspaper articles. See also the article by the same author in the *Journal of Southern African Studies* (q.v.).

198 **Pluralism and elite conflict in an independence movement: FRELIMO in the 1960s.**
Walter C. Opello, Jr.   *Journal of Southern African Studies* vol. 2, no. 1 (Oct. 1975), p. 66–82.

Opello argues that the crisis in FRELIMO, which he dates virtually from the foundation of the organization in 1962 up to 1969, 'was primarily the result of competition among elite factions' and was not a 'tribalist' struggle at all. Certainly, the crisis cannot be explained in terms of hypothetical 'tribal' rivalries, but an 'elite factions' theory does not take us much further, since neither concept takes full account of the genuine *political* differences between the two lines, nor of the class positions which underlay them. Nonetheless, Opello provides us with a detailed circumstantial description of the events of the crisis – the Mateus Gwenjere-inspired student revolt at the Mozambique Institute in Tanzania, the attack by disaffected militants on FRELIMO's headquarters in May 1968, and the assassination of Eduardo Mondlane, the first president, in 1969.

199 **Terror in Tete: a documentary report of Portuguese atrocities in Tete District, Mozambique, 1971–72.**
London: International Defence and Aid Fund, 1973. 48p. maps.
(IDAF Special Report, no. 2:1973).

On 10 July 1973 *The Times* of London carried an appalling account of a massacre of about 400 villagers in Wiriyamu, south of Tete, by Portuguese colonial troops. The information upon which the report was based came from a group of foreign priests, especially Father Adrian Hastings, and caused a furore, especially as the story broke just before Dr. Marcello Caetano's arrival in London on an official visit. The impact on Western public opinion was considerable, and FRELIMO's case was placed in the centre of public attention; an important victory on the diplomatic front. This IDAF report includes material on several other massacres and atrocities in Tete, and seven documentary appendixes. For a report in

Portuguese, see the clandestine publication by 'A group of defenders of peace', *Guerra colonial em Moçambique: torturas, destruição de aldeias, massacres: testemunho do Pe. Afonso da Costa* [Colonial war in Mozambique: torture, destruction of villages, massacres: testimony of Father Afonso da Costa] (N.p.: Um Grupo de Defensores da Paz, 1973. 34p.); and the later *Documentos secretos: massacres na guerra colonial: Tete, um exemplo* [Secret documents on massacres in the colonial war: Tete, an example] (Lisbon: Ulmeiro, 1976. 172p.), which reproduces facsimiles of Portuguese military documents proving the accusations of massacres.

200 **25 de Setembro.** (25th of September.)
Dar es Salaam: Frente de Libertação de Moçambique; Maputo: Comissariado Político das Forças Populares de Libertação de Moçambique, [1965–82]. irregular.

The first armed attacks on Portuguese colonial posts were launched by FRELIMO on 25 September, which is commemorated in Mozambique as Armed Forces Day. This venerable but fugitive magazine began as a fighters' political, military and cultural news-sheet, appearing in mimeographed form until independence. It carried poetry, essays, letters and articles. The Museum of the Revolution in Maputo holds an almost complete set, starting with no. 10 (23 June 1966), which it uses in many of the displays. After independence *25 de Setembro* was revived as a glossy magazine (no. 83, July 1976), and continued in publication for a further six years.

201 **The Zambesi salient: conflict in southern Africa.**
Al J. Ventner. London: Robert Hale, 1975. 395p. bibliog. maps.

The reactionary South African journalist Ventner researched this volume in Mozambique, Angola and Zimbabwe in 1973, and so was overtaken by the defeat of the Portuguese army at the hands of FRELIMO and the movements in the other Portuguese colonies. Ventner views the various liberation wars as part of a general struggle, and puts the blame for almost everything on Chinese and Soviet agitators. Although mainly on the Zimbabwe struggle, there also is a considerable amount of material on Mozambique. The work contains ten appendixes, one of which is an interview with the FRELIMO traitor Miguel Murupa.

Population and Demography

General

202 **To seek a better life: the implications of migration from Mozambique to Tanganyika for class formation and political behaviour.**
Edward A. Alpers. *Canadian Journal of African Studies* vol. 18, no. 2 (1984), p. 367–88.
Looks at the impact of labour migration from northern Mozambique to colonial Tanganyika (Tanzania) on the society, economy and politics of the local population. The process was a complex one, and Alpers devotes some space to a discussion of the theoretical framework. The region along the Ruvuma River had been split in the 19th century by the Portuguese-German colonial border, and local people adopted various strategies to overcome the problems that this created. As a result, class formation and political behaviour in the area appear strange and unpredictable. All these factors were important for the growth of Mozambican nationalism. Oddly, the work by Bertil Egerö on Tanzanian migration patterns (*Colonization and migration: a summary of border-crossing movements in Tanzania before 1967* Uppsala, Sweden: Scandinavian Institute of African Studies, 1979. 45p. map. bibliog. (Research Report, no. 52); and *Population movement and the colonial economy of Tanzania* Dar es Salaam: Bureau of Resource Assessment and Land Use Planning, University of Dar es Salaam, 1974. 79p. maps. bibliog. (BRALUP Research Paper, no. 35)) does not appear in Alpers' bibliography.

203 **A evolução demográfica da cidade de Lourenço Marques, 1895–1975.**
(The demographic development of the city of Lourenço Marques,
1895–1975.)
Eduardo Medeiros. *Revista Internacional de Estudos Africanos*
no. 3 (Jan.–Dec. 1985), p. 231–39.

A short survey article on demographic sources and secondary works on the
population of the town of Lourenço Marques. Medeiros covers the censuses
themselves, sources for population data from the period before the 1894 census,
and the growth of the population over the eighty years between the 1894 census
and independence. He also prints a table on population growth and a four-page
bibliography. For a more critical approach, see Colin Darch's 'Notas sobre fontes
estatísticas oficiais referentes à economia colonial moçambicana' (q.v.), and
Manuel Jorge Correia de Lemos' careful and detailed piece 'Recenseamentos
populacionais em Moçambique colonial' [Population censuses in colonial
Mozambique] *Arquivo* [Maputo] vol. 1, no. 1 (April 1987), p. 15–24.

Censuses

204 **A população de Lourenço Marques em 1894 (um censo inédito).**
(The population of Lourenço Marques in 1894: an unpublished
census.)
Carlos Santos Reis. Lisbon: Centro de Estudos Demográficos,
1973. 136p.

A facsimile of the manuscript of one of the earliest headcounts, conducted in
Lourenço Marques at the end of the 19th century. The census consists essentially
of a list of names and land-holdings, and is an important historical, as well as
demographic, source. The original manuscript is in the collections of the
Historical Archive of Mozambique.

205 **Recenseamento da população do Concelho de Lourenço Marques
referido a 17 de Abril de 1904.** (Census of the population of the
Conselho of Lourenço Marques on 17 April 1904.)
Boletim Oficial de Moçambique no. 48, supplement (1 December
1904), p. 1–12.

Consists of a series of tables giving the demographic breakdown by race,
nationality, literacy, religion, marital status and profession. There is also
information about houses: in 1904 there were 1,890 in the district, of which 1,346
were built of wood and zinc. See also, for the same census, *Recenseamentos da
população e das habitações do Concelho de Lourenço Marques e da população
das circumscripções do mesmo districto* [Censuses of the population and housing
of the Conselho of Lourenço Marques and of the population of the
circumscriptions of the same district] (Lourenço Marques, Mozambique:
Imprensa Nacional, 1904. 14p.).

206 **Recenseamentos da população e das habitações da cidade de Lourenço Marques e seus subúrbios, referidos à 1 de Dezembro de 1912.** (Censuses of the population and housing of the city of Lourenço Marques on 1 December 1912.)
Secretaria Geral da Província de Moçambique. Lourenço Marques: Imprensa Nacional, 1913. 21p.

For the first time in Mozambican census-taking, this coverage includes a brief report on the work of the census, as well as tables giving the population breakdown by race, age, nationality, religion, profession and length of stay in the city. The suburbs are dealt with separately, from p. 17 onwards. There is also information on housing.

207 **Censo da população e arrolamento do gado: ano de 1922.** (Census of population and inventory of cattle for 1922.)
Companhia de Moçambique. Beira, Mozambique: Imprensa da Companhia de Moçambique, 1923. 19p. (Anexo ao *Boletim* no. 19, 1923).

This is a census for the territory under the control of the Mozambique Chartered Company, which consisted of what are now Manica and Sofala provinces. Tables give the white population breakdown by sex and nationality, district by district, and similar figures for Asiatic, mixed-race and black populations; population growth 1912–22; and summaries by racial category. There are also two tables on the population of head of cattle and its growth between 1912 and 1922.

208 **Primeiros resultados do censo da população não indígena realizado em 31 de Dezembro de 1928.** (First results of the census of the non-native population on 31 December 1928.)
Companhia de Moçambique. Beira, Mozambique: Imprensa da Companhia de Moçambique, 1929. 5p. (Anexo ao *Boletim* no. 10, 1929).

There is considerable confusion in the secondary sources over the 1928 census. This census of the non-African population took place in three stages: 29 December 1927, Lourenço Marques and suburbs; 3 May 1928, the rest of the colony, including Cabo Delgado and Niassa, but excluding Manica and Sofala; and 31 December 1928, territory of the Mozambique Chartered Company (i.e. Manica and Sofala). The publication cited above is a preliminary report on this last stage, and includes summary breakdowns by sex, race, nationality and district. This was the first census, even for non-Africans, which covered the whole of Mozambique, and was co-ordinated by the Bureau of Statistics which had been set up in 1924. Some of the results from 3 May 1928 were first published in four tables which appeared in the *Anuário estatístico* for 1926–28 (p. 32–33, 40–41), for 1929 (p. 58–59) and for 1930 (p. 40–43). The full report on this census is 'Censo da população não indígena da colónia de Moçambique em 29 de Dezembro de 1927 e 3 de Maio de 1928', (Census of the non-native population of Mozambique colony on 29 December 1927 and 3 May 1928) *Boletim Económico e Estatístico* special series, no. 10 (1930), of more than 300 pages.

Population and Demography. Censuses

209 **Censo da população indígena da colónia de Moçambique.** (Census of the native population of Mozambique colony.) Repartição de Estatística. *Boletim Económico e Estatística* special series, no. 11 (1932), p. 1–45.

From the 1930s until the abolition of the Native Statute in 1961, the censuses of whites, *assimilados*, persons of mixed race, Chinese and Indians (that is, the 'civilized' population) were held in years ending in '5'; for Africans they were held in years ending in '0'. The '0' series has been continued up to the present. This census of Africans gives tables by sex, age, district, level of education, profession, place of origin and physical defect (blind, idiot, deaf-mute, cripple, leper, invalid).

210 **Censo da população não indígena em 2 de Maio de 1935.** (Census of the non-native population on 2 May 1935.) Repartição Central de Estatística. *Boletim Económico e Estatística* special series, no. 13 (1936), p. 1–99.

The first of the '5' series of censuses of the non-African population, this publication gives detailed tables breaking down the population by age, sex, race and geographical distribution. See also the Mozambique Chartered Company's *Censo da população não indígena realizado em 2 de Maio de 1935* [Census of the non-native population made on 2 May 1935] (Beira, Mozambique: Imprensa da Companhia de Moçambique, 1937. 67p. [Anexo ao *Boletim* no. 20, 1937]), which was co-ordinated with the census for the rest of the colony, and gives data by age, sex, race, religion and nationality.

211 **Censo da população em 1940.** (Census of the population in 1940.) Repartição Técnica de Estatística. Lourenço Marques, Mozambique: Imprensa Nacional, 1942–45. 5 vols.

The first modern census of Mozambique. The first volume of this large report is devoted to the 'non-native' population, and the remaining four to the 'native' population. See also the Mozambique Chartered Company's last census (the company was wound up in 1942), *Censo da população não indígena realizado em 1 de Fevereiro de 1939* [Census of the non-native population made on 1 February 1939] (Beira, Mozambique: 1940. 65p. [Anexo ao *Boletim* no. 14, 1940]), which seems to have been out-of-step with the '0' and '5' series already established.

212 **Recenseamento da população não indígena em 12 de Junho de 1945.** (Census of the non-native population on 12 June 1945.) Repartição Técnica de Estatística. Lourenço Marques, Mozambique: Imprensa Nacional, 1947. 235p.

Before the establishment of the modern series of population censuses, of which the above is an example, the Portuguese had devoted some time and effort to the study of demographic trends and problems. At least two important studies were published in the earlier period: Mário Costa's 'Da população de Moçambique: achegas para a estatística da colónia' [Of the population of Mozambique: supplementary materials on the statistics of the colony] *Boletim Ecónomico e Etatístico* special series, no. 6 (1929); and Alexandre Lobato's University of

Population and Demography. Censuses

Coimbra (Portugal) dissertation, 'Ensaio de uma história demográfica da cidade de Lourenço Marques' [Attempt at a demographic history of the city of Lourenço Marques] *Boletim Económico e Estatístico* special series, no. 17 (1938), p. 1–65, which is based mainly on the 1912 and 1928 censuses.

213 **Recenseamento geral da população em 1950.** (General population census, 1950.)
Repartição de Estatística Geral.   Lourenço Marques,
Mozambique: Imprensa Nacional, 1953–55. 3 vols.

Generally referred to as the second census. For a discussion of the characteristics and uses of these counts in different phases of the colonial period, see Colin Darch's 'Notas sobre fontes estatísticas oficiais referentes à economia colonial moçambicana' (q.v.).

214 **Recenseamento geral da população civilizada em 1955.** (General census of the civilized population in 1955.)
Direcção dos Serviços de Economia e de Estatística Geral.
Lourenço Marques, Mozambique: Imprensa Nacional, 1958.
1,206p.

The last of the racially separate censuses of the '5' series; note that by this time the non-Africans were no longer 'non-natives', but had become the 'civilized' population. The abolition of the Native Statute in 1961 removed the legal basis for the two separate census series, although it did nothing to improve the lot of the majority of Mozambicans.

215 **III recenseamento geral da população na Província de Moçambique.** (Third general population census in Mozambique Province.)
Direcção Provincial dos Serviços de Estatística.   Lourenço Marques, Mozambique: Imprensa Nacional, 1969. 9 vols.

For a useful summary of the masses of data in these report volumes, see *III recenseamento geral da população: censo resumo da população da Província* (Third general population census: summary census of the population of the Province) prepared by the Direcção Provincial dos Serviços de Estatística, (Lourenço Marques, Mozambique: Imprensa Nacional, 1969. 79p.). Note also the frequent changes in the official title of the Bureau of Statistics throughout this series of census publications.

216 **IV recenseamento geral da população, 1970.** (Fourth general population census, 1970.)
Lourenço Marques, Mozambique: Direcção Provincial dos Serviços de Estatística, 1973–74. 9 vols.

The last of the colonial censuses, and the last Mozambican census data to be widely available. Volumes deal with what are now provinces, for example, Volume One is about Lourenço Marques; Volume 5 about Gaza; and Volume 7 about Inhambane. Data from the most recent (1980) census, the first undertaken after independence and in difficult conditions, has only been released in part, or in limited distribution publications. The first concrete information was contained in Marcelino dos Santos' speech to the 10th session of the People's Assembly (see *Tempo* no. 625 [1982], p. 18–21), but according to *Notícias* (28 March 1983), it was only a year later that data processing was completed. At the time of writing, volumes of provincial data from the 1980 census have begun to appear, published by the National Planning Commission in Maputo. See also *1° recenseamento geral da população: informação pública* [First general population census: public information] (Maputo: Conselho Coordenador de Recenseamento, 1983. 48p.).

Anthropology and Ethnography

217 **The Yaos.** *Chiikala cha wayao.*
Compiled by Yohanna B. Abdalla, edited by Meredith
Sanderson. London: Cass, 1973. 2nd ed. [120]p. (Cass Library of
African Studies. Missionary Researches and Travels, no. 25).

A reprint of the English and Yao editions of 1919 (both published by the
government in what was then Nyasaland, now Malawi), with a sixteen-page
introduction by Edward Alpers, a leading historian of the Mozambique-Malawi-
Tanzania border area where the Yao-speaking people live. Abdalla's work, says
Alpers, is one of the earliest 'East African efforts in the writing of African
history', and is therefore important even for readers not specifically interested in
northern Mozambique. The English text has recently been translated into
Portuguese and published in a mimeographed edition of 150 copies by the
Mozambican Historical Archive: *Os Yaos* (Maputo: Arquivo Histórico de
Moçambique, 1983. [156]p.), with a new introduction and explanatory notes.
There is some ethnographic literature on the Yaos of Malawi; for a specifically
Portuguese anthropological view from colonial times, see the two theses by
Manuel Gomes da Gama Amaral (q.v.) and by António Raimundo da Cunha
(q.v.).

218 **O povo yao (*mtundu wayao*): subsídios para o estudo de um povo do
noroeste de Moçambique.** (The Yao people (*mtundu wayao*):
elements for the study of a northwestern Mozambican people.)
Manuel Gomes da Gama Amaral. Licenciatura dissertation,
Instituto Superior de Ciências Sociais e Política Ultramarina,
Universidade Técnica de Lisboa, 1968. 283p. bibliog. maps.

A detailed Portuguese Master's thesis, covering the geographical and historical
background, individual and family life, and political, administrative, social and
economic organization of the Yao-speaking people. For another, similar thesis,
see António Raimundo da Cunha's 'Contribuição para o estudo do povo 'Wayao''

Anthropology and Ethnography

[Contribution to the study of the Yao people]. The Yao-speaking people have been much studied, especially in Malawi. See for example J. Clyde Mitchell's *The Yao village: a study in the social structure of a Nyasaland tribe* (Manchester, England: University of Manchester Press, 1956. 236p. Reprinted, Humanities Press, 1971); and Mary Tew's more general *Peoples of Lake Nyasa region* (London: Oxford University Press, 1950. 131p. [Ethnographic Survey of Africa. East Central Africa, part 1]).

219 **Antropologia cultural: algumas referências.** (Cultural anthropology: some references.)
Boletim do Centro de Documentação Científica [de Moçambique] vol. 14, no. 1 (Jan.–March 1971), p. 56–64.

Published in the bibliographical bulletin of the Mozambican Institute for Scientific Research (IICM), this checklist consists of 117 assorted citations in alphabetical author order, with no introduction, indexes or annotations. Oddly, the numbering of this bibliography continues in Ilídio Rocha's 'Bibliografia científica de Moçambique: linguística e literatura' (q.v.), published in the following issue, even though the titles differ and some items are repeated in both works. Although António Rita-Ferreira's anthropological bibliography (q.v.) is a much more systematic and serious effort, this list does include supplementary material.

220 **Stalemate: a study of cultural dynamics.**
Martha Butler Binford. PhD dissertation, Michigan State University, East Lansing, Michigan, 1971. 459p. bibliog.

This study of the ethnography of the Ronga-speaking (or, in Binford's spelling, Rjonga-speaking) people is organized in two parts. The first two chapters constitute a general ethnography of the Ronga, who Binford carefully distinguishes from the Tsonga; in this and in several other respects she disagrees with Henri Junod (q.v.), and she does not hesitate to correct the earlier writer whenever she considers it necessary. The second part of the thesis is a case-study, based on field-work and presented within a 'process theory' *problématique* of the marital problems of one Malangatana Ngwenya Valente, principally a dispute over his taking a second wife. This involves, at various stages, informal local intervention, the Church and the Portuguese authorities. The lengthy analysis of the conflicts is written in a very readable style.

221 **Contribuição para o estudo do povo 'Wayao'.** (Contribution to the study of the Yao people.)
António Raimundo da Cunha. Licenciatura dissertation, Instituto Superior de Ciências Sociais e Política Ultramarina, Universidade Técnica de Lisboa, 1966. 369p. bibliog.

A general description of the Yao, concentrating on their ethnography rather than their history. Cunha covers housing, agriculture, trade, family life, food, dress, social life and literature (folk-tales, proverbs and guessing-games), as well as religious beliefs and taboos.

Anthropology and Ethnography

222 **African anthropology and history in the light of the history of FRELIMO.**
Jacques Depelchin. *Contemporary Marxism* no. 7 (Fall 1983), p. 69–88.

Depelchin mounts a vigorous attack on what he terms the 'anthropological problematic', which, as he points out, is by no means the exclusive preserve of the anthropologists. Ranging widely over recent southern African history, Depelchin cites the example of the refusal of the first Zairean Prime Minister, Patrice Lumumba to be locked into an ethnographic mould, and quotes a telling passage from Junod's *The life of a south African tribe* (q.v.) to make the same point. He discusses whether a Marxist anthropology is really possible, concluding that Marxism may have 'radicalized anthropology, but it is far from calling it into question'. Pointing out that the Atlantic slave-trade left African societies decimated, he argues that what anthropologists actually do is to 'look at broken vases, buildings in ruins as the real and whole things'. The main section of the article moves on to a detailed account of how FRELIMO arrived at an analysis of Mozambican realities which was to enable it to conduct a victorious struggle against Portuguese colonialism. Depelchin concludes that even a radicalized anthropological *problématique*, because of its inherent assumptions about the specific nature of African social formations, should have no place in Mozambique – unfortunately, however, academics 'naturally turn to anthropology as the most adequate science to study the peasantry'. The paper was originally presented at a 1982 Mozambican anthropology conference.

223 **Os macondes de Moçambique.** (The Makondes of Mozambique.)
Jorge Dias, Margot Dias, Manuel Viegas Guerreiro. Lisbon: Junta de Investigações do Ultramar, Centro de Estudos de Antropologia Cultural, 1964–70. 4 vols. bibliog.

These lavishly produced volumes constitute essential reading for anybody interested in the Makonde-speakers of northern Mozambique, whether for purely ethnographic reasons, or to see how the Portuguese sought to understand their African subjects. Jorge Dias was a Portuguese ethnographer of international distinction, and this massive study was his African masterwork. It may reasonably be asserted that, together with the ethnographic writings of António Rita-Ferreira, and the classic studies of Junod on the Tsonga, these volumes constitute virtually the entire worthwhile ethnography produced on Mozambique. They were published by one of the major research institutes of colonial Portugal, the Board for Overseas Studies' Centre for Cultural Anthropology. The first volume, by Dias himself, deals with history and economics; the second, written together with his wife, with material culture; the third, and last to be published, again by the Diases, is the anthropological core of the work, on social and ritual life; and Guerreiro's volume on wisdom, language, literature and games completes the set. A fifth volume, apparently an album of photographs of Makonde carvings with an introduction by Margot Dias, was planned, but has never appeared (but on this subject, see Jorge Dias, 'Les sculptures makondes', *Revue Française* [Paris] no. 261 (1973), p. 34–37). The quality of the illustrations and the comprehensiveness of the enterprise make this an essential work, even for those readers with little Portuguese. For a further aspect of Dias' work, see his political reports for the Portuguese government on conditions on the Mueda plateau: for example Jorge Dias, Manuel Viegas Guerreiro, Margot Dias, *Missão de estudos das minorias étnicas do ultramar Português: relatório da campanha de 1959 (Moçambique, Angola, Tanganhica e União Sul Africana)* [Mission to study ethnic minorities in overseas Portugal: report for the 1959 season (Mozambique, Angola, Tanganyika and the Union of South Africa)] (Lisbon: Centro de Estudos Políticos e Sociais, Junta de Investigações do Ultramar, 1960. 56p.). This prints (on p. 53–56) the constitution of the Tanganyika-Mozambique Makonde Union, a precursor of MANU. On Dias himself, see the memorial Festschrift *In memoriam Jorge Dias* (Lisbon: Instituto de Alta Cultura, Junta de Investigações do Ultramar, 1974. 2 vols.), especially the biographical introduction, in English, by Ernesto Veiga de Oliveira (vol. 1, p. 11–20) and the bibliography of Dias' writings (p. 21–28).

224 An ethnohistoric study of continuity and change in Gwambe culture.

Charles Edward Fuller. PhD dissertation, Northwestern University, Illinois, 1955. 277p. bibliog. maps.

The Gwambe people come from an area north of the Inharrime River up to the Inhassume River. Fuller lived there for twelve years as a Methodist missionary. His thesis is an attempt to construct an historical anthropology for the area, and covers the history of the Gwambe from the arrival of the Portuguese in the 16th century to the 20th century. 'Continuity and change' has long been recognized as a central theoretical problem for the anthropological approach to the study of human society, and Fuller includes both a lengthy ethnography of contemporary Gwambe, and a discussion of the theoretical problems. There are two brief appendixes on the vowels and consonants of the language. Another anthropological thesis completed in the same year is Johannes Bruwer's 'Die verwantskapsbasis van sosiale organisasie by matriliniere bantoegemeenskappe met besondere verwysing na die Kunda', [The family basis of social organization among matrilinear Bantu populations, with special reference to the Kunda] (PhD dissertation, University of Pretoria, 1955).

225 Mozambique: the Africanization of a European institution: the Zambesi *prazos*, 1750–1902.

Allen F. Isaacman. Madison, Wisconsin; London: University of Wisconsin Press, 1972. 260p. bibliog. maps.

After the revival of Shona power under the Rozwi dynasty had pushed the Portuguese off the Zimbabwe plateau for the last time, a few hundred settlers established themselves on the *prazo* estates or crown lands of the Zambezi Valley. In this book, much praised at the time of publication, Isaacman submits the estates to an anthropological examination. The book is based on Isaacman's doctoral research (see 'The historical development of the *Prazos de Coroa*, 1750–1902' PhD dissertation, University of Wisconsin, Madison, Wisconsin, 1970. 562p.).

226 The life of a south African tribe.

Henri A. Junod. London: Macmillan, 1927. 2nd ed. 2 vols. map.

Junod worked for the Swiss Romande Mission in Lourenço Marques in the late 19th and early 20th centuries, and had published a small study of the people of the region, entitled *Les Ba-Ronga* (The Ronga people) in 1898. This lengthy account is based on the testimony of three principal informants, with supplementary material from others associated with the mission. The second edition was published after seven years' further work, and differs substantially in the accounts of the kinship system, hunting rites, and ancestor worship. The first volume deals with social life, describing the clan system, the life of the individual (birth, circumcision, marriage, old age and death), village life, the character of chieftainship, and military organization. The second volume deals with the life of the psyche, discussing agriculture and industry, folklore, music, religion and superstition, and taboo and morality. Junod does not attempt to disguise his disapproval or approval of what he is describing, and is, at times, indignant over what must have appeared to him to have been highly immoral customs. He is also most confident of his own cultural superiority. The first edition of this important work was published in Switzerland before the First World War (Neuchatel: Imprimerie Attinger Frères, 1912–13. 2 vols.), and the second edition remains in print (New York: AMS Press, 1977. 2 vols.) The work has been translated into Portuguese, from the French: *Usos e costumes dos bantos: a vida duma tribo sul-africana* [Manners and customs of the Bantu: the life of a southern African tribe] (Lourenço Marques: Imprensa Nacional, 1944–47. 2 vols.), and this in turn was reprinted after independence in 1975. For a detailed critique of Junod's defects and virtues as an historical source, see Patrick Harries' 'The anthropologist as historian and liberal: H. A. Junod and the Thonga', *Journal of Southern African Studies* vol. 8, no. 1 (1981), p. 37–50. A bibliographical list on H. A. Junod was published in the Swiss journal *Genève–Afrique* vol. 4, no. 7 (1965) p. 271–77.

227 **The Shona.**
Hilda Kuper. In: *The Shona and Ndebele of Southern Rhodesia*.
London: International African Institute, 1954. p. 9–40.
(Ethnographic Survey of Africa. Southern Africa, part 4).

Although Kuper's work, a conventional piece of ethnography from the mid-1950s, deals mainly with the Shona-speakers of Zimbabwe, it also covers the sub-groups of Mozambique, principally the Ndau- and Rozwi-speakers who live between the Sabi and Pungwe rivers. Kuper discusses the Shona language, with remarks on literature and music, social organization, economic life, local politics, religion, rituals and magic; the chapter concludes with a four-page bibliography. See also M. F. C. Bourdillon's *The Shona peoples: an ethnography of the contemporary Shona, with special reference to their religion* (Gwena, Zimbabwe: Mambo Press, 1982); the author is 'unrepentant about leaving out the Shona in Mozambique', but the book nevertheless does contain relevant information.

228 **An ethnographic classic brought to light.**
M. G. Marwick. *Africa* vol. 34, no. 1 (Jan. 1964), p. 46–56.

Marwick discusses Ian Cunnison's translation of António Candido Pedroso Gamitto's extraordinary narrative *King Kazembe* (Lisbon: Junta de Investigações do Ultramar, 1960. 2 vols.). Gamitto was commander of the Sena garrison, and in 1831–32 was appointed second-in-command of a Portuguese expedition to try to open up trade with the eastern Lunda state of Mwata Cazembe, thus opening up the possibility of a link to Angola. Marwick is at pains to point out the value of Gamitto's account of the ethnography of the Nyanja-Maravi-Chewa people, since he was a careful observer and makes explicit comments on his methodology. This is one of the earliest of such accounts, and moreover dates from before the arrival of the Nguni at the Zambezi. See also Burton's *Lands of Cazembe* (q.v.).

229 **Bibliografia etnográfica macua: subsídios para uma bibliografia dos estudos sociais em Moçambique.** (Bibliography of Makua ethnography: contributions to a bibliography of social studies in Mozambique.)
Eduardo Medeiros.   Maputo: Faculdade de Letras, Universidade Eduardo Mondlane, 1980. 18p. (Universidade Eduardo Mondlane. Faculdade de Letras. Bibliografia temática, no. 1).

A simple checklist of material relating to the social life of the Makua-speaking people of northern Mozambique (and Mozambique's largest language-group), consisting of 198 entries in alphabetical author order. Citations follow a consistent format, but there are no indexes.

230 **O sistema linhageiro macua-lómwè.** (The Makua-Lomwe lineage system.)
Eduardo Medeiros.   Maputo: Faculdade de Letras, Universidade Eduardo Mondlane, 1985. 50p. maps.

A working paper by a Maputo researcher, presenting his ideas on the periodization of the economic history of the Makua-Lomwe social formation, and with notes on their lineage system, the clan and clan organization, matrilineage and the segments thereof, family units and extended kinship, and the great chiefs and junior chiefs. On the ethnography of the Makua, see also the extremely detailed work by Mello Machado (q.v.), and the thesis by Edgar Adriano Nasi Pereira, 'Aspectos da vida macua: considerações etnosociais, socioeconómicas e sociopolíticas sobre a vida dos povos do norte de Moçambique' [Aspects of Makua life: ethno-social, socio-economic and socio-political considerations of the life of the peoples of the north of Mozambique] (Licenciatura dissertation, Instituto Superior de Ciências Sociais e Política Ultramarina, Universidade Técnica de Lisboa, 1964. [176]p. bibliog.).

231 **Entre os Macuas de Angoche.** (Among the Makuas of Angoche.)
A. J. de Mello Machado.   Lisbon: Prelo Editora, 1970. 734p. bibliog. maps.

An extremely detailed account of the Angoche area, covering geography, ethnology, languages, history, demography, economics and social life. Angoche is predominantly Muslim, and predominantly Makua-speaking, and was only conquered by the Portuguese, with some difficulty, in 1910–12. The author tends to accept Portuguese information at face value, and he includes too much data of a general character, but the work is informative and important.

232 **Bibliografia etnológica de Moçambique, das origens a 1954.**
(Ethnological bibliography of Mozambique, from its origins to
1954.)
António Rita-Ferreira.   Lisbon: Junta de Investigações do
Ultramar, 1961. 254p.

An annotated bibliography of 968 items, with an introduction, an author index
and a key to abbreviations of periodical titles. The entries are classified according
to a system devised by the author, beginning with southern and eastern Africa in
general, then dealing with countries bordering Mozambique, the Monomotapa
Empire and the Zimbabwe culture, and then ethnic groups, with subdivisions.
These are: the Nguni (with three subdivisions); Tonga (with four); Chope with
three); Shona (nine); lower Zambezi complex (five); Marave (four); and, without
subdivisions, Makua-Lomwe, Yao, Makonde and Swahili. Rita-Ferreira revised
and updated this valuable bibliography in the late 1970s, but unfortunately the
revised edition has never appeared. See also José Júlio Gonçalves' *Bibliografia
antropológica do ultramar português* [Anthropological bibliography of the
Portuguese colonies], (Lisbon: Agência-Geral do Ultramar, 1960. 95p.), which
was first published in the March–April and Oct.–Dec. 1961 issues of the *Boletim
Geral do Ultramar*; and also the *Bibliografia do Centro de Estudos de Etnologia
do Ultramar* [Bibliography of the Centre of Overseas Ethnological Studies], by
Maria Emília de Castro e Almeida, Maria Cecília de Castro and José D. Lampreia
(Lisbon: Centro de Estudos de Antropobiologia, 1964. 163p.).

233 **Etno-história e cultura tradicional do grupo Angune (Nguni).** (The
ethno-history and traditional culture of the Nguni group.)
António Rita-Ferreira.   *Memórias do Instituto de Investigação
Científica de Moçambique* vol. 11, series C (1974), p. 1–247.

António Rita-Ferreira, now retired in Lisbon but still working on documentary
research, was one of the most productive of the Portuguese scholar-administrators
at work on Mozambique during the colonial period, bringing out books and
articles on ethnography, economics, sociology and bibliography, and opening
debates with both Portuguese-speaking and foreign opponents (see his exchanges
on migrant labour with Marvin Harris in *Africa* (q.v.), for instance, or more
recently, with Yussuf Adam (et al.) over Rhodesia in *História* (q.v.)). Not
especially progressive, he nevertheless wrote his mind; when his writings were
refused publication in Lourenço Marques, he brought them out in Lisbon. This
extensive ethnography and history is divided into three parts. The first discusses
the origins of the Nguni, dealing with traditional life, demography, the politics
and economics of their expansion, military life, and the new politico-military
organization. Part two describes the new political units which emerged from the
Nguni migrations: the Swazis, Matabele, N'qaba, Zwanguendaba and Ngoni. The
third and central section is an account of the Gaza Empire, starting with the story
of Soshangana, its founder, and moving on to a conventional ethnography
covering political organization, the economy, military life, the life of the
individual, kinship and law, magic and religious belief, and material life. The
work ends with a useful bibliography of 175 numbered items.

234 **The peoples of southern Mozambique: an historical survey.**
Alan Kent Smith. *Journal of African History* vol. 14, no. 4
(1973), p. 565–80.

A useful and interesting survey on the ethnography of southern Mozambique. He
looks at the positions of such earlier anthropologists as Junod père (q.v.), Fuller
(q.v.), and Binford (q.v.), as well as Henri-Philippe Junod's 'Notes on Tshopi
origins', *Bantu Studies* vol. 3, no. 1 (July 1927) and his later 'The Vachope of
Portuguese East Africa', in: *The Bantu tribes of south Africa*, edited by
A. M. Duggan-Cronin (Cambridge, 1936), with their arguments for and against
large ethnic groupings. Smith himself argues that by the 18th century three groups
occupied the area, namely the Tsonga, the Tonga and the Chope. State formation
among the Tsonga-speakers began early, under the influence of the Shona-
speakers, but neighbouring peoples, with one exception, did not fall under this
influence. See also Smith's dissertation, 'The struggle for the control of southern
Mozambique, 1720–1835' (PhD dissertation, University of California at Los
Angeles, 1970, 391p.).

Languages

General

235 Sínopse das línguas e dialectos falados pelos autoctones de Moçambique. (A synopsis of the languages and dialects spoken in Mozambique.)
Manuel Simões Alberto. *Boletim do Instituto de Investigação Científica de Moçambique* vol. 2, no. 1 (1961), p. 51–68.

Alberto writes that his article is intended to help systematize the census categories for Mozambique. He refers to two earlier attempts to classify the Mozambican languages: J. Santos Peixe's 'Línguas indígenas de Mocambique: estudo comparado' (Native languages of Mozambique: a comparative study) *Boletim da Sociedade de Estudos de Moçambique* no. 87 (1954), p. 87–115, which is based on the Guthrie classification; and António Rita-Ferreira's *Agrupamento e caracterização étnica dos indígenas de Moçambique* [Ethnic grouping and character of the natives of Mozambique] (Lisbon: Junta de Investigações do Ultramar, 1958, 133p., especially p. 89–102), which is based on the Doke classification. Alberto identifies fifteen linguistic groups, as follows: I. Swahili, II. Makonde, III. Yao, IV. Makua, V. Chuabo, VI. Nyanja, VII. Senga, VIII. Tawara, IX. Shona, X. Tswa, XI. Thonga, XII. Ronga, XIII. Chope, XIV. Tonga, and XV. Swazi-Zulu. He includes an alphabetical list of all the languages and dialects in these groups, with the area where they are spoken. It is not at all clear what the scientific basis for this work may have been.

236 A comparative study of the Bantu and semi-Bantu languages.
Sir Harry H. Johnston. Oxford: Clarendon Press, 1919–22.
2 vols. bibliog. maps. Reprinted, New York: AMS Press, 1977.

The first volume of this pioneering work consists almost entirely of lengthy comparative vocabulary tables for 366 Bantu and 87 semi-Bantu languages, including Makonde, Mavia, Yao, Makua, Lomwe, Chuabo, Sena, Nyanja and

Ronga from Mozambique. In the second volume, see especially chapter four on the southern Bantu languages.

237 **MLA International Bibliography of Books and Articles on Modern Languages and Literature.** New York: Modern Language Association, 1922–. 5 annual vols.

The second of the five annual volumes, on 'European, Soviet, Asian and African literatures'; the third, on linguistics; and the fifth, on folklore, may be assumed to list material related to major Mozambican languages and literature. This bibliography is a collective undertaking, and is a model of its kind. Until 1981 it was arranged in three volumes, along different principles. As a current supplement to the major retrospective bibliographies on African languages and literature, the main virtues of the MLA bibliography are its extensive and up-to-date coverage, and its ease of use. Useful not only for linguists, but also for historians, ethnographers and anthropologists. See also the *Linguistic Bibliography for the Year [. . .] and Supplement for Previous Years* (Dordrecht, The Netherlands: Martinus Nijhoff, 1949–. annual), which was preceded by a retrospective two-volume issue covering 1939–47. The volume for 1983, published in 1985, including eighty-six references on Bantu languages, including some on Tsonga, Shona and Makua.

238 **Empréstimos linguísticos nas línguas moçambicanas.** (Linguistic borrowings in Mozambican languages.)
António Carlos Pereira Cabral. Lourenço Marques, Mozambique: Empresa Moderna, 1975. 78p.

An entirely unscientific work, actually about loanwords rather than linguistic borrowings in general, in which Pereira Cabral begins by acknowledging that English and Afrikaans 'undoubtedly had a strong influence on our languages', and goes on to assert that Portuguese influence is on the upswing. The nature of these influences are not defined, however, and we are left to assume that they can only be at a lexical level. The first part of the book consists of a series of extracts from the introductions to various grammars and dictionaries of Yao, Shangaan, Nyanja, Chope, Makonde, Makua, Sena and Manyika. This is followed by a list of Portuguese words which have supposedly been adopted into African languages. Wild folk etymologies abound, such as the claim that Portuguese *festa* (party) entered Swahili as *fedha* (money) which Pereira Cabral spells *feta*. He explains this by saying that a party can't be held without money!

239 **Bibliografia científica de Moçambique: linguística e literatura.**
(Scientific bibliography of Mozambique: linguistics and literature.)
Ilídio Rocha. *Boletim do Centro de Documentação Científica [de Moçambique]* vol. 14, no. 2 (April–June 1971), p. 110–18.

For reasons that are unclear, the items in this bibliography begin at no. 118 and continue to no. 240, picking up from the last item in the checklist entitled 'Antropologia cultural: algumas referências' (q.v.), published in the previous issue of the same journal. Some citations are repeated in both lists. Like all the bibliographies in this journal, this is a simple checklist, in author order, with no introduction, indexing or annotations. The focus of the work is principally on books and articles in or about the national languages and thus only a couple of references to Portuguese-language literature are included. Rocha gives details of some obscure early missionary readers (see his items 178–79 or 238, for instance), and, oddly, includes two Soviet publications in Russian (nos. 127, 240).

240 **Bibliografia linguística de Moçambique: línguas nacionais.**
(Linguistic bibliography of Mozambique: national languages.)
Eugeniusz Rzewuski. Maputo: Departamento de Letras
Modernas, Universidade Eduardo Mondlane, 1979. 27p. map.

This 251-item bibliography of material on the African (or 'national') languages of Mozambique identifies the principal groups, following the Guthrie classification, as follows: Swahili (the Mrima and Mgao dialects); Yao (including Makonde and Mavia); Makua (including Lomwe and Chuabo); Nyanja; Senga-Sena; Shona (Ndau, Korekore and Manyika); Tswa-Ronga; and Chope. There is a map of the areas where these languages are spoken. In a thoughtful seven-page introduction, Rzewuski points out that the distinction between a language and a dialect in Guthrie's classification is often unsatisfactory; he also comments on the frequently derogatory and always unscientific use of the expression 'dialect' in Portuguese to mean simply a language spoken by Africans. The bibliography, the first of its kind since independence, is arranged around the identified groups, and consists of the following sections: Nyanja (81 items in 2 numbered sequences); Yao (16 items); Makonde (2); Makua (16); Lomwe (3); Chuabo (3); Shona (50); Nsenga (1); Nyungwe (8); Sena (8); Chope (8); Tonga (4); Tsonga (27); Tswa (4); and Ronga (20). Rzewuski, a Polish researcher on Bantu languages, trained at the University of Warsaw and worked in Mozambique for a number of years (see the interview with him in *Notícias da Beira*, 31 July 1979).

241 **A comparative grammar of the south African Bantu languages,
comprising those of Zanzibar, Mozambique, the Zambezi,
Kafirland, Benguela, Angola, the Congo, the Ogowe, the
Cameroons, the Lake Region, etc.**
Júlio Torrend. London: Kegan Paul, Trench, Trübner, 1891.
336, [4]p.

A pioneering work of missionary linguistics, with a considerable amount of information on Mozambican languages, in which Torrend tries to develop a classification for this huge language family. Torrend was a Jesuit, author of a study of Sena (q.v.), and worked in the Zambezi Mission under Father Depelchin. This area of comparative and classificatory Bantu linguistics has made considerable advances through the work of such scholars as Harry Hamilton Johnston, C. M. Doke, Malcolm Guthrie, and more recently Derek Fivaz and Patricia E. Scott.

Makua-Lomwe

242 **Apontamentos sobre a língua èmakua: gramática, vocabulário, contos, e dialecto de Angoche.** (Notes on the Makua language: grammar, vocabulary, stories and the Angoche dialect.) Francisco Manuel de Castro. Lourenço Marques, Mozambique: Imprensa Nacional, 1933. 184p.

Makua was not a much-studied language. According to the preface to de Castro's book the first wordlist of Makua was published in 1891 by Almeida e Cunha; a second list was compiled by the *capitão-mor* of Mossuril, Camisão, in 1898–99, but was never published; and the only previous grammatical notes were José Vincente do Sacramento's *Apontamentos soltos da língua macua* (Notes on the Makua language) of 1906. Castro thus seems to be unaware of the information in the pioneering work by W. H. J. Bleek, *The languages of Mosambique [sic]: vocabularies of the dialects of Lourenzo Marques, Inhambane, Sofala, Tette, Sena, Quellimane, Mosambique, Cape Delgado, Anjoane, the Maravi, Mudsau, etc., drawn up from the mss. of W. Peters and from other materials* (London: Harrison, 1856. 403p.), which certainly includes material on Makua. In addition, there was a Portuguese word-list in print as early as 1887: see Ayres de Carvalho Soveral's *Breve estudo sobre a Ilha de Moçambique acompanhado d'um pequeno vocabulário portuguez-macua* [A short study on Mozambique Island, with a short Portuguese-Makua vocabulary] (Oporto, Portugal: Livraria Chardron, 1887. 31p.). A catechism was translated into the language by M. Duarte Barata. This volume is a 'teach-yourself' manual, with extensive descriptive grammar, exercises, a vocabulary (p. 119–60) and some folk-tales in parallel Makua-Portuguese texts. There is a final note on the language spoken in Angoche, which Castro says is a mixture of Makua and Swahili. There is also a poignant footnote protesting the fact that the publishers, a state enterprise, would not allow Castro to spell the name 'Angôxe', although, as he says, it is good Makua and better Portuguese: this is a point of contention even today.

243 **A preliminary description of sentence structures in the e-Sáaka dialect of e-Mákhuwa.** José Mateus Muária Katupha. MPhil dissertation, School of Oriental and African Studies, University of London, 1983. 317p. bibliog.

Makua-Lomwe is probably the most widespread of the Mozambican language-groups, and its e-Saaka dialect is spoken in Erati district in Nampula and in parts of Chiúre district in Cabo Delgado. Katupha's pioneering thesis is a highly technical study of the language, dealing with phonology and tonology, with the morphology of the nominal and verbal, and the structure of the group, clause and sentence. Katupha is the first Mozambican scholar to have been trained in scientific linguistics, and is now the head of the Faculty of Letters at Eduardo Mondlane University in Maputo.

244 **Dicionário português-macua.** (Portuguese-Makua dictionary.)
António Pires Prata. Cucujães, Portugal: Sociedade Missionária
Portuguesa [1973]. 374p.

A large dictionary, with only a brief guide to usage given in the entries, which are,
in any case, quite short. Pires Prata, who died in September 1984, does, however,
provide an introduction covering phonetics, orthography (in which he argues
against using ny- or ly- for the equivalent Portuguese transcriptions nh- and lh-),
nasalization, the use of apostrophes, and accents. The same author has,
apparently, also compiled a Makua-Portuguese dictionary, but this has not been
published. Pires Prata's missionary-style linguistic work has been superseded by
professional research in recent years. See especially C. C. Cheng and C. W.
Kisseberth, 'Ikorovere Makua tonology', *Studies in Linguistic Sciences* no. 9
(1979), p. 31–63; no. 10 (1980), p. 15–44; no. 11 (1981), p. 181–202; S. U.
Stucky, 'Word variation in Makua: a phrase structure grammar analysis' PhD
dissertation, University of Illinois, 1981; and the Mozambican scholar J. M. M.
Katupha's 'A preliminary description of sentence structures in the e-Sáaka dialect
of e-Mákhuwa', MPhil dissertation, School of Oriental and African Studies,
University of London, 1983. (q.v.).

245 **Gramática da língua macua e seus dialectos.** (Grammar of the
Makua language and its dialects.)
António Pires Prata. Cucujães, Portugal: Escola Tipográfica das
Missões, 1960. 442p. map.

Father Pires Prata confidently identifies, on a coloured map, the following
principal dialects of Makua: Meto, Chirima, Lomwe, Marrevone, Nampamela,
Mulai, Naharra and Chaca; the map also shows areas marked Ruvuma, Cabo
Delgado and Central, but it is not clear from the text whether these are also
intended to be taken as dialects. The map also shows the Koti-speaking area, and
Kimwani (which is now considered to be a Swahili dialect). The grammar is very
detailed, and covers phonetics, morphology and syntax. Pires Prata's work
appears to be still well-thought-of in Portugal, although his reputation has
suffered recently in other countries.

246 **An outline of Makua grammar.**
H. W. Woodward. *Bantu Studies* vol. 2. (Oct. 1926), p. 269–325.

A fairly substantial revision of, and advance upon, Chauncey Maples' *Collections
for a handbook of Makua* (1879). Woodward's article is organized in ninety-eight
grammatical sections, and includes a 2,500-word vocabulary. Woodward points
out that there is wide variation among Makua dialects.

Nyanja-Sena

247 **Dicionário português-chisena e chisena-português.** (Portuguese-Sena and Sena-Portuguese dictionary.)
Albano Emílio Alves. Beira, Mozambique: Escola de Artes e Ofícios, 1957. 2nd ed. 263p.

The first edition of the dictionary, which includes examples of usage, appeared in 1939 (Lisbon: Casa Portuguesa, 213p.), but the pioneering Father Alves died before the revision could be published, and it seems to have been prepared by Rafael dos Santos. Alves was a prolific worker in Sena studies, translating the catechism (1931), a children's Bible (1939) and a small book of prayers (1939) into the language, as well as producing a short grammar, *Noções gramaticais da língua chisena* [Grammatical notes on the Sena language] (Braga, Portugal: Missões Franciscanas, 1939, 164p.). The Historical Archive of Mozambique has a copy of the first edition of the dictionary, apparently issued bound up with the *Noções gramaticais* as one volume, under the cover title *Gramática e dicionário da língua chisena* [Grammar and dictionary of the Sena language] (AHM shelf-number C1216p), but it should not be supposed that this is a different work.

248 **A visitor's notebook of Chichewa.**
M. V. B. Mangoche. Blantyre, Malawi: Times Book Shop [n.d.]. 72p.

Chewa is essentially the same language as Nyanja, and as it is the official language of Malawi, as well as having speakers in Mozambique, Tanzania and Zambia, the most useful grammars for the English-speaking learner come from that country. This is a tourist's guide, consisting of some brief grammatical observations and notes on expressions of courtesy, the currency, numerals and quantitative words, expressions of length, days of the week, relationships, beliefs, greetings, imperative forms, car travel, at the shop, and so on. The second half of the book (p. 43–72) consists of a brief English-Chewa dictionary.

249 **Dicionário cinyanja-português.** (Nyanja-Portuguese dictionary.)
Missionários da Companhia de Jesus. Lisbon: Junta de Investigações do Ultramar, 1963. 291p.

The introduction to the dictionary is signed by João de Deus Gonçalves Kamtedza, S. J. and deals with pronunciation, plurals, etc. A part is also printed in Nyanja. See also the companion volume *Dicionário português-cinyanja* (Portuguese-Nyanja dictionary) by the same author(s) (Lisbon: Junta de Investigações do Ultramar, 1964. 266p.), which has an introduction with some references to previous work on the language, and some grammatical information. See also the important thesis by Deborah Ann Harding. 'The phonology and morphology of Chinyanja', (PhD dissertation, University of California at Los Angeles, 1966); George Meredith Sanderson and W. B. Bithrey's *An introduction to Chinyanja* (Zomba, Malawi: [n.p.], 1925. 99p.); and the Missionários de Companhia de Jesus' *Elementos de gramática cinyanja* [Elements of Nyanja grammar] (Lisbon: Junta de Investigações do Ultramar, 1964. 146p.). A useful manual is the *Chinyanja basic course* (Washington, DC: US Department of State,

Foreign Service Institute, 1965). The most complete bibliography on Nyanja/ Chewa is S. M. Made, M. V. B. Mangoche Mbewe and R. Jackson's *One hundred years of Chewa in writing: a select bibliography* (Zomba, Malawi: University of Malawi, 1976. 87p.), which includes over 1,000 unannotated entries. For a succinct and annotated guide, see Robert B. Boeder's volume in the World Bibliographical Series, *Malawi* (Oxford: Clio Press, 1979), p. 119–21, which gives eight principal and eight secondary references on the language.

250 **Practical grammatical notes of the Sena language.**
Alexandre Moreira. St. Gabriel-Mödling, Austria: Anthropos; London: Sena Sugar Estates, 1924. 168p. ('Anthropos' Linguistic Library, vol. 3).

Father Moreira was a Jesuit who worked at the Chipanga mission on the Zambezi. The introduction to his grammar correctly characterizes Sena as a *lingua franca* of the Zambezi Valley, closely related to Nyanja. At that time, it was spoken by an estimated 300,000 people along the banks of the river from Chinde up to Tambara. This is a descriptive grammar, with chapters on substantives, adjectives, numerals, pronouns, verbs and invariable words. There are no exercises. The earliest grammar of Sena, a fairly well-studied language, dates from the 17th century; see Paulo Schebesta, 'Eine Bantu-Grammatik aus dem 17. Jahrhundert' [A Bantu grammar from the 17th century], *Anthropos* vol. 14–15 (1919–20), p. 764–87.

251 **Vocabulário do dialecto chi-sena.** (Vocabulary of the Sena language.)
António A. Parreira. *Boletim da Agência Geral das Colónias* no. 62–63 (Aug.–Sept. 1930), p. 71–106.

This article, by a former land surveyor of the Mozambique Chartered Company, consists of a brief introduction; a discussion of Sena's relationship to neighbouring languages (with a map of the area where it is spoken); sections on orthography, pronunciation and conventions; the vocabulary itself (p. 80–103, in simple alphabetical order); some grammatical and ethnographic notes; and a quasi-theological comment on the supposed African concept of the soul. The author's name is sometimes cited under the modern spelling 'Pereira'.

252 **The elements of Nyanja for English-speaking students.**
Thomas Price. Blantyre, Malawi: Church of Scotland Mission, 1959. 282p.

This work, the preface to which is dated 1941, is divided into two sections. The first is a simple teach-yourself guide to elementary Nyanja for those who need to learn a small amount quickly. The second section is more advanced and complicated. There are appendixes on English loanwords, on the courtesies and on relationships. There are also indexes.

253 **Dictionary of the Chichewa language, being the encyclopaedic dictionary of the Mang'anja language.**
David Clement Scott, edited by Alexander Hetherwick. Blantyre, Malawi: Christian Literature Association in Malawi (CLAIM), 2nd ed. 1970. 612p.

First published as the *Dictionary of the Nyanja language* (London: Lutterworth Press, 1929). The dictionary fully deserves the description 'encyclopaedic', including an extensive commentary on meanings, usage and folklore. The tone of the commentary is sometimes disapproving, for example on p. 294, in the section on *mfiti* 'witch or wizard' we find a long paragraph on 'these midnight wretches [and] . . . their awful orgies'.

254 *Gramática de chisena*: **a grammar of the language of the lower Zambezi.**
Júlio Torrend. Chipanga, Zambezia: Typographia da Missao de Chipanga, 1900. 176p.

Júlio Torrend was a Jesuit priest, and his grammar is tri-lingual – printed in columns of Portuguese, Sena itself, and English. Torrend's attitudes are not always those of a scientist: ' . . . compared with its brothers, the Chi-Manganja [Nyanja] of the Upper Chire and the language of Tete, it yields the impression of a less primitive, but more polite, language'. The book consists of chapters on substantives, strong and weak adjectives, pronouns, verbs, the -i conjugation, pre- and post-positions, interjections, and what Torrend styles 'informal' words. The first edition of this grammar is now a bibliographical rarity; there is a copy in the Historical Archive of Mozambique. References have also appeared to a 1960 reprint. It should perhaps be noted that Sena is considered by Fivaz and Scott in their modern classification to be closely related to Mang'anja, a Nyanja dialect; earlier linguists had also noticed the similarities.

255 **The student's English-Chichewa Dictionary.**
Zambezi Mission Inc. Blantyre, Malawi: Christian Literature Association in Malawi (CLAIM), 1972. 173p.

A simple wordlist-type dictionary, originally published by the Zambezi Mission as *English-Nyanja dictionary*. The work is based on southern Malawi usage, and employs the orthography used before the standardization of the -ŵ- sound.

Shona

256 **An analytical grammar of Shona.**
George Fortune. London: Longmans Green, 1955. 443p.

This is the published version of Fortune's University of Cape Town doctoral dissertation, submitted in 1950, and deals principally with Zezeru. However, it has some usefulness for Manyika. See also M. Hannan's *Standard Shona dictionary* (Salisbury: Rhodesia Literature Bureau, 1972. 2nd ed. 996p.) and D. Dale's *Shona companion* (Gwelo, Rhodesia: Mambo Press; Salisbury: Rhodesia Literature Bureau, 1972. 2nd ed. 337p.).

Tsonga

257 **Pocket dictionary Thonga (Shangaan)-English, English-Thonga (Shangaan), preceded by an elementary grammar.**
Ch. W. Chatelain, H. A. Junod. Lausanne, Switzerland: George Bridel, 1909. 98p., 151p.

Two independent works issued in one volume: the grammar by Junod and the dictionary by Chatelain. A copy of the grammar is available as a separate volume, but with no title-page. Junod makes some strange assumptions: he writes that 'mastering a Bantu dialect is by no means a trifle. One must consecrate to that study at least six months of hard work!' The grammar is for learners, with exercises. The dictionary is based on Henri Berthoud's work and is in the long line of Swiss Mission material on this language.

258 **Tsonga-English dictionary.**
Compiled by R. Cuenod. Braamfontein, South Africa: Sasavona Publishers, 1967. Reprinted, 1976. 286p.

A substantial and apparently carefully-compiled dictionary, based on a manuscript by Henri Berthoud, considerably augmented and revised. Cuenod worked on the revision of the Bible in Tsonga, and with the help of several informants contrived to add 'many thousands' of words to his father-in-law's manuscript over the years. He also collaborated with the University of South Africa's Department of Bantu Languages, and with the governmental Bantu Education Department. He points out that the dictionary is 'practically limited to the Tsonga spoken in the Transvaal. The Mozambique Tsonga would add thousands of words.' There are short sections on morphology, the parts of speech, and the Meinhof noun classification, as well as an appendix of the official South African Tsonga Language Committee's list of terminology. Entries give examples of usage, explanatory definitions and the scientific names of birds and plants. The tone is indicated.

259 **English-Tsonga, Tsonga-English dictionary.**
Braamfontein, South Africa: Sasavona Publishers, 1978. 7th ed. 214p.

The Swiss Mission's pocket dictionary, first published in 1907, and last revised extensively for the sixth edition in 1974. Apparently the publication of Cuenod's dictionary (q.v.) had led the Swiss Mission to suppose, erroneously, that there was no longer a market for this small volume. The style is much more that of a wordlist, with little explanation and no usage or indication of tones. In the field of

Languages. Minor languages (Chope-Bitonga, Makonde, Swahili-Kimwani, Yao)

Mozambican languages, where bibliographers deal mainly in arcane rarities, this volume has the great advantage that it is in print and available.

260 Everyday Tsonga.
M. Ouwehand. Braamfontein, South Africa: Sasavona, 1965. Reprinted, 1978. 107p.

A highly recommended teach-yourself manual for those who wish to learn Shangaan. The author writes that his work 'makes no pretentions [sic] to be a scientific work or to give a complete description of the language . . . ' Thirty-one lessons occupy the first eighty-seven pages; the second half of the work is a reference section on some thirty-two topics which have presumably caused difficulties to past learners.

261 Gramática changana (Tsonga). (Shangaan or Tsonga grammar.)
Armando Ribeiro. Kisubi, Uganda: Marianum Press, 1965. 510p.

A very detailed descriptive grammar of Shangaan by a missionary with pronounced opinions about African languages and Portuguese (see the extraordinary appendix two on the 'Portuguesifying' of 'native' words). Ribeiro covers the orthography, grammatical categories (nouns, adjectives, numerals, pronouns, verbs etc.), syntax and usage of Shangaan exhaustively.

262 Dicionário prático português-tshwa. (Practical Portuguese-Tswa dictionary.)
[Ralph L. Wilson, Elias Mucambe]. Braamfontein, South Africa: Sasavona, 1978. 193p.

A very simple dictionary of the language spoken in Inhambane around Vilanculos, based on the first 4,000 or so words in a Spanish word-frequency list compiled by Buchanan at the University of Toronto; no such list apparently exists for Portuguese. Some common local expressions (for tools, birds, flowers, etc.; and words used in hymns) were added by the authors. Paternalistically, the dictionary is intended to help 'all natives who might know how to read' to tackle Portuguese texts 'with intelligence'.

Minor languages (Chope-Bitonga, Makonde, Swahili-Kimwani, Yao)

263 Swahili grammar.
E. O. Ashton. London: Longman, 1947. 2nd ed. 398p. bibliog.

Swahili is spoken in one form or another all the way down the eastern African littoral from Mogadishu to Quelimane, and on the islands, including the Comoros. Despite the fact that the Kimwani dialect of the Mozambican coastal

105

Languages. Minor languages (Chope-Bitonga, Makonde, Swahili-Kimwani, Yao)

areas has some marked differences from the Zanzibar-based 'standard' Swahili, the available grammars and dictionaries serve well enough for use in northern Mozambique, especially nowadays. Mrs. Ashton's clearly laid-out grammar is based on her 'ideas approach' to Swahili. Somewhat academic in style, the book uses traditional grammatical terminology. Exercises and vocabulary are included, and, more importantly, characteristic intonation patterns of the language, often the weakest part of foreigners' pronunciation. Despite the 1947 publication date for the latest edition, the book has been reprinted many times.

264 **Pequeno vademecum da língua bantu na Província de Moçambique, ou, Breve estudo da língua chi-Yao ou Adjaua, comparada com os dialectos de Sena, Tete e Quelimane e seguida d'um vocabulário da mesma língua e da Quelimane.** (Short guide to the Bantu language of Mozambique, or, Short study of Yao compared to the dialects of Sena, Tete and Quelimane and followed by a vocabulary of Yao and of Quelimane.)
Pedro Dupeyron. Lisbon: Administração do Novo Mensageiro do Coração de Jesus [n.d.]. 168p.

An interesting 19th-century comparative study by a missionary, consisting of a forty-page description of the Yao language: a comparison of Yao with Sena, Nyungwe and Chuabo; and short Chuabo and Yao wordlists, this last section containing thirty-seven pages. On Nyungwe, spoken in Tete and quite close to Sena, see also, both by Victor José Courtois: *Dicionário cafre-tetense-portuguez: ou idioma falado no distrito de Tete e na vasta região do Zambeze inferior* [Tete-Kaffir-Portuguese dictionary: or the language spoken in Tete district and in the vast region of the lower Zambezi] (Coimbra, Portugal: Imprensa da Universidade, 1900. 81p.); and *Elementos de gramatica tetense: lingua chi-nyungue, idioma falado no distrito de Tete e em toda a vasta região do Zambeze inferior* [Elements of the grammar of Tete: the chi-Nyungwe language, spoken in Tete district and all over the vast area of the lower Zambezi] (Coimbra, Portugal: Imprensa da Universidade, 1899. new ed. 231p.).

265 **A standard Swahili-English dictionary founded on Madan's Swahili-English dictionary.**
Inter-Territorial Language Committee for the East African Dependencies. Nairobi: Oxford University Press, 1939. 548p.

Reprinted many times, this dictionary has remained the standard reference for foreigners learning Swahili. It is organized by roots, with extensive cross-referencing. The preface, by the then Bishop of Zanzibar, makes the origins of the work quite explicit: like so many other studies in African linguistics it began through missionary interest in translation. The comments and definitions sometimes make racist assumptions, for example, 'the value of [high-denomination coinage] cannot be easily understood by some natives' (p. 187). The dictionary prints many examples of usage, proverbs and sayings, and includes information on manners and customs. Derivations from Persian, Arabic and Urdu are given in Arabic script.

Languages. Minor languages (Chope-Bitonga, Makonde, Swahili-Kimwani, Yao)

266 A study of Gitonga of Inhambane.
Leonard W. Lanham. Johannesburg: Witwatersrand University
Press, 1955. 264p. map. (Bantu Linguistic Studies, no. 1).
This mimeographed technical publication was Lanham's MA thesis at Witwatersrand University in 1955. It is a grammar divided into two general chapters on phonetics, phonology, orthography, and grammatical analysis; followed by nine further chapters on the noun, pronoun, qualificative, verb, copulative, adverb, ideophone, conjunctive and interjective, with a final chapter on syntax. There are appendixes on the descriptive possessive, on the relationship of Tonga to other Bantu languages, and on oriental loanwords. The book was critically reviewed by D. Z. in *African Studies* vol. 15, no. 2 (1956), p. 89–91.

267 The Swahili: reconstructing the history and language of an African society, 800–1500.
Derek Nurse, Thomas Spear. Philadelphia, Pennsylvania:
University of Pennsylvania Press, 1985. 133p. bibliog. maps.
(University of Pennsylvania. Publications in Ethnohistory).
One of the innovative aspects of this work as far as Mozambican studies are concerned, is that virtually for the first time, it identifies the Kimwani language of the Quirimba Islands and the nearby coastline as a Swahili dialect. In linguistic terms Kimwani has both conservative and progressive features, and was probably one of the first dialects of the southern group to emerge. Its historical development has been deeply affected by close contacts with such neighbouring languages as Makua, Makonde and Yao. For a thoughtful review of this book, see Randall L. Pouwels in the *International Journal of African Historical Studies* vol. 19, no. 1 (1986), p. 93–95.

268 A influência da língua portuguesa sobre o suahíli e quatro línguas de Moçambique. (The influence of Portuguese on Swahili and on four Mozambican languages.)
António Pires Prata. Lisbon: Instituto de Investigação Científica Tropical, 1983. 149p.
A collection of studies on loanwords in Swahili, Makua, Koti (the language of Angoche), Chuabo and Sena. Despite the title, the work effectively limits itself to a discussion of lexicographical influence. This work was severely criticized by the Polish scholar Eugeniusz Rzewuski as an 'apologia, Camoense in tone' for the beneficial effect of Portuguese on African languages, in a review article, 'A língua português e as línguas africanas de Moçambique' (Portuguese and the African languages of Mozambique), *Revista Internacional de Estudos Africanos* no. 3 (Jan.–Dec. 1985), p. 213–20. Rzewuski also points out that the essay on Swahili was first published as long ago as 1961. See also the work of Pereira Cabral (q.v.). This field is still wide open as far as scientific work is concerned.

269 A dictionary of the Yao language.
G. Meredith Sanderson. Zomba, Malawi: Government Printer,
[1954]. 440p.
Sanderson's dictionary is a continuation of Bishop Steere's *Collections for a handbook of the Yao language* (1871), on which A. Hetherwick based his

Languages. Minor languages (Chope-Bitonga, Makonde, Swahili-Kimwani, Yao)

Introductory handbook (1889: 2nd ed. 1902). Sanderson began work in 1910, but had the misfortune to lose the manuscript in 1922. By 1930, with patience beyond that of most men, he had managed to recompile what he had lost. The work includes a grammatical outline, a Yao-English vocabulary, and an English-Yao index.

270 **Dicionário português-chope e chope-português.** (Portuguese-Chope and Chope-Portuguese dictionary.)
Luís Feliciano dos Santos. Lourenço Marques, Mozambique: Imprensa Nacional, 1949. 223p.

A pocket-sized dictionary by a Franciscan missionary, with an introduction on the language, which was spoken at that time by about 200,000 people, mainly in Zavala and Inharrime, but also in Manhiça, Sábiè, Homoine, Morrumbene and Vilanculos. Santos identifies three dialect groups, of which the northern is the most distinctive. He also discusses English and Portuguese loanwords (e.g. -puni, spoon; -timela, steamer; -kudo, escudo) as well as kinship terminology and its significance.

271 **Gramática da língua chope.** (Grammar of the Chope language.)
Luíz [sic] Feliciano dos Santos. Lourenço Marques, Mozambique: Imprensa Nacional, 1941. 306p.

A descriptive grammar of Chope. Part one covers phonetics (divided into phonology and orthography, and orthography and prosody); part two discusses morphology – nouns, adjectives, pronouns, verbs, prepositions, adverbs and conjunctions.

272 **Guia de conversação português-chope.** (Portuguese-Chope phrase book.)
Luís Feliciano dos Santos. Braga, Portugal: Tipografia 'Missões Franciscanas', 1953. 71p.

A straightforward phrasebook with no apparatus at all. The chapters offer phrases under the following rubrics: greetings and common expressions; questions; polite expressions; asking somebody's name, age and address; hiring workers; working in the kitchen; at the shop; servants; sleeping and waking up; journeys; hunting; illnesses and everyday problems; boat journeys; at school; in the courtroom; and conversation between friends. The class relations implicit in these exchanges comes out clearly – the worker cries out 'Aiiee, [the box] fell on my foot!' and the boss replies unsympathetically 'That's nothing. I'll give you some medicine.'

273 **Rudimentos de língua maconde.** (Rudiments of the Makonde language.)
M. Viegas Guerreiro. Lourenço Marques, Mozambique: Instituto de Investigação Científica de Moçambique, 1963. 152p.

This Portuguese grammar and reader is one of the few available sources for a general account of Makonde sounds and syntax. It may be just possible to be able to speak the language on the basis of this work, although some critics have doubted it. In practice, modern Makonde speakers tend to mix a lot of Swahili

Languages. Minor languages (Chope-Bitonga, Makonde, Swahili-Kimwani, Yao)

into their speech, a fact which Viegas Guerreiro, writing in the early 1960s, leaves out of account. Included are eight pages of simple phrases ('Come here.' 'What is this?' 'Who are you?'), some folk-tales and some riddles. The Makonde-Portuguese and Portuguese-Makonde vocabularies, while not of dictionary status, are nevertheless usable. See also the earlier sketch of the language by Lyndon Harries, 'An outline of Maviha grammar' *Bantu Studies* vol. 14, no. 2 (1940). The derogatory expression *maviha* apparently means 'the angry ones', a reference to the Makonde reputation for ferocity; there is disagreement about whether Maviha is a dialect of Makonde or not.

274 **A study of Yao sentences.**
W. H. Whiteley. Oxford: Clarendon Press, 1966. 289p.

A fairly technical work in African structural linguistics, important both for its conceptual approach and for the material it provides on the Yao language, which is widely spoken in northern Mozambique as well as in Malawi and southern Tanzania. Whiteley describes the elements which are used to build sentences, their grammatical relationships, and a range of sentence types. See also: G. M. Sanderson's *A Yao grammar* (London: Society for the Promotion of Christian Knowledge (SPCK), 1922. 2nd ed. 211p.); the same author's *A dictionary of the Yao language* (Zomba, Malawi: Government Printer, 1954); A. Hetherwick's *Introductory handbook and vocabulary of the Yao language* (London: SPCK, 1889); and Edward Steere's *Collections for a handbook of the Yao language* (London: SPCK, 1871. 105p.).

Religion

275   **Subsídios para uma bibliografia missionária moçambicana
(católica).** (Contribution towards a Mozambican (Catholic)
missionary bibliography.)
Filipe Gastão de Almeida de Eça.   Lisbon: The author,
[distribution: Livraria Petrony, Rua de Assunção, 90], 1969. 157p.

This bibliography is in author order and includes 543 main entries. Full
descriptions are given, albeit in an idiosyncratic style (e.g., the dimensions given
refer not to the volume, but to the *mancha tipográfica* or printed area). Eça
includes information about indexes and illustrations, and whether the work is
printed in columns. He also adds a lot of hard information and colloquial
annotations, but too often these are eulogistic, along the lines of 'An historical-
biographical study which does great honour to its illustrious author, a dedicated
and honoured poet, writer and journalist.' Nor are there any doubts here about
the 'civilizing mission' – Eça quotes a few statistics about mission education and
claims that they 'bear witness to the exceptional enthusiasm [of the missionaries,
and] . . . greatly dignify the Province of Mozambique and greatly honour the
good name of Portugal'. The introduction explains that the author had planned to
produce two volumes: one on Catholic and one on Protestant missions, but took
fourteen years just to complete the volume on the Catholics, and so gave up. Eça
died in Lisbon in 1972 at the age of 77; he had written a number of bibliographies,
including works on Mouzinho de Albuquerque, and a supplement to Mário Costa.
Two incidental points of interest: the work is dedicated to, among others, Father
Daniel Boormans, who was killed by a MANU splinter group at Nangololo in
Cabo Delgado on 24 August 1964. In addition, Eça refers to Alfredo Freire
de Andrade's *Relatórios sobre Moçambique* [Reports on Mozambique] (Lourenço
Marques, Mozambique: Imprensa Nacional, 1907–10. 6 vols), which has a short
author and title checklist of the publications of the Swiss Mission between 1880
and 1909 (vol. 5, p. 323–24). These add up to fifty-six items.

Religion

276 **Towards a history of the expansion of Islam in East Africa: the matrilineal peoples of the southern interior.**
Edward A. Alpers. In: *The historical study of African religion.*
Edited by Terence O. Ranger, I. N. Kimambo. Berkeley,
California: University of California Press; London: Heinemann,
1972. p. 172–201.

In this paper Alpers analyses the process of the expansion of Islam in northern
Mozambique, Malawi and southern Tanzania during pre-colonial and colonial
times. Alpers comments, with some justification, that 'One of the annoying
preoccupations of many scholarly discussions of Islam in Africa, in general, has
been an unwarranted concern over the 'unorthodox' nature of African Islam.' He
shows how Arab traders and teachers in the north helped to spread their faith
along the long-distance trade routes which linked the coast to the interior, and
concludes with some comments on the conditional and selective acceptance of
foreign religions by African societies in general.

277 **Africains, missionnaires et colonialistes: les origines de l'Église Presbytérienne du Mozambique (Mission Suisse), 1880–1896.**
(Africans, missionaries and colonialists: the origin of the
Presbyterian Church in Mozambique (the Swiss Mission),
1880–96.)
Jan van Butselaar. Leiden, The Netherlands: E. J. Brill, 1984.
230p. bibliog. (Studies on Religion in Africa: supplements to the
Journal of Religion in Africa, no. 5).

Butselaar taught for some months in 1980 at the seminary of the Presbyterian
Church of Mozambique, where he was able to interview church elders on the
history of the Swiss Mission for his PhD thesis. He also conducted interviews in
the Transvaal, and consulted archives in Lausanne, Geneva, Lisbon, Pretoria and
Rome, as well as examining missionary journals and reviews. He begins with a
survey of the three peoples and three cultures which met at the Swiss
Mission – the Tsonga, the Portuguese and the Swiss. The bulk of the narrative
consists of the story of the establishing of the Swiss Mission, and the Portuguese
war (or 'pacification campaign') of 1896 against Ngungunyane (Gungunyane) and
his Gaza Kingdom. The Swiss Mission, of course, survived to employ such
personalities as Henri Junod (1863–1934), the great ethnographer of the Tsonga
people, and to teach Eduardo Mondlane and others. Eventually the Mission
became the Presbyterian Church of Mozambique.

278 **Dossier: documents from a meeting in Maputo between the Mozambican Party and state leadership and representatives of religious organizations in Mozambique, December 14 to 17 1982.**
Maputo: Agência de Informação de Moçambique, 1983. 56p. (*AIM Information Bulletin* no. 78. supplement).

Relations between Church and State in post-independence Mozambique have
been sensitive, and there has been a particular mistrust of the Catholic hierarchy,
both because of their close relations with the colonial state in the past, and
because of their ambivalence towards the armed bandits at the present time. A

111

considerable amount of misleading propaganda about restrictions on religious freedom has been disseminated, but the government's position is, broadly, that religion is a private matter. Religious organizations have no right to intervene, for instance, in health or education. At the end of 1982 Samora Machel and other leaders met with Catholic, Protestant, Moslem and Hindu representatives to clarify some of the points of dispute; this dossier is a record of the proceedings. It was published in Portuguese as *Consolidemos aquilo que nos une: reunião da direcção do Partido e do Estado com as representantes das confissões religiosas, 14 a 17 de Dezembro de 1982* [Let us build upon that which unites us: meeting of Party and Government leaders with representatives of the religious beliefs, 14–17 December 1982] (Maputo: Instituto Nacional do Livro e do Disco, 1983. 100p. [Colecção 'Unidade Nacional', no. 1]). See also the vigorous exchange between (an unidentified) Sérgio Vieira and the Catholic bishops in 'The church in Mozambique: the colonial inheritance. Minutes of a discussion between the Roman Catholic bishops and the government of Mozambique' *IDOC Bulletin* no. 7–9 (July–Sept. 1979), p. 1–67, originally published in Spanish by IEPALA (Instituto de Estudios Politícos para América Latina y Africa) in Madrid. For the Catholic viewpoint on Mozambique, see Cesare Bertulli's *A cruz e a espada* (The cross and the sword) translated from Italian by Mário Costa (Lisbon: Portugàlia Editora [n.d.], 413p.).

279 **The Tshwa response to Christianity: a study of the religious and cultural impact of Protestant Christianity on the Tshwa of southern Mozambique.**
Alf Gustav Helgesson.   MA thesis, Witwatersrand University, Johannesburg, 1971. 286p.

Much of the writing in English on religion in Mozambique consists of academic or seminary studies of the activities of the various Catholic and Protestant missions. The role of the Protestant missions in the south was extremely important, but has not been adequately researched. Studies by the missionologists themselves are often most useful for the ethnographic or linguistic material which they contain; Helgesson's thesis, for instance, cites local proverbs.

280 **Colonisation portugaise et discours religieux.** (Portuguese colonialism and religious conversations.)
Preface by François Houtart.   Louvain-la-Neuve, Belgium: Centre des Recherches Socio-Religieuses, Université Catholique de Louvain, Reprinted 1978. 214p.

A progressive Catholic analysis, in sociological terms, of the tensions between (Portuguese) priests and (foreign) missionaries during the last years of the colonial system. Although not specifically about Mozambique, the work has an obvious relevance. See also by Houtart and André Rousseau, *A igreja e os movimentos revolucionários: Vietname, América Latina, colónias portuguesas* [The church and the revolutionary movements in Vietnam, Latin America and the Portuguese colonies] (Lisbon: Arcádia, 1976. 164p.).

Religion

281   *Madzi-manga, mhondoro* and the use of oral traditions: a chapter in
Barue religious and political history.
Allen Isaacman.   *Journal of African History* vol. 14, no. 3 (1973),
p. 395–409.

The Barwe Kingdom was founded in the 16th century, and perished only in 1918
after a bloody confrontation with the Portuguese. An offshoot of the
Monomotapa Empire, it controlled the Sena-Manica trading network, and
effectively blocked Portuguese ambitions in the area for many years. Curiously,
although it has not been intensively studied as a social formation, there is ample
documentation on one aspect of the society, the custom of 'baptizing' the kings
with holy water (*madzi-manga*) brought from Sena by a Portuguese official.
Control of the source of holy water gave the Portuguese some leverage to gain
access to the Manica market (*feira*) on the other side of Barwe. By the 1880s,
however, the Barwe had begun to obtain water from another source, independent
of the Portuguese. In this article Isaacman attempts to redefine the ritual
significance of *madzi-manga* by using evidence from oral traditions; and further,
to examine the process of investiture in Barwe society and the role of the
guardian spirit (*mhondoro*), as well as the light all this sheds on Barwe-
Portuguese relations. Isaacman concludes that the holy water was not used for a
Catholic-style 'baptism' as the Portuguese wanted to believe, nor was it a
syncretic religious practice, as other scholars have argued.

282   **Islam in Mozambique (East Africa).**
Islamic Literature vol. 15 (Sept. 1969), p. 45–53.

An odd, anonymous article, which begins at a very general level, explaining
where Mozambique is located, and within a few pages is providing relatively
detailed information about, for example, clandestine Islamic associations in
northern Mozambique in the 1950s, and the role of the Cabo Delgado nationalist
Kibiriti Diwani in the foundation of MANU. The author is anti-FRELIMO, and
gives the date for the launching of the armed struggle as 28 August (rather than
25 September) 1964. This refers to the incident in which a small group of MANU
dissidents killed a Dutch missionary, Father Daniel Boormans, in Cabo Delgado.
The piece ends with an attack on FRELIMO's supposed 'anti-Islamic' position,
and with reference to a Muslim League (Umoja wa Waislamu wa Msumbiji).

283   **Peuple mmeto et christianisme: partenaires d'un dialogue.** (The
Mmeto people and Christianity: partners in dialogue.)
Policarpo Lopes.   Licenciatura dissertation, Institut International
de Catéchèse et Pastorale, Université Catholique de Louvain,
Belgium, 1975. 207p. bibliog. maps.

The Mmeto people are Makua-speakers living in Cabo Delgado. After a
confused, and at times wrong, introduction to the linguistics and ethnography of
the area, with some remarks on political power and on contacts with the Arabs,
Indians and Portuguese, Lopes discusses the difficulties these people have found
in their dialogues with the Church. Apart from his odd ethnographic ideas (he
thinks that the Makonde-speakers are a Makua subgroup), Policarpo Lopes'
political views are quite reactionary. He speaks of using the 'little spaces of
freedom which exist', and characterizes the Mozambican government as
'totalitarian', presumably because it does not allow missionaries a free hand; and

113

Religion

he advocates that the missionary should 'go among the Mmeto in an absolutely secular way, as a worker, as a qualified employee . . . [so that] he can create a new Church presence'. Another missionary-style thesis on Mozambique presented to this institution is Ernesto Pereira's 'Croyances du peuple shangane et christianisme' [The beliefs of the Shangaan people and Christianity] (1971, 144p.). A doctoral dissertation on the religious beliefs of the Mmeto group was presented to the University of Nijmegen in Holland by G. M. M. Cuppen, an unpublished Portuguese translation of which can be found in the Historical Archive of Mozambique (call no. C 522j).

284 Portuguese East Africa: a study of its religious needs.
Eduardo Moreira.   London; New York: World Dominion Press, 1936. 104p. maps.

A survey mainly of Protestant missionary activity in Mozambique. Five chapters deal with the history of the colony, the spread of Christianity, relations between missions and the Mozambique Chartered Company, mission activities, and relations between the state and the missions. The role of the missions and Moreira's far-from-radical views can be summed up by his comment that 'Clearly it is impossible that any Christian worker [i.e. missionary] who is true to the Bible should fail to teach respect and submission to the authorities, obedience to the laws and the established order, payment of taxes, and so forth.' (p. 67). The last thirty pages consist of statistical appendixes and translations of the legislation on mission activity then in effect. The situation changed dramatically after the publication of this book, with the Concordat and the Missionary Statute of the early 1940s. Moreira includes some interesting but brief information on the Ethiopian churches, important for the growth of nationalist feeling at that time.

285 O nhamussoro e as outras funções mágico-religiosas. (The soothsayer and other magical-religious functions.)
Luís D. Polanah.   Licenciatura dissertation, Instituto Superior de Ciências Sociais e Política Ultramarina, Universidade Técnica de Lisboa, 1965. 171p. bibliog.

Polanah was a literary figure in Lourenço Marques during the 1950s (see his *Saga of a cotton capulana* (q.v.)), and later devoted himself to anthropology, completing his doctorate in Portugal at the age of nearly sixty. This thesis is a study of the *nhamussoro* (soothsayer) and related phenomena. Polanah discusses illness and what he terms the 'primitive mentality', agents of the sacred (i.e. different types of healers), the soothsayer and his functions, with an account of spirit possession in the light of psychopathology, the process of becoming a soothsayer among Nguni- and Ndau-speaking people, and the religious cult of the *nhamussoro*. He concludes with an analysis of shamanism.

286 **The history and political role of the M'Bona cult among the Mang'anja.**
Matthew Schoffeleers. In: *The historical study of African religion*. Edited by Terence O. Ranger, I. N. Kimambo. Berkeley, California: University of California Press; London: Heinemann, 1972. p. 73–94.

For six hundred years the M'Bona cult was influential throughout a huge area in present-day Mozambique and Malawi, north of the Zambezi up to the Tchiri (Shire) Highlands, bounded in the west by Tete and across to the coast. The M'Bona cult was similar in its ideological content and its organization to other neighbouring religions such as Chauta, Chisumphi, Mwari and Chaminuka. Schoffeleers traces the history of the cult among Mang'anja-speakers, from its origins to the present day. At times it spread among neighbouring groups, such as the Makua-Lomwe and the Kololo. Schoffeleers concludes that 'The success of the cult . . . as a religious institution, should be measured . . . in its ability to . . . maintain relative harmony throughout the main phases of Mang'anja history.' For a discussion of Shona and Nyanja territorial cults on the northern bank of the Zambezi, between Tete and Sena, and up into southern Malawi, see Terence Ranger's 'Territorial cults in the history of central Africa', *Journal of African History* vol. 14, no. 4 (1973), p. 581–97.

287 **Short notes on an east Indian group in Mozambique: the Ismailian Moslem community.**
D. J. Soares Rebelo. *South African Journal of Science* vol. 58, no. 2 (Feb. 1962), p. 41–44.

Very little has been published on Islam in Mozambique: Samir Zoghby in his important bibliography *Islam in sub-Saharan Africa* (Washington, DC: Library of Congress, 1978. 318p.) lists only three items, one of them the Portuguese version of this article. According to the 1955 census about fourteen per cent of the non-African population of Mozambique were Muslim, excluding the large Yao- and Swahili-speaking Muslim populations of the north. Of the Mozambican Muslims of Indian descent, who at that time numbered about 6,000, under 2,000 were Ismaili Shi'ias. Soares Rebelo describes their educational system, economic and community activities, marriage customs and social status within colonial society. The Ismailis, unlike other groups, were willing to adapt to Portuguese dress and other customs. The Portuguese version of this article was published as 'Breves apontamentos sobre um grupo de indianos em Moçambique: a comunidade ismaília maometana' *Boletim da Sociedade de Estudos de Moçambique* no. 128 (July–Sept. 1961), p. 83–89.

288 **Bibliotheca missionum.**
Edited by Robert Streit, Johannes Dindinger, John Rommerskirchen. Freiburg, FRG: Institut für Missionswissenschaftliche Forschung [various publishers], 1916–. vols. 1–[30].

Portugal is generally considered to be one of the most devout of the Catholic countries, and Roman Catholic missions played an important part in the history of Portuguese colonial activity in Mozambique throughout five centuries. This voluminous bibliographical and biographical series is the basic guide to literature on Catholic missionary activity all over the world up to the mid-1960s. Volumes 15–20 are devoted to Africa and are organized chronologically (vols 15–18), or by missionary order (vols 19–20). They cover the following periods: 1600–99 – vol. XVI; 1700–1879 – vol. XVII; 1880–1909 – vol. XVIII; 1910–1940 – vols XIX–XX. David Henige has estimated that the work includes about 250,000 Africa-related citations (see his 'A comprehensive bibliography of Catholic materials relating to Africa: the *Bibliotheca missionum*,' *African Research and Documentation* no. 18 (1978) p. 20–22; Henige has also published '*Bibliotheca missionum*: a case of benign neglect' *History in Africa* vol. 5 (1978), p. 337–44). At least until recently there were only two sets of this work in research libraries in the United Kingdom, at the British Library in London and at the Bodleian Library in Oxford. See also on this subject the annual *Bibliografia missionária* (1933–.), and the *Dictionary catalog of the Missionary Research Library, New York*, edited by M. H. Harrison (Boston, Massachusetts: G. K. Hall, 1969. 17 vols).

Social Conditions

General

289 Ethnicity, politics and history in Mozambique.
Edward A. Alpers. *Africa Today* vol. 21, no. 4 (1974), p. 39–52.

Alpers looks at the problems caused by the attempts to exploit Mozambican regional or tribalist animosities by reactionary political groups after the 1974 coup in Portugal, and earlier. These manoeuvres combined 'divide-and-rule' tactics with a high level of self-deception about political realities, e.g., the idea that FRELIMO was a Makonde organization. Alpers provides a detailed historical refutation of the Portuguese notion that the Makua-speakers were 'a loyal tribe'; his main point is that the division between revolutionary and reactionary is the most important of political distinctions.

290 Race relations in the Portuguese colonial empire, 1415–1825.
Charles Ralph Boxer. Oxford: Clarendon Press, 1963. 136p.

The myth that the Portuguese were in some way less racist in their colonial activities than other European nations has a long history and dies hard. This book consists of the Richard Lectures delivered at the University of Virginia (Charlottesville, Virginia) in 1962. Boxer shows that the truth was far more complex, and that attitudes on race varied widely in different times, places and circumstances. Chapter II (p. 41–85) is devoted to Mozambique and India (during most of this period Mozambique was administered as part of Goa): Boxer writes that ' . . . the majority of European-born Portuguese were convinced upholders of white superiority . . . '. The question of the emigration of white women to the colonies is central to this particular *problématique*, and Boxer shows that, for instance, one Portuguese scholar overestimated the number by a factor of between 10 and 100. He also briefly discusses the *prazo* system, and the social position of the *mestiço* (of mixed black African and white descent) and the Goan families who ran it. A well-argued book on this topic, but dealing with Angola, is Gerald Bender's *Angola under the Portuguese: myth and reality* (London: Heinemann, 1978. 287p.).

291 **Chitlangou, son of a chief.**
André D. Clerc, translated by Margaret A. Bryan, with a foreword by Alan Paton.   London: Lutterworth Press, 1950. Reprinted, Westport, Connecticut: Negro Universities Press, 1971. 208p.

André Clerc worked as a missionary in southern Mozambique, and Chitlangou, the small boy who is the hero of this story, was none other than Eduardo Mondlane, who was Clerc's informant and student ('this story was told to the author by Chitlangou himself'). The name, properly spelled Xitlhàngú, means 'a shield'. The book is a lightly-fictionalized account of village life in the south during the 1920s and 30s; it is readable and well translated, but as a source of information, other than of the most impressionistic kind, should be treated with great caution. Nevertheless, it is an important if unclassifiable book.

292 **Bairros do caniço da cidade da Beira: tentativa de interpretação humana.** (The reed-house townships of Beira city: an attempt at a humane interpretation.)
Ramiro Duarte Henriques Coimbra.   Licenciatura dissertation, Instituto Superior de Ciências Sociais e Política Ultramarina, Universidade Técnica de Lisboa, 1970. 121p. bibliog. maps.

African housing in Mozambican colonial townships was typically built from reeds; hence the Portuguese expression *caniço* to designate those parts of the city. This sociological thesis deals with the rapid growth of Beira city, including the reed-townships; the composition of the population in terms of origin, and occupational structure; patterns of the sexual division of labour; and social problems associated with water-supply, transport, drainage and hygiene, light, education, and human relations (including relations between 'culturally differentiated' communities). Coimbra concludes that life in the *caniço* is socially marginal, and that the situation of most of the inhabitants is 'terrible', with no social system or effective administration; moreover, the majority of the population of Beira lives there.

293 **Public policies to improve the living conditions of the poor: a comparison of Mozambique and Zimbabwe.**
Elaine A. Friedland.   Washington, DC: American Political Science Association, 1984. 20p.

This interesting conference paper, prepared for the Annual Meeting of the APSA, examines the general socio-economic situation during colonial times, and then moves on to a comparison of the policies of independent Mozambique and Zimbabwe on income distribution, land distribution, and the provision of social services. Friedland concludes that the Frelimo government in Mozambique has in fact been more successful in improving general living standards for both urban and rural poor, than their counterparts of Zimbabwe, despite the latter country's markedly better economic performance.

294 **Social banditry in Zimbabwe (Rhodesia) and Mozambique,**
1894–1907: an expression of early peasant protest.
Allen Isaacman. *Journal of Southern African Studies* vol. 4, no. 1
(Oct. 1977), p. 1–30.

Isaacman uses Eric Hobsbawm's widely criticized concept of 'social banditry' to
try to analyse the careers of two Shona-speaking local leaders in the Zambezi
Valley. Both Dambukashamba and Mapondera (or Kadungere) operated along
the Zimbabwe-Mozambique border around the turn of the century. Isaacman
argues that 'resistance historiography' should pay more attention to such localized
phenomena, and should rely less on archival research among the colonial
documents and more on oral sources. Incidentally, Isaacman is often cavalier with
the spellings of his colleagues' names: Henry Slater becomes Slatter; Marc Wuyts
becomes Wurtz; and António Nogueira da Costa becomes Noguiera. It is to be
hoped that African terms are more carefully transcribed.

295 **Third world lives of struggle.**
Hazel Johnson, Henry Bernstein, with Raúl Hernán Ampuero;
Ben Crow. London: Heinemann, in association with the Open
University, Milton Keynes, Buckinghamshire, England, 1982.
271p.

This reader for the Third World Studies course at the Open University includes
three chapters based on the important interview material collected by Alpheus
Manghezi of the Centre for African Studies over several years in Mozambique.
Manghezi, who trained as a sociologist in Scandinavia, speaks Shangaan as his
mother tongue, and is especially well placed to collect oral data in southern
Mozambique. The chapters are 'Forced labour in colonial Mozambique: peasants
remember', which includes material on forced road-construction and on forced
cotton-cultivation; 'Work songs of Mozambican miners', with the two songs
Maghalangu, leaving for the mines, and *Xikwembu xa muhliwa*, working on the
mines; and 'Interviews with Mozambican peasant women', three interviews about
rural conditions. See also the annotations to Manghezi's other articles.

296 **Beyond the skin: how Mozambique is defeating racism.**
Chris Searle. London: Liberation, 1979. 32p. map.

The teacher and poet Searle has several publications to his credit on aspects of the
struggle in the East End of London, in Mozambique and in the West Indies. In
this pamphlet he draws on his two years' experience as a teacher in Nampula, and
on his knowledge of the history of FRELIMO, to produce an account of the fight
against racism, tribalism and regionalism in all their forms (including so-called
'jokes') in independent Mozambique. He points out that FRELIMO's acceptance
of the idea that Portuguese colonial racism had corrupted many black
Mozambicans' ideas on race represented a big step forward. Racism, for Searle, is
quite simply a crime; and his strength of feeling comes over clearly, even if his
style sometimes suffers. He uses telling illustrations, such as the role of the
'Portuguese' footballer Eusébio in the early 1960s: when they saw him play, writes
Searle, 'millions of English people first saw, but never knew and recognised,
Mozambique – bleached white for Portuguese colonialism, unrecognised and
invisible, just as Salazar had conceived him'.

119

297 **FRELIMO militant: the story of Ingwane from Mozambique, an ordinary, yet extraordinary, man, awakened . . .**
Ndabaningi Sithole. Nairobi: TransAfrica, 1977. 187p. map.

Based on interviews with a Mozambican, Julius Paunde Shimangane Ingwane, this book purports to describe the life of an African under Portuguese colonial rule in Mozambique. Written in a chatty and conversational style, with virtually no political analysis, the text is notably imprecise as to dates, names and places, and has, therefore, little value as an historical document. It is hard to tell, for instance, to what extent Sithole's own prejudices inform the discussion of 'tribal characteristics' on pages 59–62. In addition, Sithole's history of political opportunism within ZANU in Zimbabwe would largely discredit his views on Frelimo for many readers, to say nothing of the recent co-operation agreement which his political group have signed with the armed bandits of Mozambique.

298 **The Mozambican revolution and the national question: for the nation to live the tribe must die.**
Spectator. *African Communist* no. 89 (Second quarter 1982), p. 30–48.

The pseudonymous author starts from the proposition that the fundamental question of the Mozambican revolution is that of people's power, which he or she defines as 'the organized form of rule by the masses', and which is unitary. The nation is not simply a collection of its parts; hence the Assembleia Popular (People's Assembly) does not have local constituency representation. Similarly, there are no minorities, and no special rights or duties for particular sections of the population. The idea of Negritude, which was progressive in specific historical circumstances, is now regarded as reactionary and is rejected. The author discusses why and how Portuguese became the national language and the language of the revolution. The internationalist is the best patriot, according to Frelimo doctrine. The article ends with nine propositions, of which the first is that the struggle creates the nation, and not the other way around.

Children

299 **Family planning in Mozambique.**
Calane da Silva. *LSM News* no. 17 (Winter 1978), p. 33–37.

The family planning and abortion policy in Mozambique is a complex area in which 'traditional' rural values clash with modern medical opinion and with the somewhat puritanical FRELIMO ethos, developed of necessity during the armed struggle. Existing policy is not, in fact, widely publicized or debated, even by the women's organization, the OMM. This piece is a translation of a superficial *Tempo* article on abortion, misleadingly retitled. In general, Mozambican peasant women are uninformed about family planning methods, and their husbands are often actively opposed to any such measures; thus 'secret' abortions are quite commonly performed in the countryside as well as in the cities. The article does not analyse any of this in depth, but it does hint at some of the problems involved, and at the government's solutions.

300 **Preventive health care for mothers and children: a study in Mozambique.**
Diana Jelley, Richard J. Madeley. *Journal of Tropical Medicine and Hygiene* vol. 86 (1983), p. 229–36.

Evaluates the delivery of preventive health services for mothers and children in three contrasting urban health centres in Maputo city. The technical level of operation of the preventive services was considered to be efficient, since over two-thirds of the target population was covered. There was, however, a lower level of attendance in poorer areas, and high-risk cases were rarely given the necessary support. Indeed, nurses and midwives often took punitive measures against those at most risk. But Jelley and Madeley point out that this situation must be seen in the context of the very rapid development of these services in post-independence Mozambique; in colonial times health services were curative and commercial. Jelley and Madeley have published several other articles of similar content and tone (q.v.).

301 **Reduction of child hospital mortality in Mozambique through a nurse training programme.**
Alfredo Pisacane. *Annals of Tropical Paediatrics* vol. 5 (1985), p. 7–10.

Child mortality among cases admitted to hospital in developing countries is usually high; at the Provincial Hospital of Xai-Xai in Gaza, serving a population of about 40,000, the yearly average was about nine per cent between 1976 and 1980. This paper looks at the impact on the child mortality-rate of a six-month paediatric nurse training-programme, which was carried out during the normal ward timetable. The results were positive – the rate dropped from eight per cent to three per cent in the period of the study, which meant in absolute terms that out of an expected forty-four deaths twenty-seven were avoided. Pisacane is an Italian paediatrician.

302 **Avaliação nutricional da população infantil banto (0–5 anos) de uma zona suburbana da cidade de Lourenço Marques.** (A nutritional survey of the infant African population under five of a suburban area of Lourenço Marques.)
Norberto Teixeira Santos. *Revista de Ciências Médicas* [Lourenço Marques, Mozambique] vol. 17, series B (1974), p. 1–400.

A technical study on nutritional levels among young children in the African slums or 'reed-townships' around Lourenço Marques, here described as 'suburban zones'. Teixeira Santos surveyed 112 households, and focused on 72 of these, giving a population of 118 under-fives. He discovered extremely high levels of protein-caloric malnutrition in this age-group (an average of forty-eight per cent; twenty-seven per cent in the first year of life; fifty-five per cent subsequently), and he identifies the causes as poverty, ignorance, bad living-conditions and poor sanitation. No political conclusion is drawn. Teixeira Santos says that he was unable to discover any similar survey that had been attempted elsewhere in Africa, and so could not compare his results with others. There is a 328-item bibliography, maps and several illustrations. A (bad) English summary is printed on p. 331–33. This was originally a doctoral dissertation, but there is no indication of the university to which it was submitted. See also on child development Deolinda da Costa Martins' 'Association of physical maturation and visual acuity in school-children of Lourenço Marques, Mozambique' (Doctor of Public Health dissertation, University of Pittsburgh, Pennsylvania, 1963. 137p.).

Health

303 **Drugs and the Third World: the Mozambique pharmaceutical policy.**
Carol Barker. *The Lancet* (1 Oct. 1983), p. 780–82.
Carol Barker worked in Mozambique from 1976 to 1979, and was a member of the Technical Committee for Therapeutics and Pharmacy which developed Mozambique's drugs policy, generally considered to be a major achievement in the Third World health sector, and the subject of a growing literature. In this article Barker discusses the question of generic-name prescribing, pointing out that in a typical Western country as many as 100,000 drugs are formulated from around 250 active ingredients. Mozambican doctors have encountered no serious difficulties with the generic names, although it is sometimes argued that they are hard to remember. See also Barker's essay 'Are 300 drugs too many?' in *Mozambique: towards a people's health service* (q.v.), p. 131–43; and the more general piece 'Bringing health care to the people' in *A difficult road: the transition to socialism in Mozambique*. Edited by John Saul. (New York: Monthly Review Press, 1985. p. 316–46), with a bibliography that is especially useful on colonial sources on health.

304 **Health in Mozambique: a select bibliography, 1950–1980.**
Julie L. Cliff. London: Mozambique, Angola and Guiné Information Centre, 1980. [37]p.
The title of this bibliography is slightly misleading, since the articles included are mainly of a technical medical nature, rather than dealing with health care as a social issue. The 357 citations are organized into eight main chapters, further subdivided, and the work includes author and subject indexes. It is difficult to ascertain from the brief introduction what the criteria for selection were.

305 **Cuidados de saúde primários em Moçambique: outros níveis de atenção de saúde.** (Primary health precautions in Mozambique and other levels of attention to health.)
[Maputo]: Ministério da Saúde [1978]. 128p.
A general manual in Portuguese on primary health care (PHC), with chapters on the historical background of PHC; the principal health problems in the country

and the resources available to tackle them; the concept and strategy of PHC; levels of attention to health; and the involvement of the community with their local health centre. There are also appendixes, including statistical data on the health sector. This work has been translated into French and published in Paris by L'Harmattan.

306 **Health care in Mozambique: five years later.**
Andy Epstein, Paul Epstein. *Southern Africa* vol. 13, no. 7 (Sept.–Oct. 1980), p. 23–24, 28.

A fairly lightweight piece, consisting of an interview with two health professionals who had worked in Beira between 1978 and 1980. According to the article, ninety per cent of doctors working in Mozambique at the time of the announcement of the nationalization of health services in 1975, left within six months; the entire country, with a population of 9 or 10 million, remained with less than fifty doctors. Large numbers of qualified and politically committed health workers were quickly recruited from abroad, and in November 1977 a law was passed providing for free emergency and preventive care, and for nominal charges for other consultations (presently these charges are fixed at 7.50 meticais). The interviewees discuss the policy of emphasizing preventive medicine, the role of the women's organization and of the 'Dynamizing Groups' in health programmes, health planning, medical supplies, the situation in the rural areas and the open official attitude towards traditional or herbal medicine. They conclude with the optimistic hope that Zimbabwe's independence will improve the food situation in the region and help to eliminate some of the more serious health problems.

307 **A review of health care in Mozambique: issues, analyses, and recommendations.**
Family Health Care, Africare. Washington, DC: Family Health Care, Africare, 1978. 101p. bibliog. (Health and Development in Southern Africa, vol. 6).

This document was submitted to the Southern Africa Development Analysis Program of the US Agency for International Development in Washington, DC and is based on secondary documentation in US libraries; no research visit to Mozambique was made by the authors. Nevertheless, health professionals in Mozambique consider the review to be one of the most useful summaries available on the health sector in the late 1970s. The obligatory survey of the Mozambican economy is followed by an overview of the health situation, covering morbidity and mortality patterns, food and nutrition, the environment and health, population and family planning, and mental health. The delivery system is discussed, with material on the colonial legacy, post-independence measures, expenditure, and preventive and industrial health. There are chapters on foreign aid, and opportunities for health assistance. The review also prints, in an appendix, an English translation of the resolutions of the Eighth Session of the FRELIMO Central Committee on health conditions in Mozambique. Despite the Congressional prohibition on direct aid to Mozambique which was then in effect, the review concludes that 'The United States should join in the international effort to assist in improving the health of Mozambicans and their health care system; it should explore ways and means for collaborating effectively with the Government of Mozambique and with other donors that have been active in providing health assistance.'

123

308 **Revolutionary practice in health; the health care services in Mozambique.**
Martin Hobdell, Nigel Leigh, Naomi Richman, Pamela Smith. *People's Power in Mozambique, Angola and Guinea-Bissau* no. 13 (Spring 1979), p. 13–51.

This article, or group of articles, was prepared by British health-workers with first-hand experience of Mozambican working conditions. It begins with an 'historical perspective', describing the discriminatory hospital system in colonial times, in which the white middle classes received all the best treatment and conditions, while the African urban poor had to scrabble for what was left over. Private practice, too, was based on medical services in Portugal and South Africa, which, as the authors comment, were 'hardly likely to provide models for the radicalization of health care . . . '. As in the case of the judicial system, FRELIMO's experience of health care in the liberated areas served as a basis for later policy, and the second section describes this experience in its political context. This is followed by sections on 'The politics of health: fighting for change in Maputo's Central Hospital'; an attempt to define what the health problems in Mozambique are (i.e., malnutrition, respiratory infections, diarrhoea, measles, whooping cough and parasites); a description of the structure of the health care services; a section on medical and paramedical training; accounts of preventive medicine, oral health and dental services; a very brief discussion of the new drug policy (see also the article by Joe Hanlon (q.v.)); and lastly, a page on the role of *cooperantes* or foreign experts. The article is illustrated and includes statistical tables.

309 **Plantas medicinais: seu uso tradicional em Moçambique.** (Medicinal plants: their traditional use in Mozambique.)
P. C. M. Jansen, Orlando Mendes. Maputo: Ministério da Saúde, Gabinete de Estudos de Medicina Tradicional, 1983–. vol. 1–.

This is a technical reference work on herbal medicine, by the Dutch botanist Jansen and the Mozambican scientist and poet Orlando Mendes. It consists of entries in alphabetical order by scientific name of the plants described, followed by detailed descriptions, observations, medical information, bibliographical references, detailed herbarium references, and distribution maps and drawings. There are indexes of scientific and vernacular names, and of medical terms. This is described as Volume 1, but no further issues have yet appeared.

310 **The advent of primary health care in Mozambique.**
Richard Madeley, Diana Jelley, Phil O'Keefe. *Ambio* vol. 12, no. 6 (1983), p. 322–25.

The authors point out in a brief introduction that the major killers in the Third World are not exotic tropical diseases, but the well-understood illnesses of poverty, which were controlled in the industrialized countries in the last century. Poorer nations, which have to use large numbers of paraprofessional health workers, have therefore opted for the 'risk approach' to preventive medicine, which involves training workers in health centres and clinics to recognize, in advance whenever possible, and according to objective diagnostic criteria, cases which should be referred higher up the system. This is especially important in child-care and maternity cases, since they constitute the majority. Mozambican policy has been to tackle health care and general social issues together, emphasizing prevention and the training of paramedics. Priority areas for intervention have been identified as nutrition, water-supply, environmental hygiene, communicable diseases, and infant mortality. Madeley, Jelley and O'Keefe describe the 'triage system of care' in Mozambique, focusing on a case-study of pre-natal identification of high-risk pregnancies in Maputo, to show how the system works. See also the article by Jelley and Madeley, 'Antenatal care in Maputo, Mozambique: an analysis of risk factors and action taken', *Journal of Epidemiology and Community Health* vol. 37 (1983), p. 111–16.

311 In the words of the minister.
Helder Martins. *World Medicine* (26 January 1977), p. 22.

A one-page interview about health policy, by Geoff Watts, with Dr. Helder Martins, the controversial Minister of Health from independence until March 1980, printed together with Watts' article 'What to do when the doctors leave' (q.v.). Martins comments briefly on the colonial inheritance, present priorities within the health sector, health in the scale of national priorities (it came after agriculture and education, but before defence), the liberation struggle as a source of ideas, and the question of overseas aid. Helder Martins is also the author of *Apontamentos de estatística sanitária e hospitalar* [Notes on health and hospital statistics] (Maputo: The author, 1985. 2nd ed. 148p.).

312 Pharmaceutical policy in independent Mozambique: the first years.
Helder Martins. *IDS Bulletin* vol. 14, no. 4 (1983), p. 62–70.

Before independence Mozambique had about 13,000 drugs on the market, and approximately one drug-company salesman for every five doctors. All drugs were imported, mainly from Portugal, Switzerland, the Federal Republic of Germany, South Africa, France and Britain. This number of drugs was reduced in two phases, first to some 2,600 items with the co-operation of the pharmaceutical companies, and later to less than 500. The first edition of the Mozambican *Formulário nacional de medicamentos* [National formulary of medicines] (Maputo: Ministério da Saúde, 1977. [pagination unknown].) made prescriptions by generic name compulsory and listed 430 therapeutic substances, 20 diagnostic agents and 14 dressings; the second edition (Maputo, 1980) reduced this still further to 343 therapeutic items, 19 diagnostic agents and 12 dressings. At the same time, procurement was centralized and the budget for pharmaceuticals increased four-fold. The author of this article was born in Lourenço Marques in 1936, and qualified as a doctor at the University of Lisbon in 1961, also taking courses at the Institute for Tropical Medicine in Lisbon. In the same year he was drafted into, and deserted from, the Portuguese navy, going into exile first in Morocco and then in Algeria. In early 1965 he joined FRELIMO in Tanzania, and the following year became Director of Health Services. In 1968, as a white, he was caught up in the FRELIMO crisis, and had to leave Tanzania, first returning to Algeria and then going to Sweden. In 1975 he became Minister of Health for Mozambique, a position he held until 1980.

313 **Drug selection: Mozambique.**
Carlos Marzagão, Malcolm Segall. *World Development* vol. 11,
no. 3 (1983), p. 205–16.

Only a few hundred generic drugs are essential for general health care, but the
international market is flooded with hundreds of thousands of brand-name
products, many of them imitative, combinations of drugs, simple duplications, or
even items with low therapeutic value or with bad side-effects. Mozambique has
reduced the number of registered products to around 1,200, and the national
formulary contains less than 350 substances, all referred to by generic name.
There is a growing literature on Mozambican drug policy; apart from other items
annotated in this chapter, see also on this topic S. Velásquez' 'Mozambique's new
pharmaceutical policy proves its worth' *World Health Forum* vol. 4 (1983),
p. 248–50; S. Velásquez, Joaquim Durão and Carlos Marzagão's *Pour une
politique du médicament: l'expérience du Mozambique* [Towards a drug policy: the
Mozambican experience] (Paris: L'Harmattan, 1985 [pagination unknown].); and
Joe Hanlon's 'Essential drugs in Mozambique', *World Health* (June 1983),
p. 26–29.

314 **The zone of influence of some rural health centres in Mozambique.**
Gertrudes Mendonça. *Ethiopian Journal of Health Development*
vol. 1, no. 1 (1984), p. 41–46.

Evaluates the area of influence of five different rural health centres in widely
separated districts of the country during the first half of 1982. Results showed that
the mean radius of patient activity was 8–13 kilometres, and from half to over
four-fifths of the patients lived within 10 kilometres of the centres.

315 **Report of the People's Republic of Mozambique.**
Ministry of Health, Maputo. Nazareth, Ethiopia: World Health
Organization, 1982. 37p. (WHO/UNICEF Primary Health Care
Workshop, Narareth [sic] Ethiopia, 8–18 February 1982).

Although this is a mimeographed paper from a conference held in an African
country – which as any librarian will immediately recognize, means an item very
hard to get hold of – it is an extremely clear and concise statement of
Mozambican primary health care (PHC) policy, and is included for that reason.
The paper is divided into eight parts, dealing with the evolution of the concept of
PHC from the armed struggle onwards; with national health policy in the context
of PHC; the management of programmes within PHC; strengthening the national
infrastructure; the orientation of local infrastructures; integrated rural development; integrated urban development; and lastly, information systems, indicators,
monitoring and evaluation. There are several statistical annexes.

316 **The medicinal and poisonous plants of southern and eastern Africa: being an account of their medicinal and other uses, chemical composition, pharmacological effects and toxicology in man and animal.**
John Mitchell Watt, Maria Gerdina Breyer-Brandwijk.
Edinburgh, London: E. & S. Livingstone, 1962. 2nd ed. 1457p.

A detailed, if sometimes old-fashioned reference work whose content is accurately described by its title. Mozambique falls within the area covered by the book. The text takes the form of a continuous essay, with plant-names printed in bold type for easy retrieval. The book is organized in two sections, on phanerogams (the flowering, seed-producing plants), and on cryptogams (plants without flowers which produce spores), with a series of appendixes. The first of these deals with hydrocyanic acid in non-gramineous (grassy) plants; this is followed by a fifty-one-page bibliography, in double columns, a list of plant-names in European and African languages, with their scientific equivalents, a list of active ingredients, and a detailed index. The work is illustrated with black-and-white and coloured photographs and drawings.

317 **Revista Médica de Moçambique.** (Mozambique Medical Journal.)
Maputo: Ministério da Saúde, Jan. 1982–. biannual.

Mozambique's medical journal, in Portuguese, with English summaries and an English contents page. The content is a mixture of the purely technical medical paper and pieces of more general interest; for example, the first issue contains an article on infant mortality in five suburbs of Maputo city; the third issue has a paper on a cholera epidemic in Sofala. See also the more regular news-sheet *Boletim: a saúde em Moçambique* (Bulletin: health in Mozambique) from the same ministry.

318 **Variacão humana na resposta farmacológica: estudos de farmacogenética em Moçambique.** (Variations in human response to drugs: studies in pharmaco-genetics in Mozambique.)
Lesseps José António Lourenço Reys. Doctoral dissertation, Faculty of Medicine, University of Lourenço Marques, 1971. 284p. bibliog.

Reys' dissertation discusses the need to take into account local genetic characteristics (at a biochemical level) when administering potentially harmful drugs to African patients. There is a short English summary on p. 261.

319 **Forward march, left, right? Health care in liberated Mozambique.**
Malcolm Segall. *Medicine in Society* vol. 6, no. 2/3 (1980), p. 12–16.

An updated version of a paper originally presented to a conference on the theme 'Southern Africa: the Year of the Child' organized by the Committee on Southern Africa at the University of Michigan's Center for Afro-American and African Studies. Segall describes the pre-independence situation, and the development of health policy under Frelimo. In particular, he gives a version of the sacking of Health Minister Helder Martins in early 1980, for allowing 'widespread liberalism

Social Conditions. Health

and (ultra-left) populism' in the sector. The emphasis on preventive medicine had
led to the neglect of curative medicine, and the elected councils had eroded the
doctors' technical and administrative authority. Segal says that the crucial issue is
not really prevention or cure, but rather the relationship between primary health
care and the more expensive levels which involve hospitalization. He indicates
that there has been some decentralization of resources since independence. Segall
is also the author of 'Health and national liberation in the People's Republic of
Mozambique', *International Journal of Health Services* vol. 7, no. 2 (1977),
p. 319–25; and, with Carol Barker and Carlos Marzagão, 'Economy in drug
prescribing in Mozambique', *Tropical Doctor* vol. 10, no. 1 (1980), p. 42–45.

320 **The struggle to build a healthy Mozambique.**
Mozambique Revolution (Dar es Salaam) no. 55 (April–June
1973), p. 17–18.
There is very little hard data on the health services set up by FRELIMO in the
liberated zones during the armed struggle; they must have been rudimentary in
the technical sense, yet their political impact was enormous. This is a report on
the important Conference of the Health Services held by FRELIMO from
16 February to 2 March 1973. The conference was the first of its kind, and it
underlined 'the principle that in the relationship between politics and technique,
politics comes first'. Once this has been properly understood, the comrades in the
health services must 'cultivate love for the masses with whom they are in direct
contact'. However, technical and organizational levels must also be improved;
even the most remote villages should receive medical care. *Mozambique
Revolution* was FRELIMO's English-language monthly magazine during the
armed struggle, and while many of its articles are public relations exercises, it
remains an irreplaceable source for the period.

321 **III. Jornadas de Saúde, Chongoene, 9 a 13 de Novembro de 1981.**
(Third Health Workshops, Chongoene, 9–13 November 1981.)
Maputo: Ministério da Saúde, [1981]. 72p.
The health sector is not only more efficient than most in Mozambique, but it
continues with some traditions that have been abandoned in other areas; for
instance, the Medical Faculty continues with the 'July Activities', when students
are supposed to forget their privileged position and go out to serve the people.
Similarly, the health workshops have been held regularly since just after
independence. The series runs as follows: 1st, Nampula, 1976; 2nd, Beira, 1979;
3rd, Chongoene, Gaza, 1981; 4th, Namaacha, 1983; 5th, Inhambane, 1985. These
proceedings from the third workshop include various details of the participants,
sessions, messages from well-wishers, and so on, and more importantly, fifty-
seven abstracts of research reports presented to the workshop (p. 40–63), which
make the brochure useful as a small reference work. The quite impressive number
of papers submitted shows clearly that medical research in Mozambique is in a
reasonable condition.

322 **National decision-making for primary health care: a study.**
UNICEF/WHO Joint Committee on Health Policy. Geneva:
World Health Organization, 1981. 69p.

A useful and well-produced booklet on the primary health care (PHC) systems of seven countries – Burma, Costa Rica, Democratic Yemen, Finland, Mali, Mozambique and Papua New Guinea. Material on Mozambique is integrated with that on the other countries throughout the text. There are seven chapters, dealing with the background and aims of the study, decision-making for PHC, politics, government and planning, community involvement, the practical impact of PHC decisions, resource allocation, and a final set of eight recommendations by the Joint Committee.

323 **La problématique de la santé mentale au Mozambique.** (The
problematic of mental health in Mozambique.)
Ernesto Venturini. *Psychopathologie Africaine* (Dakar, Senegal)
vol. 16, no. 3 (1980), p. 285–307.

Venturini argues that in the five years between independence in 1975 and 1980, when he concluded his research, certain problems of mental health policy became clearly evident. Because the new Government adopted a democratic and progressive medical policy, contradictions arose between the medical disciplines inside the rigid institutional framework of the hospitals, and those outside. Thus, the importance of mental health problems is generally underrated in comparison with serious sanitary problems, for example. This is a dangerous situation, but Venturini feels that the process of development is nevertheless promising. There is a rather poor summary in English on p. 307.

324 **The dynamics of health policies in Mozambique, 1975–85.**
Gill Walt, Julie Cliff. *Health Policy and Planning* vol. 1, no. 2
(1986), p. 148–57.

The tenth anniversary of Mozambican independence in 1985 took place in the midst of a severe crisis: the country was under attack by the South African-backed MNR bandits, and at the same time was suffering severely from drought, food shortages and the world-wide economic recession. The armed bandits have chosen to attack not only economic targets, but health centres and rural hospitals, as well as health workers themselves. Medical supplies cannot be delivered or stored because roads are mined and electricity supplies are cut. Lives are at risk from food and water shortages. Health policy is itself the object of fierce struggles; as Walt and Cliff point out ' . . . Frelimo will be very reluctant to divest itself of its credibility in this area by giving in to possible IMF demands for a return to private medical care'. *Mozambique health holding the line* by Julie Cliff and fellow health workers Najmi Kanji and Mike Muller (*Review of African Political Economy* no. 36 (Sept. 1986), 7–23) also describes the health situation in the context of the struggles against armed banditry and foreign destabilization. The authors stress that even aid programmes have a disruptive effect, since they prevent effective government planning. They conclude that 'If [there] is a reason for Mozambique to be attacked, [there] is also good reason to defend it. It is vital now, when fortunes are at their lowest ebb, to protect the edifice which has been built with such sacrifice in the last ten difficult years, to hold the line.' President Samora Machel, who was trained as a paramedic, has made several important speeches which lay down the principal lines of health policy. See the November 1971 speech to trainee health cadres 'Our health service's role in the revolution', published in English in his collection *Mozambique: sowing the seeds of revolution* (q.v.), p. 46–55, and also as 'Our hospital's role' in his *The tasks ahead* (q.v.), p. 19–32; the speech of 6 October 1976 at the Central Hospital of Maputo, published in English as 'Transform the Central Hospital into a people's hospital' in *Samora Machel: an African revolutionary* (q.v.), p. 142–55; and the speech of 4 December 1979 'We must strengthen people's power in our hospitals' in the same volume, p. 156–68.

325 **Health policies in Mozambique.**
Gill Walt, David Wield.   Milton Keynes, Buckinghamshire, England: Open University Press, 1983. 35p. bibliog. maps. (U204 Third World Studies. Case Study, no. 3).

An excellent short text designed as a reader for Britain's Open University, where teaching is done mainly through television and radio programmes. Both of the authors have extensive first-hand knowledge of Mozambique. The book is organized around three central chapters, dealing with the war of liberation and the struggles over FRELIMO's development strategy, with health conditions in the country, and with the construction of the new health services after independence. The tone of the brochure is generally positive, and it is clear where the authors' sympathies lie; nonetheless, difficulties are not glossed over. The text is well illustrated with maps, photographs, and statistical graphs and tables.

326 **Mozambique: towards a people's health service.**
Edited by Gillian Walt, Angela Melamed.   London: Zed Books, 1983. 150p. map.

An important collection of pieces on such topics as health policy (Gill Walt), nurse training (Christine Webb), rural health care (David Bell) and pharmaceutical policy (Carol Barker). Basil Davidson writes in his foreword that the nine papers in this volume, all by health professionals with experience of working in Mozambique, 'have nothing to do with propaganda on one side, or, on the other, with the corruptions of orthodox cynicism'. Of particular interest, too, are the articles on democratization in the hospitals and the health service up to 1980, by Richard Williams; and the description of two years in a small provincial hospital in the remote north, 'If you don't know Niassa, you don't know Mozambique' by Moira Dick. This collection is certainly the best entry-point in English, alongside *Health policies in Mozambique* (q.v.), for the general reader interested in the subject from a non-technical angle.

327 **What to do when the doctors leave.**
Geoff Watts.   *World Medicine* (26 January 1977), p. 17–20, 25–26, 28.

Watt begins with what he describes as a 'ridiculously bald outline' of the country's recent history; he points out that FRELIMO had a health policy long before seizing state power. In Niassa in 1971, for example, FRELIMO was already running two regional hospitals, fourteen district medical posts, and eighteen first aid posts in the liberated zones. After independence the new government nationalized medicine and medical education; doctors were invited to stay on, but they had to accept a government salary (a high one by local standards). Nonetheless, out of about 500 doctors, only 50 or so stayed. The Central Hospital of Maputo is full of high-tech machinery which cannot be serviced because the departing technicians tore up the maintenance manuals. Thus, while access to health services and preventive medical policy have improved, scientific medicine is in crisis. Watts points out that shaping the motley collection of buildings and installations inherited from the Portuguese into a rational health system is much easier on paper than in practice. He concludes optimistically that four factors augur well for the future: the tranquil atmosphere (since destroyed by the South African-backed armed bandits, however); the erosion of the extremes of privilege; the realism of the planners; and the general correctness of the policies adopted.

Hunger

328 *Ku thekela*: **estratégia de sobrevivência contra a fome no sul de Moçambique.** [*Ku thekela*: strategy of survival against hunger in southern Mozambique].
Alpheus Manghezi. *Estudos Moçambicanos* no. 4 (1983–85), p. 19–40.

Ku thekela is the Shangaan term for 'survival'; Manghezi argues that famines are not 'natural disasters', but arise in the context of a complex of economic and political factors. He uses songs and interviews from his own rich collection of materials to illustrate the various tactics employed by the southern peasantry to obtain food in times of hunger, and he discusses various historical famines, here called by their local names, for example: 'the famine of the small bucket'. Manghezi's previous articles for this journal have been montages, leaving the reader to draw his own conclusions; here he deploys his materials to make a telling argument.

329 **Mozambique.**
Jacques M. May, Donna L. McLellan. In: *The ecology of malnutrition in seven countries of southern Africa and in Portuguese Guinea.* Jacques M. May, Donna L. McLellan. New York: Hafner, 1971. p. 233–97. (Studies in Medical Geography, vol. 10).

May wrote a series of studies on the ecology of malnutrition in Africa, of which this is the last volume. Not surprisingly, in such an ambitious enterprise, he and his collaborators tended to take the assertions and viewpoints of their sources very much at face value. In the case of Portuguese colonial sources on Mozambique this proved disastrous, especially when combined with a set of paternalistic and naïve ideas about Africa as a whole. May and McLellan start this essay from a conception of Mozambican rural society that is almost a parody of ethnographic over-simplification; they make the bizarre claim that Mozambique's

Social Conditions. Hunger

African population is 'one of the most varied and mixed in Africa' and that the 'tribes' live in villages 'comprised mostly of people related to one another'. They assert that 'Portugal has attempted to create a multiracial society with opportunities for all', and that the 1961 labour laws 'firmly established free choice of work for the African'. Nevertheless, while practically worthless in analytical terms, the piece does bring together in English a considerable amount of ecological and nutritional data from over fifty, mainly Portuguese, sources. For a bibliography on nutrition in all the Portuguese colonies, published just before independence, see Carlos Santos Reis' *A nutrição no ultramar português: subsídios para uma bibliografia* [Nutrition in overseas Portugal: a preliminary bibliography] (Lisbon: Instituto Nacional de Estatística, 1973–74; 2 vols. [Centro de Estudos Demográficos; Publicações]).

330 **Nutritional surveillance: morbidity and mortality from the 1983 famine.**
National Commission for Natural Disasters. *Weekly Epidemiological Record* (Geneva) no. 37 (14 September 1984), p. 284–87.

A report on a survey conducted in drought-stricken Inhambane and Gaza provinces in October and November 1983 to determine the prevalence of acute malnutrition, and the causes and rates of morbidity and mortality. 656 children were examined; twelve per cent were acutely malnourished in Gaza and twenty-eight per cent in Inhambane. Similarly, 207 families were surveyed to discover the death-rates, which were highest (at 145.5 per 1000) in the under-one-year-old age group. These are high rates: the Sahel famine of the early 1970s produced an acute malnutrition average of between nine and twenty-three per cent. However, there were some difficulties with the sampling because of military considerations. The estimated total number of deaths in 1983 may have been as high as 72,000 among the approximately 750,000 displaced persons in the two provinces. An emergency food and rehabilitation programme was an urgent necessity.

331 **Food policy and production in Mozambique since independence.**
Philip Raikes. *Review of African Political Economy* no. 29 (July 1984), p. 95–107.

By the mid-1980s Mozambique's food crisis had become one of the worst in Africa, as well as one of the most intractable. Raikes identifies structural causes – the way in which the inherited colonial agricultural system was organized, combined with the impact of the flight of the Portuguese settlers around the time of independence. This potentially dangerous situation was turned into a real crisis by prolonged and systematic South African destabilization, either direct, or through their proxies, the armed bandits; and by a series of unusually poor rainy seasons in the late 1970s. Raikes follows the line of analysis of Frelimo's IV Congress, pointing out that policy errors also played a part in all this – over-investment in the conversion of settler agriculture into massive and unproductive state farms, and a pricing policy which kept food prices down in support of an urban and Portuguese dietary pattern. The peasantry, thus, suffered most.

332 **Cassava, cyanide and epidemic spastic paraparesis: a study in
     Mozambique on dietary cyanide exposure.**
     Hans Rosling.   Uppsala, Stockholm: Almqvist & Wiksell, 1985.
     [pagination varies]. bibliog. maps. (Acta Universitatis Upsaliensis.
     Comprehensive Summaries of Uppsala Dissertations from the
     Faculty of Medicine, no. 19).

Cassava roots, or *mandioca*, are normally dried in the sun for some time before
they are eaten. In 1981, during a period of severe drought and hunger in
Nampula, peasants were reduced to eating cassava without the necessary
preparation, with tragic results. Rosling was district medical officer in the area
affected and this is a technical report on the disaster. The book includes a fifty-
page abstract of his thesis, plus six papers, including the Mozambican Ministry of
Health's 'Mantakassa: an epidemic of spastic paraparesis associated with chronic
cyanide intoxication in a cassava staple area of Mozambique', *Bulletin of the
WHO* vol. 62, no. 3 (1984), p. 477–84, 485–92; 'Association of high cyanide and
low sulphur intake in cassava-induced spastic paraparesis' by Julie Cliff (et al.),
The Lancet (30 November 1985); a technical article on blood analysis, and two
unpublished papers.

333 **Military attacks, drought and hunger in Mozambique.**
     Vincent Tickner.   *Review of African Political Economy* no. 33
     (Aug. 1985), p. 89–91.

In this short note, which should be read by all concerned with hunger in
Mozambique, Tickner takes the Western media and the relief agencies to task for
adopting a so-called 'non-political' attitude towards the South African-backed
armed bandits, who have in fact played a major role in the serious famine in Tete
Province. At one point, according to Tickner, it was even suggested that the
bandits should be included in the food-distribution system. Western television has
presented the famine as a situation that Frelimo could not – or would not – do
anything about, when in fact the struggle against the bandits was precisely over
the movement of local surpluses and foreign food aid from one part of the country
to another.

Women

334 **Valenge women: the social and economic life of the Valenge women
     of Portuguese East Africa: an ethnographic study.**
     E. Dora Earthy.   London: Oxford University Press for the
     International African Institute, 1933. Reprinted, Cass, 1968. 251p.
     map. (Cass Library of African Studies, General Studies, no. 59).

Dora Earthy was a missionary in southern Mozambique from 1917 to 1930, and
based this classic ethnographic monograph on the women of the Langa clan in the
region between Manjacaze and the coast in Gaza Province on her observations
during those years. It deals with the origin and history of the people in that

133

Social Conditions. Women

region, their social organization and kinship system, women and their home-steads, the agricultural calendar, material culture, birth rites, early education, games, string figures, tattooing and scars, puberty and initiation, marriage, death, dances, religion, folklore and proverbs. In an appendix Earthy gives an amplified list of the names of chiefs and *régulos* in the area, with their districts, as an amplification of the information provided by Henri Junod's list in *Bantu Studies* vol. 3 (1927), p. 57–71. The phonetics are very carefully transcribed with special characters for phonemes which cannot be represented easily in Roman script. The case-studies are livened up with illustrative anecdotes. It remains a valuable work, taking its period and the religious views of its author into account.

335   **The state, the Party and the female peasantry in Mozambique.**
Sonia Kruks, Ben Wisner.   *Journal of Southern African Studies*, vol. 11, no. 1 (Oct. 1984), p. 106–27.

Kruks and Wisner left Mozambique in 1980, and their article relies heavily on secondary sources in English. They provide an overview of Mozambique since independence, characterizing the economic crisis precipitated by FRELIMO's victory in 1974–75, and analysing briefly the Party's position on the worker-peasant alliance. A weak section on rural women under colonialism follows, repeating a number of anthropological myths (e.g., that Mozambique has many 'ethnic groupings'); this is followed by sections on FRELIMO's policy on women's emancipation during the armed struggle, on the OMM (Mozambican Women's Organization), on domestic social relations, and on Mozambican women's role in non-domestic production. The tenor of the argument is that FRELIMO's analysis of the 'woman question' is far too orthodox, in Marxist-Leninist terms, and needs substantial rethinking. The authors conclude that an analysis of the crisis of rural production is inseparable from an analysis of women's role as producers.

336   **Mozambican women's conference.**
People's Power in Mozambique, Angola and Guinea-Bissau no. 6 (Jan.–Feb. 1977), p. 5–26.

The first conference of the Mozambican Women's Organization (OMM) was held in Tanzania in 1973, during the struggle for independence. The second conference was held in Maputo in November 1976, with the central theme of the role of women in the new socialist society. This article consists of the full text of the conference resolutions, dealing with illiteracy; obscurantism and superstition; tribalism, regionalism and racism; rumour, intrigue and slander; superiority and inferiority complexes; single mothers; divorced women; idle women; and abortion. Under the heading urban social problems the conference discussed liberalism; adultery; prostitution; divorce; abandoned children; and unemployment. Rural social problems included initiation rites; premature marriage; forced marriage; hereditary marriage; *lobolo* (bridewealth); polygamy; adultery; and divorce. Includes explanatory notes by the translator. On the Extraordinary Conference of the OMM, see among various press reports Etevaldo Hipólito's 'A familia e a sociedade' (Family and society), *Cadernos do Terceiro Mundo* no. 74 (Feb. 1985), p. 74–76.

337 **Mulher moçambicana: boletim da OMM** (Mozambican woman:
bulletin of the Mozambican Women's Organization).
Maputo (PO Box 4015): Secretariado Nacional da OMM, March
1986–. quarterly.

Edited by Sabina Santos, this bulletin replaces the earlier women's publication 'A
mulher na transformação da sociedade: página quinzenal da OMM' (Woman in
the transformation of society: fortnightly page of the Mozambican Women's
Organization), which first appeared in *Notícias* on 6 February 1978 and which ran
for three or four years into well over sixty numbers (I have not been able to
ascertain the date of the last issue). The first issue of the new bulletin, which is
not part of any other periodical, includes short exhortatory pieces on the OMM's
Extraordinary Conference in November 1985, on child-care, and on a seminar
held by the OMM's departments (namely of Mobilization, Social Work and
Administration, and Finances). Other features include an article entitled
'Woman: she who produces and feeds fighters' which, it is to be hoped, does not
represent the OMM's vision of women's role in Mozambican society. For
comments on the OMM, see the annotations to other articles in this section.

338 **Making our own way: women working in Lourenço Marques,
1900–1933.**
Jeanne Penvenne. Boston, Massachusetts: African Studies
Center, Boston University, 1986. 20p. (Boston University. African
Studies Center. Working Papers. no. 114).

Penvenne, as always, spots a theme which other writers have missed; in this case
the question is why, in view of the enormous effort which migrant workers devote
to the accumulation of cash for *lobolo* (bridewealth), so many wives (representing
large capital investments) were abandoned by their husbands. From the mid-1940s
onwards, the flow of women from the whole Sul do Save area into the towns was
a major problem for the colonial administrators. Yet, as Penvenne describes it,
they managed to 'make their way'. In the process, she cautiously claims in this
preliminary paper that 'Women working for wages in Lourenço Marques shared
important day-to-day experiences as women and mothers which cut across their
diverse class and ethnic identities.' Penvenne focuses on the 'local African and
Afro-European female elite' and their strategies of survival. The work is based on
archival sources and interviews as well as the published literature.

339 **Rural transformations: women in the new society.**
Stephanie Urdang. *Africa Report* vol. 30, no. 2 (March–April
1985), p. 66–70.

Stephanie Urdang is known for her sympathetic and analytical studies of women
in Guinea-Bissau as well as Mozambique. In this article, based on a case-study of
the '3 February' communal village, she concludes that while the Mozambican
Party and government have defined the emancipation of women as a top-priority
policy objective, there are still considerable difficulties to be overcome. See also,
for a more detailed study on women *A mulher moçambicana no processo de
libertação* [The Mozambican woman in the process of liberation] (Maputo:
Instituto Nacional do Livro e do Disco, 1984. 135p.) by Barbara Isaacman and
June Stephen, which was originally published by the United Nations Economic

135

Social Conditions. Women

Commission for Africa in Addis Ababa, in both English and Portuguese editions under the title *Moçambique: a mulher, a lei e a reforma agrária* (Mozambique: women, the law and agrarian reform). Also of interest is Urdang's article 'The last transition: women and development in Mozambique', *Review of African Political Economy* no. 27/28 (Feb. 1984), p. 8–32.

340   **Fertility and famine: women's agricultural history in southern Mozambique.**
   Sherilynn J. Young.   In: *The roots of rural poverty in Central and southern Africa.* Edited by Robin Palmer, Neil Parsons.   London: Heinemann, 1977. p. 66–81.

This paper was actually written before Young began to do field-work in southern Mozambique; she attempts to study 'women as a division of labour' and to see how this influenced their wider social role in the Sul do Save. She begins with a section on the situation in the 16th century, based on accounts by priests who probably failed fully to understand what they were describing. She then moves on to an account of changes in the women's role as cultivators up to the end of the 19th century. In the 20th century Tsonga and Chope women took over cash-crop production as well as continuing to expand food production. Income from crop sales gave them considerable independence. Women's participation in spirit possession cults, for example, was an assertion of their control over community ritual, not a compensation for low status, according to Young. See also her unpublished conference papers, 'Changes in diet and production in southern Mozambique, 1855–1960' (Presented to the ASAUK Conference on Agricultural Change in Africa, Durham, England, 1976. 12p.); and 'Women in transition: southern Mozambique 1975–76: reflections on colonialism, aspirations for independence' (Presented to the Conference on the History of Women, College of St. Catherine, Minnesota, Minneapolis, 1977. 24p.).

Political Economy

341 **Colonial dependence and regional integration.**
Luís de Brito. *Mozambican Studies* (Amsterdam) no. 1 (1980),
p. 23–32.

Brito's short article argues that previous authors have tended to overestimate the
impact of Portuguese Fascism on the history of the colony, and to underestimate
the importance of Mozambican integration into the South African-dominated
regional subsystem. Brito writes that 'The error lies in attempting to analyse
policies before . . . making a prior study of colonial society in terms of capitalist
domination . . . ' He argues that Portuguese Fascism had a 'limited impact' on
this basic structure of regional dependence.

342 **Moçambique economic survey: special edition for the independence.**
Direcção-Geral do Comércio Externo. Lourenço Marques,
Mozambique: Tempográfica, [1975]. 64p. map.

A useful official survey, in English, of the economic situation at independence,
intended mainly for foreign importers. The work consists of a general description
of the country; a section on foreign trade; a chapter entitled aspects of the
economy; and a summary of foreign trade regulations. There are statistical tables
and photographs. For a much drier and grimmer account of the economy in later
years, see especially the official government publications: *A situação actual no
nosso país* [The current situation in our country] (Maputo: Partido Frelimo, 1982.
39p.); *Informação económica* (Maputo: Comissão Nacional do Plano, Jan. 1984.
77p.); and for an up-to-date statistical publication see *Informação estatística
1975–1984* [Statistical information, 1975–84] (q.v.).

343 **Economia de Moçambique.** (Economy of Mozambique.)
Lourenço Marques, Mozambique: Centro Social; Beira,
Mozambique: Companhia Editorial de Moçambique, Dec.
1963–July 1974. no. 1–vol. 9, no. 7. monthly.

'EM', as it called itself on its masthead, was of a popular and newsy character
with short scientific articles, and was the first economics magazine to be published
in Mozambique. In 1971 it moved from Lourenço Marques to Beira, after being
taken over by the right-wing industrialist Jorge Jardim, with what was rumoured
to be Portuguese government money. The magazine was a self-proclaimed
'vehicle for official information' about economics and business in the colony.

344 **A political, economic and social bibliography on Moçambique, with
main emphasis on the period 1965–1978.**
Thyge Enevoldsen, Vibe Johnsen.   Copenhagen: Centre for
Development Studies, 1978. 60p. ([CDR paper no.] C 78.9).

This bibliography by two young Danish researchers was based on material
available at the time in their Centre's library, and is thus in many respects an
arbitrary list, including, for example, a number of trivial press clippings. The
references are unnumbered and there are no indexes. There are many errors and
poor citations, and even the annotations are not consistently in any given
language. The bibliography is organized into eight chapters, with subdivisions, as
follows: Mozambique in general; history; economy; foreign relations; social
sector; state and party; planning; and mobilization. See also the critique of this
work in 'Writings and research on Mozambique, 1975–1980'.

345 **Roots of counter-revolution: the Mozambique National Resistance.**
Paul Fauvet.   *Review of African Political Economy* no. 29 (July
1984), p. 108–21.

In the original manuscript of this article, which was cut for publication, Fauvet
quotes Amílcar Cabral to the effect that a revolution is like a train journey – 'at
every stop some people get off, and new passengers get on'. The ones who 'got
off' were picked up like loose ends and moulded into the diverse collection of
gangs – the MNR – to make an 'opposition' to Frelimo. Fauvet identifies three
main strands: the groups defeated in internal struggles during the liberation war;
the remnants of the defeated colonial forces; and anti-Frelimo elements who
emerged after independence. He then provides a detailed account of how, where
and when these groupings were brought together by the Rhodesians and then
taken over by the South Africans after 1980. The article was written in 1983, and
was not only cut heavily for publication, but also came out after the initial pre-
Nkomati contacts between South Africa and Mozambique in 1983–84. See also
Fauvet's earlier piece with Alves Gomes, 'The 'Mozambique National
Resistance'' *AIM Information Bulletin* no. 69 (1982), supplement.

346 **The political economy of colonialism in South Africa and Mozambique.**
Elaine A. Friedland. *Journal of Southern African Affairs* vol. 2, no. 1 (Jan. 1977), p. 61–75.

In this rather confusing article, Friedland starts off from the proposition that settler colonialism is the same as something she calls 'racial-colonialism', and that it is found in both Mozambique and in South Africa, where it 'may be referred to as an 'estate system''. From here she moves on to a series of abstract definitions of the estate system, involving 'a hierarchy of two or more social groups which are differentiated in both law and social custom', and private ownership of land. The system was set up by the process of European alienation of land from African control, and was sustained by allowing Africans to hold land only in reserved areas (presumably she is here talking about South Africa), and by political regulations 'Such as special forms of taxation, pass laws . . . , a differentiated educational system, residential segregation, and special criminal statutes . . . '.

347 **Bibliografia sobre a economia portuguesa.** (Bibliography on the Portuguese economy.)
Edited by Amaro D. Guerreiro. Lisbon: Instituto Nacional de Estatística, 1958–. annual.

The first thing to be said about this important bibliographical source is that the title means 'Portuguese' in the Salazarist sense, that is, including the so-called 'overseas provinces'. The bibliography is, therefore, a first-rate source on Mozambique, at least up until 1974. It is easy to find all the Mozambican references in one place, since the arrangement follows a systematic topical classification under main geographical divisions (continental Portugal, the Azores, Madeira, overseas territories in general, and then the colonies one-by-one). The bibliography includes large numbers of analyticals from Portuguese journals and newspapers, many of which have never been indexed elsewhere. The first issue, covering 1948/49, includes nearly 300 numbered items on Mozambique; and the issue covering 1971, published in 1973, has nearly 800. Each issue includes an introduction, a section entitled 'Standards used in compiling the bibliography', an outline of the classification, a list of the abbreviations of periodical titles, and of issues indexed, subject and author indexes (the former referring to the classification, not the references), and a detailed contents page.

348 **Economic policy context and adjustment options in Mozambique.**
Maureen Mackintosh. *Development and Change* vol. 17 (1986), p. 557–81.

Maureen Mackintosh worked on marketing problems in Zambezia Province at the Centro de Estudos Africanos in the early 1980s, and returned to Mozambique in 1985 on a consultancy mission funded by the Nordic aid agencies, visiting Chokwe in Gaza Province. In this article she examines the concept of 'adjustment' (meaning living within your national means), and sharply terms it 'a deliberate euphemism in many economic contexts in which it is used'. She also looks at the constraints and options in economic policy for Mozambique, as the country struggles against South African aggression, the breakdown of agriculture and trade, and the drought which is afflicting large parts of southern Africa. She concludes that deregulation of the economy is not a viable alternative to

139

decentralized planning. The government must set up an 'effective, partially planned wartime economy with a more efficient state sector and functioning fragmented local markets'. There is, she writes, 'no efficient market solution to the re-establishment of a devastated economy in wartime'.

349 Mozambique: to Nkomati and beyond.
David Martin, Phyllis Johnson. In: *Destructive engagement: southern Africa at war.* Edited by Phyllis Johnson, David Martin. Harare: Zimbabwe Publishing House for the Southern African Research and Documentation Centre, 1986. p. 1–41, notes p. 341–50.

The Mozambican government's refusal to acknowledge that their guerrilla opponents constitute any kind of domestic political opposition is sometimes presented in the Western press as a stubborn denial of reality. Martin and Johnson present the view that Mozambique's analysis of the situation is, in fact, entirely reasonable. This is the most detailed circumstantial account available of the creation of the armed bandits by the Rhodesians and their subsequent handing-over to South Africa. Based on a mass of documentation and on extensive interviews with former Rhodesian intelligence officials, the article presents incontrovertible evidence that the MNR, or Renamo, is entirely a creation of Mozambique's enemies, without any social or political base or legitimacy. In their summing up, Martin and Johnson quote a Mozambican official, defending his country's refusal to negotiate with the bandits, but only with South Africa, as saying 'We talk to the organ-grinder, not the monkey.'

350 Towards a political economy of northern Mozambique: the Makua hinterland, 1600–1900.
Joseph Frederick Mbwiliza. PhD dissertation, Columbia University, New York, 1980. 360p. bibliog. maps.

Mbwiliza, a Tanzanian historian, traces the development of commodity production and its effect on the history of the Makua plateau over three centuries. He describes the struggle for political and commercial control between Swahili traders, Makua leaders and the Portuguese, a struggle which the Portuguese were only able to win in the late 19th and early 20th centuries through military expeditions financed by loans from Britain and Germany. Mbwiliza concludes with the reasonable suggestion that, in the history of colonialism, resistance and collaboration 'are not necessarily polar opposites'.

351 Mozambique: the political economy of development.
James H. Mittelman. *Journal of Southern African Affairs* vol. 3, no. 1 (Jan. 1978), p. 35–54.

Mittelman is an American political scientist who has worked in eastern Africa and has paid a couple of visits to Mozambique. He tries to assess 'the history of productive resources' and to evaluate Frelimo policies since independence, although the emphasis is on the latter. Mittelman questions how a liberation movement attempted 'to challenge the structures of underdevelopment and fundamentally alter the basis of social relations'. Although his footnotes feature such insider's references as 'private diplomatic source', 'international agency,

140

internal working documents', and even 'restricted document', it appears clear that the piece includes a certain amount of supposition.

352 **Underdevelopment and the transition to socialism: Mozambique and Tanzania.**
James H. Mittelman. New York; London: Academic Press, 1981. 277p. bibliog. maps. (Studies in Social Discontinuity).

Mittelman has taken a slight idea and attempted to stretch it out into a full-length book, on the basis of thin empirical work. Essentially he takes two key conjunctures in the history of the two countries, and analyses them comparatively. Unhappily, the two conjunctures chosen – FRELIMO's seizure of state power in Mozambique, and the post-Arusha Declaration bank nationalizations in Tanzania – are quite dissimilar, and so we end up with a juxtaposition of two journal articles rather than a comparative analysis. The section on Mozambique is based largely on secondary sources and interviews with journalists, and so does not represent any advance either in knowledge or in interpretation. The theoretical introduction, in which Mittelman attempts to disarm criticism by disclaiming any comparative pretensions, uses Marxist terminology to reach perfectly conventional conclusions.

353 **The struggle for Mozambique.**
Eduardo Mondlane; introduced by John Saul, biographical sketch by Herbert Shore. London: Zed Books, 1983. 225p. (Reprint of first edition, Harmondsworth: Penguin Books, 1969. 224p.).

This posthumously published book by the first president of FRELIMO, who was brutally murdered in February 1969 in Dar es Salaam by a parcel bomb, is essential reading for anyone who wishes to understand the Mozambique of the armed struggle, of FRELIMO and Frelimo, and of the post-independence period. Mondlane was born in Gaza in 1920, and attended a mission primary school. Self-taught in English, he managed to complete his secondary schooling in the Transvaal, and won a place at the University of the Witswatersrand in Johannesburg. He was expelled back to Mozambique, and the Portuguese sent him to study in Lisbon. He eventually transferred to a US university, and completed his doctorate at Northwestern, near Chicago. After working as an academic and as a civil servant for the UN, he established contact with various Mozambican nationalists, and became the president of the newly-formed Mozambique Liberation Front (FRELIMO) at its first meeting in 1962. He then devoted himself to the preparation for the armed struggle, and spent much of his time in Cabo Delgado after its launching, until his untimely death at forty-nine years of age. This work is divided into two main sections, of which the first is a description of the Portuguese colonial system – colonization, the social structure, the role of education and the economic reality underlying the ideology. The second part is a history of the growth of the nationalist movement and the foundation of FRELIMO, the launching of the war, the aspirations of the Mozambican people for the future, and their attitude towards other countries. John Saul writes in his introduction that 'If the first part of *The struggle for Mozambique* repays reading, the second part *demands* it.'

141

Political Economy

354 The MNR: opponents or bandits?
José Mota Lopes. *Africa Report* vol. 31, no. 1 (Jan.–Feb. 1986), p. 67–73.

Mota Lopes, a veteran Mozambican journalist, is a former National Director of Information; when he wrote this exclusive article he was Deputy Director of the Centre of African Studies in Maputo. He points out that despite its claims to be a genuine opposition movement, the MNR has never been able to establish 'an effective link with the people', has never recognized 'the predominance of political factors over purely military aspects', and has never been able to form 'provisional administrative structures and alternatives to the established power'. Instead, it relies on 'brutality, kidnapping, armed coercion, and blackmailing'. The group has never attracted intellectuals or exiles in large numbers into its membership because it has never offered any solutions to the real problems facing Mozambique; indeed, it often refers to colonial times with nostalgia. Mota Lopes traces the origins of the MNR back to 1968–72 in Southern Rhodesia. In an interview with Kenneth Flower, a former director of Rhodesian security, Mota Lopes was able to establish that special Mozambican units had been set up by the CIO (Central Intelligence Organization) as long ago as 1968 in Tete Province. This later became 'the Resistance', and then the Mozambican National Resistance (MNR, or, in Portuguese, Renamo). The article closes with a telling comment from the Mozambican side: 'We have already spoken with the true leaders of the MNR – the South Africans – at Nkomati . . . There is no one else to talk to.' See also in the same issue of *Africa Report* Mota Lopes' interview with Robert Mugabe on the question of Zimbabwe-Mozambique military co-operation against the bandits (p. 74–76). See also the long newspaper interview with José Mota Lopes by Rodrigues da Silva, in which he points out that Renamo does not exist as a *political* movement, but is merely a convenient fiction for South African policy-makers (*Diário Popular* [Lisbon], 13 May 1986).

355 Mozambique: the revolution and its origins.
Barry Munslow. London: Longman, 1983. 195p. bibliog. map.

Munslow was a researcher at the Centre of African Studies in Maputo in the mid-1970s, and this slightly disappointing book is based on his doctoral thesis 'FRELIMO and the Mozambican revolution' (PhD dissertation, University of Manchester, Manchester, England. 1980). Munslow is clearly happier as a sociologist than as a historian. The book is openly partisan, and Munslow makes no secret of his admiration for and sympathy with the FRELIMO leadership. He has been heavily criticized for this by such diverse scholars as Gervase Clarence-Smith (*Portuguese Studies* vol. 1 [1985], p. 225–27); Landeg White (*Journal of Southern African Studies* vol. 11, no. 2 [April 1985], p. 320–32); and Jeanne Penvenne (*International Journal of African Historical Studies* vol. 18, no. 1 [1985], p. 109–38), although this last reviewer is more upset by his cavalier attitude to historical sources. The book was, however, praised in the non-specialist pages of, for example, *International Affairs* (vol. 60, no. 4 [1984], p. 722) and *Third World Book Review* (vol. 1, no. 1 [1984], p. 24–25). Munslow has also written on post-independence political economy; see, for example, *The fly and the spider's web: Mozambique in the southern African regional subsystem* (Manchester, England: University of Manchester, 1981. 19p. [Manchester Discussion Papers in Development Studies, no. 8103]).

142

356   **Quarterly Economic Review of Tanzania, Mozambique.**
London: Economist Intelligence Unit.   1952–. quarterly.
This is probably one of the most widely available sources of economic information
for businessmen, being part of a series covering most countries of the world. The
Quarterly Economic Review consists of over seventy different country series, and
began publication in 1952. Mozambique is covered in a subseries which also
includes Tanzania. Each issue normally consists of a one-page summary, a section
entitled 'Outlook' dealing with short-term economic prospects in both countries,
and the review itself. This is divided, in a typical issue, into such topics as the
political scene, the economy, agriculture, industry and mining, transport and
communications. The review includes graphs on general trends in, for example,
the cost-of-living index, export performance, and banking activity. Appendixes
may give data on quarterly indicators and foreign trade. Like most publications of
this type, the quality of the information published depends very much on who the
(anonymous) contributors are at any given moment; the *Review* was first, in one
memorable scoop, to publish the statistical data from the Mozambican Comissão
do Plano's *Economic Report* (Maputo: National Planning Commission, Jan. 1984.
62p. appendixes).

357   **A difficult road: the transition to socialism in Mozambique.**
Edited by John Saul.   New York: Monthly Review Press, 1985.
420p.
A difficult road is a difficult book, to assess rather than to read. Arguing that the
process of socialist transformation in Mozambique follows neither a Soviet nor a
Chinese model, Saul and his co-authors posit a 'different' and 'difficult' road. The
book opens with two lengthy, informative and perceptive essays by Saul himself,
on the context and the content of the Mozambican revolution. The 'content' is
defined as a transition to socialism. This is followed by shorter essays by Judith
Marshall on education, Helena Dolny on agriculture, Peter Sketchley on industry,
Barry Pinsky on urbanization, Carol Barker on health and Stephanie Urdang on
women. The book concludes with a piece on post-Nkomati Mozambique, again by
Saul himself. A lengthy review of the book, by the late Aquino de Bragança and
Jacques Depelchin, has been published in Zimbabwe: see 'From the idealization
of Frelimo to the understanding of the recent history of Mozambique', *African
Journal of Political Economy* no. 1 (1986), p. 162–80.

358   **FRELIMO and the Mozambique revolution.**
John Saul.   In: *Essays on the political economy of Africa.*
Giovanni Arrighi, John S. Saul.   New York, London: Monthly
Review Press, 1973; Nairobi: East African Publishing House, 1974.
p. 378–405.
Saul attempts to focus on the 'recent development' of FRELIMO, arguing
forcefully that the leadership crisis after the death of Eduardo Mondlane in 1969
'was a mark of the movement's *growing strength* not of its weakness.' This is to
say that the Front's ability to confront its own internal contradictions and to
resolve them through struggle resulted in the emergence of a coherent and mature
leadership group, who were clear about their political goals and were able to
pursue them in a principled fashion. Saul also addresses himself usefully to the
question of the logic of protracted struggle, and FRELIMO policy in general. The

paper was written in 1970, and Saul revised it in 1972 just after his visit to the liberated areas of Tete Province. His sources, as given, are the familiar ones of the period, but the article is no less well argued for that.

359   **The state and revolution in eastern Africa.**
John S. Saul.   London, Nairobi: Heinemann, 1979. 454p.

John Saul was associated with FRELIMO in Dar es Salaam from the early days, visited the liberated areas during the struggle, was a guest at the independence celebrations, has visited the country a number of times, and worked in the Universidade Eduardo Mondlane's Faculty of Marxism-Leninism and the Party School in 1981–82. This is a book of essays which continues the reflections published by Saul in his joint collection with Giovanni Arrighi under the title *Essays on the political economy of Africa* (q.v.). This volume includes material addressed directly to Mozambican as well as to East African questions. Part One consists of six essays on Portuguese colonialism grouped together under the title 'Mozambique and the struggle for southern Africa', of which two are specifically devoted to Mozambique. They are 'Inside Mozambique' (p. 59–78, first published as 'Portugal and the Mozambican revolution' in *Monthly Review* [Sept. 1974]); and 'Free Mozambique' (p. 79–92, first published in Toronto in *This Magazine* [Nov.–Dec. 1975] and in *Monthly Review* [Dec. 1975]). The second essay is a moving description of the euphoric mood in the country at the time of the independence celebrations. The book also includes a postscript entitled 'Mozambique: the new phase' (p. 429–46, originally from *This Magazine* [March 1979] and *Monthly Review* [March 1979]). Moving back to the social system, of which Saul witnessed the death-throes, there are two fundamental works in Portuguese on the political economy of colonialism. See Eduardo de Sousa Ferreira's *Aspectos do colonialismo português: análise de economia e política sobre as colónias portuguesas, África do Sul e Namíbia* [Aspects of Portuguese colonialism: an analysis of economics and politics in the Portuguese colonies, South Africa and Namibia] with a preface by Basil Davidson (Lisbon: Seara Nova, 1974. 363p. [Colecção de Leste a Oeste, no. 11]); and Armando Castro's *O sistema colonial português em África: meados do século XX* [The Portuguese colonial system in Africa in the mid-20th century] (Lisbon: Ed. Caminho, 1978. 434p. [Temas políticos e sociais]).

360   **Mozambican development: a bibliography covering social science literature with emphasis on the period after 1965.**
Ole Stage, assisted by Ole Norgaard.   Copenhagen: Centre for Development Research, 1982. 68p. (CDR Library Service. Paper C82.11) (Occasional Bibliographies and Guides, no. 5).

An updated and revised (in fact, corrected) edition of Enevoldsen and Johnsen's erratic 1978 compilation (q.v.). It includes 438 numbered references to items in English, Portuguese, French, German and the Scandinavian languages, on contemporary social sciences. As much as possible Stage excludes works on history or on technical aspects of agronomy, although some guidance is given for the interested reader. The work is organized around a series of topics – general works (including statistics, bibliography, and current sources); history; the economy; politics; the social sector (education and health); foreign relations; and religion. Many entries carry brief explanatory annotations, and non-English titles are translated. There is an author index. This is an important and useful select

144

bibliography on social sciences, although it does not entirely replace Enevoldsen and Johnsen, which, despite its manifest defects, continues to give clues to obscure material.

361 Assistance to Mozambique: report of the Secretary-General.
United Nations General Assembly. New York: United Nations, Oct. 1976–June 1980.

In March 1976, less than one year after independence, Mozambique applied sanctions against the illegal Smith régime in Southern Rhodesia, and appealed to the international community for help. By the end of April a UN Mission had prepared and published a proposal for a programme of financial, economic and technical assistance (UN document no. E/5812 and Corr. 1 and Add. 1). Thereafter these regular review reports to the General Assembly's sessions (31st to 35th) were prepared by a series of missions sent to see how things were progressing (document nos A/31/266, Oct. 1976; A/32/96, June 1977; A/32/268, Oct. 1977; A/33/173, July 1978; A/34/377, Aug. 1979; A/35/297, June 1980). They are an excellent and convenient source of general economic and social information for a crucial period in Mozambican history; a typical issue of thirty or so pages will contain sections on, for example, the budget, balance-of-payments, international assistance and natural disasters, including statistical tables.

362 The political economy of east-central Africa.
Leroy Vail. In: *History of Central Africa*. Edited by David Birmingham, Phyllis M. Martin. London, New York: Longman, 1983. vol. 2, p. 200–50.

'One must guard against identifying colonialism, imposed in the 1890s, with the growth of capitalist relations', writes Vail, recounting the 'dolorous tale' of the past century in Mozambique, Malawi and Zambia. This chapter comes from an undergraduate textbook on Central Africa, and presents a summary of present knowledge, without, unfortunately, always making explicit the areas of debate. Beginning with the series of ecological disasters of the late 19th century (rinderpest, and the spread of the jigger flea), Vail moves on to describe the impact of capitalism from the south (the Rand gold fields) and the setting up of the system of labour migration. He deals with each of the three countries in separate sections, focusing in the Mozambique paragraphs on the Niassa and Mozambique companies, and on the characteristics of the Salazar period to 1960.

363 Mozambique: late colonialism and early problems of transition.
David Wield. In: *Revolutionary socialist development in the Third World*. Edited by Gordon White, Robin Murray, Christine White. Brighton, Sussex, England: Wheatsheaf Books, 1983. p. 75–113.

A lengthy exposition, originally prepared in 1979 for a seminar in Brighton, of a series of positions developed at the Centro de Estudos Africanos in the late 1970s. Wield begins with a brisk discussion of the colonial period, arguing that the weakness of Portuguese capital, and its inability to exploit the labour and natural resources of Mozambique effectively, led to the 'leasing out [of] Mozambique to foreign investors', and to the systems of forced labour and compulsory cultivation of cash crops; Wield states that forced labour was 'widespread in Mozambique until the mid-1960s'. He then discusses the formation and development of FRELIMO, adhering closely to an analysis based on the 'struggle between the two lines'. The most interesting part of the article, however, is the twenty-page section based on Wield's own work in Mozambique between 1976 and 1978 – on the crisis of the colonial economy, 1974–76; on the restructuring of the Party and state; and on the struggle to reach former levels of production again, between 1976 and 1981. Wield characterizes these phases as the breakdown of the colonial economy and the early period of reconstruction. The article concludes with a country profile in tabular form, and a chronology of such brevity and generality as to be almost useless.

364 **The political economy of Portuguese colonialism in Mozambique.**
Marc Wuyts.   *Mozambican Studies* [Amsterdam] no. 1 (1980),
p. 10–22.

Wuyts' article is an attempt to periodize the development of colonialism in Mozambique during the phase of imperialism. The periodization is based on the phases of the class struggles within the colony, with respect to the relations between labour and capital and between fractions of capital. The approach is theoretical rather than historical, and the broad periodization arrived at is as follows: 1885–1926, domination of foreign, non-Portuguese capital; 1926–60 economic nationalism; 1960–(1963/64)–1973, the crisis and restructuring of capital. Recent research has tended to move the beginning of the second phase forward, and the beginning of the crisis slightly backward, however.

Constitution and the Legal System

365 **Boletim Oficial** (Government Gazette.)
Lourenço Marques, Mozambique: Imprensa Nacional, 13 May
1854–21 June 1975. Several times per week. Succeeded by: *Boletim
da República*. Lourenço Marques (Maputo): Imprensa Nacional,
25 June 1975–.

First published on Mozambique Island in the middle of the 19th century, this was
the official government gazette as well as the first publication ever to be printed in
the colony. The details of the title and the numbering varied over the years.
During most of this century the 'BO' has appeared in three series: legislation;
appointments and official announcements; and classified announcements, which
could be either official or private. The *Boletim da República* continues with the
same three series.

366 **The Constitution of the People's Republic of Mozambique.**
[Maputo: Instituto Nacional do Livro e do Disco], 1980. 35p.

The Constitution was approved by the FRELIMO Central Committee on 20 June
1975, five days before independence. It has been amended twice, on 13 August
1978, and in July 1986 to incorporate the functions and duties of the system of
People's Assemblies (Parliament and local councils), which operates from local up
to national level, and to define the functions of the Prime Minister. This English
translation, which was issued locally in a tiny print-run of only 500 copies,
includes the amendments. For the text of the original Constitution, and of the
controversial nationality law (which deprives Mozambican women who marry
foreigners after independence of their citizenship), see the pamphlet *Constituição
da República Popular de Moçambique, Lei de Nacionalidade, e Constituição do
primeiro Governo* [Constitution of the People's Republic of Mozambique, the
Nationality Law, and the composition of the First Government] (Lourenço
Marques, Mozambique: Imprensa Nacional, 1975. 5th ed. 62p.), and various
other editions.

367   **Portuguese law and administration in Mozambique and their effect on the customary land laws of three tribes of the Lake Nyasa region.**
Maria Leonor Correia de Matos.   PhD dissertation, University of London, 1969. 373p. bibliog. maps.

This thesis for the School of Oriental and African Studies covers virtually the whole history of the colony. Correia de Matos tries to show, in chapters dealing with Portuguese colonial administration in the *donatórios* (land-holding divisions) or *capitanias* (captaincies) in the late 15th–16th centuries; the *prazo* system in the 17th–18th centuries; and on colonial policy and the land-tenure system in the 19th and 20th centuries, that the statutory land-law in effect in Mozambique in the 1960s had evolved out of Portuguese experience elsewhere. The perpetual leaseholds resemble the former *prazos*, and the *prazos* in turn can be traced back to mediaeval Portugal and even to the classical world; the feudal *donatórios* go back to the 15th century in the Portuguese islands of the Atlantic and later on in Brazil and Angola, and they contributed to the *prazo* system. Nonetheless, the impact of all this on the customary land-law of the 'three tribes' mentioned in the title (the Ngoni-, Chewa- and Yao-speaking peoples) was minimal.

368   **Criminals into 'new men': penal justice in Mozambique.**
Tony Gifford.   *People's Power in Mozambique, Angola and Guinea-Bissau* no. 17 (Spring 1981), p. 37–43.

Lord Tony Gifford supported the struggles in the Portuguese colonies for many years, and founded the Committee for Freedom in Mozambique, Angola and Guinea-Bissau (CFMAG, later MAGIC, and now, as far as Mozambique is concerned, MIO); *People's Power* was the magazine of the support group after independence. In this essentially descriptive article Gifford reports on criminal justice in Mozambique, explaining the present situation in terms of the experience of the armed struggle and the liberated zones. Except for the most serious security-related crimes, the basic principle of that experience was to deal with offenders in terms of re-education, through public meetings, discussion, self-criticism and productive work under popular surveillance. After independence, however, this system had to be adapted to deal with vast new problems – the virtual collapse of the old apparatus, as the settlers fled back to Portugal, cities full of beggars, prostitutes, thieves, drug addicts and drunks. FRELIMO's response was to set up Dynamizing Groups of political militants, who introduced and applied the experience of the liberated zones to the new situation. Re-education Centres were established in remote areas for the more serious offenders. Gifford describes a visit to the former centre at Unango in Niassa, where a new city is to be built. The article also deals with the network of people's tribunals, or local courts, which was established in 1978 to deal with non-custodial offences. Mozambican policy has always been opposed to the idea of prison as simply punishment, 'a factory for the production of criminals'. Gifford's article ends with a survey of the prison system and a description of his visit to Nampula Prisoners' Centre in August 1980.

Constitution and the Legal System

369 **Transforming the foundations of family law in the course of the Mozambican revolution.**
Gita Honwana Welch, Francesca Dagnino, Albie Sachs. *Journal of Southern African Studies* vol. 12, no. 1 (Oct. 1985), p. 60–74.
The authors start off by stating that while some of the values of traditional law have influenced the emerging system of justice in Mozambique, it has not entered formally into the system, which applies uniquely and equally to all citizens. The article poses two questions: first, how is it possible to have a unified system of family law in Mozambique, when family life itself takes on such diverse forms? There are matrilineal systems, the Muslim system, Christian marriage and civil registry marriage. Additionally, new forms of family relationships are beginning to emerge in the communal villages. Second, what is the social and political meaning of traditional law for the Mozambican people? Traditional law survives in three ways: it is integrated into the system of popular justice; it exists at the level of the cultural traditions of the people; and its positive values must be carried over into the new system. The authors write, for instance, that 'The intricate and delicate procedures of *lobolo* [bridewealth], if shorn of their associations with the commercialization of women, continue to dignify the marriage process and to encourage inter-family solidarity.' See also Gita Honwana Welch's Master's thesis on the politics of *lobolo*: 'O lobolo: por uma estratégia adequada' [Bridewealth: towards an adequate strategy] (Licenciatura dissertation, Faculty of Law, Eduardo Mondlane University, 1983. 35p.).

370 **Creating a new legal system.**
Allen Isaacman, Barbara Isaacman. *Africa Report* vol. 26, (Jan.–Feb. 1981), p. 19–22.
The Isaacmans have been writing on various aspects of Mozambican life for over a decade, and have played an important role, especially in their journalistic writings, in bringing the country to the attention of a wider public. Their popular booklets aimed at a wide readership, such as *A luta continua: creating a new society in Mozambique* (Binghamton, New York: Fernand Braudel Center for the Study of Economies, Historical Systems and Civilizations, 1978. 131p.) and the more recent *Mozambique: from colonialism to revolution* (q.v.), have been criticized as scholarship, but have nonetheless played their part in mobilizing support abroad for Mozambique's positions. This piece, contributed to the glossy American magazine *Africa Report* and to which Mrs Isaacman, who is a lawyer, presumably made a major contribution, offers a preliminary assessment of the emerging popular legal system in Mozambique. See also *A socialist legal system in the making: Mozambique before and after independence* (q.v.).

371 **A socialist legal system in the making: Mozambique before and after independence.**
Barbara Isaacman, Allen Isaacman. In: *The politics of informal justice*, vol. 2. Edited by Richard Abel. New York: Academic Press, 1982. p. 281–323.
An attempt to examine 'the development of popular justice and the tensions inherent in institutionalizing and formalizing it on a national scale' during the first five years of independence. The paper begins with an overview of the legal system

149

under colonialism, pointing out that the formal system was transplanted with only minor modifications from Portugal, while at the same time a so-called 'traditional' law system was maintained through the local administrators and the chiefs (*régulos*) who worked with them. The Isaacmans move on to a discussion of FRELIMO's legal practice in the liberated zones in a section subtitled ' . . . the birth of an informal legal system'. Since the colonial system was 'both irrelevant and inoperative' and since the chiefs were trying to reintroduce a form of customary law, FRELIMO had to create a system of popular justice, although this did not have top priority in war conditions. The article discusses the transitional phase from 1974 to 1975, and the role of the Dynamizing Groups in the extension of popular justice all over the country. The final section, on the institutionalization of this experience in a formal system after independence, begins with a discussion of the Constitution (q.v.), and includes material on the controversial Re-education Centres based on visits and interviews; the establishment of new district courts with elected lay judges; and a detailed examination of the draft family law. The Isaacmans conclude that the process of formalizing a popular system of justice involves a complex dialectic between theory and practice.

372 **Justiça Popular** (People's Justice.)
     Maputo: Gabinete de Estudos, Ministério da Justiça, Nov./Dec.
     1980–. 6 issues per year.

Mozambique's only law journal, including some case reports, historical studies, political information, photographs and news items. It is clearly intended for a mass audience. It should be noted that the University Law Faculty has been closed for some years, so that the Ministry was the only body in existence able to publish this serial.

373 **Tribunais populares.** (People's courts.)
     João Filipe Martins, Machatine P. Munguambe. [N.p.]:
     Ministério da Informação, 1976. 17p.

A discussion, within the terms of constitutional law, of the theory of people's courts, citing such examples as the Cuban and Guinea-Bissau practices, as well as the experience of the liberated zones during the armed struggle in Mozambique, Angola and Guinea-Bissau. The authors include a brief discussion of the judgement at Nachingwea (FRELIMO's training-camp in Tanzania) at the end of the war, when such FRELIMO traitors and deserters as Uria Simango, Nkavandame, Paulo Gumane, Joana Simião, Adriano Gwambe and Verónica were presented to a large meeting of combatants. In these cases FRELIMO adopted a policy of clemency.

374 **Principal legislação promulgada pelo Governo [da República**
     Popular de Moçambique] (Main legislation passed by the
     Government of the People's Republic of Mozambique.)
     Lourenço Marques, Mozambique: Imprensa Nacional, 1975–.
     vol. 1–.

The first two volumes of this exceedingly useful and substantial reference series were entitled *Principal legislação promulgada pelo Governo de Transição* (Main

Constitution and the Legal System

legislation passed by the Transitional Government) and covered the period from September 1974 to June 1975, when FRELIMO and the Portuguese held power jointly during the run-up to independence. Each volume is a useful digest of the most important laws and decrees, and they appear 'annually', with substantial delays – in fact the later volumes have not carried a publication date. The laws and resolutions of the Assembleia Popular (People's Assembly, the Mozambican parliament) are included, as are the legislative acts of its Standing Commission, as well as of the Presidency, the Council of Ministers, and minor decrees and proclamations.

375 **Sumários do *Boletim Oficial de Moçambique*, 1ª. série, anos de 1855–1965.** (Contents of the *Official Gazette of Mozambique*, 1st series, for the years 1855–1965.)
José Caramona Ribeiro.   Braga, Portugal: Barbosa e Xavier [n.d.]. 924p.

A comprehensive alphabetical subject index to over a century of colonial legislation; the first series of the gazette was the principal one for laws, decrees and *portarias* (executive orders). Ribeiro gives a descriptive title for each piece of legislation, its number, and the date and pages of the gazette in which it was published. Unfortunately, these essential details are often incorrect or incomplete. On cotton, for instance, see pages 53–56, with references to two related topics. For very similar subject indexes to legislation for the colonial period, see Alberto Cota Mesquita, *Índices alfabético e cronológico da principal legislação publicada nos Boletins Oficiais da Colónia de Moçambique desde 1854 a 1920* [Alphabetical and chronological indexes to the main legislation published in the *Official Gazette of Mozambique* from 1854 to 1920] (Lourenço Marques, Mozambique: Imprensa Nacional, 1941. 663p.) which also includes a year-by-year listing; and Francisco Pinto Ramos, *Resumo sinóptico de legislação da Província de Moçambique* (Synoptic summary of legislation of Mozambique Province), of which the main volume covers 1900–54 (Lourenço Marques, Mozambique: Artes Gráficas, 1955. 611p.); with continuation volumes for 1955–56 (Lisbon: Grafitécnica, 1957. 106p.); 1957–58 (Lisbon: Grafitécnica, 1959. 80p.); 1959–63 (Nampula: Sociedade do Niassa, 1964. 231p.); and 1964–65 (Nampula: Sociedade do Niassa, 1966. 89p.).

376 **Liberating the land – liberating the law.**
Albie Sachs.   In: *Essays on Third World perspectives in jurisprudence*. Edited by M. L. Marasinghe, William E. Conklin. Singapore: Malayan Law Journal, 1984. p. 355–74.

The law abolishing private titles in land was adopted by the People's Assembly (Mozambique's Parliament) at its Fourth Session in 1979, and was published, together with explanatory apparatus, in a widely distributed pamphlet under the title *Lei de terras* (Maputo: Instituto Nacional do Livro e do Disco, 1980. 47p. [Assembleia Popular. 4a. Sessão. Documentos, no. 1]). In Albie Sachs' words 'With one legislative stroke . . . land law passes from private law to public law.' The article argues that the suspicion with which lawyers tend to regard the concept of 'revolutionary legality' is misplaced, and uses the case of the Mozambican land-law to show that, on the contrary, the revolutionary state must use new law to destroy old. A large part of the article consists of a translation of the 'Explanation of the land-law' from the Mozambican pamphlet referred to above. The article has also been published in English as *Mozambique land law: an official document*, translated under the auspices of the Committee on African Studies, Harvard University, with an introduction by Albie Sachs (Cambridge, Massachusetts: The Committee, 1981. 36p.).

377 **Principles of revolutionary justice: the Constitution and other documents on law and state from the People's Republic of Mozambique.**
[Edited by Albie Sachs with the assistance of the Mozambique Information Agency, AIM]. London: Mozambique, Angola and Guiné Information Centre, 1979. 62p. (State Papers and Party Proceedings, series 2 [1979], no. 2).

An anthology of political and legal texts in English translation which remains useful although out of date. The volume includes Samora Machel's Independence Day message; a speech by Justice Minister Rui Baltazar Alves on the colonial judiciary; an article by Sérgio Vieira on law in the liberated zones; an extract from Samora Machel's 'Establishing people's power to serve the masses'; the Constitution; an editorial from *Mozambique Revolution* on nationalization; Óscar Monteiro on the state apparatus; an AIM text on revolutionary justice; Samora Machel again, this time on the prison-system and reform; a FRELIMO circular on crime; the labour law, Decree No. 14/75; an extract from the Central Committee report to the III Congress; Machel's speech to the First Session of the People's Assembly; another AIM article, on the Justice Brigades which set up the court system; and the text of the law on judicial organization.

378 **The two dimensions of socialist legality: recent experience in Mozambique.**
Albie Sachs. *International Journal of the Sociology of Law* vol. 13 (1985), p. 133–46.

Albie Sachs writes, in a characteristic passage in the opening paragraph of this workshop presentation, that 'When things are going well in Mozambique as far as the legal system is concerned, we speak about 'popular justice', and . . . when we have problems, we speak about 'socialist legality'.' The article is a transcription of a more-or-less improvised talk with the title 'Beyond formal justice' given to a workshop held in Antwerp, Belgium, in 1983. Sachs describes the enthusiastic popular reaction to the closure of Eduardo Mondlane University's Law Faculty, and analyses the reasons for it – principally that the legal system, and the legal profession, were completely out of touch with popular feeling and local conditions. He says at the end of the talk that he has 'left out the whole theme of Popular Justice, that's the bright side . . . '. A useful, if impressionistic survey of the role of law in a society attempting to transform itself.

Party and Government Administration

Colonial administration

379 **Alguns aspectos da colonização agrícola de Moçambique.** (Some aspects of the agricultural colonization of Mozambique.)
Francisco Manuel Rui Peres Vaz de Araújo. Dissertation, Curso de Altos Estudos Coloniais, Lisboa, 1953. 127p. bibliog.

Covers colonial agricultural policy, especially the importation of large numbers of Portuguese peasants (*colonos*), in Mozambique. The thesis deals with the objectives of colonization, the emigration of the *colonos* from metropolitan Portugal, and the virtues of 'organized' as opposed to 'native' agriculture. It is virtually all theoretical argument, with no footnotes and little empirical content; it is, therefore, only usable as evidence of the way the Portuguese colonial administrators saw and justified their own role.

380 **Antecedentes históricos da Reforma Administrativa da Província de Moçambique de 1907.** (Historical antecedents of the Administrative Reform in the Province of Mozambique in 1907.)
Francisco Xavier Basílio. Licenciatura dissertation, Instituto Superior de Ciências Sociais e Política Ultramarina, Lisboa, 1965. 359, 168p.

The year 1907 was an eventful one in Portugal. João Franco seized power in a coup d'état, dissolved Parliament and instituted a reactionary dictatorship. The 1907 colonial administrative reform, which was introduced by the Minister for the Colonies and the Navy, Aires de Ornelas, was followed immediately by decrees in 1908, 1911 and 1912, which had the effect of weakening the legislation and increasing local autonomy. Basílio's account begins with a chapter on the influence of António Enes' *Moçambique: relatório apresentado ao Governo* (q.v.), and of the ideas of Mouzinho de Albuquerque on Ornelas; there follow sections

153

Party and Government Administration. Colonial administration

on the National Colonial Congress of 1901, and on Ornelas' career. The third chapter deals with the history of the Reform Act itself, including Manuel António Moreira Júnior's 1904–05 inquiry into colonial administration. The fourth chapter looks at preceding colonial legislation from the Carta Orgânica (Organic Charter) of 1836 onwards. The last 168 pages present the texts of the legislation referred to in the thesis.

381 **Corporatisme et colonialisme: approche du cas mozambicaine, 1933–1979.** (Corporatism and colonialism: the Mozambican case, 1933–1979.)
Michel Cahen. *Cahiers d'Études Africaines* vol. 23, no. 4 (no. 92) (1983), p. 383–417; vol. 24, no. 1 (no. 93) (1984), p. 5–24.

A two-part article abridged from an unpublished text prepared for the Centro de Estudos Africanos in July 1981. The two parts appear under the subtitles 'Une genèse difficile, un mouvement squelettique' (A difficult birth, a skeleton movement) and 'Crise et survivance du corporatisme colonial, 1960–1979' (Crisis and survival of colonial corporatism, 1960–79). The article attempts to analyse the Frelimo Party's characterization of Mozambican society before independence as 'colonial-Fascist'. Cahen poses three questions – what was the impact on Mozambique of Fascism in Portugal? Can one speak of a colonial-Fascist social formation? What was the economic and political impact of colonial-Fascism on the integration of Mozambique into the southern African subsystem? Cahen attempts to use the expression 'Fascism' with some rigour, and examines the way in which the Estado Novo (New State) legislated for the setting up of producers' associations (*grémios*), national trade unions, and state corporations (*juntas*). He characterizes the climate of European opinion in the colony, at least until 1961, as 'relatively liberal', and unsuitable for the growth of a real Fascist Party. In the second part of the article Cahen examines the Labour Code and the effect of the repeal of the Estatuto Indígena (Native Statute) in 1961 on the corporate state. He concludes that 'In the strict sense of the term, there was no colonial Fascism, simply because colonialism did not need a Fascist dictatorship to impose its domination.'

382 **Autoridades tradicionais de Magude, 1895–1975: repertório de documentos.** (Traditional chiefs in Magude, 1895–1975: a guide to the documents.)
José Armando Vidal Capão. Trabalho de diploma for the Licenciatura, Arquivo Histórico de Moçambique, Universidade Eduardo Mondlane, 1985. 134p.

Magude lies on the frontier between Maputo and Gaza provinces, and has belonged to both of them at different periods in its history. This Master's-level thesis is a guide to material from several different collections (*fundos*) in the Historical Archive of Mozambique – of the 19th-century Governo do Distrito de Lourenço Marques (Government of the District of Lourenço Marques); of the Administração da Circunscrição de Magude (the Local Administration of Magude); of Negócios Indígenas (Native Affairs); and of the Direcção dos Serviços de Administração Civil (Directorate of Civil Administrative Services), augmented by a list of relevant legislation. The main list of documents has 301 items; the list of legislation has 109. The principal usefulness of the work, however, lies in the detailed index (p. 59–133) of *régulos* and *indunas* (chiefs), organized by chiefdom (*regedoria*), with references to the documents in the main list, and with dates and biographical information. This last is usually very limited, for example, 'Induna of Chobela, imprisoned in 1929 for beating the chief'.

383 **As reformas de 6 de Setembro de 1961 e a sua incidência político-social em Moçambique.** (The reforms of 6 September 1961 and their political and social effects in Mozambique.)
César Augusto Ferreira de Castro Coelho. Licenciatura dissertation, Instituto Superior de Ciências Sociais e Política Ultramarina, Universidade Técnica de Lisboa, [1964]. 169p. bibliog.

This thesis, written before independence, deals with the impact of the repeal of the Native Statute. It covers settlement policy, migration, urbanization, the importation of *colonatos* as a way of stimulating and strengthening interracial relations, the administration and organization of the *regedorias* [chiefdoms], and the recognition of local customs and their legal force.

384 **Moçambique: relatório apresentado ao Governo.** (Mozambique: report to the Government.)
António Enes. Lisbon: Agência Geral das Colónias, 1946. 3rd ed. 625p.

António Enes (in the older spelling Ennes) was, together with Joaquim Mouzinho de Albuquerque (1855–1902), one of the national heroes of Portuguese colonialism. A former Minister of 'the Navy and Overseas', he was appointed Royal Commissioner for Mozambique, and wrote this report, first published in 1893; a second edition was printed by the Geographical Society of Lisbon in 1913. The report exposed corruption and advocated the appointment of dedicated civil servants to colonial posts, as well as the granting of some local autonomy. The document continued to be quoted for decades. The book includes a series of thirty-six proposals on such topics as the budget, taxes, administration, the police, health, customs and excise, the armed forces, agronomy, judicial reform, tobacco, wine, and so on. The final section consists of a budget proposal and an outline of a budgetary law. See also, in Portuguese, Mapril de Jesus Gouveia's *António Enes e o tratado de 1891–1892* [António Enes and the treaty of 1891–1892] (Lourenço Marques, Mozambique: 'mimeo' 1968. 251p.), first submitted as a licenciatura thesis to the Instituto Superior de Ciências Sociais e Política Ultramarina at the Technical University of Lisbon in 1964 under the title 'António Enes, Comissário Régio para a execução de tratado de 1891–1892' [António Enes, Royal Commissioner for the execution of the treaty of 1891–92, 286p.

385 **Evolução histórico-administrativa do distrito de Moçambique, 1895–1934.** (The historico-administrative evolution of Mozambique district, 1895–1934.)
Dagoberto Garcia. Licenciatura dissertation, Instituto Superior de Ciências Sociais e Política Ultramarina, Universidade Técnica de Lisboa, 1964. 364p. bibliog. maps.

Mozambique district is the present-day Nampula Province. This is a straight-forward colonial historical account, with a general description of the area, an account of its administrative history until 1894, the occupation of the territory after 1895 (the year of Mouzinho's campaigns), and a short history of its administration from 1895 to 1934.

386 **As autoridades tradicionais e a organização das regedorias de 1961: alguns aspectos político-administrativos na Província de Moçambique.** (The traditional authorities and the organization of the chiefdoms in 1961: some politico-administrative aspects of Mozambique.)
Rafael Carcomo de Almeida Rosa Lobo. Licenciatura dissertation, Instituto Superior de Ciências Sociais e Política Ultramarina, Universidade Técnica de Lisboa, 1966. 125p. bibliog. maps.

A not very useful thesis from the Lisbon course for colonial administrators. There are chapters on the 'traditional authorities' as the Portuguese liked to call them, although they were not in fact traditional, nor did they have much authority; on the 'tribe' and the 'chief'; on traditional authorities from the arrival of the Portuguese up to the Conference of Berlin (1884–85); on the period from the end of the 19th century to the legislative reforms of 1926–33; on the 1961 legislation; and on the present organization of the *regedorias* (chiefdoms).

387 **Moçambique, 1896–1898.**
Joaquim Augusto Mouzinho de Albuquerque. Lisbon: Manoel Gomes, 1899. 433p.

Mouzinho (1855–1902) succeeded António Enes as Royal Commissioner in Mozambique in 1896, and joined in his vehement condemnation of the excessive centralization of administrative power in Lisbon. He was also an aggressive champion of Portuguese colonial interests, ruthlessly extending Portuguese control in the south, and personally capturing the Gaza King Ngungunyane, a feat which he boasts of in this book. A white supremacist, he eventually resigned in 1898 in protest over a decree which limited his powers as Commissioner. The ideas of Enes and Mouzinho led eventually to the reform of 1907, which devolved considerable power to the colonies and set up the administrative system which, in essence, was to survive until the end of the colonial period. An equestrian statue of Mouzinho dominated the main square of Lourenço Marques, and was one of the first symbols of Portuguese rule to be pulled down after independence. This book was reprinted by the Ministry of Colonies and the Geographical Society of Lisbon in 1913 (415p.), and again in 1934 in vol. II of *Mousinho de Albuquerque* (Lisbon: Agência Geral das Colónias, 1934).

Party and Government Administration. Colonial administration

388   **The Nyassa Chartered Company, 1891–1929.**
Barry Neil-Tomlinson.   *Journal of African History* vol. 18, no. 1
(1977), p. 109–28.
In this interesting article, Neil-Tomlinson puts forward a periodization of the
Niassa Company into three main phases. During the first of these, from 1894 to
1898, the directors were mainly interested in speculation, and despite the formal
requirement that the company should develop Niassa, its real influence was
limited to a few coastal enclaves. The second phase lasted from 1899 to 1914, and
it was at this time that the company became a force of occupation; by 1909 the
main economic activity was the supply of migrant labour. In the final period, after
the First World War, from 1919 to the end of the charter in 1929, the Company
had lost interest in investment from which it could expect no return, and
concentrated on increasing revenue through the collection of hut-tax.

389   **Aspectos da divisão e ocupação administrativa em Moçambique a
norte de Zambeze (1885–1910).** (Aspects of administrative division
and occupation in Mozambique north of the Zambezi, 1885–1910.)
Euclides Mendes Pinhal.   Licenciatura dissertation, Instituto
Superior de Ciências Sociais e Política Ultramarina, Universidade
Técnica de Lisboa, 1971. 242p. bibliog. maps.
This thesis, together with that by Francisco dos Reis Ribeiro (q.v.), deals with the
evolution of Portuguese administration in the colony of Mozambique in the late
19th century; Pinhal covers the north, Ribeiro the south. The topics covered
include frontier delimitation, the *prazos*, the concessionary companies, and the
administrative division of the area (the creation of the districts, or present-day
provinces). As is common in Portuguese academic work of this period, the last
section of the work (p. 199–226) consists of transcribed documents.

390   **Alguns aspectos da ocupação e divisão administrativa de
Moçambique a sul do Zambeze (1885–1910).** (Some aspects of the
occupation and administrative division of Mozambique south of the
Zambezi, 1885–1910.)
Francisco dos Reis Ribeiro.   Licenciatura dissertation, Instituto
Superior de Ciências Sociais e Política Ultramarina, Universidade
Técnica de Lisboa, 1972. 203p. bibliog.
Studies the administrative history of the southern half of Mozambique (for the
north, see the similarly titled work by Euclides Mendes Pinhal). The topics
covered include the historical antecedents to the effective occupation and
administrative reorganization of Mozambique; the territorial definition of
Mozambique south of the Zambezi (including the so-called 'pacification'
campaigns, and frontier negotiatons with neighbouring powers); the *prazos*; the
concessionary companies; and the evolution of the administrative divisions from
the chaotic situation of 1885, including the measures laid down by Mouzinho
de Albuquerque.

391   **Rural development schemes in southern Mozambique.**
      J. L. Ribeiro-Torres.   *South African Journal of African Affairs*
      vol. 3, no. 2 (1973), p. 60–69.

Ribeiro-Torres studied various settlement and community development schemes in the Sul do Save region from 1964 to 1973. He states from the outset that he does not want to defend the Portuguese from their critics, but simply to correct the inaccuracies of other writers. He discusses schemes for the establishment of white Portuguese peasants on smallholdings; mixed-scale schemes for whites and Africans; and land consolidation and villagization schemes for African peasants. He describes in detail the administrative structures (*missões*, *juntas*, *brigadas*, etc.) for all these plans. He is cautious about evaluating the success of Portuguese colonial policy, and claims that it is necessary 'to eschew the use of coercive measures of any kind' in implementing these schemes.

392   **Some settlement schemes in the Gaza district of southern**
      Mozambique.
      J. L. [Ribeiro-] Torres.   *South African Journal of Economics*
      vol. 35, no. 3 (1967), p. 244–55.

An early account by Ribeiro-Torres of the *colonato* (settlement scheme for Portuguese peasant farmers) Limpopo, which he calls 'the Guijá Scheme', and of a similar settlement scheme at Inhamissa, further down the river. He is favourably inclined towards Portuguese settlement policy, although he does make some criticisms of details of its implementation. Several theses have been written on the subject of Portuguese colonial policy and its historical, economic and political development. See, for example, Anselmo Alves' 'Política colonial: alguns aspectos políticos de Moçambique' [Colonial policy: some political aspects of Mozambique] (Dissertation, Curso de Altos Estudos Coloniais, Lisbon, 1951); R. S. de M. Fernandes' 'Portugal and its overseas territories: economic structure and policies' (PhD dissertation, Harvard University (Cambridge, Massachusetts), 1960); António Marques' 'Dimensão ultramarino: análise de alguns aspectos de problematicá moçambicana' [The overseas dimension: an analysis of some aspects of the Mozambican problem] (Licenciatura dissertation, Instituto Superior de Ciências Sociais e Política Ultramarina, Universidade Técnica de Lisboa, 1962); Rui E. B. Lacerda's 'Subsídios para o estudo da política ultramarina em Moçambique, 1820–1851' [Elements for the study of overseas policy in Mozambique, 1820–51] (Licenciatura dissertation, Instituto Superior de Ciências Sociais e Política Ultramarina, Universidade Técnica de Lisboa, 1968); Fernando Amaro Monteiro's 'Contribution à l'étude de la colonisation portugaise au Mozambique', [Contribution to the study of Portuguese colonization in Mozambique] (Doctorat de l'université, University of Aix-Marseille (Marseille, France), 1968. 313p. map).

393   **Colonato do Limpopo: aspectos sociais do povoamento.** (The
      colonato of the Limpopo: social aspects of the settlement.)
      Manuel dos Santos Lopes.   Licenciatura dissertation, Instituto
      Superior de Ciências Sociais e Política Ultramarina, Universidade
      Técnica de Lisboa, 1968. 538p. bibliog. map.

Santos Lopes worked in Mozambique in the colonial civil service, in a sector dealing with Portuguese immigration to the *colonato*. His thesis is devoted to a detailed account of the selection and recruitment of settlers in Portugal, their rights and duties, state assistance, the 'farming couple', reasons for breaking contract, socio-cultural integration, organization of space, transport and communications, water and energy, banking and credit, industry and commerce, education, religion and health. There are photographs and forty-nine statistical tables.

394 **Mozambique's chartered companies: the rule of the feeble.**
Leroy Vail. *Journal of African History* vol. 17 no. 3 (1976), p. 389–416.

At the end of the 19th century Portugal was facing a financial crisis and was also under pressure from other imperialist powers in Africa who were anxious to make a claim on her colonies. In the 1890s the Portuguese government began an experiment of governing large stretches of territory cheaply through the two chartered companies, the Companhia do Nyassa and the Companhia de Moçambique. On two counts, writes Leroy Vail, the results were disastrous. First, instead of pouring in investment capital the companies devoted all their energy to the maximization of profits through the exploitation of cheap African labour. Second, since shares were for sale to individuals, both Britain and Germany used proxies to further their own interests, through the companies, at Portugal's expense. In the late 1920s Portugal's Premier António Salazar finally put an end to the anachronistic experiment.

The Frelimo Party

395 **O Marxismo de Samora.** (Samora's Marxism.)
Aquino de Bragança. *Três Continentes* [Lisbon] no. 3 (Sept. 1980), p. 43–50.

In this paper, prepared for a sociology conference in Uppsala, Sweden, the late Director of the Centre of African Studies in Maputo traces the development of Marxist practice in FRELIMO, arguing that before independence the Front was 'essentially a peasant movement led by a Marxist-inclined group', although Eduardo Mondlane himself had suggested turning it into a Party before his death in 1969. Bragança concludes by quoting the FRELIMO catch-phrase 'The society which we built in the liberated zones remains our only model, our scientific laboratory.' The piece was first published in French as 'Le Marxisme de Samora', *Afrique-Asie* no. 217 (7–20 July 1980).

396 **Published documentation of the Party Frelimo: a preliminary study.**
Colin Darch. *Mozambican Studies* no. 2 (1981), p. 104–25.

A preliminary survey on sources about FRELIMO and the Frelimo Party. The piece is divided into sections on bibliographical sources and collections of documents; texts of the Central Committee and the Congress; writings of Eduardo Mondlane and Samora Machel; texts of other leaders and structures; and Frelimo serials. There is a 33-item bibliography, and two tables, on important

Party and Government Administration. The Frelimo Party

meetings from 1962 to 1980 and on the publishing history of the two serials *Mozambique Revolution* (q.v.) and *Voz da Revolução* (q.v.), listing all the issues published.

397 **Documentos base da FRELIMO, 1.** (Basic documents of FRELIMO, 1.)
Maputo: Tempográfica, 1977. 211p.

Distributed to delegates and others at the III Congress of Frelimo in February 1977, this is an excellent collection of texts from various conferences, congresses, central committee meetings, and so on. Some copies have made their way on to the Africana book market in Portugal and the United States, so it is worth citing here. Unfortunately there is no introduction, index, or apparatus. A typed English translation of the same texts was circulated to English-speaking invited guests at the congress, but that is a much rarer bibliographical item.

398 **Frelimo III Congress, Maputo, 3–7 February 1977.**
People's Power in Mozambique, Angola and Guinea-Bissau no. 7/8 (June 1977), p. 16–29.

The III Congress, attended by 379 Mozambican delegates and 39 foreign delegations, changed FRELIMO the liberation front into Frelimo the Marxist-Leninist vanguard party, at least in formal terms (the restructuring of the Party did not begin until 1978). The Congress adopted several documents, including economic and social directives for the next five years. A summary translation of the directives is printed here (p. 18–29), with a brief introduction. The translation is sometimes careless (for example, 'commercialized' for 'marketed'). The document covers agriculture, livestock, forestry, renewable natural resources, industry, fishing, tourism, internal and external trade, transport and communications, energy, public works and building, finances, banking, insurance, the state apparatus, and health and housing. The III Congress also heard the important report of the Central Committee, the first chapter of which remains an important source for Frelimo's view of its own history. For an accessible English version of this view, see the study aid prepared in 1978 by the Frelimo Party's Department of Ideological Work, and subsequently translated as *A history of FRELIMO* (Salisbury: Longman Zimbabwe, 1982. 27p.).

399 **Samora Machel, an African revolutionary: selected speeches and writings.**
Edited by Barry Munslow, translated by Michael Wolfers.
London: Zed Books, 1985. 210p.

The most up-to-date collection in English of Samora Machel's speeches, mainly from the post-independence period, carefully translated by Michael Wolfers. Machel's sense of history, and his ability to articulate popular criticism of the negative aspects of government policy comes through strongly in these texts. The first section of the book deals with general problems of the Party and the state; the second with national reconstruction, production and economic development, health and education, women and youth. There is a biographical introduction by Barry Munslow, a bibliographical note on Samora's writings by Colin Darch, and a useful index. President Samora Moisés Machel died in suspicious circumstances on 19 October 1986, along with thirty-three members of his delegation returning

160

from a summit meeting in Zambia, when the presidential aircraft crashed into a hillside in South Africa, near the border with Mozambique. *Mozambique and South Africa: death of a president* by Rob Davies (*Work in Progress* no. 45 (Nov.-Dec. 1986), p. 3–9) was one of the first assessments of what the death of President Samora Machel might mean both to Mozambique itself, and to the relations between Mozambique and the rest of the region, especially South Africa. Other assessments of Machel's life are now beginning to appear; one of these is Iain Christie's portrait of Samora, provisionally entitled *Machel of Mozambique*, and due to be published in Harare by the Zimbabwe Publishing House late in 1987. *Samora: why he died* (Mozambique News Agency. Maputo: AIM – Mozambique News Agency, 1986. 95p.) is 'not a considered reflection on the death of President Samora' but is a compilation from the daily telex service of the Mozambique News Agency and includes several moving photographs.

400   **FRELIMO and socialism in Mozambique.**
Azinna Nwafor.   *Contemporary Marxism* no. 7 (Fall 1983), p. 28–68.

A longer version of this wide-ranging article appeared in the Fall 1982 issue of *Omenana*. Nwafor is enthusiastically pro-FRELIMO, but he is not a hagiographer. He discusses the transformation to a vanguard party, the worker-peasant alliance, ideological unity forged in the armed struggle, women, democratic centralism and the People's Assembly, the colonial heritage, relations with South Africa, and internationalism in Frelimo's practice. He devotes some space to the question of the role of culture, quoting several poems in translation.

401   **Building socialism: the people's answer.**
Partido Frelimo.   Maputo: Frelimo Party, 1983. 63p. (Fourth Congress series, no. 3).

This booklet contains three Congress reports: on the preparations for the Congress; from the Credentials Commission (responsible for the delegates); and from the Economic and Social Directives Commission. For the run-up to the IV Congress, see the pamphlets *Documento final da Conferência Nacional do Partido* [Final document of the National Party Conference] (Maputo, May 1982. 32p.) on the decision to hold the Congress in 1983; and *Projecto das teses para o 4° Congresso do Partido Frelimo* [Proposed theses for the IV Congress of the Frelimo Party] (Maputo, Oct. 1982. 42p.), both issued in Portuguese only, as part of the Colecção '4° Congresso'.

402   **Directivas económicas e sociais.** (Economic and social directives.)
Partido Frelimo.   Maputo: Partido Frelimo, 1983. 79p. (Colecção '4° Congresso').

The economic and social directives were the subject of considerable debate at the IV Congress; they are the basic policy guidelines for Mozambique for the periods between congresses. The 'small projects' approach to development questions was eventually adopted for the period 1983–85 which is covered by this document. There is no English edition, presumably because the directives were published later than the other Congress documents.

403 **Frelimo Party programme and statutes.**
Partido Frelimo. Maputo: Frelimo Party, 1983. 54p. (Fourth
Congress series, no. 2).

Two basic documents of Frelimo, in their latest revised form. The programme is
the fundamental political statement of the Party, to which all members must
adhere. The statutes are the rules and regulations of Party conduct.

404 **Intervenções dos delegados [ao 4⁰ Congresso].** (Speeches of the
delegates to the IV Congress.)
Partido Frelimo. Maputo: Partido Frelimo, 1985. 262p.

The IV Congress of the Frelimo Party in 1983 was characterized by the openness
of the discussion of the problems facing the country. Delegates from the
countryside, speaking unsophisticated Portuguese, criticized the Government and
its policies, and even claimed that there were *infiltrados* (or moles) inside the top
echelons of the Party. This collection of speeches is a mixture of formal tributes
and frank attacks on past errors, from top leaders and from workers and peasants.
Interestingly, when the new (and greatly enlarged) Central Committee was
elected at the end of the Congress, it included virtually all of the critics, and
workers and peasants made up a majority of the 130-person membership. See
especially such speeches as that by Zeca Lampião. (Speeches from the earlier
III Congress in 1977 were only ever published in the Mozambican newspaper
Notícias.)

405 **Out of underdevelopment to socialism: report of the Central
Committee.**
Partido Frelimo. Maputo: Frelimo Party, 1983. 166p. (Fourth
Congress series, no. 1).

The Central Committee's report to the Congress is its last formal act, and is the
principal retrospective analysis of the economic, social and political progress of
the country between congresses. It is thus a document of considerable authority.
This 1983 report was delivered as Mozambique entered a period of grave crisis,
and after several national campaigns around issues such as 'legality' and
'organization and politics' had been waged. The report deals with the colonial
situation; the main problems of economic and social development; the main lines
of development; the class struggle in Mozambique; the role of Frelimo; the tasks
of the state; defence; popular participation; and foreign policy.

406 **Voz da Revolução.** (Voice of the Revolution.)
Dar es Salaam: Frente de Libertação de Moçambique; Maputo:
Comité Central do Partido Frelimo, June 1965–. irregular.

This is an historical and political source of·considerable importance. It is the
principal FRELIMO journal in Portuguese, and replaced the earlier and less-
memorably titled *Boletim Nacional* and *Boletim de Informação*. It was issued in
three series. The first was mimeographed and ran for about five years, including
several unnumbered issues: like all liberation movement serials, it is a
bibliographer's nightmare. The second, printed series comprised twenty-two
numbered issues and three specials. In May 1978, after independence, *Voz da
Revolução* was revived, beginning for some reason with issue no. 57. For more

details, see Darch, 'Published documentation of the Party Frelimo' (q.v.), and António Sopa's catalogue of periodicals (q.v.).

The People's Republic

407 **Mozambique: the post-colonial state and the consolidation of people's power.**
Gary Baker. *The Pan-Africanist* (Evanston, Illinois) no. 9 (Jan. 1982), p. 58–66.

There is a fairly substantial body of literature on Mozambique which the Mozambicans themselves describe as 'triumphalist'; that is, which adopts an uncritically supportive position towards the country, often rooted in a very superficial knowledge of Mozambican reality. The absence of Portuguese-language references in the text is often, though not always, a danger sign. Entirely based on American academic and newspaper sources, this piece argues that, after five years of independence, 'Mozambique's struggle represents a real possibility for breaking the historical pattern of capitalist dependency for states in Africa'. Baker characterizes the Portuguese régime as 'colonial-capitalist', and follows Houser and Shore (q.v.) in arguing that culture, rather than colour, was the determining factor in Portuguese racism. He goes on to describe the role of the Dynamizing Groups in political activity after independence, and of the communal villages in the rural economy. The article's principal weakness lies in Baker's uncritical acceptance of policy statements as representing an accurate description of reality; hence he comments, after quoting the President's opening speech at the first session of the People's Assembly, that the formation of the Assembly *'represented a decisive stage* in the consolidation of class power in the state' (my italics). The history of the People's Assembly since then scarcely bears this out.

408 **Mozambique: the politics of liberation.**
Tony Hodges. In: *Southern Africa: the continuing crisis.* Edited by Gwendolen M. Carter, Patrick M. O'Meara. London: Macmillan, 1979. p. 57–92. (Contemporary African Issues series).

Hodges is an economic journalist known mainly for his writings about the struggle of the POLISARIO Front of Western Sahara against the Moroccan occupation, and he has also written on Angola. In this article he attempts to present an overview of the Mozambican political and economic situation at the end of the 1970s, in the context of the history of the liberation war and the period of transition. No specific references are given, and Hodges appears to have used some disinformation stories from very doubtful sources; for example, he takes seriously some stories about the entirely spurious 'Cabo Delgado Front', allegedly set up by Lazaro Nkavandame in early 1976 (when Nkavandame was, in fact, still in detention). There are sections on colonial oppression, FRELIMO reforms, nationalization and labour policy, the one-party state, opposition to FRELIMO, non-alignment, Mozambique and the regional crisis, relations with South Africa and with Rhodesia, and on the country's economic crisis.

163

409 **Consolidating people's power in Mozambique.**
Samora Machel. *The African Communist* no. 72 (First quarter,
1978), p. 32–49.

This is Machel's speech to the first session of the People's Assembly, which at that
time consisted of appointees. The President describes the significance of the
forthcoming elections, the first general elections ever to have been held in the
country, and goes on to discuss class and state power. He also covers the nature
of class dictatorship, proletarian internationalism (especially in the region) and
democratic centralism.

410 **The People's Republic of Mozambique: the struggle continues.**
Samora Machel. *Review of African Political Economy* no. 4
(Nov. 1975), p. 14–25.

The text of the speech delivered by Samora Machel, as President of the People's
Republic, on Independence Day, 25 June 1975, in Lourenço Marques, as it still
was then (now Maputo). The translation is the official Ministry of Information
version. The President gives a concise summary of the colonial heritage, the
armed struggle and the tasks ahead.

411 **Structures of power in Mozambique.**
People's Power in Mozambique, Angola and Guinea-Bissau no. 11
(1978), p. 22–28.

The first of a two-part series on the results of the first general elections held
between September and December 1977. These resulted in the election of 894
local assemblies, 112 district assemblies, 10 assemblies at city and provincial level,
and a National Assembly (in Portuguese the National Assembly is known as the
Assembleia Popular; other levels are termed Assembleias do Povo). Elections
were by direct suffrage only at locality level; above that, the assemblies
themselves elected the members of the next level up, from a list approved by the
Party. The article reproduces without analysis official data and definitions of tasks
and principles. A table on the composition of the assemblies, for instance,
suggests that 'significant numbers of women [were] elected at every level', but
closer examination reveals that the *proportion* of women deputies falls as one
moves up the system. Thus, at locality level roughly one deputy in four is a
woman (28.30 per cent); in the Assembleia Popular only one in eight is female
(12.39 per cent). The National Assembly has held fifteen sessions altogether,
although the first session was made up of appointed deputies. New elections were
held in late 1986, but were suspended briefly after the death of President Samora
Machel. The first session of the second legislature in early 1987 introduced
sweeping reforms in the Economic Recovery Programme: see *Notícias* (31 January
1987, supplement. 8p.) and in English, 'The Economic Recovery Programme',
Mozambique News (formerly *AIM Information Bulletin*) no. 127 (1987),
supplement. p. 1–11.

Foreign and Economic Relations

General

412 **African international relations: an annotated bibliography.**
Mark W. DeLancey. Boulder, Colorado: Westview, 1981. 365p.
An extensive 2,840-item bibliography, with very short annotations, organized around eleven non-geographical subject categories. It includes forty-four references specifically about Mozambique, but much more relevant material about the region as a whole. There is a subject index. DeLancey references Robert d'A. Henderson's 'Principles and practice in Mozambique's foreign policy' (q.v.); and William Minter's 'Major themes in Mozambican foreign policy' (q.v.).

413 **Principles and practice in Mozambique's foreign policy.**
Robert d'A. Henderson. *World Today* vol. 34, no. 7 (July 1978), p. 276–86.
A general assessment of Mozambican foreign policy after three years of independence. Henderson characterizes that policy as being both idealistic and cautious (he also uses 'pragmatic' as a code-word, in journalistic style, to mean friendly, or not overtly hostile, to the West). He also refers to the Mozambican Constitution, which defines the objectives of foreign policy as the consolidation of national independence, internationalism and the setting-up of a strong economic grouping in the region.

414 **Mozambique's widening foreign policy.**
Norman MacQueen. *World Today* vol. 40, no. 1 (Jan. 1984), p. 22–28.
MacQueen writes that the present epoch is one in which Western (and especially US) foreign policy towards the developing world is dictated principally by an

Foreign and Economic Relations. General

elementary and reductionist kind of anti-communism. He attempts to explain how Mozambique, which was originally 'a neo-conservative *bête rouge* of the deepest hue', has been able to approach the West, establishing reasonably friendly relations not only with Scandinavian countries, but also with France, Britain and even the US itself. The reasons, says MacQueen, are various.

415 **Major themes in Mozambican foreign relations, 1975–1977.**
William Minter. *Issue* vol. 8, no. 1 (Spring 1978), p. 43–49.

A cool and intelligent look at Mozambique's foreign policy in the first two years of independence. Minter studiously avoids characterizing Mozambican policy in 'the image [of] . . . a ricocheting course from one external sponsor to another . . .' which seems to be typical of much Western academic analysis. Instead, he looks to FRELIMO itself and its stated goals and objectives, for an explanation of the positions adopted, not reading imaginary 'pro-Soviet' or 'pro-Chinese' shifts into routine relations. This number of *Issue* is devoted entirely to Mozambican topics. Minter has recently published a major (although clumsily titled) study of Western policy in the whole region, from a committed historical perspective, which has had a mixed reception but which certainly deserves careful reading: see *King Solomon's Mines revisited: Western interests and the burdened history of southern Africa* (New York: Basic Books, 1986. 401p. bibliog.)

416 **FRELIMO's foreign policy and the process of liberation.**
Whitney J. Schneidman. *Africa Today* vol. 25, no. 1 (Jan.–March 1978), p. 57–67.

A much-condensed version of Schneidman's Master's thesis in political science, submitted to the University of Dar es Salaam in 1977. Based on rather thin documentary sources, all in English and few of them from Mozambique, the article is mainly concerned with FRELIMO's correct identification of the importance of the diplomatic arena for the liberation struggle: as Schneidman puts it, 'Winning diplomatic support at the United Nations was as important to FRELIMO as acquiring supplies for the liberated areas and arms for the guerrillas.' The international isolation of Portugal and the neutralization of its propaganda were also major goals. The article is mainly useful for its descriptive overview of FRELIMO's foreign policy as a liberation movement, before coming to power in Mozambique, but it provides very little analysis. Two doctoral dissertations on US policy towards the Portuguese colonies in general were written at the time of independence. See M. Dexheimer's 'American policy towards Portuguese Africa' (PhD dissertation, Boston University, Massachusetts, 1974. 359p.); and A. R. Raposa's 'American foreign policy and the Portuguese territories' (PhD dissertation, University of Massachusetts, 1975. 331p.).

417 **Die mozambiquanische Aussenpolitik, 1975–1982: Merkmale, Probleme, Dynamik.** (Mozambican foreign policy, 1975–82: characteristics, problems, dynamics.)
Bernhard Weimer. Baden-Baden, FRG: Nomos Verlagsgesellschaft, 1983. 213p. bibliog. map. (Aktuelle Materialen zur Internationalen Politik, no. 2).

The only full-length study on Mozambican foreign policy since independence, by a moderate West German academic associated with the Foundation for Science and Politics, a security-related government institute. The book covers the bases for Mozambican foreign policy; the role of political ideology; administration and development objectives; commercial policy; relations with Western governments (the US, Portugal and South Africa); with socialist governments (especially the Soviet Union and the German Democratic Republic); and with neighbouring independent states (Tanzania, Zimbabwe and Zambia). The concluding chapter evaluates the Mozambique policy of the West German government.

With the West

418   **Le Portugal et l'Afrique: le cas des relations luso-mozambicaines (1965–1985): étude politique et bibliographique.** (Portugal and Africa: the case of Luso-Mozambican relations 1965–85. A political and bibliographical study.)
Michel Cahen. *Afrique Contemporaine* no. 137 (Jan.–March 1986), p. 3–55.

Cahen's informative article also includes 19 statistical tables and 108 bibliographical references, many of them with brief annotations. More than a study in international relations, Cahen's piece moves rapidly through the history of the process of decolonization, touching on the realities of economic relations between Portugal and its colonies, and the shock to the colonists when they realized that the Portuguese army could not defend them (in January 1974, after FRELIMO attacks in Manica, settlers demonstrated in Chimoio and Beira *against* their own military). After independence, the first five years of Mozambican-Portuguese relations were characterized by provocations (the attempt to arrest Sérgio Vieira for desertion from the army in the 1960s), and dogmatism (Portuguese claims for compensation for the *retornados* (Portuguese settlers who fled back to Portugal upon independence)). In January 1980, however, the Sá Carneiro government abandoned claims for compensation, and there began a phase of what Cahen calls 'right-wing Third-Worldism'. By September the first Mozambican minister had visited Portugal, by October an accord had been signed. This policy of *rapprochement* continued until the election of Mario Soares' centre-left coalition in 1983, which was followed by a visit to Lisbon by President Machel and the signing of a Treaty of Friendship and Co-operation, and accords on economics, finance and industry. Between 1981 and 1984 trade increased sharply, but only with what were, in effect, Portuguese state subsidies. It became clear, however, by 1983, that Mozambique was in serious difficulties, and the early growth dropped away. Cahen discusses Lisbon's pretentions to the role of intermediary between Maputo and Washington, Pretoria, and the EEC, as well as the government's consideration of the question of military co-operation between Portugal and its former colony. He concludes that the structural difficulties for economic co-operation are enormous, but cultural links will continue. He criticizes the French government for abandoning the area to the South Africans, instead of supporting Portuguese policy, and suggests an opening for French intervention in higher education. Why not, Cahen asks, a French-Portuguese *lycée* in Maputo?

167

419 **American policy options.**
Michael Clough. *Africa Report* vol. 27, no. 6 (Nov.–Dec. 1982),
p. 14–17.
Despite the general title, this article is about US policy towards Mozambique.
Much analysis of international and regional relations in southern African is based
on the idea that a superpower conflict between the US and the USSR for
influence in the subcontinent is the main motive for almost everything that
happens. In essence, Clough argues here that the increased activity of the armed
bandits inside Mozambique since 1980, undertaken at South African instigation,
may well force the United States to take a position on relations with
Mozambique. If the US administration continues with present policy, says
Clough, then there is a risk that Mozambique, and other countries in the region,
will turn more and more to the Soviet Union for support.

420 **United States policy towards Mozambique since 1945: 'the defense
of colonialism and regional stability.'**
Allen Isaacman, Jennifer Davis. *Africa Today* vol. 25, no. 1
(Jan.–March 1978), p. 29–55.
This carefully documented article is divided into sections on US policy towards
Mozambique both before and after the Portuguese coup in 1974. Policy before
1974 was based on the strategic importance of the US bases in the Azores,
Salazar's militant anti-communism, and a willingness to accept the claims of
'lusotropicalism'. The United States consistently voted in support of Portugal in
the United Nations, maintained close relations with the Portuguese government
through official visits at the highest levels, supplied weapons, training and aircraft
to the Portuguese armed forces either directly or through funding agreements,
and rebuffed attempts by FRELIMO to obtain support for the liberation struggle.
Immediately after the coup in Lisbon, the United States hesitated to open direct
lines of communication with FRELIMO, and only did so when it was clear that
FRELIMO would take power in Mozambique. After independence, Mozambique
was portrayed in an orchestrated campaign in Congress and in the American press
as a Soviet pawn, and as the aggressor in the war for Zimbabwean independence.
Isaacman and Davis conclude that 'Little in United States policy towards
Mozambique appears to be . . . produced in response to peculiarly Mozambican
conditions.' Rather, it is defined in terms of US economic interests in the region
as a whole; of US desire to maintain stability, that is, to keep reactionary régimes
in power; of the need to stay on good terms with Portugal because of the Azores
bases; and of the perception of South Africa as the key regional power, which
must be supported at all costs. As long as Washington analyses regional politics in
global terms, conclude the authors, there is little prospect for real improvements
in US-Mozambican relations.

421 **European powers and south-east Africa: a study of international
relations on the south-east coast of Africa, 1796–1856.**
Mabel V. Jackson Haight. London: Routledge & Kegan Paul,
1967. rev. ed. 368p. bibliog. maps.
Submitted to the University of London in 1938 as a doctoral dissertation (under
the author's maiden name of Jackson), with the title 'International relations on

the south-east coast of Africa, 1796–1856', the first edition of this study was published in 1942 as no. 18 of the Royal Empire Society's Imperial Studies Series by Longmans Green. The study is a conventional Eurocentric one within an international relations *problématique*, in which Mozambique is seen as an arena for the resolution of various types of conflict between the Western powers – in this case France and Britain, with Portugal trailing in third place. Mrs Jackson Haight recognizes this in her preface to the new edition, where she writes that 'Since it was first published the history of international relations has ceased to be an account of the exploits and actions of European powers.' She discusses the state of the Portuguese possessions, French interests in the region, the voyage of Captain W. F. W. Owen and its repercussions, and the significance of the Great Trek for Mozambique.

422 **Broken promises?**
Sam Levy. *Africa Report* vol. 31, no. 1 (Jan.–Feb. 1986),
p. 77–80.
Levy is an American freelance journalist of right-wing views who spent six months in Mozambique on a scholarship from the Institute of Current World Affairs, and as a correspondent for the *Christian Science Monitor*. He also wrote a series of newsletters for the Institute, which appear to have been intended for limited distribution, and which were more openly hostile to Frelimo than this piece on US-Mozambique relations. Even here, however, the technique is one of unverifiable assertion – 'the Soviets are *generally* dismissed as surly racists who 'only send us arms'' (my italics). Later we meet 'some Mozambicans' predicting that Soviet technicians will be expelled, and 'average Mozambicans' who are grateful for US aid. Levy thinks that Mozambique has followed 'Soviet agricultural models' with 'disastrous results'; he also labels criticism of US policy as 'hostile political rhetoric'. He concludes wistfully that although the State Department has never recognized MNR's legitimacy, most analysts 'recognize that the war can only be ended by some form of mutual political accommodation' – a recognition which would, in fact, imply legitimacy.

423 **Portugal and Africa: the politics of re-engagement.**
Norman MacQueen. *Journal of Modern African Studies* vol. 23,
no. 1 (March 1985), p. 31–51.
MacQueen looks at Portuguese relations with the former African colonies, which he describes as having been occasionally suspicious and even acrimonious, but with a general and accelerating tendency towards *rapprochement*. He first of all examines the role of the Portuguese Armed Forces Movement (MFA) in the decolonization process, pointing out that the radical soldiers operated outside the political parties and maintained a high level of public credibility which enabled them to oversee the rapid process. He then discusses relations with the different Portuguese-speaking countries. The Mozambican nationalizations of July 1975, February 1976 and January 1978 affected relations with Portugal badly, and by early 1979 they were at their lowest point. However, with the fall of Carlos Mota Pinto from government things began to improve, and visits by Joaquim Chissano and Samora Machel on one side and Ramalho Eanes on the other, marked the beginning of a new period. However, the 'Portuguese connection' with armed banditry remains a problem.

424 **Portugal and Africa, the politics of indifference: a case study in American foreign policy.**
John A. Marcum. Syracuse, New York: Program of Eastern African Studies, Maxwell School of Citizenship and Public Affairs, Syracuse University, 1972. 41p. (Eastern African Studies, no. 5).

Throughout the period of the struggles for independence in Portugal's African colonies, the United States kept its distance from the liberation movements. Preoccupied above all with access to the bases in the Portuguese Azores, US policy-makers supported Portugal and to a very large extent enabled the colonial power to keep going, prolonging the wars in Mozambique, Angola and Guinea-Bissau. In the 1972 Eduardo Mondlane Memorial Lecture, John Marcum, known mainly for his massive two-volume history of the Angolan revolution, covers this ground efficiently; the last ten pages of this publication consist of the question-and-answer session which followed the lecture.

425 **Portuguese Africa and the West.**
William Minter. Harmondsworth: Penguin, 1972. 176p. maps.

Minter's survey remains a useful account of US policy on the question of Portuguese colonialism from the end of the Second World War up to the early 1970s. Policy in this area was subordinated to the requirements of a generalized struggle to 'contain communism' and US verbal support, in the abstract, for the idea of self-determination was never translated into any concrete measures. Much more important than the African colonies to the US government's perception of American interests was the strategic significance of their airfields in the Azores. Minter also covers the policies of other Western countries such as Britain, France, West Germany and Brazil, as well as South Africa, but these sections are less authoritative. For a recent general analysis of US policy in the region by this author, see 'Destructive engagement: the United States and South Africa in the Reagan era', in: *Destructive engagement: southern Africa at war*, edited by Phyllis Johnson and David Martin (Harare: Zimbabwe Publishing House for the Southern African Research and Documentation Centre, 1986. p. 281–320).

426 **Portugal-África: que cooperação?** (Portugal-Africa: what co-operation?)
Cadernos do Terceiro Mundo no. 50 (Jan. 1983), p. 51–84.

The term *cooperação*(co-operation)is used in Portuguese to cover aid, trade and economic relations in general. This piece consists of a series of articles, written from a Portuguese perspective, at a high-point of optimism about possible future developments within the Portuguese-speaking world (which one diplomat called, with romantic accuracy, the 'community of suffering'). The pieces are: António Rosa Coutinho's 'Da descolonização à solidariedade' (From decolonization to solidarity); Sérgio Ribeiro's 'Reflexões sobre cooperação técnica' (Reflections on technological aid); Luís Moita's 'Por um correcto relacionamento' (For proper relations); Octávio de Matos' 'Formação profissional, questão central da cooperação' (Professional training, the crux of aid); Guiomar Belo Marques' 'Prosseguir o diálogo' (Continue the conversation); Natal Vaz' 'Cooperação da Gulbenkian tem áreas definidas' (Gulbenkian Foundation aid has defined areas); Francisco Teixeira de Mota's 'A experiência de uma realidade diferente' (Living a different reality); and Afonso Melo's 'Só por si a boa volontade não resolve os problemas' (Goodwill doesn't solve problems by itself). This last is on scholarships offered by Portugal, and shows that Mozambique had taken up only 22 of 240 places offered up to the end of 1983. See also Eduardo de Sousa Ferreira and Paula Fernandes dos Santos' *Portugal, paises africanos, CEE: cooperação e integração. Workshop realizado no Centro de Estudos de Dependência – CEDEP* [Portugal, African countries and the European Economic Community: co-operation and integration. Workshop held at the Centre of Dependency Studies – CEDEP] (Lisbon: GRADIVA, CEDEP, 1985. 174p.).

427 **Le Portugal et l'Afrique.** (Portugal and Africa.)
Querculus [pseudonym]. *Marchés Tropicaux* no. 1990, vol. 39 (1983), p. 3143–62.

A detailed account of Portugal's relations with her former African colonies, with sections on the place of Africa in Portuguese history; the 'rediscovery' of Portugal by the independent Portuguese-speaking countries; Portugal between the Americas, Europe and Africa; Samora Machel's visit to Portugal in 1983; and cultural and technical exchanges. There are also sections on Portuguese-African commerce, including Mozambique; the organization of Portuguese co-operation; the agreements between South Africa and Mozambique on transport and migrant labour; and Portuguese emigrés in Africa. Statistical tables are included.

428 **Healing old wounds.**
Victor de Sá Machado. *Africa Report* vol. 31, no. 1 (Jan.–Feb. 1986), p. 81–83.

Sá Machado is at present senior administrator of the Calouste Gulbenkian Foundation in Lisbon; he has been foreign minister of Portugal, and is also currently Vice-President of the conservative Christian Democrats. This article on Portugal's relations with its former colonies is diplomatic in the sense of conciliatory. Sá Machado identifies two 'trends' – Portuguese willingness 'to overcome the traumas that accompanied decolonization' on the one hand, and, to different degrees, an equivalent desire for good relations on the part of the ex-colonies. However, Sá Machado says that he regrets 'there is no such thing as a pleasant decolonization process . . . Portugal's . . . was initiated within the context of the revolution in *continental* [sic] Portugal'. He also thinks that 'Instability resulting from old conflicts between ethnic groups is an important factor' in the present difficulties in Mozambique and Angola. He does not devote much space to the specifics of each individual ex-colony, but he does feel that in terms of development, 'Portugal's contribution is indispensable to Lusophone Africa'.

429 **Anglo-Portuguese relations in south-central Africa, 1890–1900.**
Philip R. Warhurst. London: Longmans Green for the Royal Commonwealth Society, 1962. 169p. bibliog. maps. (Imperial Studies, no. 23).

The 1890s were a period of strained relations between Britain and Portugal, who were formally allies and thus could not resolve by force their differences over Central Africa (present-day Zambia and Malawi), or over Rhodesian access to the sea. This book tells the story of Cecil Rhodes' attempt to negotiate in 1890–91 with Umtasa, a Manica chief, in order to gain an Indian Ocean port for the new settlement in Mashonaland. The Portuguese, whose rights over the coast from Delagoa Bay to Cabo Delgado had been recognized at the Berlin Conference, protested vigorously; however, they had no legal claim to the Manica plateau or to Umtasa's chiefdom. Rhodes next tried to make a treaty with Ngungunyane, but in 1891 Britain formally recognized him as a Portuguese vassal. The final result of a decade of tension was, therefore, Portugal's obtaining of formal British guarantees of all their territory in the region.

With Socialist countries

430 **Sowjetische Afrikapolitik in der 'Aera Gorbatschow': eine Analyse ihrer grundlegenden Probleme Mitte der 80er Jahre, ausgehend von den Entwicklungen in Mozambique, Angola und Aethiopien.**
(Soviet Africa policy in the Gorbachev era: an analysis of its fundamental problems in the mid-1980s, based on developments in Mozambique, Angola and Ethiopia.)
Winrich Kühne. Ebenhausen, FRG: Forschungsinstitut für Internationale Politik und Sicherheit, Stiftung Wissenschaft und Politik, 1986. 146p. bibliog.

Kühne distinguishes between 'normal' diplomatic relations, which the Soviet Union currently has with about forty-seven African countries, and relations based on 'pro-Soviet influence'. The starting point for his analysis is that Soviet foreign policy is in deep crisis as far as its 'ideological, power political aspirations' are concerned. He tries to see how the nature of the Soviet-Mozambique relationship led to Mozambique's *rapprochement* with the West; to periodize Soviet African policy since Khrushchev, describing the present scepticism among Soviet analysts about the 'irreversibility' of revolutionary gains in the Third World; to characterize present difficulties, and to describe the present state of Soviet Third World policy. Kühne emphasizes the importance of the Soviet refusal to accept African states into membership of Comecon (the CMEA). Of Gorbachev, he writes that he holds a 'clear-sighted and matter-of-fact position on the question of ideological expansion', but still wants the Soviet Union to be recognized as a superpower. The Foundation for Science and Politics is a West German government think-tank with connections to the security establishment. English summary, p. 137–46.

431 **The USSR and southern Africa.**
Keith Somerville. *Journal of Modern African Studies* vol. 22, no. 1 (March 1984), p. 73–108.

South African analysts frequently portray the Soviet Union as having an aggressive policy in southern Africa. However, there is strong evidence that the region has traditionally been regarded by the USSR as an area in which it has no crucial interests. In this article Somerville looks at Soviet strategy from 'an

African perspective', focusing especially on relations with Mozambique (see p. 85–91), Angola and Zimbabwe, as well as looking at the USSR's role in developments in Namibia and South Africa. He concludes that there are three main components in Soviet policy in the region: support for the liberation movements and for the states of 'socialist orientation'; opposition to a Chinese role or influence; and an attempt to reduce Western influence in the area. Somerville sees little change during the period of the Brezhnev-Andropov-Chernenko transitions. For an account of Soviet policy much more compatible with the conventional South African view, see also Peter Vanneman's 'Soviet foreign economic policy in the Third World: the case of Mozambique after Nkomati', *ISSUP Strategic Review* (Dec. 1984), p. 1–4.

With southern Africa

432 **Portugal's attitude to Nyasaland during the period of the partition of Africa.**
Eric Axelson.   In: *The early history of Malawi*. Edited by Bridglal Pachai.   London: Longman, 1972. p. 252–62.

In the late 19th century Portugal occupied only the coast and the Zambezi Valley in Mozambique, but regarded the hinterland, as far as Angola if necessary, as a kind of reserved territory for future expansion, 'by virtue of Portuguese discovery and prior interest'. However, in 1875 the British began to send missionaries to the Zambezi, threatening this Portuguese reserve. Portugal did not have the military power at its disposal *in situ* to secure the Tchiri (Shire) River (flowing into the Zambezi), or even to make the missionaries pay their customs duties. Axelson recounts the complicated story of British-Portuguese manoeuvring and nego-tiations over such issues as navigation rights on the Zambezi, and who was to control the Tchiri Highlands. In the end, even though the Portuguese succeeded in occupying the Tchiri, and in beating the Kololo, they were overcome by British threats in Europe and withdrew. The essay is based on Lisbon archives.

433 **Angola and Mozambique vis-à-vis South Africa.**
Gerd D. Bossen.   *Aussenpolitik* (English ed.) vol. 35, no. 3 (Third quarter 1984), p. 281–94.

An unpleasant piece of writing, representative of a certain uninformed right-wing line on southern Africa. Bossen uses the old clichés about the causes of Mozambique's economic crisis (the 'white exodus' and 'close ties with the East Bloc'). He presents armed banditry in terms of the MNR which 'enjoys public support due to dissatisfaction with the country's catastrophic economic position . . . and considerable material backing from South Africa . . . '. The Nkomati Accord (1984) is presented as 'a political defeat' which has nonetheless 'laid a groundwork from which further progress can be made'. Bossen's anti-Soviet position becomes clear when he repeats a rumour that perhaps the Angolan President Agostinho Neto 'did not die a natural death in the Soviet capital'.

Foreign and Economic Relations. With southern Africa

434 **Notes pour une lecture économique de l'Accord de Nkomati.** (Notes
for an economic reading of the Nkomati Accord.)
Michel Cahen. *Estudos de Economia* (Lisbon) vol. 6, no. 3
(April–June 1986), p. 421–49.

Cahen has published several articles on Mozambique, and he clearly enjoys
polemic and provocation; in this piece he argues that the Nkomati Accord was *not*
the result of a conjuncture made up of South African aggression, natural
calamities, and Frelimo's own errors; on the contrary, Mozambican independence
had not allowed the Mozambican state itself to change the pre-existing
dependency relations between South Africa and Mozambique. Moreover,
Frelimo's policy initiatives, in this interpretation – such as negotiations over
Maputo port and the Maputo-Johannesburg railway, the establishment of a
national currency, or *ad hoc* nationalizations – were inadequate, and in Cahen's
words, allowed the 'laws of the market' to return in force. Cahen sees Frelimo
policy as cyclic, and is profoundly pessimistic about the situation. What is missing
from the article is a sense of the Mozambican crisis as being part of the general
regional destabilization caused by South Africa's own capitalism.

435 **Nkomati before and after: war, reconstruction and dependence in
Mozambique.**
Horace Campbell. *Journal of African Marxists* no. 6 (Oct. 1984),
p. 47–73; *Third World Quarterly* vol. 6, no. 4 (Oct. 1984),
p. 839–67.

In this article, which appeared, oddly, in two different academic journals in the
same month, Campbell takes a critical but confused position towards Frelimo and
the events which led up to the signing of the Nkomati Accord with South Africa
in 1984, writing, for instance, that 'The repressive tendencies which are expressed
in the forms of state oppression hinder the full mobilization of the people and
represent the anti-democratic politics and practices which are to be found all over
the underdeveloped world.' Relying almost entirely on English-language sources,
Campbell constructs an account of the phenomenon of armed banditry, which,
despite characterizing it initially as 'a pseudo-guerrilla movement supported by
South Africa' (almost right), ends up by describing the bandits as 'rebels' (quite
wrong, since it implies that they are a Mozambican political movement).

436 **As relações económicas entre Moçambique e a África do Sul,
1875–1964: edição crítica dos acordos e regulamentos principais.**
(Economic relations between Mozambique and South Africa,
1875–1964: a critical edition of the main accords and regulations.)
Luís António Covane. Trabalho de diploma for the Licenciatura,
Arquivo Histórico de Moçambique, Universidade Eduardo
Mondlane, 1985. 113p. bibliog.

An excellent thesis from the two-year postgraduate course at the Historical
Archive in 1984–85 to train historian-documentalists. The dissertation presents
virtually all the (mainly Portuguese, but some English) texts of the principal
agreements between Portugal and South Africa, from the Treaty of Peace and
Friendship of 1869 up to the 1940 agreement by the exchange of notes. Covane

174

adopts a four-part periodization: 1875–96; 1897–1909; 1910–25; and 1926–64. The documents, which deal principally with migrant labour, the railway and Lourenço Marques harbour, are linked by a substantial critical commentary, with the objective of producing a usable teaching text. The spelling is left unmodernized; there is, however, a chronology and a bibliography.

437 **South African strategy towards Mozambique in the post-Nkomati period: a critical analysis of effects and implications.**
Robert Davies. Uppsala, Sweden: Scandinavian Institute of African Studies, 1985. 71p. (Research report, no. 73).

In this penetrating analysis, based on a careful reading of both Mozambican and South African sources, Davies concludes that all the evidence points to the fact that 'the apartheid regime is not prepared to live in 'peaceful coexistence' with its neighbours in southern Africa' unless they accept incorporation into a constellation of southern African states under South African domination. However, he identifies certain real limits to Pretoria's freedom of action; in the case of Mozambique, for instance, South Africa's need to show that co-operation produces results contradicts Pretoria's unwillingness to allow economically strong states to develop in the region. In addition, South Africa itself is in the midst of a severe economic crisis, which restrains its options. By assigning a 'key role . . . to the "private sector" ' in the post-Nkomati phase, Pretoria put itself at the mercy of businessmen who were only willing to co-operate if it was profitable for them to do so; Davies comments that 'overall involvement is likely to be limited'. For more detail on the theoretical context of this pamphlet, see also Davies' paper with Dan O'Meara, 'Total strategy in southern Africa: an analysis of South African regional strategy since 1978', *Journal of Southern African Studies* vol. 11, no. 2 (April 1985), p. 183–211; the central argument of which is that the 'destabilization' *problématique* oversimplifies the range of tactical options open to the Pretoria régime, and wrongly elevates military and quasi-military destabilization to the level of a strategic option. (See also, by the same authors, 'The state of analysis of the southern African region: issues raised by the Total Strategy', *Review of African Political Economy* no. 29 (1984), p. 64–76.).

438 **Relations of neighbourliness: Malawi and Portugal, 1964–74.**
Robert d'A. Henderson. *Journal of Modern African Studies* vol. 15, no. 3 (1977), p. 425–55.

Of Mozambique's neighbours, Malawi shares the longest land border, and from the time of the armed struggle right up to the present (late-1986) crisis, relations have always been complex and sensitive. Henderson's article remains the most informative general account in English of the uneasy course which President Banda tried to steer between the demands of solidarity with FRELIMO's nationalism and the economic necessity to collaborate with the Portuguese while they controlled access to his landlocked country. See also R. d'A. Henderson's 'Portuguese settlement policy in Mozambique, 1929–61' (BPhil thesis, University of York, York, England. 1974), and Oswald Toindepi Ndanga's 'Zambia's relations with Malawi, Botswana, Mozambique, Zimbabwe and South Africa: an analysis within the context of southern Africa' (PhD dissertation, American University, Washington, DC. 1984.).

439 **Südafrika und seine Nachbarn: Durchbruch zum Frieden? Zur Bedeutung der Vereinbarungen mit Mozambique und Angola vom Frühjahr 1984.** (South Africa and her neighbours: breakthrough to peace? On the importance of the agreements with Mozambique and Angola from spring 1984.)
Winrich Kühne.   Baden-Baden, FRG: Nomos Verlagsgesellschaft, 1985. 166p. (Aktuelle Materialen zur Internationalen Politik, no. 7).

Kühne is a prolific and conservative writer on inter-state relations in the region, and in this volume he deals with the impact of the Nkomati Accord (between Mozambique and South Africa) and the Lusaka Agreement (between Angola and South Africa) on the security strategy of the white minority régime. The Nkomati Accord was a 'model solution for South Africa's fundamental legitimation problems, as well as a means of breaking international isolation via the frontline states'. Kühne concludes that the 'unending economic recession' is a major threat to South African strategy, since South Africa may be able to impose her hegemony, but she will not be able to 'prevent domestic unrest, violent upheavals and other instabilities in the region'. There is an English summary on p. 163–66. For information on the idea that any attempt by Mozambique to break off relations with South Africa would be tantamount to 'economic suicide', see Mário J. Azevedo's 'A sober commitment to liberation? Mozambique and South Africa, 1974–1979', *African Affairs* no. 317, vol. 79 (1980), p. 567–84.

440 **Stop the war against Angola and Mozambique: chronological account of acts of aggression against the Front Line States by apartheid South Africa, 1975–1981.**
Jan Marsh.   London: Campaign to Stop the War against Angola and Mozambique (SWAM), 1981. 48p.

Jan Marsh does not devote very much space in this useful reference work to a discussion of South Africa's destabilization tactics within the general 'Total Strategy' as elaborated after 1977. Instead she simply chronicles the appalling series of direct and indirect South African aggressions against its neighbours, especially Mozambique and Angola, during the first seven years after the independence of the former Portuguese colonies. The facts are left to speak for themselves. For two much more developed accounts of South Africa's subversive activities (whether economic, military, diplomatic or simply terroristic) and their effects on Mozambique, see the collection entitled *Destructive engagement: southern Africa at war* edited by Phyllis Johnson and David Martin (Harare: Zimbabwe Publishing House for the Southern African Research and Documentation Centre, 1986. 378p.) and Joseph Hanlon's *Beggar your neighbours: apartheid power in southern Africa* (London: CIIR with James Currey; Bloomington, Indiana: Indiana University Press, 1986, 352p.). Pages 131–50 of this latter work are particularly interesting.

441   **Independent Mozambique and its regional policy.**
Keith Middlemas.   In: *Southern Africa since the Portuguese
coup.* Edited by John Seiler.   Boulder, Colorado: Westview Press,
1980. p. 213–33.

Middlemas's article is 'based almost entirely on interviews with officials, Frelimo
members, and Portuguese advisers . . . I have not cited these sources indi-
vidually'. This infuriating and suspect procedure apart, Middlemas produces an
article in two distinct sections. The first is a general survey of the immediately
post-independence socio-economic and political situations. This is followed by a
discussion of Mozambican foreign and regional policy. Middlemas recognizes
that, at the time of writing, the resolution of the conflict in Zimbabwe was the
central issue for Mozambique at a regional level. Ironically, he underestimates
South Africa's aggressiveness when he predicts that after Zimbabwean independence, Mozambique will be 'free to pursue its long-term interests'.

442   **Mozambican foreign policy and the West, 1975–1984.**
Luís Benjamim Serapaio [sic].   *Munger Africana Library Notes*
no. 76 (Aug. 1985), p. 1–14.

A disgraceful publication by a self-exiled Mozambican who has lately compromised
himself by associating with the armed bandits' propaganda activities in the United
States. Serapião openly pushes a racist line, identifying a so-called 'Gang of
Argel' [sic, presumably for Algiers] within FRELIMO, made up of 'Whites,
Indians/Goans, and Mulattoes'. He asserts that Mondlane was never a Marxist,
ignoring evidence to the contrary, and claims that the armed bandits have
achieved 'acceptance among the black people in the country' because 'the non-
black Marxists . . . still control virtually all of the powerful positions in
government and politics'. Thus are Mozambique's complex problems reduced to a
question of skin colour. It is fortunately uncommon to find this kind of
publication in English, and it is included here as an example of its type.

443   **Mozambican socialism and the Nkomati Accord.**
Eduardo da Silva.   *Work in Progress* [Braamfontein, South
Africa] no. 32 (1984), p. 16–29.

The Nkomati Accord, signed between South Africa and Mozambique in March
1984, was greeted with shocked incomprehension by many commentators. In this
piece, one of the first articles to appear after the signing, the writer clearly has
some knowledge of Mozambican history and conditions, and uses the idea of
destabilization in a sophisticated total strategy *problématique*. The author takes a
critically sympathetic look at the history of relations between the two countries,
and attempts to analyse the sequence of events which led up to the Accord. The
development of South Africa's 'Total Strategy' (which involved the deployment of
a range of economic, political, ideological and military resources), is periodized
into four phases: launching the idea of a constellation of southern African states
(1978–80); generalized and indiscriminate destabilization (mid-1980 to 1981);
selective responses (1982–84); and Nkomati (1984–   ). Similarly, there is an
attempt to periodize post-independence Mozambique, as follows: 1975 to 1977,
the attempt at socialist planning; 1977 to 1979, the failure of the economy; 1979 to
1983, the strategy for the development decade and its failure; and 1983 onwards,

Foreign and Economic Relations. With southern Africa

the response to the crisis. The writer concludes that Frelimo's response to the crisis has been made up of a retreat from state and co-operative forms of property, cuts in the social services, and the acceptance of the permanent presence of foreign capital; but these measures by themselves are inadequate.

178

Finance and Banking

444 **II plano de fomento, 1959–1964.** (Second Development Plan, 1959–64.)
Assembleia Nacional.   Lisbon: Imprensa Nacional, 1959. 3 vols.
The First Plan (1953-58, with a budget of 16.5 million contos) had as its main objective the construction of an economic infrastructure (e.g., a railway to Rhodesia); the second (1959–64, with a budget of 31 million contos) was intended for industrialization. This document consists of the proposal itself, reports and the National Assembly's evaluation. See also the Inspecção Superior do Plano de Fomento's *Relatório final preparatório do II, plano de fomento* [Final preparatory report on the Second Development Plan] (Lisbon: Imprensa Nacional, 1958. 5 vols.), of which section 9, vol. 5 deals with 'overseas'. Some seminars were also held, at which papers on colonial planning were presented covering sectors such as industry, agriculture, telecommunications and electrification, as well as policy, finance and economic development in general. For such a view of planning through Portuguese eyes, see *Colóquios sobre o II. Plano de Fomento (Ultramar)* [Seminars on the Second Development Plan for Overseas] (Lisbon: Junta de Investigações do Ultramar, 1959. 191p. [Estudos de Ciências Políticas e Sociais. no. 21]). On Mozambique specifically, see the series *Relatório de 1962–[1964?]* by the Mozambican Comissão de Estudos de Plano de Fomento (Lourenço Marques, Mozambique: CEPF, 1964–   . annual.).

445 **Angola and Mozambique: a short economic survey.**
Neil Bruce.   *Bolsa Review* (Bank of London and South America) no. 72, vol. 6 (Dec. 1972), p. 660–68.
Such bank reviews as those produced by Barclays and Lloyds during the colonial period are often a useful source of condensed economic information from the hard-headed business community about prospects in Mozambique. This article, by a University of Keele politics lecturer and former BBC Africa correspondent, includes a short summary of the business climate in the early 1970s: Bruce reports

179

Finance and Banking

that 'Lourenço Marques, in the extreme southern corner, has hardly been aware of [operations against guerrillas] except through press reports.' See also, for example, *Economic Report: Mozambique (Portuguese East Africa)* (London: Lloyds Bank, Overseas Department, Export Promotion Section, annual), and the *Annual Economic Review: Mozambique* (London: Standard Bank, Economic Department, annual).

446 **Relatório final da execução do I. Plano de Fomento.** (Final report on the implementation of the First Development Plan.)
Inspecção Superior do Plano de Fomento.   Lisbon: Imprensa Nacional, 1959. 900p.

A general report which includes information for Mozambique on the general context of financial implementation, sources of finance, use of resources, and communication and transport. The crucial point about the Portuguese development plans before 1974 is that they were for the benefit of Portugal, and dealt with Portugal-and-the-colonies as a whole. 'Overseas' Portugal was simply a section, albeit often a substantial one (in this volume, for instance, it occupies p. 667–900). There exists a vast amount of technical literature on the plans, much of it of doubtful value. There are two categories of publication: general items published in Lisbon, in which Mozambican data *may* appear under the 'overseas' heading; and the often-mimeographed reports produced in Lourenço Marques, which have also frequently escaped the bibliographers. See also, on the First Plan, *Plano de fomento [para 1953–1958]* [Development plan, 1953–58]. (Lisbon: Edição dos Ministérios da Economia e do Ultramar, 1953. 2 vols.).

447 **Breve estudo sobre a balança de pagamentos de Moçambique.**
(Short study on the balance of payments of Mozambique.)
António dos Santos Labisa, Maria de Lurdes Barata.   In: *Estudos de economia, vol. 1* (Economic studies, vol. 1). Lisbon: Centro de Estudos Políticos e Sociais, Junta de Investigações do Ultramar, 1961. p. 151–243. (Estudos de Ciências Políticas e Sociais, no. 47).

In the late 1950s Mozambique faced an economic crisis, the roots of which are only just beginning to be understood by historians working on the period; the crisis continues until the present day. In 1958 the colony had for the first time a negative balance of payments; in 1959 the situation grew markedly worse. This Portuguese study was one of the first reactions to the situation just after the beginning of the crisis, but before the launching of the liberation war; it discusses, with plenty of statistical information, the trade balance, the balance in invisibles, the general balance of payments and its development, and ways of controlling the natural tendencies of the balance of payments. It is a useful source of data.

448 **Problemas do ultramar no plano intercalar de fomento.** (Overseas problems in the Intermediate Development Plan.)
Mário de Oliveira.   Lisbon: Agência-Geral do Ultramar, 1964. 92p.

The Intermediate Development Plan (1965-67, with a budget of 49.18 million contos) was oriented towards exports, and it has been argued that it had been made necessary by the launching of the colonial wars, especially in Angola. This text does not say so, of course, since it is a report by the Under-Secretary for Overseas Development to the session of the Overseas Council on 5 November 1964. On Mozambique see particularly the series *Plano intercalar de fomento, 1965–1967: relatório de [1965–]* (Lourenço Marques: Comissão Técnica de Planeamento e Integração Económica, 1966–[1968?]), which are detailed accounts of about 200 pages each on all aspects of the intermediate plan.

449 **Estimativa do produto interno de Moçambique, 1970–73–75.** (Estimate of the internal product of Mozambique, 1970–1973–1975.)
Francisco Pereira de Moura, Maria Fernanda Amaral. Maputo: Curso de Economia, Universidade Eduardo Mondlane [n.d.]. 27p.
Published in the late 1970s, this work by the Portuguese economist Pereira de Moura is one of the few serious technical works on the Mozambican economy to have been published since independence. It includes a discussion of methods of calculation, and how to avoid double-counting either by using industrial production plus raw material exports as the basis for reckoning, or by calculating value-added. This was probably the last period for which such an exercise could have been performed by an independent observer, since detailed statistical information on production is released only intermittently by the Mozambican government.

450 **Vinte anos de finanças moçambicanas e seu reflexo na economia da colónia.** (Twenty years of Mozambican finances and their effect on the colonial economy.)
Tómas Maria Rafael. Dissertation, Escola Superior Colonial, Lisbon, 1949–50. 233p. bibliog.
'Good finance is good policy', writes Rafael in the epigraph to this extremely detailed account of the colonial state's sources of income and its expenditures in the two decades of the 1930s and 1940s. Useful principally as a reference source, with lots of statistical tables.

451 **Money, planning and rural transformation in Mozambique.**
Marc Wuyts. *Journal of Development Studies* vol. 22, no. 1 (1985), p. 180–207.
Wuyts, formerly senior economist at the Centro de Estudos Africanos in Maputo, argues that rural transformation should proceed on a broad front, linking the development of the state sector to the co-operativization of peasant agriculture. He presents a short discussion of the colonial legacy, and then periodizes post-independence economic development into pre-III Congress, and inter-Congress phases. In fact, Mozambican government planners concentrated on the state farms, which received the bulk of investment resources to the detriment of the family sector. The imbalance between planned needs and the real availability of resources upset the relationship between the two sectors, and hence blocked any chance of transforming peasant agriculture. The imbalance is expressed in money terms, but cannot be solved through monetary policy; it requires a rethinking of the planning process itself. Wuyts is careful to point out that he is not arguing against the state sector, nor in favour of 'freeing the market vis-à-vis the peasantry'.

Trade

452 **Trade, state and society among the Yao in the nineteenth century.**
Edward E. Alpers.   *Journal of African History* vol. 10, no. 3
(1969), p. 405–20.

The Yao-speaking (or, in Portuguese, *Ajáua*-speaking) people inhabit a corridor
between Lake Nyasa and the east coast, which includes parts of northern
Mozambique, southern Tanzania and central Malawi. Alpers looks at the way in
which the Yao involvement with Swahili traders in long-distance commerce from
the lake to the coast, led to an increased volume of trade, and thus permitted the
growth of larger Yao states. He moves from an examination of the pre-19th-
century situation to a study of the slave-trade and the rise of large territorial
chiefdoms, and such related developments as the growth of towns, and the spread
of Islam.

453 **O vinho para o preto: notas sobre a exportação do vinho para
Africa.** (Wine for the black man: notes on the export of wine to
Africa.)
José Capela (pseudonym).   Oporto, Portugal: Afrontamento,
1973. 170p.

An anthology of texts on the Portuguese wine-trade to Africa, by the industrious
writer Soares Martins. On this subject, see also Sandro Sideri's important study
Trade and power: informal colonialism in Anglo-Portuguese relations (Rotterdam,
The Netherlands: Rotterdam University Press, 1970. 256p. bibliog.), which
examines the relationship between international labour specialization and
economic development over a long time-span. Sideri argues that the Portuguese
specialization in the wine-trade hindered her economic development. The
question of the African colonies only comes into the last three chapters of Sideri's
book, however, when he discusses the 1890 crisis between Portugal and Britain
over land occupation, and the Portuguese terms of trade with her colonies. In a
short dissertation written at the Portuguese Colonial School, Evandro J. Vieira

Rodrigues advocated the absolute prohibition of the local distillation of spirits in
Mozambique, or their importation, and the continuation of wine imports (below
thirteen degrees), but no sales to the 'natives'; see his 'Bebidas cafreais', [Native
drinks] (Dissertation, Escola Superior Colonial, Lisbon, 1950. 89p. bibliog.
map.).

454 **O comércio externo de Moçambique.** (The foreign trade of
Mozambique.)
Lourenço Marques, Mozambique: Câmara do Comércio de
Lourenço Marques, 1968. 24p.

An informative pamphlet on the foreign trade situation in Mozambique in the
mid-1960s. There is some discussion of the importance of foreign trade, its
development, average prices, the terms of trade, Mozambican transactions with
Portugal, with other colonies, with neighbouring countries (i.e. South Africa),
and with the rest of the world. The brochure also includes material on the
structure of trade by territory and by commodity. There are forty-five statistical
tables taken from well-known official sources.

455 **External traders in the hinterland of Sofala, 1810–1889.**
Kholisile David Dhliwayo.   MPhil dissertation, University of
London, 1977. 166p. bibliog. maps.

A School of Oriental and African Studies dissertation, supervised by Richard
Gray and based on archival sources in Portugal, Rhodesia and England, on the
trade relations of the eastern Shona and the Nguni peoples with the Portuguese,
and on the relations between Gaza and Madanda, Kiteve and Kisanga states. In
the early 19th century, caravans were sent from Sofala to these three eastern
Shona states, and from 1830 to 1839, the hinterland of Sofala became an area of
conflict between the Nguni groups. The Gaza state emerged victorious, and tried
by various means to gain control of the local trade-systems for gold and ivory.
Portuguese control of the coast was grudgingly accepted. From the 1870s
onwards, however, Gaza began to try to play off the British against the
Portuguese; when this stratagem failed, they made a deal with the Portuguese,
and moved southwards to the lower Limpopo, leaving the eastern Shona polities
exposed.

456 **Pre-colonial African trade: essays on trade in Central and eastern
Africa before 1900.**
Edited by Richard Gray, David Birmingham.   London: Oxford
University Press, 1970. 308p. maps.

This collection of historical essays on trade in such staples as salt, iron and pottery
is an important one for the historian of the Portuguese Empire, and is of interest
to students of Mozambican history. Chapters 7–13 contain references to Angola
or Mozambique, with chapter 13 by Alan Smith, on 'Delagoa Bay and the trade
of south-eastern Africa' (p. 265–89) having particular relevance, and, less directly
so, chapter 11, 'Zambian trade with Zumbo in the eighteenth century' by Nicola
Sutherland Harris. The editors contribute an introductory chapter in which they
argue for a more rigorously economic analysis of trade history, against a static,
subsistence agriculture model of African societies. Pre-colonial African economies

Trade

usually followed, as Gray and Birmingham point out, 'a mode of economic organization midway between subsistence and a fully-fledged market economy'. This book marked the end of the phase of trade-and-politics in African history.

457 Trade, society and politics in northern Mozambique, ca. 1753–1913.
Nancy Jane Hafkin. PhD dissertation, Boston University, Massachusetts, 1973. 423p. bibliog.

An important contribution to the history of Swahili merchant capital in present-day Nampula Province, formerly known as Mozambique district. See also on the history of this area, Mbwiliza's 'Towards a political economy of northern Mozambique' (q.v.), and a recent survey article by Gerhard Liesegang, 'A first look at the import and export trade of Mozambique, 1800–1914' in a special issue on 'Figuring African Trade' of the *Kölner Beiträge zur Afrikanistik* no. 11 (1985).

458 Trade and politics in southern Mozambique and Zululand in the eighteenth and early nineteenth centuries.
David Hedges. PhD dissertation, School of Oriental and African Studies, University of London, 1978. 277p. bibliog. maps.

This much-praised doctoral dissertation by a respected historian, deals with some thorny historiographical problems through a detailed study of the area between the Tugela River in Natal and Delagoa Bay, from the mid-16th to the early 19th centuries. The area had access to foreign trade from the 16th century, and in the 18th century this trade increased, the commodities dealt in changed, and the geographical pattern of commerce altered. Hedges looks at the way all this was related to the social structures and ecology of the southern Ronga and northern Nguni polities, showing how their relations with each other changed at the end of the 18th century, and how this in turn affected the emergence of the great 19th-century Zulu state. Among works heavily influenced by Hedges' approach can be cited Philip Bonner's *Kings, commoners and concessionaires: the evolution and dissolution of the nineteenth-century Swazi state* (Cambridge, England: Cambridge University Press; Johannesburg: Ravan, 1983. 315p.); Bonner writes of the 'subtlety and complexity of Hedges's analysis' and praises his 'persuasive' argument. Another, although less enchanted commentator, who seems to have missed the point of Hedges' work, is W. D. Hammond-Tooke in his article 'Descent groups, chiefdoms and South African historiography', *Journal of Southern African Studies* vol. 11, no. 2 (April 1985), p. 305–19, but especially p. 310 ff.

459 Comércio e acumulação: a comercialização de milho na Alta Zambézia. (Trade and accumulation: maize marketing in Upper Zambézia.)
Maureen Mackintosh. *Estudos Moçambicanos* no. 4 (1983–85), p. 77–102.

An important article on grain-marketing policy before the IV Congress, with a considerable amount of historical background. Mackintosh identifies four ways in which grain is marketed in the area, and remarks critically that 'These four activities do not make up an active and coordinated marketing policy in support of the socialization of the rural areas.' The piece is based on her consultancy

Trade

report *Agricultural marketing in the district of Alto Molócue, Zambézia Province* (Maputo: Centro de Estudos Africanos, 1982. 137p.), from which three other documents were prepared. They are: *Comercialização agrária: métodos de planificação* [Agricultural marketing: planning methods] (Maputo: Centro de Estudos Africanos, 1982. 59p.); *O sistema de informação sobre a comercialização agrária* [The system of information about agricultural marketing] (Maputo: Centro de Estudos Africanos, 1982. 55p.); and *Comercialização agrária ao nível distrital* [Agricultural marketing at the district level] (Maputo: Centro de Estudos Africanos, 1982. 58p. [CEA Relatório no. 82/7]).

460 **The trade of Delagoa Bay as a factor in Nguni politics, 1750–1835.**
Alan Smith. In: *African societies in southern Africa: historical studies*. Edited by Leonard Thompson. London: Heinemann, under the auspices of the African Studies Center, Los Angeles, 1969. p. 171–90.

Smith argues that the usual reduction of the motivating force behind 'Zulu' politics down to expansion because of land hunger is inadequate, and that the trade with Delagoa Bay was also a factor in the development and spread of the northern Nguni. Published sources on the subject are, however, limited and difficult to locate. In addition, they do not take account of events in northern Natal. During the 18th century the trade with Delagoa Bay, which served a 'vast interior' was maintained at high levels.

461 **Trade patterns and institutional aspects of trade: an empirical study of trade in southern Africa.**
Gunnar Sollie. Bergen, Norway: Chr. Michelsen Institute, 1982. 67p. (DERAP Working Paper, no. A267).

A useful preliminary working paper by a Norwegian researcher, which summarizes a considerable amount of information on Mozambican and regional trade. At independence there were around 2,000 private import-export companies in Mozambique; now about eighty per cent of Mozambican foreign trade is controlled by a handful of state corporations, including ENACOMO (general commodities), PETROMOC (petroleum products), PESCOM and EFRIPEL (shrimps), INTERMACOM (cement), INTERMETAL, and so on. Two state companies are concerned only with imports; they are MEDIMOC (pharmaceuticals and medical supplies) and INTERQUIMICA (chemical products). Sollie refers to two papers which apparently contain useful information on trade. They are 'Mozambique: on the road to reconstruction and development' (Geneva: Business International SA, 1980); and 'Evaluation of technical cooperation needs in trade promotion on behalf of the People's Republic of Mozambique' ([N.p.]: International Trade Centre, UNCTAD/GATT, 1979).

Industry

462   **Manufacturing industries in Mozambique: some aspects.**
J. M. Blum. *Wissenschaftliche Beiträge* (Berlin, GDR)
Sondernummer 2 (1976), p. 69–81.

A summary version of a paper prepared in Mozambique shortly after
independence. Among other fugitive, 'grey', or semi-published papers on
industry, a seriously under-researched area for the 1970s and 1980s, see David
Wield's 'Some characteristics of the Mozambican economy particularly relating to
industrialization' (Maputo, [n.d.]), and M. R. Bhagavan's 'Some aspects of
industrial development in Mozambique' (1977).

463   **The mineral industry of Mozambique.**
Miller W. Ellis. In: *Minerals Yearbook 1980.* Washington, DC:
US Government Printing Office, 1982. vol. 3. p. 691–95.

Despite Mozambique's undoubted mineral wealth, there is relatively little
published on mineral resources. This short piece, one of a series of general survey
articles in the American yearbook, is available as a separate pamphlet. Earlier
articles by David Miller appeared in the issue for 1975 (vol. 3, 1978, p. 703–08);
1976 (vol. 3, 1980, p. 751–54); and 1977 (vol. 3, 1981, p. 661–63). Ellis took over
from the double issue of 1978–79 (vol. 3, 1981, p. 663–66). More recent issues of
the yearbook have dropped Mozambique as a country chapter, and included such
information as is available under East African countries. However, for a detailed
and well-informed survey by a mining engineer with several years of experience
inside Mozambique, see Paul Jourdan's 'The minerals industry of Mozambique',
Raw Materials Report vol. 4, no. 4 (1986), p. 31–45. Jourdan, who seems to have
read everything on the subject, covers all the important minerals, with maps,
tables and graphs, as well as discussing legislation and showing clearly the impact
of armed banditry in reversing the recovery which began around 1980. His notes
and references will be especially useful for other professionals in the field who
wish to read further.

464 **Energy development in the People's Republic of Mozambique.**
In: *SADCC: energy and development to the year 2000.* Edited by
Jorge Tavares de Carvalho Simões. [Luanda]: SADCC Energy
Sector; Stockholm: Beijer Institute; Uppsala, Sweden:
Scandinavian Institute of African Studies, 1984. p. 141–49.

An anonymous but informative survey article, covering the administration of
national energy, which is undertaken by a variety of enterprises and ministries,
including the state mining corporation CARBOMOC, the National Coal
Directorate, the Ministry of Energy and Industry, and so on. The article discusses
national energy demand and potential, both commercial and non-commercial; this
section covers hydro-power (with a current installed capacity of nearly 12 million
kilowatts in sixty sites); coal, gas and oil, including the huge high-quality coal
reserves at Moatize in Tete Province; fuel-wood for rural domestic energy and for
tea-drying; agricultural waste residues from cotton, sugar, cashew and rice; and
charcoal. The survey also discusses geothermal energy sources (hot springs),
future projects, and Mozambique's participation in bilateral and multilateral aid
and co-operation agreements in this sector.

465 **Indústria de Moçambique.** (Industry of Mozambique.)
Lourenço Marques, Mozambique: Serviços Técnicos da Associação
Industrial de Moçambique, Jan. 1968–June 1975. monthly.

The voice of a certain section of Portuguese industrial capital in Mozambique,
with informative articles by such writers as António Rita-Ferreira. See also the
longer and much more detailed pieces in the three issues of the *Colectânea de
estudos do Gabinete de Estudos Técnicos* [Collection of studies by the Technical
Research Office] (Lourenço Marques, Mozambique: Associação Industrial de
Moçambique, July 1967–Dec. 1970. nos 1–3).

466 **Cabora Bassa: engineering and politics in southern Africa.**
Keith Middlemas. London: Weidenfeld & Nicolson, 1975. 367p.
bibliog. maps.

The huge Cabora Bassa dam in Tete Province was (and still is) one of the major
feats of hydroelectric engineering in Africa, and it took on great symbolic, as well
as economic, importance for the Portuguese colonialists and their allies.
Middlemas took four years to write this book, during which time FRELIMO won
independence for Mozambique. He says that he conducted more than 300
interviews between 1970 and 1974, but unfortunately these sources are not cited
for reasons of their personal safety. The book is organized around four themes:
consortia and contractors; the building of the dam; the role of the dam in
Mozambique; and lastly, Mozambique's role in southern Africa, the Portuguese
crisis and the future of Cabora Bassa. Middlemas concludes that imperial
Portugal's only monuments may eventually consist of a few crumbling castles
along the Indian Ocean, and the huge dam on the Zambezi. See also, in an
extensive litrature, F. Abecassis' 'The social cost-benefit analysis of the Cabora
Bassa project' (DPhil dissertation, Oxford University, 1978); and Claire Ollivier's
'Cabora Bassa, Mozambique: géopolitique et aménagement' [Cabora Bassa,
Mozambique: geopolitics and trade-offs] (Doctorate of the 3rd Cycle, University
of Paris VII, 1982. 318p.).

Industry

467 **The Zambezi Development Scheme: Cabora Bassa.**
Wolf Radmann. *Issue* vol. 4, no. 2 (Summer 1974), p. 47–54.

The Portuguese colonial régime began planning to develop the Zambezi Valley and to populate it with up to one million white settlers as early as the mid-1950s. With the launching of the armed struggle and its advance southwards, the Zambezi Valley settlement and the huge Cabora Bassa dam, with its vast artificial lake, came to be seen more and more as a vital *cordon sanitaire*, to protect the already settled central and southern parts of the country. Radmann's article outlines the general history of the Missão de Fomento e Povoamento do Zambezi (Zambezi Development and Settlement Commission); provides details of multinational tenders and financing; and discusses the arguments for and against the construction of Cabora Bassa. After discussing FRELIMO's opposition to the project, and the mobilization of African and international opinion behind this position, Radmann, a Texan academic, concludes that 'The timing of dam construction may be undesirable from the African point of view; the opportunity should not, however, be rejected. In due time, the advantages of a powerful source of electric energy will be appreciated throughout Africa.'

468 **Casting new molds: first steps toward worker control in a Mozambique steel factory.**
A conversation with Peter Sketchley and Frances Moore Lappé. San Francisco: Institute for Food and Development Policy, 1980. 60p.

A moderately interesting volume, which is actually rather less specialized than the title implies. Written for a generally radical audience, and presented in what some readers may find an irritating conversational format, the book covers, in a relatively short space, the colonial inheritance, the role of foreigners and technical assistance, the role of the Party and its leadership, the question of tactics (compromises or retreats?), and planning. The tone is a mixture of realism and triumphalism. Sketchley, who is British, worked in Mozambique as a systems analyst at the steel factory in question; Lappé is an American radical researcher. See also *Forging the new society*. For a less rosy picture, see Herbert Schröer's *Frelimo und Industriearbeiter in postkolonialen Konflikten: zur Politik der mosambikanischen Befreiungsfront seit ihrer Machtübernahme* (Frelimo and industrial workers in post-colonial conflicts: on the policy of the Mozambican Liberation Front since coming to power] (Saarbrücken, FRG; Fort Lauderdale, Florida: Breitenbach, 1983. 317p. [Sozialwissenschaftliche Studien zu internationalen Problemen, no. 86].).

469 **Forging the new society: steel making in Mozambique.**
Peter Sketchley *Southern Africa* vol. 13, no. 7 (Sept.-Oct. 1980), p. 2–4, 29.

A short piece in a popular magazine by a committed writer, describing the struggles and difficulties in the CIFEL steel mill just after independence. Sketchley writes that when he arrived at CIFEL, his experience there '. . . exploded one of my myths about the transformation of the social relations of production . . . the idea that it was all simply a question of the revolutionary spontaneity of the masses freed from the shackles of capitalist exploitation'. He concludes with a series of questions which he himself does not answer, simply pointing out, in Frelimo's most basic slogan, that the struggle continues.

470 **Hammer and hoe: local industries under state socialism in Mozambique.**
David Sogge. MPhil thesis, Institute of Social Studies, The Hague, 1985. 347p. bibliog.

A study of local industrialization 'under post-revolutionary state socialism'. After some theoretical discussion of the European experience in capitalist and socialist societies, Sogge looks at Mozambican industrialization, taking as his case-studies the farm-tool, building materials and footwear sectors. He reviews the performance of twenty-nine production units, and compares his data with those from six other industrial sectors. He concludes that present policies frequently result in frustration rather than in the development of the forces of production, and can put in doubt the feasibility of present industrialization plans. A note states that ISS theses 'are not made available for outside circulation by the Institute'.

471 **Industrial planning and development in Mozambique: some preliminary considerations.**
Jens Erik Torp. Uppsala, Sweden: Scandinavian Institute of African Studies, 1979. 57p. bibliog. (Research report, no. 50).

One of the few studies that were published after independence on Mozambican industry, by a Danish researcher. Torp points out that Mozambican industry was quite a substantial sector in African terms – Mozambique was one of the top eight countries on the continent, with four per cent of the total production, and an industrial workforce of over 99,000. The first part of this short work sketches out a periodization of industrial development: 1885–1926, an export-oriented phase, dominated by non-Portuguese capital; 1926–45, simple import-substitution for the Portuguese settlers, but with continued emphasis on exports as well; 1945–60, industrial consolidation for the local market, but still export-oriented; 1960–74, the growth of intermediate goods industries, a period of intense growth. The second part of the study deals with industrial development after independence, and the third section discusses, without suggesting a strategy, the question of industrial planning and development in both the long and short terms.

Agriculture and
Co-operatives

472 **Agronomia Moçambicana.** (Mozambican Agronomy.)
Lourenço Marques, Mozambique: Instituto de Investigação
Agronómica de Moçambique, Jan. 1967–June 1974. quarterly.

A technical agronomy journal which reflects to some extent the preoccupations of
the colonial régime with cash crops such as cotton. For a much more popular and
newsy agricultural magazine, see the *Revista agrícola* (Lourenço Marques,
Mozambique: Oct. 1958–Nov. 1974. monthly).

473 **Aspectos da produtividade da agricultura em Moçambique:
primeira parte.** (Aspects of agricultural productivity in
Mozambique: part 1.)
Alfredo Baptista Barros. Licenciatura dissertation, Instituto
Superior de Ciências Sociais e Política Ultramarina, Lisboa, 1965.
179p. bibliog. maps.

A plodding statistical analysis of agricultural productivity. The author identifies
the determining factors in agricultural productivity as industrialization, marketing,
transport, techniques and the agrarian system. He then moves on to an analysis of
'traditional' agricultural productivity, in terms of population density and available
area, administrative division by administrative division, with nearly fifty statistical
tables and coloured maps. Barros' schematic conclusions, in summary, are: that
areas of low productivity do not correspond neatly to administrative divisions;
that labour migration, fishing and cattle-farming have to be taken into account;
that smuggling and poor communications are serious problems; and that climate
affects productivity. Barros seems to think that Nampula and Zambézia provinces
are key agricultural zones because of 'the superiority which . . . the peoples from
north of the Zambezi . . . have over those of the south' (p. 172). He recommends
the shipping over of more *colonos* (Portuguese peasants), and more contacts
between them and 'traditional' farmers.

190

474 **A cultura algodoeira na economia do norte de Moçambique.**
(Cotton cultivation in the economy of northern Mozambique.)
Nelson Saraiva Bravo. Lisbon: Centro de Estudos Políticos e
Sociais, Junta de Investigações do Ultramar, 1963. 252p. bibliog.
maps. (Estudos de Ciências Políticas e Sociais, no. 66).

Nelson Bravo worked as a colonial administrator in various parts of Mozambique for fifteen years, and presented this work as his Master's dissertation at the Institute for Social Sciences and Overseas Policy in Lisbon in 1962. The published version appears to have undergone no alteration whatsoever. Nevertheless, it constitutes a useful source on a vitally important subject, since forced cotton-cultivation was at the centre of Portuguese colonial policy in Mozambique from the 1940s onwards. Bravo, after chapters on the agronomy of cotton and its worldwide and local importance, provides a schematic but informative account of the general agricultural and commercial economy of northern Mozambique, with production statistics, a description of pricing practice, and a discussion of the impact of forced cotton-production on other economic sectors, such as transport, agriculture in general, industry and even 'native life'. He quotes approvingly the comment made by another analyst in 1952, that 'cotton saved the economy of northern Mozambique from disaster'. For more recent analyses, outside the colonial *problématique*, see the reports by the Centro de Estudos Africanos, and the papers by Allen Isaacman (q.v.). See also José G. Taveira Pereira's 'O algodão na economia da província de Moçambique' [Cotton in the economy of the province of Mozambique] (Licenciatura dissertation, Instituto Superior de Ciências Sociais e Política Ultramarina, Universidade Técnica de Lisboa, 1951).

475 **A terra e o desenvolvimento comunitário em Moçambique.** (Land
and community development in Mozambique.)
Alexandre Cancelas. Licenciatura dissertation, Instituto Superior
de Ciências Sociais e Política Ultramarina, Universidade Técnica
de Lisboa, 1965–66. 307p. bibliog.

Despite its general title, the central part of this colonial dissertation consists of a study of land policy in Bilene. There is a general discussion of the question of land tenure in Mozambique, and of the relationship between land tenure and community development. Cancelas also identifies the obstacles to the establishment of a better system.

476 **A agricultura tradicional de Moçambique. 1. Distribuição
geográfica das culturas e sua relação com o meio.** (The traditional
agriculture of Mozambique. 1. Geographical distribution of crops
in relation to the environment.)
Mário de Carvalho. Lourenço Marques, Mozambique: Missão de
Inquérito Agrícola de Moçambique, 1969. 67p. maps.

Despite its age, this is still the best and most detailed overview of the agriculture of what would now be called the 'family' or peasant sector in Mozambique. The maps are well printed in colour and clearly show the relationship of food cultures to climate and other factors. Like all Portuguese colonial work in this subject area, however, nothing is said of the close inter-relationship between the family sector and commercial cash-crop farming. It appears that no other volumes were ever published.

477 **Fontes para o estudo do algodão em Moçambique: documentos de arquivo, 1938–1974.** (Sources for the study of cotton in Mozambique: archival documents, 1938–74.)
Manuel Jorge Correia de Lemos. Trabalho de diploma for the Licenciatura, Arquivo Histórico de Moçambique, Universidade Eduardo Mondlane, 1985. 125p.

A Master's thesis which is intended both as an historical analysis of the institutions which controlled cotton-production from the end of the 1930s to independence (the Junta de Exportação do Algodão [Cotton Export Board]; the Centro de Investigação Científica Algodoeira [Centre for Scientific Cotton Research]; the Instituto do Algodão de Moçambique [Mozambique Cotton Institute]; the Fundo de Fomento Algodoeiro [Cotton Development Fund]; and the Instituto de Investigação Agronómica de Moçambique [Agronomy Research Institute of Mozambique]), and as a guide to the documentation. The work is divided into chapters dealing with the historical background, the institutions themselves, the series which they published, legislation and a detailed chronology. Despite the limiting dates of the title, there is much information on earlier periods – the chapter on legislation begins at 1838.

478 **O problema das oleaginosas: posição de Moçambique.** (The problem of the oil-producing plants: Mozambique's position.)
Raúl Ribeiro dos Santos Delgado e Silva. Dissertation, Curso de Altos Estudos Coloniais, Lisbon, 1952. 250p. bibliog.

Deals with the production of vegetable oils in Mozambique, from such crops as cashew, coconut, ground-nuts, sesame, cotton-seed, copra, castor-beans and palm-oil. The work also contains much statistical data.

479 **Agricultural pricing policy in Mozambique, Tanzania, Zambia and Zimbabwe: study commissioned by the Nordic aid agencies.**
Frank Ellis (et al.). Brighton, Sussex, England: Institute of Development Studies at the University of Sussex, 1985. 261p.

The World Bank's *Berg Report* (1981) assigned the blame for poor development performance in sub-Saharan Africa firmly to 'domestic policy inadequacies', while conceding that other factors may have made their contribution. Subsequently, the Nordic countries, who are major aid donors, exerted pressure for a review of pricing policy in certain countries, including Mozambique. The chapter on Mozambique (p. 12–70) in this volume is by Maureen Mackintosh (q.v.), a former CEA researcher, and points out that reform has, in fact, already started, even if its direction is not entirely clear. She surveys the available data on prices and quantities of the produce marketed; provides two case-studies (on maize marketing in Zambezia Province and on the situation in Chokwe, Gaza Province, in 1984); and finally looks at the demands of a war economy. The section on conclusions (p. 237–40) argues that there is no realistic policy alternative, in a war situation, other than continued support for the state sector.

480   **Endeavor and achievement of cooperatives in Mozambique.**
Ralph von Geresdorff.   *Journal of Negro History* vol. 45, no. 2
(April 1960), p. 116–25.

This study is devoted principally to the Zavala African co-operatives in
Inhambane which were active in the late 1950s. They are often mentioned
alongside the Linguilanilu cotton co-operative of Cabo Delgado, in operation
during the same period, but there is some controversy among Mozambican and
foreign scholars as to whether the two are really comparable. What is certain is
that the Zavala co-operative was under firm state control, and can scarcely be
considered an African initiative – planning and accounting were both under
government supervision, for instance, and finance came from the state.
Von Geresdorff rather reveals his own bias when he concludes that the
improvement in living standards among the members of this co-operative would
produce democratic (read 'pliable') African leaders. See also the important
contemporary publication *Relatório da administração da circunscrição de Zavala
sobre as cooperativas da sua área* [Report of the administration of the
circumscription of Zavala about the co-operatives in the area] (Lourenço
Marques, Mozambique: Imprensa Nacional, 1958. 34p.).

481   **Cotton: from concentrations to collective production.**
Kurt Habermeier.   *Mozambican Studies* no. 2 (1981), p. 36–57.

In 1979–80 the CEA conducted a large-scale two-year research project on cotton-
production in Mozambique. In the first year fieldwork concentrated on Nampula
Province; in 1980 investigations were carried out in Zambézia, and some work
was also conducted on cotton-ginning and on textile factories. For a complete list
of reports produced by the cotton project, see M. Cahen's 'Publications du
Centro de Estudos Africanos de l'Université Eduardo Mondlane (Maputo,
Mozambique)' *Politique Africaine* no. 5 (Feb. 1982), p. 113–15. Habermeier's
article is based on the report *A transformação da agricultura familiar na província
de Nampula* [The transformation of family agriculture in Nampula Province]
(Maputo: Centro de Estudos Africanos, 1980. 91p. [Relatório no. 80/3]), and
discusses the transformation of an abandoned settler farm into a collective
settlement in Assuate Circle, Netia locality in 1977, and the ensuing events.

482   **Does modernisation = mechanisation?**
Joe Hanlon.   *New Scientist*, 24 August 1978, p. 562–65.

In mid-1978 the Minister of Agriculture, Joaquim de Carvalho, was sacked and
disgraced because, among other things, he had failed to implement the official
policy of supporting communal villages. Instead, his Ministry had devoted huge
resources to the mechanization of state farms. Whether Carvalho did not want to
put the policy into practice, or was simply unable to, remains unclear; certainly
his successors have not done much better. In this informative article Joe Hanlon,
for several years the Manchester and London *Guardian* correspondent in Maputo,
analyses the background to the mechanization debate in Mozambique and looks
at alternatives such as 'appropriate technology'. As Hanlon points out, the
mechanization campaign was both expensive (£20 million on agricultural
equipment in 1977 alone) and inefficient (30,000 volunteers were needed to
harvest rice in the Limpopo Valley in June 1978). Hanlon's tone in this article is
optimistic, and he argues that 'The problems are all those of inexperience, and
the [state] farm managers seem to be learning fast.' A much more technical

Agriculture and Co-operatives

discussion of the mechanization experience in Mozambique is Marc Wuyts' 'The mechanization of present-day Mozambican agriculture' (q.v.).

483   **Agricultural cooperatives and development policy in Mozambique.**
Laurence Harris.   *Journal of Peasant Studies* vol. 7, no. 3 (1980), p. 338–52.

Harris' article is based on fieldwork done in 1978. He begins by summarizing the recent history of FRELIMO policy on agricultural co-operatives. In the second part of the article Harris looks at the class composition of a particular co-operative, the 'Eduardo Mondlane Co-operative' in Gaza Province; he then examines the relations of production in the same village. The fourth and concluding section tries to bring out the relationship between class composition and relations of production in co-operatives, and to look at the role of co-operatives in socialist transformation in Mozambique.

484   **Contemporary land struggles on the Limpopo: a case study of Chokwe, Mozambique, 1950–1985.**
Kenneth Hermele.   Uppsala, Sweden: Working Group for the Study of Development Strategies, Department of Development Studies, University of Uppsala, 1986. 26p. maps. (AKUT series, no. 34).

The Swedish researcher Hermele presents a succinct account of the history of the *colonato* of the Limpopo Valley, Mozambique's most fertile rice-growing area and the so-called 'bread-basket' of the nation. In the 1920s the Portuguese had planned to settle large numbers of white peasants, but the scheme only got under way, rather unsuccessfully, in the 1950s; at its peak the *colonato* had only just over 1,000 white settlers and under 500 black ones. After independence the situation was frozen, and eventually the Government created the giant state farm CAIL (Agro-Industrial Complex of the Limpopo) there. By 1983 it was obvious that CAIL in its turn was a failure, and the huge enterprise was broken up into ten separate farms of 1,500 hectares each. Hermele concludes that the difficulties encountered were not simply of a technical nature, but were intimately linked to struggles over land and to the system of migrant labour to the South African mines.

485   **Moçambique.** (Mozambique.)
Compiled by Göran Högblom.   Uppsala, Sweden: International Rural Development Division, Swedish University of Agriculture, Forestry and Veterinary Medicine, 1977. Preliminary ed. 65p. (RU-Develop Documentation. Series Country).

A thematically organized agricultural and rural development bibliography, unfortunately now rather outdated; although this is given as a 'preliminary' edition, there does not seem to be a later one. There are thirty-six categories, including several cash and food crops, but some of these sections contain only a handful of entries. The entries are not numbered, and there are no indexes. Some citations of articles include abstracts, apparently taken from the original journal. Locations in Swedish research libraries are indicated. The list is strongest on material from the late colonial period.

486 **Colonato do Limpopo: contribuição da cooperativa agrícola no desenvolvimento socio-económico.** (The *colonato* of the Limpopo: contribution of the agricultural co-operative in socio-economic development.)
António Lopes de Almeida. Licenciatura dissertation, Instituto Superior de Ciências Sociais e Política Ultramarina, Universidade Técnica de Lisboa, 1970. 448p. bibliog. maps.

A Master's thesis, organized into three chapters, on the general character of the *colonato*, and on the Limpopo agricultural co-operative, with nearly seventy statistical tables and a wealth of detail; from the special course for colonial administrators held at the Institute for Social Sciences and Overseas Policy in Lisbon. Before 1961, when the Institute became part of the Technical University of Lisbon, the diploma was known as the 'Course of Higher Colonial Studies' and did not have the status of a licenciatura (or MA); nevertheless, as many of these dissertations as possible have been listed in the relevant subject chapters. For recent work on the state farm CAIL, which succeeded the *colonato* of the Limpopo, see Kenneth Hermele's article, *Contemporary land struggles on the Limpopo* (q.v.).

487 **Esboço para uma monografia agrícola do post-sede dos Muchopes e de alguns regulados do Chibuto, Moçambique.** (Outline of an agricultural monograph on the main village of the Muchopes and on some chieftainships in Chibuto, Mozambique.)
J. Montalvão Marques. *Memórias da Junta de Investigacão do Ûltramar*, 2nd series, no. 22 (1960), p. 7–130.

This essay has a modest title and with good reason; even by the standards of the average administrator's report of this period it is a rather inadequate piece of work. Montalvão Marques does not seem to have a very clear idea of the boundaries of the region he is discussing, and he leaves out at least as much information (about the people for instance) as he puts in. He does describe, in fairness, the physiography, geology, climate, soil structure, vegetation, demography, water-supply, agriculture and animal husbandry of the area. The work was commissioned by the Cotton Export Board, and was evidently well enough thought of to be published. It is included here as an example of the vast mediocrity of much of the colonial literature.

488 **Mozambique: communal villages.**
People's Power in Mozambique, Angola and Guinea-Bissau no. 5 (Nov.–Dec. 1976), p. 23–35.

This English-language summary is based on two articles published in the Mozambican press. (For readers with a knowledge of Portuguese the original references are as follows: 'Gaza: Aldeia Comunal Herois de Moçambique' *Tempo* no. 283 [7 March 1976], p. 16–23; and 'Aldeias Comunais em Inhambane' *Tempo* no. 284 [14 March 1976], p. 46–55.) The two articles were based on visits to communal villages in February 1976, and include, as well as photographs, plans of the layout of the settlements; the English version omits these. The English text is of interest principally for the inclusion of translated extracts from the Resolution on Communal Villages passed at the Eighth Session of the FRELIMO Central

Agriculture and Co-operatives

Committee, held in February 1976. This very detailed policy document remained a basic text for some time afterwards, although modified and adapted by national meetings of Party and state structures.

489   **Mozambique: food and agriculture sector, preliminary study.**
       Uppsala, Sweden: International Rural Development Division,
       Swedish University of Agriculture, Forestry and Veterinary
       Medicine, 1976. [pagination varies].

A general survey of the rural sector as a whole; two versions of this report were issued, in April and November, of which the latter is to be preferred. The work is a compilation, based on documentary sources and on a study visit in April 1976; at that point the Swedish International Development Authority also added some comments. The first chapter on the general background is followed by the rural sector; agriculture (by crop: sugar-cane, cotton, cereals, sisal, cashew, citrus, coconut and tea) and animal husbandry (cattle, sheep and goats, pigs, poultry and wildlife); fisheries; forestry; and development options. The report is under-theorized, and is mainly useful as a summary of data for its period; for instance the last chapter reproduces uncritically, presumably from Portuguese colonial documents, the idea of a 'dualism' in Mozambican agriculture – even using the expressions 'modern' and 'traditional' sector.

490   **Mozambique: report of the UNDP/FAO/Nordic Agricultural
       Formulation Mission, 9 June–7 July 1976.**
       Rome: United Nations Development Programme, Food and
       Agriculture Organization of the United Nations, 1976. 153p.
       bibliog. maps. (DD:DP/MOZ/76/002, Mission report).

United Nations' agency reports are often a very convenient source of statistical and other information on developing countries such as Mozambique. Nonetheless, users should remember that, while UN missions do have access to top officials, they are also given the information which the Government concerned wishes to disseminate, and that can be both an advantage and a disadvantage. This was one of the earliest of such reports, and was prepared before the First Development Plan, in an atmosphere of some urgency. In particular, the mission examined the situation in the areas of livestock-production and health, crop production and protection, small-scale irrigation, land-use planning, agricultural machinery, rural development institutions, inland fisheries development, and forestry development. Because the report was written only one year after independence, however, the statistical information is taken largely from the quite different conditions of the last years of the colonial régime. The mission leader was M. Gonzalez de Moya of the FAO (Food and Agriculture Organization).

491   **State intervention in agriculture: the Mozambican experience.**
       Barry Munslow.   *Journal of Modern African Studies* vol. 22, no. 2
       (1984), p. 199–221.

An account of the history of Mozambican agricultural policy, which tries to explain the major shifts of the early 1980s; Munslow begins with a favourable description, based on rather thin evidence, of FRELIMO's experience in

196

organizing agricultural production in the liberated zones of Cabo Delgado and
Niassa during the war: 'Centres of agricultural experimentation were established
at major military bases, where a combination of modern science and traditional
experience was brought to bear . . . ' After independence in 1975, Frelimo did
not develop a detailed agricultural policy until the III Congress, in February 1977.
In a situation requiring urgent crisis management measures, a policy developed
'which stressed both the formation of co-operatives and communal villages and
the creation of large state farms. Unfortunately, the overwhelming body of
resources were poured in the latter'. As early as 1978 it was obvious to Frelimo
that emphasizing large-scale technical solutions to the problems of the huge state
farms would not work; but no changes were made in practice. Munslow says that,
'The neglect of the peasant-family sector was arguably the most damaging aspect
of agricultural policy'. The IV Congress of Frelimo formally recognized the need
to support the family sector – in the author's view 'There has clearly been a
substantial change in the nature of state intervention in agriculture . . . '.
Describing the series of natural disasters (floods, cyclones, famines) and the
ravages of the South African-backed MNR, however, he concludes that 'the
chances for agricultural development do not appear bright' unless Frelimo can
restore peace to the countryside.

492 **A questão agrária em Moçambique.** (The agrarian question in
Mozambique.)
Bridget O'Laughlin. *Estudos Moçambicanos* no. 3 (1981),
p. 9–32.

An important statement of a theoretical position which formed the basis of the
Centro de Estudos Africanos' work in the late 1970s and early 1980s: namely that
it is necessary to break decisively with dualist analyses which treat the peasantry
as in some sense pre-capitalist, or as involved in subsistence agricultural
production. It will not be possible to develop a strategy for the socialist
transformation of the state sector, without having one for family agriculture as
well, argues O'Laughlin, a senior staff member at the CEA since 1979, because
the two are interdependent. For a reasonably up-to-date descriptive account of
the policy shifts which are the background to O'Laughlin's piece, see the article
by Bruno Musti, an FAO professional, and Vanni Rinaldi, 'Mozambico: una
riorganizzazione ancora in atto' [Mozambique: reorganization still underway],
Politica Internazionale no. 8/9 (Aug.–Sept. 1984), p. 70–76.

493 **A obra hidroagrícola do Baixo Limpopo: medidas a adoptar para o
seu desenvolvimento.** (Irrigation work on the lower Limpopo:
measures for its development.)
Flávio M. Furtado de Paiva. Licenciatura dissertation, Instituto
Superior de Ciências Sociais e Política Ultramarina, Universidade
Técnica de Lisboa, 1971. 248p. maps.

Paiva worked in the lower Limpopo Valley as secretary of a settlers' association in
the *colonato* and later as a technician for the Board of Settlement, with
responsibility for the study of socio-economic conditions. Irrigation work was in
poor condition – as indeed was the *colonato* as a whole. This thesis consists of a

general description of existing hydro-agricultural works, and a set of measures recommended by Paiva for improving the situation.

494 **Cotton in the Mozambican colonial economy: a contribution to the project 'Cotton production in Mozambique': a case-study of development problems and policies.**
M. Margarida Ponte Ferreira. Oslo: Norsk Utenrikspolitisk Institut, 1982. 42p. (NUPI Notat, no. 234).

In 1979–80 the Centre of African Studies (CEA) in Maputo and the Norwegian Institute of International Affairs (NUPI) in Oslo undertook a joint two-year study of cotton production and its role in Mozambique. The CEA undertook two field-studies, one in Nampula Province and one in Zambézia, as well as working in textile factories and ginning mills. This research resulted in a series of eleven case-reports in Portuguese, and a general survey in English: *Cotton production in Mozambique: a survey, 1936–1979* (Maputo, 1981. 79p. [CEA Relatório no. 81/1]), which includes summaries of many of the Portuguese case-studies on p. 34–43. For a list of CEA reports, see the Michel Cahen article 'Publications du Centro de Estudos Africanos' (q.v.). NUPI produced this historical survey by Ponte Ferreira, and Tertit Aasland's *Development problems and development policies: cotton production in Mozambique* (Oslo, 1981. 54p.).

495 **Alguns aspectos socio-económicas da cultura do chá em Moçambique.** (Some socio-economic aspects of tea-growing in Mozambique.)
Mário Rodrigo da Fonseca Ramos. Licenciatura dissertation, Instituto Superior de Ciências Sociais e Política Ultramarina, Universidade Técnica de Lisboa, 1965. 137p. bibliog.

An informative thesis on tea cultivation in northern Mozambique. Ramos begins with a description of the general botany of tea, moving on to an account of tea in the world economy and in the Portuguese (i.e. Portuguese and colonial) economy. The central topic, tea in Mozambique, is covered from page 54 onwards. Fonseca Ramos begins with the ecology of tea, especially around Guruè, Ile, Alto Molócuè, Namarroi, Lugela and Milange, all in Zambézia Province; he then discusses the impact of tea cultivation on the area's economy and demography. The final chapter looks at plantations as settlements. For a detailed account of the economic and administrative history of the Lomwe *prazo* and Guruè district, centre of the tea economy, see also Alfredo M. Silva's 'A valorização dos montes Namuli e das populações lómuès na problematica político-administrativa da Provínçia de Moçambique' [The significance of the Namuli mountains and the Lomwe population in the political-administrative context of the Province of Mozambique] (Licenciatura dissertation, Instituto Superior de Ciências Sociais e Política Ultramarina, Universidade Técnica de Lisboa, 1965. [370]p. bibliog.).

496 **A produção no sector indígena de Moçambique.** (Production in the native sector in Mozambique.)
Armando Lourenço Rodrigues.   Dissertation, Curso de Altos Estudos Ultramarinos, Lisbon, 1960. 190p. bibliog.

Discusses the general characteristics of the 'native economy'; types of production, such as agricultural, hunting and fishing; the kinds of food crops grown by Africans; and other activities, including witchcraft, iron production, house construction and animal husbandry. There is a section on the African co-operatives at Manhiça, Chibuto, Zavala and Govuro.

497 **Peasants and collective agriculture in Mozambique.**
Otto Roesch.   In: *The politics of agriculture in tropical Africa.*
Edited by Jonathan Barker.   Beverly Hills, California; London: Sage, 1984. p. 291–316. (Sage Series on African Modernization and Development, vol. 9).

Roesch, a Canadian, conducted doctoral research for several months in 1982–83 on the lower Limpopo Valley. This paper acknowledges the influence of the ideas of the Centre of African Studies. Roesch discusses Mozambican agricultural policy from independence until 1982, identifying as an early watershed the decision taken at the 8th Session of the Central Committee in 1976 to define communal villages as the 'backbone' of Mozambique's rural development strategy. These villages were seen, not simply as a means of collectivizing agricultural production, but as an integrated social totality. Nevertheless, the communal villages were expected, especially after the III Congress in 1977, to be self-reliant, and were considered to be secondary in importance, after the state sector, in food supply. Between 1977 and 1982 only two per cent of agricultural investment went into the co-operative sector, and virtually nothing to individual peasant families. The IV Congress in 1983 recommended a major shift away from capital-intensive large-scale state projects. Roesch moves on to a discussion of the situation on the lower Limpopo, a region dominated by the large state farm UBPL (Lower Limpopo Production Unit) with seven agricultural and dairy operations. There were only about twenty co-operatives, with perhaps 3,500 members. Between 1979 and 1983 the area also had its own State Secretariat for the Limpopo-Incomati Region (SERLI). Roesch concludes that increased capital investment in the family sector may not be sufficient, for an increase in the supply of goods to the peasants will also be necessary to break the cycle of decline.

498 **Socialism and rural development in Mozambique: the case of** *Aldeia Comunal 24 de Julho.*
Otto Roesch.   PhD dissertation, University of Toronto, 1986. 248p. bibliog. map.

A careful case-study, based on field-work (sixty-five comprehensive interviews) and published literature, of a communal village in Zongoene in the lower Limpopo Valley, an important food-producing area for Maputo city. After a general introduction to the geography and history of the village, Roesch tries to analyse what he terms 'The problematic relationship that exists between production, consumption and popular voluntarism in revolutionary socialist strategies of rural development.' In chapters on the origins of the village, on

Agriculture and Co-operatives

peasant social and economic life, and on the experience of collectivization, the author shows that after independence there was a high level of popular support for collectivization. This, however, was rapidly undermined by a combination of a severe crisis of the family sector and the ineffectiveness of government policy in dealing with it. Roesch argues, quite correctly, that the allocation of investments principally to the huge state farms, while ignoring the co-operatives and the family sector, left the peasantry both incapable of participating and unwilling to mobilize itself in the collectivization process. He concludes that while 'popular voluntarism is a necessary and desirable component' of such a transformation, the importance of policy decisions which affect mobilization should not be underestimated. Another recent University of Toronto doctoral dissertation, based on field-work in the early 1980s, is by Merle Bowen, 'Let's build agricultural producer cooperatives: socialist agricultural development strategy in Mozambique, 1975–1983.'

499   **Problemática das "casas dos pescadores" em Cabo Delgado (Moçambique).** (The problem of fishing co-operatives in Cabo Delgado, Mozambique.)
Antero Francisco de Salles Pedroso de Seabra.   Licenciatura dissertation, Instituto Superior de Ciências Sociais e Política Ultramarina, Universidade Técnica de Lisboa, 1973. 162p. bibliog. maps.

Analyses traditional fishing methods in Cabo Delgado, with a general description of the province and proposals for setting up fishing co-operatives and fishing villages. It is illustrated with photographs.

500   *Tawani, machambero!*: **forced cotton and rice growing on the Zambezi.**
Leroy Vail, Landeg White.   *Journal of African History* vol. 19, no. 2 (1978), p. 239–63.

An historical study of the specific character of forced labour in the lower Zambezi Valley between 1935 and 1960. Vail and White argue that the massive recruitment of labour for the mines and agriculture in neighbouring countries created a serious labour shortage for companies inside Mozambique. From the companies' point of view, the introduction of forced cotton-cultivation in the mid-1930s only made matters worse. The authors focus especially on Sena Sugar Estates (SSE), the biggest single employer of labour in the colony, and the tactics it used to confront the problem. SSE developed a system whereby only women grew cotton, while the men worked on the sugar plantations. By the 1940s, other employers had copied this idea.

501   **The co-operative movement in Chokwe, Mozambique.**
Anna Wardman.   *Journal of Southern African Studies* vol. 11, no. 2 (April 1985), p. 295–304.

Between 1982 and 1984, Wardman worked in Chokwe, in Gaza Province, for the Ministry of Agriculture, and this essentially descriptive article is apparently based entirely on her first-hand knowledge: the only two footnotes, on the second page,

200

Agriculture and Co-operatives

refer to theoretical work by Marc Wuyts. Chokwe is important because the area produces approximately half the cereals grown in Mozambique. Wardman paints a bleak picture of the co-operatives as unwieldy, undemocratic, overdependent on unsuitable technology, and unproductive. High membership figures are explained by the members' desire to gain access to co-operative machinery for use on their private plots. Co-operatives are naturally a focus for bandit attacks, but receive insufficient material or moral support. Wardman concludes grimly that 'Under these conditions, socialism cannot survive and the future of this kind of cooperative movement looks very black.'

502   **The role of cooperative agriculture in transforming labour relations and gender relations: experiences from the Green Zones, Maputo, Mozambique.**
Christine Pelzer White, Alpheus Manghezi. [Brighton, Sussex, England: Institute of Development Studies, University of Sussex, 1985]. 218p. bibliog.

The Green Zones are a belt of small co-operative farms around Mozambique's capital city, which, it was hoped, would make a substantial contribution to the problem of food supply for the city, which has historically always been heavily dependent on food imports, especially from South Africa. The Green Zones are of interest to researchers both because of their accessibility, and because of the predominance of women and older people among the workers. This document consists of a short report (p. 1–36), a bibliography (p. 37–39), and a treasure-trove of transcriptions of interview material, mostly by Alpheus Manghezi, a Shangaan-speaking researcher at the Centre of African Studies (p. 40–218).

503   **Camponeses e economia rural em Moçambique.** (Peasants and rural economy in Mozambique.)
Marc Wuyts. *Reforma Agrária* [São Paulo, Brazil] vol. 13, no. 6 (Nov.–Dec. 1983), p. 3–17.

Originally prepared as a report for the Centro de Estudos Africanos in Maputo, this influential analysis first appeared in English as *Peasants and rural economy in Mozambique* (Maputo: Centro de Estudos Africanos, 1978, 39p.), and was later published as a booklet in Portuguese (Maputo: Instituto Nacional do Livro e do Disco, 1981, 67p.). Wuyts, whose work as senior economist at the CEA in the late 1970s and early 1980s was much criticized but, one way or another, was also used to teach a generation of Mozambican economics students, analyses the social structure of production in Mozambican agriculture at the end of the colonial period, arguing for the relative importance of peasant small-scale production. See also Wuyts' doctoral dissertation on Mozambican finance, submitted to the Open University, Milton Keynes, England in August 1986, and his 'Sul do Save: establização e transformação de força de trabalho' (South of the Sabie river: stabilization and transformation of the labour force), *Estudos Moçambicanos* no. 3 (1981), p. 33–44.

201

504 **The mechanization of present-day Mozambican agriculture.**
Marc Wuyts. *Development and Change* vol. 12 (1981), p. 1–27.

Wuyts was the senior economist at the Centre of African Studies in Maputo for several years, and this paper was written in the late 1970s as an attempt to introduce some theoretical rigour into the debate on agricultural mechanization. It was made widely available in English in mimeographed form for some time before its appearance in a journal; it was never translated into Portuguese. Wuyts starts from the assumption that choice of technique in agriculture is a political issue 'which affects the whole social structure of the rural economy'. The question cannot, therefore, be dealt with abstractly, but must be placed in the context of contemporary rural conditions. Wuyts also limits himself to a discussion of the choice of technique in food production for the internal market in the southern part of the country, arguing that cash-crop production is governed by the world market. In a complex argument, Wuyts comes down against rapid mechanization in the short term, but with the reservation that it must remain a longer-term objective.

Transport and Communications

505 **Estradas e pontes de Moçambique.** (Roads and bridges of
Mozambique.)
Maputo: Departamento de Turismo, 1976. [12]p. map.
This bilingual brochure is included here because it gives a handy factual summary
of the road transport network, with colour photographs of the major bridges, but
more importantly because it provides a detailed black-and-white fold-out road
map of the country, and a distance table for twenty-four main towns and frontier
posts. See also the *Mapa rodoviário de Moçambique* (scale 1:2,000,000), Maputo:
Direcção Nacional de Estradas, 1977.

506 **Estudo nacional de transportes: relatório final.** (National transport
study: final report.)
Copenhagen: Hoff & Overgaard; Stockholm: VIAK, 1978. 7 vols.
maps.
A large-scale consultancy report by a Danish and a Swedish firm, divided into
seven sectoral volumes dealing with the socio-economic base, the transport plan,
roads, road traffic and transport costs, ports and coastal shipping, civil aviation
and railways. A number of sub-reports of limited circulation were also prepared.

507 **South Africa and southern Mozambique: labour, railways and trade
in the making of a relationship.**
Simon E. Katzenellenbogen. Manchester, England: Manchester
University Press, 1982. 178p. bibliog. maps.
Katzenellenbogen's book is a synthesis of English and South African materials,
both official and private, on the history of the integration of southern Mozambique
into the South African-controlled regional economic sub-system. However, the
book was criticized for its failure to deal with the complexity of the interaction of
settlers and state on the Portuguese side, and for its lack of explanatory power.

Transport and Communications

Thus, Jeanne Penvenne wrote that the 'presentation of Portuguese interests . . . [is] so shallow a portrait punctuated with references to "national pride" . . . as to invoke shades of uneconomic imperialism' (*Africa* vol. 55, no. 1 [1985], p. 106–07); while David Hedges commented that 'Some of the weakest parts of the book . . . are in the introductory chapters, especially the passages dealing with the beginnings of southern Mozambican labour migration . . . there is no attempt to relate the inception of migration to the advance of capitalism in southern Africa as a whole.', (*Journal of African History* vol. 24, no. 3 [1983], p. 399–400). There is a vast literature on the economic relationship between South Africa and Mozambique. Among lesser known items, especially dissertations, see the following: for the Portuguese colonial viewpoint, Rómulo Cilindro de Oliveira Figueiredo's 'As relações económicas com a Africa do Sul e o progresso de Moçambique' [Economic relations with South Africa and progress in Mozambique] (Dissertation, Curso de Altos Estudos Ultramarinos, Lisbon, 1961. 319p. bibliog.) and Arlindo Garcia's 'A mão-de-obra portuguesa e a industria mineira da África do Sul' [Portuguese labour and the South African mining industry] (Licenciatura dissertation, Instituto Superior de Ciências Sociais e Política Ultramarina, Universidade Técnica de Lisboa, 1963); for the historical relationship as seen by researchers in South Africa itself, Barend S. C. van Tonder's 'Die verhouding tussen die Boere in die Zuid-Afrikaanische Republiek en die Portuguese van Mosambiek tussen die jare 1836–1869' [Relations between the Boers of the South African Republic and the Portuguese of Mozambique, 1836–69] (MA thesis, University of Pretoria, 1952) and Carlos Manuel Gomes da Silva Peres' 'The Mozambique economy with special reference to its interdependence with South Africa' (MBA thesis, University of the Witwatersrand, 1975. 84p.); see also W. de Beer, 'Mozambique and South Africa' (MA thesis, School of Oriental and African Studies, University of London, 1976); and finally an analysis in the journal of the South African Communist Party, Z. Nkosi's 'The S[outh] African threat to Mozambique', *The African Communist* no. 60 (First quarter 1975).

508 **Portos e Caminhos de Ferro. Ports and Railways.**
  Maputo: National Directorate of Ports and Railways (DNPCF), 1972– . quarterly.

A bibliographer's nightmare, this review changes its title with nearly every issue; variants have included *Boletim Trimestral*, *Revista Trimestral*, and in one memorable variant which lasted for one issue only, *Xitimela* (a Shangaan word for 'train'). Most of the post-independence numbers have been bilingual, although the English is sometimes a little odd; interviews originally in English have sometimes been retranslated from Portuguese, for instance. Despite all these criticisms, this mixture of news, statistics and analysis is virtually the only current source in English on the subject, and is in that sense a useful publication.

509 **Portos, caminhos de ferro e transportes de Moçambique: catálogo da 1ª. exposição bibliográfica sobre caminhos de ferro de Moçambique realizada em Nampula em Maio de 1973.** (Ports, railways and transport in Mozambique: catalogue of the first book exhibition on Mozambican railways held in Nampula in May 1973.) [Lourenço Marques, Mozambique: Caminhos de Ferro de Moçambique], 1973. 39p.

A moderately useful bibliography on railway history, with the ports relegated firmly to second place; a lot of general background material has also crept in. There are 226 numbered references, in author order, or, in the case of anonymous works (items 123–226), in title order in a special section. There are no indexes of any kind and the introduction is little more than a dedicatory paragraph, so we cannot know what the criteria for inclusion were; but the bibliographical descriptions are complete, with details of pagination, and even locations in specific libraries of colonial times (which may or may not still exist).

Employment, Manpower and Migrant Labour

510   **Mozambican labour to Rhodesia.**
Yussuf Adamo [sic], Robert Davies, Judith Head. *Mozambican Studies* no. 2 (1981), p. 58–70.

Mozambican workers did not only migrate to South Africa; they also entered Southern Rhodesia in large numbers. According to this preliminary account by Adam, Davies and Head, by 1974 there were nearly 80,000 male and over 8,000 female migrant workers on the farms and in the factories and mines of UDI Rhodesia. Rather loosely periodized and under-documented, the article was vigorously attacked by António Rita-Ferreira in 'Trabalho migratório de Moçambique para a Ródesia do Sul', *História* no. 80 (June 1985), p. 42–49. See also the following article by Robert Davies on 'The Portugal/Rhodesia Joint Trade and Economic Liaison Committee, 1965–70', based on the secret files of the committee itself, in the same issue of *Mozambican Studies*, p. 71–76.

511   **Trabalho migratório na África austral: um apontamento crítico sobre a literatura existente.** (Migrant labour in southern Africa: a critical note on the literature.)
Colin Darch. *Estudos Moçambicanos* no. 3 (1981), p. 81–96.

A critical survey article in Portuguese, based on the bibliographical chapter prepared in English for *Black gold: the Mozambican miner, proletarian and peasant* (q.v.). Sections deal with South African capitalism, the peasant base of the migrant system, the supplier states, the ILO (International Labour Organization) and the migrant labour system, health and safety in the mines, strikes and resistance, and the future of the system. The article lists eighty-four references.

512 **Black gold: the Mozambican miner, proletarian and peasant.**
Ruth First, pictures by Moira Forjaz, work-songs and interviews
recorded by Alpheus Manghezi. Brighton, Sussex, England:
Harvester Press; New York: St. Martin's Press, 1983. 256p.
bibliog. maps.

Black gold was published posthumously: on 17 August 1982 Ruth First was
murdered in her office at the Centre of African Studies in Maputo, by a South
African assassin's bomb, hidden in a letter. The book is the culmination of a six-
year process, beginning in 1977 with Ruth First's arrival in Mozambique to
organize CEA research brigades for the study of the migrant labour system and its
impact on peasant agriculture, especially in Inhambane. The first results were
presented at the Conference on Migratory Labour in Southern Africa, held in
Lusaka, Zambia in April 1978; see 'Labour migration to South Africa: the case
study of Mozambique' in: *Migratory labour in southern Africa* [Addis Ababa]:
United Nations Economic Commission for Africa, 1985. p. 401–29; the CEA
itself also issued various mimeographed texts in both English and Portuguese,
from which *Black gold* was eventually edited.

513 **Emigração indígena para o Rand: um problema que preocupa
Moçambique.** (Native emigration to the Rand: a worrying problem
for Mozambique.)
Henrique Terreiro Galha. Dissertation, Curso de Altos Estudos
Ultramarinos, Lisbon, 1952. 257p. bibliog.

Galha gives the history of early contacts from 1869 to 1901; the period of the
Modus Vivendi from 1901 up to the Convention of 1928; and the post-Convention
period up to the time of writing. He discusses the causes of emigration, giving as
major reasons higher salaries, bad treatment by the colonial state, and the
arbitrariness of the Portuguese legal system. Less important contributory factors,
according to Galha, are bad treatment by the bosses, the chance to obtain cattle,
access to land, lack of water, the forced cultivation of cotton, unscrupulous
trading practices and tax avoidance. He closes with a discussion of the effects of
the shortage of labour. On the historical causes of the migrant labour system in
the late 19th century, see Patrick Harries' 'The origins of migrant labour from
Mozambique to South Africa, with special reference to the Delagoa Bay hinter
land, ca. 1860–1897' (PhD dissertation, University of London, 1983).

514 **Labour emigration among the Moçambique Thonga: cultural and
political factors.**
Marvin Harris. *Africa* vol. 29, no. 1 (Jan. 1959), p. 50–66.

'Serious attempts to theorise the role of migrant labour in the Mozambican
economy date from the debate between Marvin Harris and António Rita-Ferreira
in the pages of *Africa* . . . Harris had argued in his original article that the
"traditional" Tsonga homestead contained within itself tensions arising from the
system of different houses for each wife; the sons of these houses were allocated
unequal shares of cattle on the death of their father, and this was said to create a
class of the dispossessed.' (Ruth First, *Black gold* (q.v.), p. 196). This article, by
the author of *Portugal's African 'wards'* (q.v.), prompted a reply from António
Rita-Ferreira, arguing that local ecology and external market incentives were

more important factors than Harris's social structure and alien oppression. The series eventually became a four-part exchange between the two of them (the other contributions were Rita-Ferreira's comments, *Africa* vol. 30 (1960), p. 141–51; Harris's reply, *Africa* vol. 30 (1960), p. 243–50; and Rita-Ferreira's comments on the reply, *Africa* vol. 31 (1961), p. 75–77.).

515 **Portugal's African 'wards': a first-hand report on labour and education in Moçambique.**
Marvin Harris.   New York: American Committee on Africa, 1958. 36p.

A polemical pamphlet on the exploitation of labour and the misuse of education to control Africans' lives. Harris attacks the idea of lusotropicalism vigorously; he writes in his preface that he 'cannot claim that this pamphlet has been written in a disinterested or unemotional frame of mind'. It is rather 'an indictment of a social and political system which demonstrably molds the minds and hearts of men into shapes that are alien to their own traditions . . . '.

516 **State, capital and migrant labour in Zambezia, Mozambique: a study of the labour force of Sena Sugar Estates Limited.**
Judith Frances Head.   PhD dissertation, University of Durham, 1980. 383p. bibliog.

Judith Head's important study of the SSE, for many years the largest employer of labour in the country, is based on careful archival research and on field-work. Head, one of the first foreign researchers to work in Mozambique after independence, asks why the migrant labour system was able to survive on the Zambezi plantations from the late 19th century up to the 1960s. She argues that until the 1930s, when the state established monopoly control over the sale of labour, there was a labour shortage in the area; in the 1940s and afterwards a new shortage arose because of the introduction of forced cotton-production and the emergence of new plantations. The system of migrant labour was allowed to continue because state control of the labour supply permitted the plantations to go on paying low wages and to resist workers' demands for more. This situation only began to change slowly in the 1950s. This thesis is currently being translated for publication in a Portuguese edition by the Universidade Eduardo Mondlane in Maputo.

517 **Over-reach: the South African gold mines and the struggle for the labour of Zambezia, 1890–1920.**
Alan H. Jeeves.   *Canadian Journal of African Studies* vol. 17, no. 3 (1983), p. 393–412.

A disturbing article. After the Anglo-Boer war, the South African mines were so desperate for cheap labour that for a brief period they even imported workers from northern China. Jeeves shows here that the ferocious competition for labour led, with the full complicity of the mine-owners, to illegal recruitment on a large scale in the northern areas of Mozambique, in what one official described as 'a kind of slave-trade'. Levels of mortality in the mines, high even for the period, were simply ignored or explained away, and it was only after a chance political scandal that improvements occurred. Unscrupulous and rapacious labour touts and criminal gangs were regularly used by the Chamber of Mines recruiters, with terrible results for the unfortunate migrants, until the South Africans eventually banned recruitment north of latitude 22° S in mid-1913.

518   **Alguns aspectos ligados a exploração da força de trabalho migrante na Província d'Inhambane entre 1897 e 1928.** (Some aspects of the exploitation of migrant labour from Inhambane Province, 1897–1928.)

Ana Maria Loforte.   Licenciatura dissertation, Universidade Eduardo Mondlane, [1983]. 80p. bibliog. maps.

This undated work, which carries no identification as a thesis, consists of a short introduction on sources, a chapter on the mobilization of labour with a discussion of the 1897, 1901, 1909 and 1928 agreements between South Africa and Portugal; a second chapter on the system of deferred payments (the appropriation of salaries by the colonial state); and a chapter on working conditions and the consequences for Inhambane of the migrant labour system.   A copy of this thesis is deposited in the Historical Archive, call no. AHM B845.

519   **The voice of the miner.**

Alpheus Manghezi.   *Mozambican Studies* no. 1 (1980), p. 75–88.

A revealing montage made up of extracts from songs and interviews with migrant workers and their wives. The miners describe in their own words the sufferings and humiliations involved in the process of recruitment, the journey to South Africa, working conditions, and the return home. There is no doubt in the minds of these speakers that the coming of FRELIMO meant an improvement in their lot. Manghezi conducted the interviews, transcribed and translated the recordings, and selected these moving extracts. For an account of the recent effects of the migrant labour system on the southern peasantry, see Kenneth Hermele's brief *Migration and starvation: an essay on southern Mozambique* (Uppsala, Sweden: Working Group for the Study of Development Strategies, Dept of Development Studies, University of Uppsala, Uppsala, Sweden, 1984. 40p. [Akut, no. 32]).

520   **The unmaking of an African petite bourgeoisie: Lourenço Marques, Mozambique.**

Jeanne Penvenne.   Boston, Massachusetts: African Studies Center, Boston University, 1982. 20p. (Boston University. African Studies Center. Working Papers, no. 57).

This paper derives from Penvenne's doctoral research, and is a study of the way in which the position of the African and Afro-European or mulatto petit bourgeoisie was undermined in the capital in the first years of the 20th century by the policies of the colonial state towards newly-arriving Portuguese immigrants. As Penvenne points out, 'local traders, artisans, commodity producers and potential bureaucrats' were needed in the 19th century for the port complex, the state structures and commerce. But the white immigrants who began to arrive in large numbers in the 20th century were mostly poor and unskilled, and the state funnelled 'even the smallest, simplest business and career opportunities to them' in exchange for political support. Thus, what Penvenne sharply terms 'Portugal's paper-pretty ideology of non-racial cultural assimilation . . . was quickly reduced to hollow window-dressing'. Divisions were fostered at all levels – religious, sexual and by skin-colour – to the point that racism cut across classes. However, Penvenne concludes, awareness of this 'was not successfully forged into a persistent strategy for community based advancement in this period'.

521 **Report on native labour conditions in the Province of Mozambique, Portuguese E[ast] A[frica].**
South African Labour Bulletin vol. 2 (July 1985), p. 14–27.
This is a reprint of a confidential report on working conditions in Mozambique, prepared by a WENELA (Witwatersrand Native Labour Association) recruiting agent for the Transvaal Chamber of Mines in 1922. It is an unvarnished account: the anonymous author writes that in the worst parts of the country 'there is no abuse, excess or crime against natives left uncommitted'. Moreover, Government policy 'is to hush up each scandal . . . Real punishment of an official for any crime whatsoever committed against natives is unknown'. However, the writer also notes that ' . . . Britain cannot escape some share of the blame for the evils here recorded', at least as far as Niassa is concerned.

522 **O movimento migratório de trabalhadores entre Moçambique e a África do Sul.** (Labour migration between Mozambique and South Africa.)
António Rita-Ferreira. Lisbon: Centro de Estudos Políticos e Sociais, Junta de Investigações do Ultramar, 1963. 193p. bibliog. (Estudos de Ciências Políticas e Sociais, no. 67).
In this monograph, published after his famous exchange with Marvin Harris over the causes of migrant labour in *Africa* (q.v.), Rita-Ferreira returns to the fray with a discussion of what he terms the spontaneous formation of the migratory labour flow, and its principal and secondary causes. He then looks at planning and legislation, the illegal flow of migrant labour (still a major factor today, twenty years later), and attempts to stabilize the situation in the rural areas through measures affecting agricultural livestock. However, for a much more coherent account of the migrant labour system as structurally part of the capitalist system in southern Africa, see Ruth First's *Black gold*. . . .

523 **The origins of migrant labour, colonialism and the underdevelopment of Mozambique.**
D. J. Webster. In: *Working papers in southern African studies*. Edited by P. L. Bonner. Johannesburg: Institute of African Studies, 1978, p. 236–79.
Although political economy provides a perfectly adequate theory, various other explanations have been advanced for the persistence of the migrant labour system in southern Africa, from the ecological to the anthropological, of which last Webster's work is an example. See also his thesis 'Agnation, alternative structures and the individual in Chopi society', (PhD dissertation, Rhodes University, 1975. 420p.); and the article 'Migrant labour, social formations and the proletarianisation of the Chopi', *African Perspectives* no. 1 (1978), p. 157–74.

Labour Movement and the Trade Unions

524 O movimento operário em Lourenço Marques, 1898–1927. (The labour movement in Lourenzo Marques, 1898–1927.)
José Capela (pseudonym). Oporto, Portugal: Afrontamento [n.d.]. 282p.

José Capela (real name José Soares Martins), cultural attaché at the Portuguese Embassy in Maputo), is the author of several historical studies and documentary collections of Portuguese colonial history. Unfortunately, it would seem that none of his work has been translated into English. In this volume he analyses trade union ideology, the role of the press, the associations, strikes and political groupings in the early years of this century, before the introduction of the Salazarist Estado Novo (New State). Capela writes that the Mozambican labour movement was not, however, genuinely or definitely 'African' and moreover ignored the growing 'sub-proletariat'. See also Capela's article on a much shorter period, 'O movimento operário em Lourenço Marques, 1910–1927', *História* [Lisbon] no. 15 (Jan. 1980), p. 26–37.

525 História da formação da classe trabalhadora em Manica e Sofala ao sul do Punguè, 1892–1926. (The history of the formation of the working class in Manica and Sofala, south of the River Pungwe, 1892–1926.)
Miguel Joaquim da Cruz. Licenciatura dissertation, Eduardo Mondlane University, 1982. 313p. bibliog. maps.

One of the first Master's dissertations in history to be written in independent Mozambique, under the supervision of David Hedges. Cruz describes the Nguni social formation in southern Manica and Sofala at the end of the 19th century, and how its ruling class was destroyed. This process was followed between 1892 (the date of the foundation of the Mozambique Company) and 1906 by the promotion of small-scale commercial production in the peasant sector, and between 1907 and 1926 by a fierce campaign against the peasantry, both periods

211

being characterized by the gradual emergence of a working class. Cruz deals with the impact of the hut-tax, land expropriation, the rule of the Mozambique Company, labour legislation, the system of labour control, recruitment and migrant labour, the intensification of the exploitation of labour between 1914 and 1922, and the class and social struggles of the early 1920s. From the 1920s onwards, we see the emergence of a class of semi-proletarianized workers depending principally on wage labour.

526 **From porters to labor extractors: the Chikunda and Kololo in the Lake Malawi and Tchiri River area.**
Allen Isaacman, Elias Mandala. In: *The workers of African trade.* Edited by Catherine Coquery-Vidrovitch, Paul E. Lovejoy. Beverly Hills, California; London: Sage, 1985, p. 209–42. (Sage Series on African Modernization and Development, vol. 11).

Isaacman and Mandala argue in this 1983 conference paper that their case-studies of the Chikunda and Kololo groups suggest a missing dimension in African labour history, that of the relationship of ethnicity and class. The Chikunda were originally slaves of the *prazo*-holders of the Zambezi Valley in Mozambique, many of whom fled north-westwards to settle among Chewa- and Mang'anja-speakers along the upper Zambezi and in the Tchiri (Shire) Valley in present-day Malawi. The Kololo were Sotho-speaking labourers who worked as porters for David Livingstone's explorations and who ended up in Tete, where they used their firearms to subjugate the local populations. Isaacman and Mandala present detailed accounts based on oral sources and archival research in Portugal, Britain and Zambia, and argue that the ethnicity of these groups 'evolved in the context of specific historical circumstances and class relationships'. They were able to transform their situation dramatically, ceasing to be labourers and becoming labour-extractors. Isaacman wrote an earlier paper on the subject, entitled 'The origin, formation and early history of the Chikunda of south central Africa', *Journal of African History* vol. 13, no. 3 (1972), p. 443–61.

527 **Forced labour by those who lived through it.**
Alpheus Manghezi. *Mozambican Studies* no. 2 (1981), p. 26–35.

The Portuguese colonial state regarded small peasant farmers as legally unemployed, and regularly staged manhunts for labour, sending the victims off to the plantations or public works. This article is made up of interviews with survivors, and reveals that Mozambican workers were not quite as passive in the face of this brutal treatment as was previously believed. Alpheus Manghezi reproduces oral testimony to two *xibalo* (forced labour) strikes, in 1943 and 1956. See also Manghezi's 'A mulher e o trabalho' [Women and work], *Estudos Moçambicanos* no. 3 (1981), p. 45–56, which is, unfortunately, not yet available in English.

528 *Chibalo* **and the working class: Lourenço Marques, 1870–1962.**
Jeanne Penvenne. *Mozambican Studies* no. 2 (1981), p. 9–25.

Chibalo (or *xibalo*, or *chibaro*), meaning 'forced labour', was the device used by the Portuguese colonial state throughout the whole of Mozambique as a response to the competition for scarce labour from stronger capital outside its borders. Mozambicans were simply 'rounded up and marched off to work by the police and the native affairs bureaucracy'. The article describes how the city of Lourenço Marques was 'largely built by *chibalo* labour', and details the effects of the system on the structure of the working class. The piece is an edited version of *Forced labor and the origin of an African working class: Lourenço Marques, 1870–1962* (Brookline, Massachusetts: African Studies Center, Boston University, 1979. 26p. bibliog. [Boston University. African Studies Center. Working Papers.]).

529   **A history of African labor in Lourenço Marques, Mozambique, 1877 to 1950.**
Jeanne Marie Penvenne.   PhD dissertation, Boston University, Massachusetts, 1982. 511p. bibliog. maps.

From the late 19th century the Portuguese attempted to control the movement of migrant labour from southern Mozambique to the industrial centres of South Africa for their own profit. The system was formalized through inter-state agreements. Penvenne argues that up to the 1950s both the Portuguese colonial government and Portuguese capital in the colony depended on 'state-conscripted cheap contract labour'. African participation in the urban society and economy was restricted to the sale of labour power; even here, Africans were not allowed to compete with whites for attractive jobs. Forced labour in Mozambique encouraged migration to South Africa, creating labour shortages which in turn reinforced the Portuguese dependence on contract labour. Workers responded to these conditions with indirect and diffuse methods of defending their interests. By 1950, however, the working class was demoralized, and the African petit bourgeoisie had been marginalized and replaced by a Portuguese one. For a piece of work on a similar topic by a Mozambican historian, see the thesis by Aurélio Rocha, entitled 'Lourenço Marques: classe e raça na formação da classe trabalhadora do sector ferro-portuário, 1900–1926' [Lourenço Marques: class and race in the formation of the working class in the port and railways, 1900–26] (Licenciatura dissertation, History Department, Eduardo Mondlane University, 1982. 137p. bibliog.). Rocha looks at the development of the port-railways sector and the creation of a cheap labour force; class struggles in the sector; and the institutionalization of the colour bar. He includes a number of useful statistical appendixes.

530   **Labor struggles at the port of Lourenço Marques, 1900–1933.**
Jeanne Marie Penvenne.   *Review* vol. 8, no. 2 (Fall 1984), p. 249–85.

In this article Penvenne focuses on the labour history of the Lourenço Marques port and railway complex in the first third of the 20th century; there had been a burst of strikes between the First World War and 1922, but the workers were unaffected by the unrest in other African countries between 1935 and 1945. Penvenne looks at these events in the context of the Sul do Save economy within the southern African subsystem, in particular the growth of the labour-hungry agro-industrial complex of the Transvaal and the Natal sugar-fields. She identifies alcohol and *xibalo* as two factors which constrained a peasantry which still had access to land to sell their labour. Within the port itself, this period saw the introduction of a colour bar between skilled and unskilled jobs, and a shift towards a labour force made up of both volunteer and *xibalo* workers under a

213

form of state control which guaranteed work to Portuguese immigrants. This was also a period when two currencies were competing in Lourenço Marques: the pound sterling from South Africa (and to some extent the gold escudo) on one hand and the paper escudo from Portugal on the other. Between 1914 and 1933 the exchange rate rose from 5$40 to 150$00 to the pound, hitting the working class especially hard. Strikes in this period met with increasingly vicious state reaction and militarization; the last strike in August 1933, over a wage cut of *quinhenta* (or 0$50), was crushed by a mixture of deceit and force, and led to riots in the city. Penvenne concludes grimly that 'workers deemed strikes inappropriate in the new political climate.'

531 **'Eingeboren-Arbeit': Formen der Ausbeutung unter der portugiesischen Kolonialherrschaft in Mosambik.** ('Native labour': forms of exploitation under the Portuguese colonial régime in Mozambique.)
Martin Schaedel.   Cologne, FRG: Pahl-Rugenstein Verlag, 1984. 511p. bibliog. maps. (Pahl-Rugenstein Hochschulschriften; Gesellschafts- und Naturwissenschaften, no. 165. Serie 'Dritte Welt').

A progressive doctoral dissertation on labour history, covering the 20th century up to independence. Schaedel's work is almost too detailed, but he is especially good on such topics as how the 1927 labour code remained a dead letter almost into the 1950s, or exactly how the ILO inspection tours went wrong. There is an extensive bibliography. It is to be hoped that this book will be translated into English or Portuguese.

532 **O trabalho indígena: estudo de direito colonial.** (Native labour: study in colonial law.)
Joaquim da Silva Cunha.   Lisbon: Agência-Geral das Colónias, 1949. 289p. bibliog.

Although not exclusively about Mozambique, this is the standard Portuguese colonial account of labour legislation in the African colonies before the reforms at the end of the 1950s. Silva Cunha gives us a dry, juridical account of the place of 'native' labour in international colonial law, and in specifically Portuguese colonial law; he also discusses the Portuguese position on various ILO conventions.

533 **Workers' control in Mozambique.**
People's Power in Mozambique, Angola and Guinea-Bissau no. 10 (Oct.–Dec. 1977), p. 21–29.

The Production Councils were set up in late 1976 as the proto-trade union organization of independent Mozambique, and were intended to play a key role in the destruction of capitalist social relations of production. They were to work alongside the elected and political Dynamizing Groups, and the factory administrations. Naturally, some private employers attempted to enlist the Production Councils as allies against the Dynamizing Groups. Throughout 1977 the Councils were very active, but by the end of the 1970s they were encountering

214

difficulties. In October 1983, the Production Councils were replaced by a full-scale trade union federation, the Organization of Mozambican Workers (OTM). See also the detailed publication of the *Resoluções do IV Plenário dos C[onselhos de] P[rodução] sobre restruturação dos sectores e estruturas* [Resolutions of the 4th Plenary of the Production Councils on reorganizing sectors and structures] (Maputo, 1977. 2 vols.).

Statistics

General

534 **Notas sobre fontes estatísticas oficiais referentes à economia colonial moçambicana: uma crítica geral.** (Notes on official statistical sources on the Mozambican colonial economy: a general critique.) Colin Darch. *Estudos Moçambicanos* no. 4 (1983–85), p. 103–25.

Argues in favour of the idea that statistical data are created within a theoretical framework which determines their form, and therefore colonial data must be analysed in terms of their original purpose before being re-used for modern studies. In addition, the Mozambican materials include cases of incompetence as well as of deliberate fudging. Darch discusses the census series and other statistical and planning serials, in terms of a periodization of the labour policies of the Portuguese colonial state.

535 **Statistics Africa: sources for social, economic and market research.** Joan M. Harvey. Beckenham, Kent, England: CBD Research, 1978. 2nd ed. 374p.

This is a useful and generally reliable listing of statistical sources, with the names and addresses of the principal organizations responsible for the collection of data, and with details of any specialized libraries or bibliographies. General statistical sources are listed on p. 1–43; and the sources for Mozambique on p. 209–214, items 913–31. Most entries are briefly annotated.

536 **Moçambique em números.** (Mozambique in numbers.) Lourenço Marques, Mozambique: Direcção dos Serviços de Planeamento e Integração Económica, 1973. 23p.

One of the handful of statistical abstracts available, published at the very end of the colonial period, and still useful as a summary of the situation just before

Statistics. Statistical sources

independence. It covers agriculture, livestock, fisheries, mining, industry, construction, electrical energy, transport, tourism, finance and credit, foreign trade, the balance of payments, and short sections on the Fourth Development Plan (Plano de Fomento), which never went into effect. It also includes a table of expected investment. A more recent pamphlet biased towards health statistics is *Dados estatísticos de base* [Basic statistical facts] (Maputo: Ministério da Saúde, 1984. 16p.)

537 **Estatística da Capitania dos Rios de Senna do anno de 1806.**
(Statistics on the Captaincy of the Rivers of Sena in 1806.)
António Norberto de Barbosa de Villas Boas Truão. Lisbon:
Imprensa Nacional, 1889. 29p. (Ministério dos Negócios da
Marinha e Ultramar. Documentos para a História das Colónias
Portuguezas).

Written in 1810, but only published in 1889, Truão's work actually includes quite a lot of 'statistical' work in the modern sense, with tables on the baptized population, the slave-trade, sugar production, exports and imports from Quelimane in 1806, industry, state revenues from the *prazos da corôa*, and on the military garrison. Most of the work, however, is in the form of an essay.

Statistical sources

538 **Anuário Estatístico. 1926/1928–1973.** (Statistical Annual
1926/28–1973.)
Lourenço Marques, Mozambique: Imprensa Nacional, 1929–76.
annual.

This is the main general source for statistical information on colonial Mozambique from the founding of the Estado Novo (New State) until just before independence. The title and issuing body vary slightly over the years; there are also some supplements. For slightly less formally presented statistical information on earlier years, see such publications as the Portuguese Ministry of the Colonies' regular *Relatório Apresentado ao Congresso da República* [Report Presented to the Congress of the Republic] (Lisbon, 1917– . annual.); and part 3 of the *Anuário Colonial* [Colonial Annual] (Lisbon, 1917– . annual.). Customs and excise statistics were also published, for Mozambique at least, as early as the nineteenth century. The Historical Archive in Maputo has *Estatística das alfândegas da Província de Moçambique no anno civil de 1884–* [Customs statistics for Mozambique Province for the financial year 1884–] up to 1887, but other issues may have been published. Note that the Portuguese Ministry of the Navy and Overseas was divided up in 1911, with 'overseas' falling to the Ministry of the Colonies. In 1951 this latter was renamed the Ministry of Overseas. Other variants of all these names appear on publications.

217

539 **Boletim Mensal de Estatística.** (Monthly Statistical Bulletin.)
Lourenço Marques, Mozambique: Imprensa Nacional, 1925–75.
monthly.

The regular current statistical source in colonial times, this bulletin continued to appear until a few months after independence, and seems to have had a chequered publishing history. It was first published as the *Boletim Económico e Estatístico* (until 1932); changed its title to the *Boletim Mensal de Estatística* (until 1938); became a quarterly *Boletim Trimestral de Estatística* until 1947, when it seems to have disappeared altogether until 1960; reappeared as the *Boletim Mensal Estatístico*, and from 1967 until 1975 was issued as the *Boletim Mensal da Direcção Provincial dos Serviços de Estatística Geral*. Note that the Mozambican Repartição de Estatística (Statistics Department) was set up in 1924, and changed its name and its affiliation many times over the years, including such variations as the Direcção dos Serviços de Economia e Estatística Geral [the Directorate of Economic and General Statistical Services]. At times it was regarded as part of the metropolitan Statistical Institute.

540 **Anuário estatístico do Território de Manica e Sofala, sob a administração da Companhia de Moçambique.** (Statistical annual of Manica and Sofala Territory, under the administration of the Mozambique Company.)
Direcção de Estatística e Propaganda da Companhia de Moçambique. Lisbon: Sociedade Nacional de Tipografia, 1930–34. 3 vols.

Large pieces of Mozambique were controlled by concessionary companies, which behaved like states, well into the 20th century. These three volumes of the major concessionary company's statistical annual were the only ones published, refer to the years 1928, 1930 and 1932, and constitute an important source for that limited period.

541 **Informação estatística 1975–1984.** (Statistical information, 1975–1984.)
Direcção Nacional de Estatística. Maputo: Comissão Nacional do Plano, 1985. 96p.

At independence the Central Statistical Bureau had a staff of around 300 people, and was producing a range of statistical publications on a regular basis. After independence the Bureau's output ground to a halt as the Portuguese staff fled, and most of the colonial series stopped with data for 1973 or even earlier. The (Portuguese) director of the Bureau left in November 1976, by which time there was a staff of thirty, not one of whom was a qualified statistician. During the early years after independence, the main source for economic statistics was the bulletin *Indicadores económicas* (Economic indicators) published by the Bank of Mozambique. The Planning Commission produced a couple of slim statistical publications, but this is effectively the first full-scale set of tables to be published since independence. A supplement for 1985 has already appeared.

542 **Estatísticas do Comércio Externo.** (Foreign Trade Statistics.)
Lourenço Marques, Mozambique: 1901–70.
The title and issuing body of this series vary. For trade statistics during the colonial period see also, for example, the following series: *Cabotagem* [Coastal Shipping] (Lourenço Marques, Mozambique: 1927–67); the *Boletim das Alfândegas* [Customs and Excise Bulletin] (Lourenço Marques, Mozambique: 1902– .) publication of which continued for a period after independence, but which now seems to have ceased; and the *Estatística do movimento comercial e marítimo no Território de Companhia* [Statistics of Commercial and Maritime Traffic in Company Territory] (Beira, Mozambique: Imprensa da Companhia de Moçambique, 1901–40).

543 **Anuário Estatístico do Império Colonial. 1943–1961.** (Statistical Annual of the Colonial Empire. 1943–1961.)
Instituto Nacional de Estatística. Lisbon: 1945–62. annual.
This was a spin-off from the more general Portuguese *Anuário Estatístico 1875–* . (Lisbon, 1877– .), which still appears. It includes geographical, demographic, economic and other kinds of statistical information for all Portuguese colonies. The title varies (. . . *do Ultramar*, 1952–1961). Note that the 1875 issue of the *Anuário Estatístico do Reino de Portugal* has only the sketchiest statistics on Africa: on p. 252, for example, the import-export figures for Africa cover only nineteen classes of product, and give no breakdown between the different territories. There are no population data. By 1942, when the Portuguese annual stopped covering African colonies, we find a wide range of economic and social topics covered – demography, justice, commerce, navigation, agriculture, industry, and so on. In 1961 the *Anuário Estatístico do Ultramar* ceased publication, and the colonial statistics were reincorporated in Portugal's *Anuário Estatístico*, but this time as a separate volume entitled *Províncias Ultramarinas* (Overseas Provinces); the last issue of which is for 1972, and was published in 1974.

544 **Anuário estatístico dos domínios ultramarinos portugueses.**
(Statistical annual of Portuguese overseas possessions.)
Ministério dos Negócios da Marinha e Ultramar. Lisbon: Imprensa Nacional, 1905. 1157p. maps.
The work is organized thematically (population, criminology, public assistance, public education, finance, commerce and shipping, posts, telephones, roads and expenditure on public works). The contents list is organized in tabular form by country, so that Mozambican statistics can be found quite easily. There is an introduction on the gaps in information, which also mentions a census of 31 December 1900.

545 **Estatística Agrícola. 1941–1972.** (Agricultural statistics. 1941–72.)
Repartição Técnica de Estatística. Lourenço Marques, Mozambique: Imprensa Nacional, 1949– . annual.
The basic agricultural statistics for the later colonial period, these data must be used with great care by modern researchers. From 1968 onwards the volumes were compiled by the Missão de Inquérito Agrícola de Moçambique. For early 20th-century agricultural statistics see, for example, the *Jornal d'Agricultura da*

219

Statistics. Statistical sources

Companhia de Moçambique [Agricultural Journal of the Mozambique Company] (Beira, Mozambique: 1911–12), most of which is in English; or the *Boletim Agrícola e Pecuário* [Agriculture and Cattle-breeding Bulletin] (Lourenço Marques, Mozambique: 1910–33), the title of which varied widely. There were also a series of agricultural inquiries and censuses of varying reliability and comprehensiveness, going back to the 1920s. See specifically 'Inquerito agrícola de 1928–29' [Agricultural inquiry of 1928–29] *Boletim Agrícola e Pecuário* no. 1/2 (1930), p. 69–79; the Direcção dos Serviços de Agricultura's *Recenseamento agrícola de 1929–1930* [Agricultural census of 1929–30] (Lourenço Marques, Mozambique: Imprensa Nacional, 1932. 220p.); on white commercial farming in the south 'Inquérito agrícola de 1930–31 no distrito de Lourenço Marques' [Agricultural inquiry of 1930–31 in Lourenço Marques district], *Boletim Agrícola e Pecuário* no. 1/4 (1932), p. 87–116; published as an appendix to the *Anuário Estatístico*, vol. 12 (1939), the *Inquérito agrícola de 1937–1938 e 1938–1939* [Agricultural inquiry of 1937–38 and 1938–39] (Lourenço Marques: Imprensa Nacional, 1941. 84p.); the *Recenseamento agrícola de 1939–1940* [Agricultural census of 1939–1940] (Lourenço Marques, Mozambique: Imprensa Nacional, 1944. 143p.); the Bureau's *Recenseamento agrícola, 1951* [Agricultural census of 1951] (Lourenço Marques, Mozambique: Imprensa Nacional, 1955. 785p.) and the Mission's *Recenseamento agrícola de Moçambique* [Agricultural census of Mozambique] (Lourenço Marques, Mozambique: Missão de Inquérito Agrícola de Moçambique, 1961–66. 11 vols.).

546 **Estatística Industrial. 1947–1973.** (Industrial Statistics. 1947–73.) Repartição Técnica de Estatística. Lourenço Marques, Mozambique: Imprensa Nacional, 1948–74. annual.

See also for information on industrial development, the *I recenseamento industrial 1971* [First industrial census, 1971] (Lourenço Marques, Mozambique: Direcção Provincial dos Serviços de Estatística, 1974. 145p.).

Ecology and the Environment

General

547 **In the mangroves of southern Africa.**
Patricia Berjak, G. K. Campbell, Barbara I. Huckett,
N. W. Pammenter. [Durban, South Africa]: Wildlife Society of
Southern Africa, Natal Branch, 1977. 73p. bibliog. maps.

The mangrove communities of the southern African Indian Ocean coastline run
from Inhaca Island, just off Maputo Bay, down to Kabonqaba at the mouth of the
Great Kei River in the Republic of South Africa. 'Mangroves' are not specific
species, but rather trees or shrubs which are the dominant members of a finely-
balanced intertidal environment. This pamphlet, although written principally with
South African mangrove environments in mind, is also used by Mozambican
biologists and ecologists with reference to southern Mozambique. The booklet
consists of sections on plant life, tree zonation, mangrove tree associates, animals
and birds, and chapters on 'do's and don'ts' for visitors to the swamps. It is well
illustrated with photographs and illustrations in both black-and-white and colour,
and with maps and tables.

548 **Studies on the ecology of Maputaland.**
Michael N. Bruton, Keith H. Cooper.   Grahamstown, South
Africa: Rhodes University; Durban, South Africa: Natal Branch of
the Wildlife Society of Southern Africa, 1980. 560p. bibliogs.
maps.

The area under study is defined geographically as the land lying between the
St. Lucia estuary in the south, the Lebombo mountains in the west and the
Mozambique-Natal border in the north – that is, Ingwavuma and Ubombo – but
in fact 'Maputaland' ecologically speaking also covers Maputo Province as far
north as Maputo Bay. The forty papers in this encyclopaedic multi-disciplinary

volume are organized into groups dealing with the environment, plant studies, vertebrate and invertebrate studies, the ecosystem, and the human environment. Individual papers discuss climate and geology, oceanography, lake hydrology, seaweeds, freshwater and terrestrial plants, the coastal dune forest, subtidal marine invertebrates, corals, freshwater invertebrates, molluscs, insects and spiders, fishes, amphibia, reptiles, sea-turtles and crocodiles, birds, mammals, palaeontology and archaeology, conservation and development, the utilization of natural resources, and human disease; there is even a paper by J. L. Ribeiro-Torres on the 'amaThonga people of Maputaland'.

549 **Guide bibliographique du Mozambique: environnement naturel, développement et organisation villageoise.** (Bibliographical guide to Mozambique: natural environment, development and village organization.)
Maria-Edy Chonchol.   Paris: L'Harmattan, 1979. 135p.
A fragmented bibliographical essay divided into chapters on resource potential, the results of colonization and its impact on the environment, the experience of villagization, a chapter on bibliographies and general works, and 'conclusions'. The unnumbered entries are embedded in the text. The work is thin (there are rather too many articles from *Tempo*), the use of Portuguese accents is somewhat idiosyncratic, and the index is so poor that it would perhaps have been better to have left it out altogether. Nonetheless, Chonchol's work is the only one in the field.

550 **The Indian Ocean.**
Stockholm: Royal Swedish Academy of Sciences, 1983. p. 284–362.
(*Ambio* vol. 12, no. 6. Special issue).
This special number of the Swedish bimonthly on the human environment focuses on the south-western Indian Ocean, an area which includes Mozambique at its southern limit, and stretches up as far as Somalia, covering the Comoros, Mauritius, Madagascar, Réunion and the Seychelles. The special number is particularly concerned with such issues as oil pollution, the use and misuse of coastal resources, tourist development and coral mining. Topics discussed by the articles include environmental stress, land use and abuse, soil erosion, pollution, public health and wildlife conservation. Two articles include material about Mozambique: see Barry Munslow et al., 'Energy and development on the African east coast: Somalia, Kenya, Tanzania, and Mozambique' (p. 332–37); and 'The advent of primary health care in Mozambique' by Richard Madeley, Diana Jelley, and Phil O'Keefe (p. 322–25) (q.v.).

551 **A general account of the fauna and flora of mangrove swamps and forests in the Indo-West-Pacific region.**
William MacNae.   *Advances in Marine Biology* vol. 6 (1968), p. 73–270.
The Indo-West-Pacific region is considered by marine biologists and ecologists to comprise a single unit as far as species distribution is concerned. This is, therefore, an account of the mangroves of Inhaca Island, and of south-east Asia, by the author of the definitive general study of Inhaca (q.v.). See also his earlier

article 'Mangrove swamps in South Africa', *Journal of Ecology* vol. 51 (1963), p. 1–25. For another study – this time on corals – which refers to the West Pacific but which contains much information of direct relevance for the marine biologist, see Hans Ditlev, *A field-guide to the reef-building corals of the Indo-Pacific* (Rotterdam, The Netherlands: W. Backhuys; Klampenborg: Scandinavian Science Press, 1980. 291p. map).

552   **A natural history of Inhaca Island, Mozambique.**
Edited by William MacNae, Margaret Kalk.   Johannesburg:
Witwatersrand University Press, 1969. rev. ed. 163p. bibliog.
maps.

Inhaca is a small island at the mouth of Maputo Bay (26° S) which is at the southernmost limit for tropical East African fauna and flora, and also on the northern limit for the species of the Natal littoral. However, the majority of the wildlife is in fact tropical; Inhaca also has the most southerly coral reefs in the world. Because of this, it always attracted intensive study by South African as well as Portuguese scientists in colonial times. The Zoology Department at Witwatersrand University regularly brought marine biology students to Inhaca before Mozambican independence. Despite the very local nature of this book, which first appeared in 1958, it is still the most useful collection of monographs on the fauna of the eastern and south-eastern African tidal area. Among the topics covered are the historical background, the ecology of algae, sea-grasses, coelenterata (corals, jelly-fish and anemones), coral reefs, crustaceans, molluscs and marine fish; there are also lists of the animals and plants collected, and an annotated checklist of flowering plants and ferns. The book can even be referred to for species found as far north as Tanzania, although those which are restricted to true tropical conditions do not occur on Inhaca Island. Nevertheless, the hardiest species, and therefore the most common ones can be found keyed and described here. On coral in general see the volume *Regional variation in Indian Ocean coral reefs* edited by D. R. Stoddart and Maurice Yonge (New York, London: Academic Press, 1971. 584p.), which includes case-studies and general pieces. For a report on a wide-ranging series of studies of different aspects of the economy, natural history and sociology of Inhaca Island, see *Plano de trabalhos integrados da Inhaca: relatório final da 1ᵃ fase* [Plan for co-ordinated studies of Inhaca: report on stage 1] (Maputo: Universidade Eduardo Mondlane, 1976. 193p.) and the *Addenda* to it (1977. 51p.).

553   **Mozambique: national report on socio-economic development and environmental problems.**
René Meeuws.   Maputo: State Secretariat for Physical Planning,
1985. 52p. maps.

Meeuws, a Dutchman with several years' experience in Mozambique, writes that his general purpose is 'to give a broad review of the overall socio-economic development and the most important environmental problems in Mozambique' (p. 50). Thus, much of the report consists of a chapter of background information, covering relief, climate, river systems and water resources, vegetation, administrative divisions and population characteristics, main economic activities, employment, gross national and domestic products, and social conditions. A second chapter deals with urban and rural development in an

Ecology and the Environment. General

environmental context, and is followed by brief treatments of agriculture and land degradation, irrigation, industrial development and population, hydroelectric energy (at Cabora Bassa), mineral resources, deforestation, maritime and coastal resources, fisheries, ports and transport, and tourism. Meeuws concludes that, since 'Mozambique still does not have enough capacity . . . to exercise a stringent control on the use of the natural resources and environment . . . environmental education [is] one of the highest priorities' (p. 50).

554 **O cancro em Moçambique: influência dos factores mesológicos.**
(Cancer in Mozambique: the influence of intermediate factors.)
F. Oliveira Torres. *Revista de Ciências Médicas* [Lourenço
Marques, Mozambique] vol. 1, série B (1969), p. 1–255.

A doctoral dissertation for the Faculty of Medicine at the University of Oporto in Portugal. Liver and bladder cancers have the highest incidence in the world in Mozambique; Oliveira Torres believes that this is due to a combination of environmental and other factors. The chapter 'Conclusions' is also printed in English (p. 217–22). A large number of health- and medicine-related theses and dissertations on Mozambique have been submitted around the world; among the relatively recent ones are A. Cattaneo's 'The national tuberculosis control programme in the People's Republic of Mozambique' (MSc in Community Health in Developing Countries, University of London, 1981); Diana Jelley's 'Primary health care in practice: a study in Maputo, Mozambique' (BMedSci dissertation, University of Nottingham, Nottingham, England. 1982); and M. F. Shapiro's 'Medical care in Portuguese Africa, 1885–1974' (PhD dissertation, University of California at Los Angeles, 1983).

555 **A bibliography of African ecology: a geographically and topically classified list of books and articles.**
Dilwyn J. Rogers. Westport, Connecticut; London: Greenwood
Press, 1979. 499p.

A potentially useful bibliography on African ecology in general, which includes lengthy sections on southern and eastern Africa. These terms are defined by reference to a map, which unhappily does not indicate as claimed the boundaries of the regions as understood by Rogers. Each regional section is subdivided into the following topics: plants, animals, aquatic ecology, abiotic environment, palaeoecology, anthropology, human health, history and geography, conservation, and lastly, general and miscellaneous. Unfortunately, the work is seriously marred by the lack of author and subject indexes; Chonchol's *Guide bibliographique* (q.v.), which also lacks adequate indexing, is to be preferred since it is specifically about Mozambique and is, moreover, cast as a bibliographical essay with substantial critical and informative commentary.

556 **Framework of the Gorongosa ecosystem.**
Kenneth Lochner Tinley. DSc dissertation, University of
Pretoria, South Africa, 1977. 184p. bibliog. maps.

Submitted to the Faculty of Science at the University of Pretoria, this doctoral dissertation studies the general ecology of the Gorongosa area in central Mozambique, north-west of Beira. Well illustrated with photographs, figures and

maps, the work is divided into ten chapters organized in three parts, entitled
'Perspective', 'Correlation', and 'Kaleidoscope', with appendixes on soil and food
plants. It is the first study of the Gorongosa ecosystem as a whole – indeed,
Tinley comments that the thesis uses an 'holistic evaluationary approach . . . in
which the emphasis is on the salient reciprocal relations and kinetic succession of
land surfaces and biotic communities, influenced by landscape processes and
prime mover components'. (Tinley does not write, clearly, with the general reader
in mind.) The central chapter is entitled 'Process and Response' and discusses the
relationship between changes in the landscape and the evolution of plant and
animal communities as they 'expand, contract and recombine' in different areas at
different times. Tinley has published some sixteen articles on aspects of
Mozambican ecology, mostly before national independence. See also, on
Gorongosa's trees, A. Rocha da Torre's brief checklist *Lista de árvores da área
do Parque Nacional da Gorongosa* [List of trees in the area of the Gorongosa
National Park] (Lourenço Marques: Imprensa Nacional, 1965; 9p.), describing 62
species; and on birds, A. A. da Rosa Pinto's *Lista sistematica das aves do Parque
Nacional da Gorongosa* [Classified list of birds of the Gorongosa National Park]
(Lourenço Marques, Mozambique: Imprensa Nacional, 1965; 35p.), listing 339
species.

557 **Biogeography and ecology of southern Africa.**
M. J. A. Werger. The Hague: W. Junk, 1978. 2 vols.
Covers the area south of the Ruvuma River (Mozambique's northern border) in
the eastern part of the continent, and south of Zaïre in the west and centre. The
first volume covers the geology, climate, soils and main vegetational forms of the
region, while the second consists of a series of monographs on the animal families
of the area; eleven of the sixteen chapters deal with insects. Other sections focus
on aquatic fauna and flora, and on special habitats.

Urbanization

558 **Aspects of urbanization and age structure in Lourenço Marques,
1957.**
Hilary Flegg Mitchell. [Lusaka]: Institute for African Studies,
University of Zambia, 1975. 49p. (University of Zambia. Institute
for African Studies. Communication, no. 11).
Originally submitted as an MA thesis at Witwatersrand University (Johannesburg)
in 1961 under the title 'Age structure in urban Africans in Lourenço Marques',
and under the author's maiden name (Flegg), this together with Maria Clara
Mendes' much-praised *Maputo antes da indepêndencia* (q.v.), António Rita-
Ferreira's 'Os Africanos de Lourenço Marques' (q.v.) and theses on Beira by Rui
Neves da Costa Rodrigues and Ramiro Coimbra (q.v.) constitute almost the total
bibliography of urbanization in colonial Mozambique.

559 **The Malhangalene survey: a housing study of an unplanned settlement in Maputo, 1976.**
Krisno Nimpuno (et al.). Gothenburg, Sweden: Chalmers University of Technology, 1977. 2 vols. maps.
This survey is one of the very few studies of post-colonial urbanization in Mozambique in English. It is very much a draft publication, both in format and content, having been prepared by some Swedish undergraduate architecture students between September and November 1976. The contents are as follows: Krisno Nimpuno, 'Introduction and background'; Ingemar Särfors, 'Reflexions on the Maputo housing situation, 1976'; Lars Nordin, 'Infrastructure and public facilities'; Ruth Näslund, 'Dwelling and space in Malhangalene'; Nea Lavén, 'The physical environment of the children in Malhangalene'; Björn Brandberg, 'Constructions'; Zounkata Tuina, 'Matériaux de construction'; and Hans Tollin, 'Workshops and crafts'.

560 **The urban problematic in Mozambique: initial post-independence responses, 1975–80.**
Barry Pinsky. Toronto: Centre for Urban and Community Studies, 1981. [58]p.
Pinsky begins by describing the selection of a neighbourhood committee in Maxaquene suburb in Maputo. He discusses the role of the Dynamizing Groups (GDs), the impact of the III Congress, the work of the National Housing Directorate, Frelimo's mobilization campaign in Hulene, and the national meeting on cities and neighbourhoods. See also Pinsky's earlier pieces 'Counting on our own forces: the Maxaquene upgrading project, Mozambique', *Habitat News* vol. 3, no. 2 (Nov. 1980), and 'Mozambique: attacking urban problems' *Southern Africa* vol. 13, no. 6 (July–Aug. 1980), p. 19–20.

561 **Os Africanos de Lourenço Marques.** (The Africans of Lourenço Marques.)
António Rita-Ferreira. *Memórias do Instituto de Investigação Científica de Moçambique* vol. 9, series C (1967–68), p. 95–491.
A book-length study of urbanization in the reed-townships (African-designated areas) of the Mozambican capital, based on 3,277 first-hand interviews in 1,024 family units, and on an extensive secondary bibliography. After a discussion of research methodology he moves on to the question of dualism in the socio-economic structure and the phenomenon of urbanization in sub-Saharan Africa in general; the reasons for the rural exodus to Lourenço Marques; the effects of this departure on public administration; the housing problem; demography (including inter-racial marriages); social aspects; social pathology (delinquency, alcoholism, drug abuse, prostitution); family life; economic and professional life; culture, sport and entertainment; health and nutrition; and religious and magical beliefs. He concludes with a series of recommendations for rural development, employment, salaries, social security, self-employment, family stability and law, education and housing. The article also includes maps, statistical tables and photographs.

562 **Um ensaio de geografia urbana: a cidade de Beira.** (An essay in
urban geography: the city of Beira.)
Rui Neves de Costa Rodrigues. Licenciatura dissertation,
Instituto Superior de Ciências Sociais e Política Ultramarina,
Universidade Técnica de Lisboa, 1967. 183p. bibliog. maps.

As is customary in the older Portuguese academic theses, the author begins with
the arrival of the Portuguese in Mozambique, but soon continues with a
description of the geology, vegetation and environment of Beira, and includes a
brief historical account of the founding of the city in the 1880s. There are chapters
on the geographical and demographic development of the city, and on
urbanization.

Education

563 A century of colonial education in Mozambique.
Mário Azevedo. In: *Independence without freedom: the political economy of colonial education in southern Africa*. Edited by Agrippah T. Mugomba, M. Nyaggah. Santa Barbara, California; Oxford: ABC-Clio, 1980. p. 191–213.

A comprehensive survey article dealing with the Portuguese colonial educational system in Mozambique from 1876 to 1974. In the first half of the article Azevedo provides a summary of factual and statistical information; in the second part he discusses the impact of the system, its nature and aims, and the role of both the missionary and state sectors. The topics covered also include the curriculum, the policy of 'assimilation' and its consequences, the educational budget, teaching methods and discipline, and the quality and condition of school premises. He concludes that the Portuguese made minimal efforts even after 1926; but that they did make a greater input in the 1960s and 1970s. There was, however, gross discrimination against Africans, and the system as a whole had virtually no quantitative impact; it simply created class divisions, and retarded the growth of nationalism. Educational opportunity, argues Azevedo, was concentrated in the towns and in the south, with results that can be seen even today.

564 The legacy of colonial education in Mozambique (1876–1976).
Mário J. Azevedo. *A Current Bibliography on African Affairs* new series, vol. 11, no. 1 (1978–79), p. 3–16.

A superficial and premature account of post-independence educational policy, which Azevedo himself terms 'a pioneering attempt'. Note that, despite the date of publication, this is, in fact, a conference paper from February 1976. The author compares the Portuguese colonial educational system with what was known of FRELIMO's intentions immediately after independence. The account is based on a few widely known secondary sources, supplemented by some press clippings for the more recent period. For a much more coherent historical version of

Mozambican colonial education, see David Hedges' working paper 'Educação, missões e a ideologia política de assimilação' (q.v.).

565 **Legislação aplicável aos serviços de educação e ensino que se ministra em Moçambique.** (Legislation applicable to the services of education and teaching which operate in Mozambique.)
João Bernardo Barata. Lourenço Marques, Mozambique: Minerva, 1973. 2nd ed. 100p.

This odd combination of anthology and index seems to be of a type which was common in Portuguese colonial literature. Pages 1–62 consist of a kind of tabular index of laws in force, with their content and a reference to the issue of the *Boletim Oficial* where they can be found. Up to p. 22 these are all 'of a general character'; pages 23–62 are specific to various types and levels of education. Pages 63–100 comprise the texts of a number of laws and regulations, printed in three columns in tiny print (the format is A5 landscape). Barata prints an introduction which claims to 'explain' how his book is to be used, but which singularly fails to do so. There are no indexes, and not even a contents page – and on top of this, the title-page differs substantially from the cover, which gives *Educação e ensino: legislação aplicável em Moçambique.* Portuguese administrators often compiled this kind of detailed but ultimately inaccessible list. There seems to be no reference earlier than the 1950s, and most seem to be from the 1960s and 1970s. There is plenty of information, but the work is of limited usefulness.

566 **Education policy in the People's Republic of Mozambique.**
Journal of Modern African Studies vol. 14, no. 2 (June 1976), p. 331–39.

This early position paper was presented by the Mozambican delegation to the Conference of Ministers of Education of African Member States of UNESCO, held in Lagos, Nigeria between 27 January and 4 February 1976, and was republished in at least one other journal, as well as in pamphlet form, as *The match that lights the flame: education policy in the People's Republic of Mozambique.* (London: Mozambique, Angola and Guiné Information Centre, 1976. 14p.). This text is principally a statement of objectives drawn up in the immediate post-independence period, identifying several key elements for future policy – emphasis on the rural areas; the development of a close relationship between work and study; and anti-élitism.

567 **The struggle continues: Mozambique's revolutionary experience in education.**
Fernando Ganhão. *Development Dialogue* (Uppsala, Sweden) no. 2 (1978), p. 25–36.

This paper was presented to the Seminar on Educational Alternatives for Southern Africa, held in Maputo in 1978. Much of the paper is devoted to a discussion of FRELIMO's experience in the liberated zones, and in particular the problems surrounding élitism. Some students refused to go to fight, on the grounds that their education made them too valuable to risk their lives; this was completely unacceptable, and later policy made a point of emphasizing an anti-élitist line. Ganhão affirms that 'It was during the armed struggle, within the

Education

context of combat against Portuguese colonialism and the building of a new type of society in the liberated zones, that we initiated FRELIMO's political line in the field of education.'

568 **Direction culturelle: education et développement au Mozambique.**
(Cultural direction: education and development in Mozambique.)
Lavinia Gasperini. *Révue Tiers Monde* no. 97, vol. 35
(Jan.–March 1984), p. 189–204.

A sophisticated and interesting article, by an Italian educationalist and journalist, which uses as its theoretical starting point the Gramscian notion of 'cultural direction' in order to analyse the educational system of independent Mozambique. In one of the few attempts to theorize the problems of Mozambican education, Gasperini discusses the 'direction' of colonial culture and the educational system; education and cultural hegemony in the liberated zones during the liberation war; and both the continuity and the break with the colonial system and the experience of the liberated areas after independence. Gasperini ends by posing some questions: can production in the schools provide a basis for a new culture, a new way of looking at the world, and a new way of transforming it? What is the relationship between coercion and consensus in the system? How do Frelimo's ideas operate in the educational system – and can it effectively promote intellectual and critical activity? She does not, however, offer any answers.

569 **Scuola e decolonizzazione in Mozambico.** (School and decolonization in Mozambique.)
Lavinia Gasperini, Elimar Nascimento. *Scuola e Città* (Rome)
vol. 31, no. 4 (1980), p. 169–78.

A well-documented survey, in Italian, of the educational system in the early years of independence. Gasperini and Nascimento deal with the situation during the colonial period, the 'new education' of the liberated zones, the socio-economic and cultural situation after independence, measures adopted in education after independence (the longest section of the article), and literacy campaigns and adult education. They end by refusing to draw any conclusions, on the grounds that the article itself is only a rapid survey and that it would also be premature to do so. They add that the next few years will allow us to see whether 'the desire for renewal will manifest itself in an organic and coherent educational system'.

570 **Il sistema educativo in Mozambico: l'uomo nuovo come obiettivo.**
(The educational system in Mozambique: the new man as an objective.)
Lavinia Gasperini. *Politica Internazionale* no. 10 (1980),
p. 57–63.

Gasperini writes that, ever since the period of the liberation struggle, Frelimo has attached great importance to the question of education; it set up a network of teaching centres in the liberated zones at that time. After independence the new Frelimo Government adopted an ambitious educational programme, in which literacy campaigns were to be given priority; the new system was to be based on participation, working in groups, and the combination of study with productive labour. A major objective of this programme was to overcome linguistic divisions and tribalist and regionalist ideology, creating national unity; in addition, of course, it would enable Mozambique to replace the Portuguese skilled personnel who had fled at independence.

571 **Educação, missões e a ideologia política de assimilação, 1930–1960.** (Education, missions and the political ideology of assimilation, 1930–60.)
David Hedges. *Cadernos de História* no. 1 (June 1985), p. 7–18.

Based on archival research, this is an important contribution to the history of Mozambican colonial education by the English historian, David Hedges. The author shows how, between 1930 and 1962, Portuguese assimilation and educational policy reflected the basic economic and political needs of the Estado Novo, extending racial barriers, guaranteeing élitist education for the settlers' children, and using the ideology of 'assimilation' to Portuguese cultural values, in its contemporary form, to justify all kinds of violence and oppression against the mass of Mozambicans, in the guise of attempting to better their socio-economic condition.

572 **O ensino indígena na Colónia de Moçambique.** (Native education in the Colony of Mozambique.)
Inspecção de Instrução Pública. Lourenço Marques, Mozambique: Imprensa Nacional, 1930. 96p.

A compilation of legislation on African education passed between 1928 and 1930. This was the crucial period when Salazarist educational policies began to be put into effect; African primary education was separated from the system for whites and handed over to the Catholic missions, which were to receive state subsidies, and which were to teach their students to know their place and that they were Portuguese. Foreign Protestant missions were not to receive support. This work includes the texts of ten regulations and syllabuses for elementary primary education; for boys' technical schools (carpentry, shoe-making, tailoring) and for girls' vocational schools (cooking and sewing); for teacher-training schools for Africans; and for private (i.e., mission) schools. There are several such collections of educational legislation. See, for example: *Legislação sobre o ensino* (Legislation on teaching), compiled by the Direcção dos Serviços de Instrucção (Lourenço Marques, Mozambique: Imprensa Nacional, 1963. 193p.), which prints three 1962 regulations on arts and crafts schools for boys, on primary education, and on private (including mission) education; *Legislação sobre ensino liceal: reforma, estatuto e programas para 1947–1948* [Legislation on grammar-school teaching: reform, statute and syllabus for 1947–48] (Lourenço Marques, Mozambique: Imprensa Nacional, 1948. 216p.), which includes six associated pieces of legislation, including the important 1947 statute on grammar schools which occupies most of the volume; *Legislação aplicável ao ensino particular: Diplomas Legislativas nos. 58/71 de 5 de Junho e 49/73 de 7 de Julho* [Legislation applicable to private education] (Lourenço Marques, Mozambique: Imprensa Nacional, 1973. 58p.), which prints two regulations of 1971 and 1973 on subsidies; and *Novas bases para o ensino de adaptação: Portaria no.15:971 de 31 de Março de 1962* [New foundations for pre-primary education] (Lourenço Marques, Mozambique: Imprensa Nacional, 1962. 12p.). The so-called 'ensino de adaptação', literally 'educational preparation' was designed to equip Africans with enough Portuguese and other skills to be able to follow primary-school courses. African languages could be used to teach Portuguese.

573 **Education in Mozambique, 1975–84: a review.**
Prepared by Anton Johnston. Stockholm: Swedish International Development Authority, 1984. 129p. bibliog. map. (SIDA Education Division. Documents, no. 15).

A useful general survey of the educational sector in Mozambique since independence, written, with the Ministry of Education's approval, by a self-confessed 'enthusiastic supporter of the Mozambique revolution and a socialist', covering the system from top to bottom. Johnston begins with the obligatory background chapter on Mozambique's geography, history and economy; and with a brief section on the colonial education system. He then moves on to a detailed account of the structure of education between 1975 and 1982, and the new National System of Education (SNE) being phased in from 1983 to 1994. The SNE has four sub-systems – general (which includes primary, secondary and university education), adult education, technical education and teacher training, and has met with considerable obstacles in its implementation. Nevertheless, as Johnston points out, it is probably true that 'education for Mozambicans (as against colonists and *assimilados*) has not declined substantially in quality', (p. 113), while at a general level 'vast quantitative and some qualitative improvements have been made . . . on the basis of a fixed and clear educational policy . . . '.

574 **Jornal do Professor.** (Teacher's Journal.)
Maputo: Ministério de Educação e Cultura, Feb.–March 1981– bimonthly.

This is Mozambique's only education periodical, and includes news items, political documents, pedagogical material, and the occasional important analytical article.

575 **Documentos de base na análise social: leis e regulamentos sobre educação e ensino durante o período colonial, 1934–1975.** (Basic documents of social analysis: laws and regulations concerning education and teaching during the colonial period, 1934–75.) [Compiled by Francisca Judite, Adolfo Casal]. Maputo: Centro de Estudos de Comunicação, Universidade Eduardo Mondlane, 1978. 24p.

This collection was produced as a textbook for second-year students of education at Eduardo Mondlane University in 1977. It includes extracts from the texts of laws and regulations governing elementary education and the organization of 'native education' (1934); education in general; the Regulation on Rudimentary Primary Education; the Concordat (with the Vatican) of 1940; the Missionary Statute; the Regulations on Official Primary Education and Primary Education, and the Native Statute of 1954; the Regulation on Elementary Primary Education, and other laws of a general character. The work is a handy short

Education

compilation of the principal legal bases of the racist and discriminatory colonial educational system.

576   **New look at Edwardo [sic] Mondlane University.**
Palamagamba Kabudi.   *Sunday News* [Dar es Salaam]
(14 September 1980).

An interview with Fernando Ganhão, the first rector of Eduardo Mondlane University (1976–86). This is one of the very few items published in English on Eduardo Mondlane University, although many of the plans described have since been abandoned because of the economic crisis and security problems. Ganhão describes the situation at independence when the University was virtually abandoned by the departing Portuguese, and the struggle to change its structure and curriculum. On 1 May 1976, during a meeting on the main campus addressed by President Samora Machel, the name was changed from the University of Maputo. For the text of Samora's speech on this occasion, see his *A classe trabalhadora deve conquistar e exercer o poder na frente de ciência e da cultura* [The working class must conquer and use its power on the scientific and cultural front] (Maputo: Imprensa da Universidade Eduardo Mondlane, 1976. 23p.). There are some publications on the colonial university: see, for example, in stark contrast to the above, the 1962 speech given to the university students by the Governor-General M. M. Sarmento Rodrigues, *Aos estudantes de Moçambique* [To the students of Mozambique] (Lourenço Marques, Mozambique: Minerva Central, 1962. 15p.); a similar exhortation by Orlando Ribeiro was published in the *Boletim da Sociedade de Estudos de Moçambique* no. 136 (July–Sept. 1963), p. 5–14. More concrete were the proposals of João Evangelista Loureiro in his 'Esquema dum plano de estudos para um curso superior de pedagogia' [Sketch of a study plan for a higher pedagogy course], *Revista dos Estudos Gerais Universitários de Moçambique* vol. 4, series 5 (1967), p. 185–207. Also of interest, if only for his later political role as a spokesman for the black petit bourgeoisie, is Domingos Arouca's *Ensaio sobre problemas de ensino e de universidade em Moçambique* (Essay on problems of education and the university in Mozambique), with a preface by Bishop Sebastião Soares Resende (Beira, Mozambique: Tip. EAO, 1961. 62p.).

577   **Education in Angola and Mozambique.**
Eugénio Lisboa.   In: *Education in southern Africa*. Edited by
Brian Rose.   London: Collier-Macmillan, 1970. rev. ed.
p. 276–333.

Trained as an engineer, Eugénio Lisboa was a fairly well-known literary critic in Mozambique in colonial times, and published a two-volume collection of essays. Born and educated in Portugal, he returned there after independence. This well-documented piece is, it is claimed, the first general description in English of the educational system in the Portuguese colonies of Mozambique and Angola. It consists of an historical and cultural survey, an account of 'present attitudes towards education as reflected in current policy', and a section headed 'final comments'. Lisboa takes a more-or-less liberal line, but, for example, defends the so-called 'rudimentary' or 'adaptation' system of education for Africans on the grounds that 'the African masses do not speak Portuguese and normally live amongst primitive unskilled peoples'. Despite the publication date, most of the

233

Education

extensively quoted statistics (nine tables) are for 1964/65. See also Lisboa's undated paper for the radical Academic Association: *O ensino em Moçambique* [Education in Mozambique] ([Lourenço Marques, Mozambique]: Associação Académica de Moçambique [n.d.]. 36p.).

578 **Literacy and adult education in the People's Republic of Mozambique.**
Vierteljahresberichte (Bonn) no. 72 (June 1978), p. 127–34.

A survey article on the literacy campaigns mounted in Mozambique after independence. Much literacy work was undertaken by secondary-school students, often using the buildings set aside for the Dynamizing Groups or the women's organization (OMM). Women were especially targeted, since they had been doubly underprivileged in colonial times. Portuguese and literacy often had to be taught at the same time, since the majority of the Mozambican population are not, in fact, familiar with the official language. Spreading and maintaining *alfabetização* as it is called in Portuguese remains a major problem, despite the advances that have undeniably been made. See also on this subject Agneta Lind's *Literacy campaigns and nation-building in Mozambique: first literacy campaign, including a case-study of one literacy center* (Stockholm: Institute of International Education, University of Stockholm, 1981. [97p.]).

579 **Panorama de educação em Moçambique, 1973.** (Overview of education in Mozambique, 1973.)
Adelino Augusto Marques de Almeida. Lourenço Marques, Mozambique: Imprensa Nacional, 1973. 30p.

Originally presented to the First Congress of the Acção Nacional Popular in Timor in 1973, this paper provides a short overview of the educational situation as seen by the Portuguese colonial authorities immediately before independence. The article is organized into two parts: the school system and educational policy, covering primary, secondary and middle-level education, with data on the education budget. The Portuguese were fond of these general surveys: for similar pieces on earlier periods, see Carlos Moreira's 'O ensino na colónia de Moçambique' [Education in the colony of Mozambique], *Moçambique: documentário trimestral* no. 5 (1936), p. 43–79; the Direcção Provincial dos Serviços de Educação's *Panorama do ensino na província de Moçambique* [Overview of education in the province of Mozambique] (Lourenço Marques, Mozambique: Empresa Moderna, 1965. 71p.); and a general article in French by Alfredo Margarido entitled 'L'enseignement en Afrique dite portugaise' [Education in 'Portuguese' Africa], *Revue Française d'Études Politiques Africaines* no. 56 (Aug. 1970), p. 62–85.

580 **História: África das origens ao século XV. Livro para os alunos da 5ª. e 6ª. classes.** (History of Africa from earliest times to the 15th century. Textbook for 5th and 6th year students.)
Ministério da Educação e Cultura. Maputo: Instituto Nacional do Livro e do Disco, 1978. 112p. maps.

After independence, the teaching of history was dramatically changed at all levels; instead of learning about the history of Portugal, students were taught the history of Mozambique in the context of Africa. For all its many weaknesses, this textbook, which was printed in a run of over 100,000 copies, represented a giant step forward for Mozambican education. Indeed, the production of working texts for teachers remains, and is likely to remain for some time into the future, one of the principal preoccupations of Eduardo Mondlane University's History Department and Historical Archive.

581 **Programa para o ensino primário.** (Programme for primary education.)
Ministério da Educação e Cultura. [Maputo]: Ministério da Educação e Cultura [1977]. 2 vols.

These volumes contain the detailed programmes introduced after independence in Mozambican primary schools, with an explanation of the main ideological problems of class education, and of scientific and political objectives. The first volume deals with the pre-primary to second-year programmes. The second volume, on the programmes for the third and fourth years, includes material on history, mathematics, geography, natural sciences, manual activities, drawing, cultural activities and physical education. Each section includes a short reading-list for the teachers. To compare these courses with those of colonial times, see, *inter alia*, the following: the Portuguese Ministério da Instrução Pública's *Novo regime de ensino e programas da instrução primária geral da Província de Moçambique* [New education system and programmes of general primary education in the Province of Mozambique] (Lourenço Marques, Mozambique: Imprensa Nacional, 1920. 72p.); Braga Paixão's 'O ensino primário em Lourenço Marques' [Primary education in Lourenço Marques], *Moçambique: documentário trimestral* no. 19 (1939), p. 63–73; and the *Programa do ensino primário elementar* [Programme of elementary primary education] (Lourenço Marques, Mozambique: Imprensa Nacional, 1970. 2nd ed. 90p.).

582 **A instrução pública em Moçambique: sua evolução.** (Public education in Mozambique: its development.)
Luís Moreira de Almeida. Lourenço Marques, Mozambique: Imprensa Nacional, 1956. 49p.

Moreira de Almeida was Head of the Public Education Department in Mozambique when he wrote this pamphlet. It deals with 'official' education for the so-called 'civilized' population, although Moreira de Almeida is at pains to point out that 'qualified natives are not excluded from attending'. The first part of the work deals with the situation before 1928, when, at least from the point of view of later Portuguese administrators, the situation had been deplorably untidy, with foreign missions, and racially-mixed schools. After 1928–30, the education of African children passed, in the system known as 'rudimentary education', into the hands of the Portuguese Catholic missions, which were given a privileged position by the state. This second chapter is divided into subsections, dealing with organization, budget, school buildings, attendance, teachers, subsidies, and the present and future.

Education

583 **O professor em Moçambique no tempo colonial: através de textos da época.** (The teacher in Mozambique in colonial times, through contemporary texts.) Júlio Moure. *Jornal do Professor* no. 10 (1982), p. 17–29.

Attempts to describe the daily life, training, material conditions and social situation of teachers in colonial Mozambique, including some statistical information. Moure covers the period up to the end of the 1960s, paying particular attention to 'official', secondary and technical education. The article is useful for its account of teacher training.

584 **A concepção da educação em Moçambique: notas introdutórias.** Elimar Pinheiro de Nascimento. *Estudos Afro-Asiáticos* (Rio de Janeiro) no. 4 (1980), p. 21–41.

In this ambitious theoretical article, Nascimento tries to analyse the development of Mozambican educational policy, using the speeches of Samora Machel as his principal source. He characterizes the Frelimo leadership as being a combination of both internationalized urban intelligentsia and military politicians. According to the author, Machel's concept of society and of the role of education are based, not surprisingly, on his experience of 'successive battles'. There are three educational 'realities' in Mozambique – the traditional, the colonial and the FRELIMO schools. The latter are organized around the 'triple unity' of production, study and combat, and follow two pedagogical principles: 'the articulation of production-study'; and the 'exchange of experience'. All this derives from the concrete experience of education in the liberated zones. See also Nascimento's lengthy thesis entitled 'Décolonisation en 'Afrique portugaise': le processus de destruction/construction hégémonique au Mozambique' [Decolonization in 'Portuguese' Africa: the process of hegemonic destruction/construction in Mozambique] (Doctoral dissertation [2nd cycle], École des Hautes Études en Sciences Sociales, Paris, 1982. 603p.).

585 **Evolução do ensino em Moçambique nos últimos 40 anos.** (The development of education in Mozambique in the last forty years.) Edmundo Andrade Pires. Lourenço Marques, Mozambique: Imprensa Nacional, 1966. 30p.

A slim pamphlet, produced for propaganda purposes, to celebrate forty years of Salazar's Estado Novo. The brochure includes some photographs of small Mozambican children in Cabo Delgado, dressed up in Portuguese peasant costumes with kerchiefs and straw hats, performing 'traditional' Portuguese songs and dances during a visit by the Portuguese Minister of Overseas Territories, Silva Cunha. It is included here as an example of its type.

586 **We're building the new school: diary of a teacher in Mozambique.** Chris Searle. London: Zed Press, 1981. 189p.

Searle is a well-known radical writer and teacher who worked in Nampula for two years (1977–79) at one of Mozambique's few secondary schools. This readable book is organized as a diary, and gives a vivid and often moving picture of daily life in a provincial town quite soon after independence. Searle's commitment to education as a means of changing society, and his support for the new educational policies of FRELIMO soon become apparent. The weakness of the work is a tendency to a kind of revolutionary sentimentality, which at times leads the writer to attribute unbelievable feelings to young Mozambicans: for example, reluctance to respond to questions in a political study group is described as shyness. Nevertheless, in Basil Davidson's words, 'a work of uncommon insight'.

587 **Strukturelle Abhängigkeit und Unterentwicklung am Beispiel Mozambiques.** (Structural dependence and underdevelopment: the Mozambican case.)
Dieter Senghaas (et al.). Bonn: Verlag Peter Wegener. 146p. bibliog. (Sozialwissenschaftliche Studientexte, Bd 1).

A syllabus for the study of Mozambique, from a dependency-theory perspective. It contains a short but useful forty-three-item bibliography of mainly German references on the country. See also S. Cohen's 'History of the colonial revolutions in Portuguese Africa: a college curriculum outline' (PhD dissertation, Carnegie-Mellon University (Pennsylvania), 1977. 526p.) for a similar guide to the study of Mozambique and other Portuguese-speaking countries.

588 **Sistema nacional de educação: linhas gerais.** (The national educational system: general outline and Law No. 4/83.)
Maputo: Instituto Nacional do Livro e do Disco, 1985. 135p.

An extremely important official policy document explaining the 'SNE' as it is known in Mozambique – the National System of Education. Its general outline was approved by the People's Assembly (Mozambique's Parliament) in Law No. 4/83. Until 1981 the basic outline of education for most pupils was four years of primary school, followed by five years of secondary school (to 9th class); a few students then continued through two supplementary years to higher education (i.e., university). The SNE, on the other hand, envisages seven years of primary school, three years of secondary, and two further years which may be pre-university, or teacher training, or middle-level technical training. Of course, there are many other aspects – ideological, political and social – to the new system, which also covers adult education. The SNE has faced tremendous problems of implementation at all levels.

589 **Escola de Artes e Ofícios da Moamba.** (Moamba School of Arts and Crafts.)
Joaquim José de Sousa. *Moçambique: Documentário Trimestral* no. 15 (1938), p. 61–70.

Included here as an example of its type, this illustrated article, strongly propagandistic in tone, is about the School of Arts and Crafts (for 'natives') at Moamba, just outside Lourenço Marques (present-day Maputo). It describes, in idealistic terms, the way the school functions: '[the students'] education is rounded off by gymnastics, by choral singing, and by reading vocational magazines which can be found in the calm of the library'. Sousa concludes that the fact that dozens of 'native lads' are fed, clothed and educated by the State 'reflects honorably on our [Portuguese] system of colonization'. There is a vast quantity of this type of material from the colonial period, and it must be read with

237

Education

great care. See also, for similar studies of individual schools: António Pina da Cunha Jardim's 'Escola de Habilitação de Professores Indígenas 'José Cabral', Manhiça-Alvor' [The José Cabral Training College for Native Teachers at Alvor, Manhiça], *Moçambique: Documentário Trimestral* no. 13 (1938), p. 67–78; *O Liceu Salazar de Lourenço Marques* [The Lycée Salazar in Lourenço Marques] (Lourenço Marques, Mozambique: Imprensa Nacional, 1956. 44p.); António David Ramos Violante's *A Escola Comercial de Lourenço Marques* [Lourenço Marques Business School] (Lourenço Marques, Mozambique: Imprensa Nacional, 1956. 14p.).

590   **O ensino missionário: uma polêmica jornalística de princípios de 1960.** (Missionary education: a debate from the newspapers in early 1960.)
Manuel Vaz.   Lourenço Marques, Mozambique: Notícias, Minerva Central, 1965. 26, 51p.

A collection of newspaper articles from early 1960, from the Lourenço Marques daily *Notícias*, of which Vaz was the owner and editor, and the Catholic papers *Diário* and *Diário de Moçambique*. The topics covered are the quality of the teaching, the cost, the results achieved, the Government's responsibility for the educational situation in the country, and the abuses practised under the name of 'rudimentary education'. By contrast, for an apologia for the missions, see António da Silva Rego's *Lições de missionologia* [Lessons in missionary studies] (Lisbon: Junta de Investigações do Ultramar, 1961. 564p. [Estudos de Ciências Políticas e Sociais, no. 56]). This is a very detailed and systematic text on Catholic missionary activity, with chapters on such topics as law, education and politics. Silva Rego argues that 'The Portuguese case . . . is completely different from the others . . . because [we] all have the same motherland, multiracial and multi-continental . . . Those who cannot accept this, for whatever reason, would be better off . . . if they went to work somewhere else.' (p. 93–6). The section on education (p. 236–70) includes much historical information on mission activity; appendixes print a series of Papal encyclicals and the Estatuto Missionário (Missionary Statute) of 1941.

Science, Technology and Research

591 **Research in Mozambique: a survey of the research sector in Mozambique with an introduction on Norwegian assistance to development research and to Mozambique.**
Tertit Aasland. Oslo: [NORAD], 1984. 69p.
A commissioned report by a Norwegian researcher with some experience of Mozambican conditions. Her terms of reference included the description of institutions and 'possible research councils as to their present research activity, capacity and financing'; a survey of support by other donors, especially Scandinavian ones; and a survey of Mozambican priorities in research and the strengthening of research capacity. After some discussion of MONAP (the Mozambican Nordic Agricultural Programme, 1976– .) and SADCC (the Southern Africa Development Coordination Conference, 1980– .), Aasland moves on to an account of the research sector in Mozambique, especially in Eduardo Mondlane University. She concludes with three short chapters on other donor organizations, regional research of relevance to Mozambique, and some notes on institutions outside the country with experience of Mozambique-related research.

592 **The work of Ruth First in the Centre of African Studies: the development course.**
Aquino de Bragança, Bridget O'Laughlin. *Review* vol. 8, no. 2 (Fall 1984), p. 159–72.
In August 1982 Ruth First, Research Director at the Centro de Estudos Africanos in Maputo, was murdered by means of a letter-bomb sent to her by South African military intelligence. In this article Aquino de Bragança, the Centre's Director, and Bridget O'Laughlin, a senior staff-member since 1979, pay tribute to Ruth through an analysis of the Development Course, which was the focus of CEA activity for over four years, and to which she devoted most of her time and energy as Research Director. The Course was based, in the authors' words, on 'a

239

distinctive and revolutionary conception of university teaching', and represented an attempt to integrate political struggle into the teaching of research method. The focus of the Course was always on questions of production in Mozambique, precisely because, in the authors' words again, 'the struggle to build socialism is a struggle to transform the organization of production'. It was the very successes of the Course which forced the South African régime to strike against Ruth 'a blow against Mozambique and against the liberation movement in South Africa, which we still feel in almost every moment'.

593 **Ciência e tecnologia.** (Science and technology.)
Maputo: Ministério da Indústria e Energia; Universidade Eduardo Mondlane, Aug. 1980– . irregular.

A general science and engineering publication produced by the Ministry of Energy and Industry, and the combined engineering and science faculties of the University. It comprises a mixture of abstract general articles and pieces with specific Mozambican interest.

594 **Construir.** (Build.)
Maputo: Ministério das Obras Públicas e Habitação; Faculdade de Engenharia Civil, Universidade Eduardo Mondlane, Oct. 1979– .

A technical engineering journal, in Portuguese, published jointly by the Ministry of Public Works and Housing and the Civil Engineering Department of the University.

595 **Mozambique and Angola: reconstruction in the social sciences.**
Bertil Egerö. Uppsala: Scandinavian Institute of African Studies, 1977. 78p. (Research Report, no. 42).

Based on a research trip undertaken by Egerö shortly after independence, this report is useful as an account of the situation at that time, although radical changes were introduced soon afterwards. The section on Mozambique describes the organization of the Instituto de Investigação Científica de Moçambique (the Scientific Research Institute); the Centro de Documentação e Informação Nacional de Moçambique, CEDIMO (the National Documentation and Information Centre); and the statistical and bibliographical centres which existed at that time. Egerö is a well-known Swedish demographer and social scientist.

596 **Mathematics education in the People's Republic of Mozambique.**
Paulus Gerdes. *Materialen zur Analyse der Berufspraxis des Mathematikers* (Postfach 8640, Bielefeld) vol. 25 (Oct. 1980), p. 127–42.

Paulus Gerdes, a mathematics professor at Eduardo Mondlane University, begins with a general account of the history of education in Mozambique; he states that by the end of the liberation war there were over 30,000 students in primary schools and over 500 students in secondary schools in the liberated areas. At independence there were under 600,000 primary school pupils; by 1978 this figure had risen sharply to over 1.4 million. This paper, which appeared before the introduction of the National System of Education (or SNE, to use its Portuguese

240

initials), discusses the training of mathematics teachers, and the pedagogical methods used, as well as mentioning the First National Seminar on Mathematics Teaching, held in May 1980 with high-level government participation. The same issue of this German publication includes another long piece by Gerdes, 'Mathematik in Mozambique: Bildung und Mathematikunterricht in Mozambique' [Mathematics in Mozambique: education and mathematics teaching in Mozambique], p. 143–274 with 117 footnotes.

597 **The social sciences and development in Africa: Ethiopia, Mozambique, Tanzania and Zimbabwe.**
L. Adele Jinadu. Stockholm: Swedish Agency for Research Cooperation with Developing Countries, 1985. 188p. (SAREC Report, no. R 1:1985).
A detailed comparative study of the relationship between social science research and development in four eastern and Central African countries, including Mozambique; in this last case it is a useful and informative compendium on recent debates. Although Jinadu is aware of the need to problematize the concept of 'development', he does not devote much space to the task; nor does his definition of the social sciences go much beyond the academic research based in university departments. All four country chapters follow the same pattern: a survey of the development of social sciences; a description of the institutional framework; and a discussion of issues, trends and 'linkage networks'.

598 **Development studies for social change in southern Africa.**
John Saul. *Review* vol. 8, no. 2 (Fall 1984), p. 173–96.
Saul taught at the Frelimo Party School and at the Faculty of Marxism-Leninism within Eduardo Mondlane University in 1981–82, and draws heavily on that experience here. He argues firstly that social science in southern Africa must associate itself 'self-consciously and unapologetically' with the struggle for genuine liberation, and must be rooted in the Marxist tradition. Secondly he argues that the Marxist tradition itself, 'so rife with dogma and cant', must be developed in terms of the specificities of the region in order to fulfill its promise. See also Saul's teaching manual, developed during his year in Mozambique, and now difficult to obtain: *O marxismo-leninismo no contexto moçambicano* [Marxism-Leninism in the Mozambican context] (Maputo: Universidade Eduardo Mondlane, 1983. 241p.).

599 **Frelimo concentrates on the practical side of science.**
Pamela Smith, David Wield. *Nature* vol. 276 (21/28 December 1978), p. 751–53.
A short journalistic survey of Mozambican science policy written just after their departure from Mozambique by Smith, who worked in the health sector, and Wield, an engineer who taught and did research in the Centro de Estudos Africanos. They point out that science policy, like all other sectors, was co-ordinated by what was then the Ministry of the Plan (now a Commission). At the time of writing, Mozambique was in the middle of the three-year Plan adopted at the III Congress of Frelimo. Since science policy is seen as an integral part of planning, there is no national scientific research council. Policy has two principal

aspects – education, with the training of competent technicians as a priority; and research in key areas, such as geology or crop production, which are obviously important economically. Smith and Wield describe the colonial educational system and the changes that have taken place since independence, and they estimate that there were (in 1978) between 200 and 400 science graduates, working mostly in agriculture, health, education and engineering. They give a short account of Eduardo Mondlane University's science courses, showing how research projects are designed to deal with immediate practical problems. The authors also refer to examples of 'spin-off': the vaccination campaign of 1976–78 provided much-needed demographic data, for instance. The article concludes that better planning is still needed, and appeals to readers with scientific skills to consider working in Mozambique.

600   **The research situation in the People's Republic of Mozambique.**
Teodósio Uate.   In: *National research councils in developing countries: SAREC seminar with collaborating agencies, Stockholm. Tammsvik, 16–21 January 1983*. Stockholm: Swedish Agency for Research Cooperation with Developing Countries, 1984. p. 54–58.

Teodósio Uate was Director of the (administrative) Department of International Relations at Eduardo Mondlane University. He outlines research activity 'in agriculture, industry and education', adding, however, that 'this does not mean that [research] is . . . restricted to these areas'. Uate then profiles the National Planning Commission's guidelines for research activity in the three specialities mentioned, referring to several projects undertaken by the Faculty of Engineering, as well as ones in archaeology and anthropology. The paper concludes that 'Research in the sciences of technology and education is thus of more advantage to the [People's Republic of Mozambique] . . . than information concerning the past.' Two years later, two further conference papers on Mozambican university research were published: Gerhard Liesegang's 'Research in the training of history undergraduates at Eduardo Mondlane University, Maputo' in: *International Conference 'Promotion of Research-Oriented Education and Training at African Universities', Nairobi, 17–26 September 1985* (Bonn, FRG: German Foundation for International Development (1985), vol. 2, p. 94–102); and Jose Negrão's 'Research and higher education in University Eduardo Mondlane (UEM)' in the same volume, p. 182–92.

Literature

Criticism and bibliography

601 **África: Literatura, Arte e Cultura.** (Africa: Literature, Art and Culture.)
Lisbon (rua de Alcântara 53): África Editora, July 1978–
biannual.

Writing in the first issue of this illustrated review, the editor, Manuel Ferreira, asked rhetorically, 'Is it necessary to say that we are anti-colonialist? Anti-fascist? Anti-imperialist? . . . Is it necessary to say that *África* is also a tribute to the national liberation movements?' Ferreira is well known as a teacher and critic of African literature in Portuguese, and has published a multi-volume anthology *No reino de Caliban* [In Caliban's kingdom] (Lisbon: Seara Nova, 1975– . vol. 1– .). The third volume is devoted exclusively to Mozambican poetry. Each issue of *África* includes articles on Mozambique, as well as on the other Portuguese-speaking African countries, and on Brazil. These are often informative biographical-critical pieces on such early figures as the poet Rui de Noronha (1909–43). The review also includes poetry, criticism, reviews of new publications, articles on the fine arts, music, archaeology, and occasionally full-colour reproductions of paintings. Various individual articles from *África* are cited elsewhere in this bibliography.

602 **Elementos para uma bibliografia da literatura e cultura portuguesa ultramarina contemporânea: poesia, ficção, memorialismo, ensaio.**
(Entries for a bibliography of contemporary Portuguese overseas literature: poetry, fiction, memoirs and essays.)
Amândio César, Mário António.   Lisbon: Agência-Geral do Ultramar, 1968. 177p.

This listing covers all the Portuguese colonies, including Macau, Timor, Goa and even Dahomey; it is organized by order of author within each colony.

Literature. Criticism and bibliography

Mozambican entries appear on p. 89–113; see also the General section on p. 155–75. The compilers indicate the type of material by code letters: P (for poetry); F (for fiction); M (for memoirs); E (for essays); and they place an asterisk by the author's name to indicate that he is a *natural* of (i.e., was born in) a particular country. The work has some defects – it includes no biographical information, citations are often to later editions rather than to first ones, there are no indexes, and, of course, it is nearly twenty years out of date. César also published a large collection of essays, *Parágrafos de literatura ultramarina* [Passages of colonial literature] (Lisbon: Sociedade de Expansão Cultural, 1967. 346p.), which includes review essays on Mozambican literature in general, and on the poet Orlando Mendes in particular.

603 **Charrua: Revista Literária.** (The Plough: a Literary Review.)
Maputo (CP 4187): Associação dos Escritores Moçambicanos,
June 1984– . bimonthly.

This review comprises a mixture of stories, interviews, poems and illustrations, mainly by the younger generation of Mozambican writers and artists such as Eduardo White, Juvenal Bucuane and Idasse Tembe. *Charrua* has also included translations of the poet Aimé Cesaire and work by Portuguese classic writers such as Fernando Pessoa. The magazine is A4 size, and each issue has about twenty pages. Both Eduardo White and Juvenal Bucuane have recently published collections of poetry: respectively, *Amar sobre o Índico* [Love on the Indian Ocean] (Maputo: Associação dos Escritores Moçambicanos, 1984. 64p. [Colecção 'Início', no. 1]); and *A raiz e o canto* [The root and the song] (Maputo: Associação dos Escritores Moçambicanos, 1984. 64p. [Colecção 'Início', no. 2]).

604 **O mancebo e trovador Campos Oliveira.** (The youth and bard
Campos Oliveira.)
Manuel Ferreira. Lisbon: Imprensa Nacional-Casa da Moeda,
1985. 134p. (Escritores dos Países de Língua Portuguesa, no. 2).

An original piece of detective research about José Pedro da Silva Campos e Oliveira (1847–1911), who was born on Mozambique Island, and who may well have been Mozambique's first poet (in Portuguese, at least). He was director of a literary journal called the *Revista Africana* and lived for some time in Goa. Ferreira publishes the texts of thirty-one poems which he has ferreted out of various 19th-century periodicals, and appends a bibliography of Campos Oliveira's literary production.

605 **Voices from an empire: a history of Afro-Portuguese literature.**
Russell G. Hamilton. Minneapolis, Minnesota: University of
Minnesota Press, 1975. 450p. (Minnesota Monographs in the
Humanities, vol. 8).

African literature in Portuguese had largely been ignored in English-language criticism before the publication of Hamilton's study (and it must be said that the situation has only improved a little in the last ten years). Apart from Luís Bernardo Honwana's 'The role of poetry in the Mozambican revolution', *Mozambique Revolution* no. 37 (Jan.–Feb. 1969), p. 23–31 and no. 38 (March–April 1969), p. 17–32, also published in *Lotus: Afro-Asian Writing* no. 8 (1971);

Literature. Criticism and bibliography

Gerald Moser's *Essays in Portuguese-African literature* (University Park, Pennsylvania: Pennsylvania State University, 1969. 88p. [Penn State Studies, no. 26]; and Donald Burness' *Critical perspectives on Lusophone literature from Africa* (Washington, 1981), the principal works of criticism have, not surprisingly, been in Portuguese, for example, the writings of Manuel Ferreira. See his *Literaturas africanas de expressão portuguesa* (Lisbon: Instituto de Cultura Portuguesa, 1977. 2 vols.). Hamilton's work is systematic and comprehensive, and omits scarcely anybody of importance. All quotations are printed in the original Portuguese, with an English translation, and these are generally of a high standard. The section on Mozambique has been published in Portuguese on p. 11–90 of a revised and updated version of the present work entitled *Literatura africana, literatura necessária. II. Moçambique, Cabo Verde, Guiné-Bissau, Saõ Tomé e Principe* (Lisbon: Edições 70, 1984. 300p.). For reviews of the work see Aron Segal in *Research in African Literatures* vol. 7, no. 2 (Autumn 1976); and Fernando Martinho in *África: literatura, arte e cultura* no. 1 (July 1978), p. 105–06.

606 **A questão da cultura moçambicana.** (The question of Mozambican culture.)
Luís Bernardo Honwana, José Craveirinha, Rui Nogar. *África: literatura, arte e cultura* no. 6 (Oct.–Dec. 1979), p. 69–72.

This paper, presented by the three-man delegation to the 6th Conference of Afro-Asian Writers in Luanda in 1979, offers in a simplified form the official literary and cultural policy of the Mozambican government. As yet, the policy remains underdeveloped. 'Culture' is given, but there is no attempt to define what is meant by the term, although the whole line of analysis is historical and demands a definition. The paper begins by describing the attempt by colonialism (another abstract term) to destroy popular culture in order to cut people off from their own history. The first written literature produced in Mozambique was a weak imitation of Portuguese writing of the period, with a few African exoticisms woven in. This was succeeded by a genuine 'settler' literature, but it still mystified the nature of the relationship between colonizer and colonized. In this context, the first 'nationalist' poetry began to appear – anti-colonialist, but addressed to the colonialist. The militant poetry of FRELIMO represented a new phase, in which 'there is an absolute identity between revolutionary practice and poetic sensibility'. After independence there was a creative explosion – poetry, drama and short stories. At present Mozambican policy is to encourage oral literature – story-telling – in villages, schools and factories. Writers must be *engagés* because 'literature has its place, its role and its function in the cultural front in the fight against the bourgeoisie, against capitalism and imperialism . . . '.

607 **Sobre literatura Moçambicana.** (On Mozambican literature.)
Orlando Mendes. Maputo: Instituto Nacional do Livro e do Disco, 1982. 189p.

In May 1980 the National Journalists' Organization in Maputo set up a meeting between a Portuguese cultural delegation led by José Carlos Ary dos Santos, and leading Mozambican writers; this was before the foundation of the Association of Mozambican Writers in 1982. At the meeting Orlando Mendes presented a lecture on Mozambican literature, of which this book is a greatly expanded

245

version. It is essentially a kind of critical anthology, commenting on and including plentiful examples of poetry, fiction and drama, and ranging from folk-tales translated from African languages to modern Portuguese-language material, much of which had not been previously published. For the reader with some knowledge of Portuguese, this is an interesting, if discursive, introduction to Mozambican literature, ranging from the poetry of Rui de Noronha up to recent fiction, and even plays for radio.

608 **Bibliografia das literaturas africanas de expressão portuguesa.**
(Bibliography of African literature in Portuguese.)
Gerald Moser, Manuel Ferreira. Lisbon: Imprensa Nacional-Casa da Moeda, 1983. 407p.

The definitive bibliography on Portuguese-language literature in Africa, by two of the best-known names in this field of study. The book is well printed and laid-out, with many photographs of the various authors, and facsimiles of the covers and title-pages of some of the rare items listed. The entries are not numbered, and are arranged by country in four main categories: oral literature (Mozambique, p. 42–46); written literature (Mozambique, p. 177–208); history and criticism (Mozambique, p. 279–86); and literary reviews (Mozambique, p. 308–10). All introductory material is printed in both Portuguese and in an occasionally quaint English translation (*Cronologia cultural* appears as 'Chronology of cultural events'). The preface is dated April 1980. There are two indexes: one biographical and the second by author and title.

609 **A tentative Portuguese-African bibliography: Portuguese literature in Africa and African literature in the Portuguese language.**
Gerald M. Moser. University Park, Pennsylvania: Pennsylvania State University Libraries, 1970. 148p. (Pennsylvania State University Libraries Bibliographical Series, no. 3).

In his preface Moser writes that the bibliography is 'tentative . . . [because] too many blank spots and question marks dot the entries'. He includes a few unpublished manuscript works, and covers the period up to the end of 1969. He comments further, that: 'Being all-inclusive, the bibliography does not reflect any value judgement; most of the authors were amateurs, some were hacks, a few were inspired artists.' The entries are not numbered; there are three main chapters – folk literature, 'art' literature, and literary history and criticism – which are then further subdivided into general and geographical sections. Mozambican folk literature is covered on p. 9–11, art literature on p. 67–87, and secondary works on p. 104–12. In this last category Moser seems to be stretching the point a little by including such general works as Mário Costa's bibliography and Eça's supplement to it, as well as a general history of the press; however, there was not very much material available in 1970. Moser also prints a few photographs of the authors. There is an author index, with brief biographical notes attached to each name, and two pages of addenda. See also the bibliography by Amândio César and Mário António (q.v.) – several items which were cross-checked between this and Moser's work revealed differences over place and/or date of publication, as well as over the treatment of publisher and series statements. Both works should, therefore, be treated with caution as far as bibliographical accuracy is concerned.

246

610 **A poesia de Rui de Noronha.** (The poetry of Rui de Noronha.) Francisco de Sousa Neves. *África: literatura, arte e cultura* no. 1 (July 1978), p. 17–18.

Noronha, together with the São-Tomense poet Costa Alegre, is generally considered to be the first African poet to write in Portuguese. Of mixed African and Indian descent, he died in 1943 at the age of thirty-four. Writing in the 1930s his works express, albeit timidly, the conflicts of being an *assimilado*, and are full of mysticism and nihilism. Neves' brief notice quotes several of Noronha's poems and laments the fact that even now there is no critical edition of the work of this pioneer of African poetry in Portuguese. Noronha's only collection was the posthumous *Sonetos* edited by D. dos Reis Costa (Lourenço Marques, Mozambique: Minerva Central, 1949. 79p.). Sousa Neves, the author of this study, has stated that he owns several unpublished poems by Noronha. In such poems as 'Surge e ambula' (Rise and walk) we can hear a call for liberation, but it is overlaid with fatalism and resignation: Noronha's identification with his oppressed people was far from complete. The poems 'Amar' (To love), 'Por amar-te tanto' (For loving you so much), 'Mulher' (Woman) and 'Quenguêlêquezè' (an untranslatable Shangaan expression, uttered when showing a newborn baby to the new moon) are printed in volume one of Mário de Andrade's *Antologia temática de poesia africana* (q.v.). But see also the penetrating and original study by Guilherme de Melo, 'Rui de Noronha: poeta incompreendido' [Rui de Noronha: a poet who is not understood], *Boletim de Sociedade de Estudos de Moçambique* no. 176, vol. 44 (April–Dec. 1974), p. 51–77; and José Rodrigues Júnior's *Ruig de Noronha, poeta de Moçambique* [Rui de Noronha: poet of Mozambique] (Braga, Portugal: Editora Pax, 1980. 56p. [Colecção 'Autores Lusiadas', no. 3]).

In Portuguese

611 **A noite dividida.** (The divided night.) Sebastião Alba (pseudonym). Maputo: Instituto Nacional do Livro e do Disco; Lisbon: Edições 70, 1981. 90p. (Colecção 'Autores Moçambicanos', no. 12).

Sebastião Alba is the pseudonym of Dinis Albano Carneiro Gonçalves, elder brother of the short-story writer, the late António Carneiro Gonçalves (q.v.). He is considered by some critics to be 'one of the most representative authors of Mozambican poetry', on a par with José Craveirinha (q.v.) or João Pedro Grabato Dias (pseudonym of António Quadros). This is, arguably, an inflated evaluation of Alba's poetry. The title of this collection comes from the lines 'In the same night divided down the middle/as if one side was reflecting the other.' The collection was reviewed in *O Diário* [Lisbon], 12 June 1983, on p. 11 of the cultural supplement by Cipriano Justo. See also Alba's earlier collection in the same series *O ritmo do presságio* [The rhythm of the omen] (Maputo: Instituto Nacional do Livro e do Disco; Lisbon: Edições 70, 1981. 119p.); this was published earlier in the series 'O Som e o Sentido' (Lourenço Marques, Mozambique: Académica, 1975). Alba's first collection, *Poesias*, was published in Quelimane in 1965 by the Sociedade Gráfica Transmontana.

Literature. In Portuguese

612 **Antologia temática de poesia africana.** (Thematic anthology of African poetry.)
Mário de Andrade. Lisbon: Sá da Costa, 1976–79. 2 vols.
(Colecção 'Vozes do Mundo').

Andrade is uniquely qualified to edit this anthology. He played a central role in the cultural and political history of the Portuguese African colonies; he worked for the Conference of Nationalist Organizations of the Portuguese Colonies (CONCP); was for a time President of the MPLA; and served as a minister in the government of independent Guinea-Bissau. In the meantime he compiled the seminal collection *La poésie africaine d'expression portugaise* (Paris: P.-J. Oswald, 1958. 103p.) and wrote histories of the wars in Angola (1971) and Guinea-Bissau (1974). More recently he has devoted himself to teaching, giving a six-month seminar on nationalism in Portuguese-speaking Africa at the Centre of African Studies in Maputo. The collection is divided into two volumes. The first 'Na noite grávida de punhais' (In the night pregnant with daggers) includes work by the Mozambicans Fernando Ganhão, José Craveirinha, Noémia de Sousa, Rui de Noronha and Kalungano (the pseudonym of Marcelino dos Santos: Kalungano's only published collection is the Russian volume *Pesnia istinnoi liubi* (Song of true love), with an introduction by the Turkish poet Nazim Hikmet [Moscow: Gospolitizdat, 1962. 101p.], of which a Mozambican edition is promised). The second volume 'O canto armado' (The armed song) prints poems by Armando Guebuza, Jorge Rebelo, Marcelino dos Santos, Mutimati Barnabé João and Sérgio Vieira. Andrade provides short introductions to both volumes.

613 **As armas estão acesas nas nossas mãos: antologia breve da poesia revolucionária de Moçambique.** (Our weapons are burning in our hands: a short anthology of Mozambican revolutionary poetry.)
Associação Portugal-Moçambique, Delegação do Porto. (Portugal-Mozambique Association, Oporto Branch). Oporto, Portugal: Edições 'Apesar de Tudo', 1976. 102p.

This anthology includes an introduction by Papiniano Carlos, in which he writes of his discovery in 1958 of the authentic voice of Mozambican poetry, already distinct from that of Portugal, where it was virtually unknown at that time. But discussion of the 'black and shocking voice' of Mozambican poetry could not be then held openly in Portugal. It was FRELIMO which began to use poetry as a weapon, as an instrument of mobilization in the struggle. This anthology includes work by Craveirinha, Kalungano, Josina Machel, Samora Machel, Dési Mora, Damião Cosme, Rosália Tembe, Daniel Maposse, Joana Nachake, Armando Guebuza, Sérgio Vieira, Mutimati Barnabé João and Maria Emília Roby, as well as FRELIMO poetry signed in the name of the front.

614 **Dos meninos da Malanga.** (The kids from Malanga.)
Raul Alves Calane da Silva. [Maputo]: Tempográfica, 1982. 64p.
(Cadernos Tempo. Colecção 'Gostar de Ler', no. 3).

Calane da Silva was born in Lourenço Marques in 1945 and grew up in the townships around the city. When he first began writing, according to an interview published in *Cadernos do Terceiro Mundo* no. 59–60 (Dec. 1983), p. 89–90, he was forced to drop the 'Calane' from his surname to disguise his mestiço (half-

248

caste) origins. These poems were written between 1962 and 1974, and deal with the social, cultural and economic divide between the white settlers inhabiting the 'concrete city' and the Africans in the 'reed city' of the townships. The division was 'a frontier which you could almost touch with your hands', in the author's words. Calane da Silva's poetry is a conscious testimony to the experience of growing up 'coloured' in racist colonial society. He himself affirms that 'I don't look for nice plays on words, or stylised poetic language . . . I describe directly, frontally and even brutally the reality which surrounds me . . . '. Thus, for instance, his 'night poems' deal with the prostitutes in Lourenço Marques' old rua de Araújo.

615 **Directo ao assunto.** (Straight to the point.)
Carlos Cardoso. Maputo: Tempográfica, 1985. 98p. (Cadernos Tempo. Colecção 'Gostar de Ler', no. 8).

Carlos Cardoso is a senior Mozambican journalist working for the Mozambican news agency AIM. He divides this collection of slight, occasional pieces into three chapters entitled 'Brief encounters beyond measure', 'Exchanges with others', and 'Trial'. The collection includes some pieces of prose and a few poems in English, written in South Africa in the mid-1970s. Not untypical of the style and content is a two-line poem (p. 62) which plays on the similarity between the Portuguese words for 'idea' and for 'village' to describe the People's Republic of Mozambique as a 'communal idea'. Another journalist with literary pretensions is the Beira-born Mia Couto, who has published a volume of poetry, *Raíz de orvalho: poemas* [Roots of mist] (Maputo: Cadernos Tempo, 1983. 78p. [Colecção 'Gostar de Ler', no. 5]), and a book of prose with an introduction by Luís Patraquim, *Vozes anoitecidas* [Darkened voices] (Maputo: Associação dos Escritores Moçambicanos, 1986, 113p. [Colecção 'Karingana', no. 1]).

616 **Contos e lendas.** (Stories and legends.)
António Carneiro Gonçalves. Maputo: Instituto Nacional do Livro e do Disco; Lisbon: Edições 70, 1980. 2nd ed. 90p.
(Colecção 'Autores Moçambicanos'. no. 5).

Carneiro Gonçalves, younger brother of the poet Sebastião Alba, was killed in a road accident near Vilanculos in 1974 at the age of thirty-two. See *Tempo* no. 146 (1 July 1973) for an interview with him. This collection of short stories was first published just after his death (Lourenço Marques, Mozambique: Académica, 1974. [Colecção 'O Som e o Sentido', no. 5]), and includes five stories and two Zambezian legends or folk-tales, as well as 'Fragments from an unfinished novel'. These works do not, in the opinion of critic Guilherme Ismael 'open up new paths for the Mozambican novelist' (*Expresso* [Lisbon], 20 June 1981, p. 29–R), but they received much more fulsome praise from Ferraz de Mota in the Mozambican weekly *Domingo* (24 January 1982), who wrote that the author was 'a complete master of form . . . the dialogue is of an awesome naturalness . . . at times we think that we hear [the characters] speaking'. High praise, and in comparison with such lightweight fiction of the same period as Eduardo Paixão's *Tchova, tchova* [Give us a shove] (Lourenço Marques, Mozambique: [n.p.], 1975. 354p.), about a broken-down jalopy, Gonçalves is, indeed, a serious writer.

Literature. In Portuguese

617 **Cela 1.** (Prison cell.)
José Craveirinha.   Maputo: Instituto Nacional do Livro e do
Disco; Lisbon: Edições 70, 1980. 94p. (Colecção 'Autores
Mocambicanos', no. 1).

Very carelessly printed (there is a whole page of errata tucked in at the back), this
was the first volume in a collaboration between the Portuguese publishing house
'Edições 70', already well-known for publishing Angolan writers, and the
Mozambican National Institute for Books and Records, which controls virtually
all publishing in the country. The series 'Mozambican Authors' has so far
produced twelve volumes, mainly of poetry. Craveirinha, Mozambique's best-
known poetic voice, in an untitled poem dated 17 May 1963 and included here
(p. 33), tries to define what it was like to be a *mestiço* intellectual in a white
colonial society: 'I'm an illiterate/The food of the bookshops/is indigestible for
me, I know./And on this subject there are unhappily only two opinions/Your
opinion when you beat me/My opinion when I catch it.' None of Craveirinha's
books have been translated, unfortunately. This collection includes poems from
the 1950s, 1960s and 1970s.

618 **Karingana ua karingana.** (Once upon a time.)
José Craveirinha.   Maputo: Instituto Nacional do Livro e do
Disco; Lisbon: Edições 70, 1982. 182p. (Colecção 'Autores
Moçambicanos', no. 9).

The expression *karingana ua karingana* was the signal for a tale to be told, and
the cover of this new edition of Craveirinha's major work carries a striking design
of a story-teller by the fire with some children listening to him. The book is
divided into 'Fabulário 1945–1950'; 'Karingana'; 'Três odes ao inverno'; and
'Tingolé', which is a type of red fruit. The edition also has a preamble, and a postscript by Rui Nogar. Craveirinha has now achieved the status of having a research
thesis devoted to his work – Ana Mafalde Leite's 'Para uma caracterização da
linguagem poética de José Craveirinha' [Towards a characterization of the poetic
language of José Craveirinha] (Licenciatura thesis, Classical University of Lisbon,
1985), principally about this very book. Mafalde Leite analyses two aspects of
Craveirinha's work: the need to define and affirm his national identity as a
Mozambican; and the need to resolve, as a *mestiço*, the perceived conflict
between two races and two cultures. In this respect there are strong affinities
between the literature of the former Portuguese colonies and that of the
Caribbean.

619 **Xigubo.** (Hoe.)
José Craveirinha.   Maputo: Instituto Nacional do Livro e do
Disco; Lisbon: Edições 70, 1980. 2nd ed. 64p. (Colecção 'Autores
Moçambicanos', no. 4).

Craveirinha is undoubtedly the major literary figure in Mozambique today, and
has been its principal and lonely poetic voice since the 1960s. This, his first
collection of poetry, was originally published as *Chigubo* (Lisbon: Casa dos
Estudantes do Império, 1964 or 1965. 35p. [Colecção 'Autores Ultramarinos',
no. 14]). According to Alfredo Margarido, it carried, against the author's wishes,
an anonymous blurb written by Margarido himself, which made quite explicit the

political content of the poems, and which Craveirinha feared would be seen by the secret police as a deliberate provocation. In fact, Craveirinha was arrested in 1965 and imprisoned until 1969. He was born in Lourenço Marques in 1922, and like virtually any Mozambican writer of his generation, began publishing in the local newspapers *O Brado Africano*, *Notícias*, *A Tribuna* and others. He subsequently published a volume in Italy under the title *Cantico a un Dio de catrame* (1966), followed by *Karingana ua karingana* [Once upon a time] (Lourenço Marques, 1974. q.v.). For interesting critical work in Portuguese on Craveirinha and other Mozambican poets and poets from Mozambique, see Jorge de Sena, Maria Lourdes Cortez and Eugénio Lisboa's *Craveirinha, Grabato Dias, Rui Knopfli* (Lourenço Marques: Minerva Central, 1973. 79p.). Lisboa also published a collection of criticism, including a number of essays on Mozambican writers, under the title *Crónica dos anos da peste* [Journal of the plague years] (Lourenço Marques: Académica, [n.d.], 2 vols). Craveirinha is also, together with António Sacramento Gouveia Lemos, one of the major chroniclers and folklorists of Mozambique, although this side of his personality is much less widely known. See his major essay 'O folclore moçambicano e as suas tendências' [Mozambican folklore and its tendencies] *O Cooperador de Moçambique*, published in seventeen instalments as follows: no. 7 (20 July 1969), p. 16, 15 [sic]; no. 8 (20 Aug. 1969), p. 5, 11; no. 9 (20 Sept. 1969), p. 16, 15; no. 10 (20 Oct. 1969), p. 12, 10; no. 11 (20 Nov. 1969), p. 12, 11; no. 12 (Dec. 1969), p. 16, 15; vol. 2, no. 1 (Jan. 1970), p. 12, 11; vol. 2, no. 2 (Feb. 1970), p. 16, 12; vol. 2, no. 3 (March 1970), p. 16, 15; vol. 2, no. 4 (April 1970), p. 16, 14; vol. 2, no. 5 (May 1970), p. 12, 11; vol. 2, no. 6 (June 1970), p. 12, 11; vol. 2, no. 7/8 (July–Aug. 1970), p. 12, 11; vol. 2, no. 10 (Oct. 1970), p. 20, 19; vol. 2, no. 11 (Nov. 1970), p. 16, 15; vol. 2, no. 12 (Dec. 1970), p. 16, 15; vol. 3, no. 4 (May 1971), p. 16, 15.

620 **Tales of Mozambique.**
Chaz Davies, Ruhi Hamid, Chris Searle. London: Young World Books, 1980. 74p.

This book of folk-tales retold for children includes work by illustrators from Europe, Asia and the Caribbean, as well as from such African countries as Tanzania, Ghana, Zimbabwe and South Africa. The stories are identified as Mozambican but not assigned to any particular region or language-group. European and American readers will recognize many of the old 'Brer Rabbit' themes in these texts. According to the translator's preface, the tales have been translated from the first volume of the two-part Portuguese-language collection published as *Contos moçambicanos* (Maputo: Instituto Nacional do Livro e do Disco, 1978–79.). However, they appear in a different order, and have been supplemented by material from the newspaper *Notícias*, and from Ministry of Education and Culture readers. All of these publications are simply light reading for adults or children; none of the material is presented in a way useful to the folklorist.

Literature. In Portuguese

621   **When bullets begin to flower: poems of resistance from Angola, Mozambique and Guiné.**
Margaret Dickinson.   Nairobi: East African Publishing House, 1972. 132p.
An important and pioneering English anthology of poetry from Portuguese-speaking Africa. From Mozambique the poets represented are Rui de Noronha, with 'Rise and walk'; Noémia de Sousa, with four poems; Craveirinha with six poems; Marcelino dos Santos with three poems; and Armando Guebuza and Jorge Rebelo each with two. Dickinson contributes a careful twenty-seven-page introduction to this poetry for the English-speaking reader; her translations are conscientious, although she occasionally misses the nuances of some of the 'Africanisms' or specifically Mozambican turns of phrase. It should be remembered that she was working under pressure and in the early 1970s, when getting hold of definitive texts of poems by FRELIMO militants was not so easy as it is today. She includes a few explanatory notes, and biographies of the poets.

622   **Norte. (North.)**
Virgílio Chide Ferrão.   Lourenço Marques: Académica, 1975. 131p. (Colecção 'O Som e o Sentido', no. 10).
Apart from Luís Bernardo Honwana, Orlando Mendes and Luís Polanah (q.v.), there is little prose from Mozambique, whose writers seem to prefer a poetic form of self-expression. From Tete Province, Ferrão was expelled from a series of mission schools and seminaries in the late 1960s and early 1970s, according to the cover of this rather ordinary novel. He 'lived through the grand realities of the colonial war, the liberation war' in the Lourenço Marques Military Hospital. His book tells the story of several characters, and the effect that the war had on them; they include Caliza, who is sent to the north in the colonial army as a punishment, after having an affair with the daughter of a member of the security services. He is seriously wounded there. The language of the book, in Portuguese, is self-consciously 'Mozambicanized'.

623   **No reino de Caliban III: Antologia panorâmica da poesia africana de expressão portuguese. 3⁰. volume: Mozambique.** (In Caliban's realm III: panoramic anthology of African poetry in Portuguese. Third volume: Mozambique.)
Manuel Ferreira.   Lisbon: Plátano, 1985. 530p. bibliog.
An important anthology of Mozambican poetry, with a general introduction and further, separate introductions to the various chapters on Rui de Noronha, the Casa dos Estudantes do Império (CEI), and such magazines as *Msaho*, *O Brado Literário* and *Paralelo 20*. Ferreira includes material from the 1960s, originally published in *Voz de Moçambique* and *Caliban*, as well as from NESAM (the Nucleus of African Secondary-School Students of Mozambique). He prints Mutimati's work, identifying it as pseudonymous but not revealing the author's true name; and the book closes with the 19th-century poet Campos Oliveira, Alexandre Lobato's discovery. There are also a couple of poems by Manuela de Sousa Lobo.

624   **We killed mangy-dog, and other stories.**
Luís Bernardo Honwana; translated by Dorothy
Guedes.   London: Heinemann, 1969. 117p. (African Writers
Series, no. 60).

Undoubtedly Mozambique's best-known prose-writer, Honwana, who was born in
1942 and is now a high-ranking member of the Mozambican government,
published this collection of short stories under the Portuguese title *Nós matamos o
cão tinhoso* in the mid-1960s, when he was still in his early twenties. They
represent an extraordinarily mature achievement. João Dias opened the way for
Mozambican prose writers with his *Godido e outros contos* [Godido and other
stories] (Lisbon: Casa dos Estudantes do Império, 1952. 102p. [Colecção 'África
Nova'. no. 1]), but apart from Luís Polanah's *The saga of a cotton capulana*
(q.v.), this appears to be the only piece of Mozambican fiction to have been
translated into English. The central theme of the collection is the 'manipulation'
which Mozambicans had to practise to survive under colonialism. The stories are
highly political, but in the words of the critic Lewis Nkosi ' . . . not once does
Honwana speak directly . . . not once does he raise his voice to harangue us'. The
publishing history of the work, which Honwana has revised from time to time, is
as follows:- 1st ed., Lourenço Marques: Sociedade de Imprensa de Moçambique,
1964. 135p. – 2nd rev. ed., Oporto, Portugal: Afrontamento, 1972. 145p. – 3rd
rev. ed., Lourenço Marques: Académica, 1975. 124p. (Colecção 'O Som e o
Sentido' no. 7). – [4th ed.], Maputo: Instituto Nacional do Livro e do Disco,
1978. 124p. (Colecção 'Tempo Novo'). – 2nd ed. [sic], Maputo: Instituto
Nacional do Livro e do Disco, 1980. 109p. [Colecção 'Tempo Novo']; 3rd ed.
[sic], Maputo: Instituto Nacional do Livro e do Disco, 1984. 109p. Note that the
INLD edition numbers are incorrect; they refer only to INLD printings. There is
also a Brazilian edition (São Paulo: Editoria Ática [Colecção 'Autores Africanos'.
no. 4]).

625   **Assim no tempo derrubado.** (In times past.)
Albino Magaia.   Maputo: Instituto Nacional do Livro e do Disco;
Lisbon: Edições 70, 1982. 53p. (Colecção 'Autores
Moçambicanos', no. 11).

Albino Magaia was born in 1947, and began to publish poetry in 1964 in such
newspapers as *A Tribuna* and *O Brado Africano*, as well as participating in the
poetry circle of the Nucleus of African Secondary-School Students of Mozambique
(NESAM). In 1971 he took up journalism, and is at present editor of the weekly
Tempo. He writes in the introduction to this first book that 'This collection of
poems is not and cannot be a revolutionary work . . . An artist in colonial
times . . . inevitably suffered from the influence of the surroundings in which he
lived . . . and unconsciously assimilated, allowed himself to be influenced by,
values which he rejected . . . *Assim no tempo derrubado* does not mark a break
with those values, insofar as a truly Mozambican form of expression does not
predominate.' See also, for an autobiographical account of those surroundings
and Magaia's experience of them, his book *Yô Mabalane* (q.v.).

Literature. In Portuguese

626 **Poetas moçambicanos.** (Poets of Mozambique.)
Compiled by Alfredo Margarido. Lisbon: Casa dos Estudantes
do Império, 1962. 140p. mimeo. (Cover title: Poetas
de Moçambique).

Margarido worked with the Casa dos Estudantes do Império (CEI) in Lisbon in
the 1950s and 1960s. The CEI provided an outlet for many African writers at that
time, publishing the first edition of Craveirinha's *Chigubo*, and putting out a
bulletin under the title *Mensagem* (Message), for instance. Craveirinha received
the Alexandre Dáskalos Prize at the CEI in 1962 for an unpublished collection
entitled 'Manifesto'. It was closed in July 1985. This early anthology includes
work by Artur Costa, Carlos Maria, Diogo de Távara, Duarte Galvão, Fernando
Couto, Fernando Ganhão, Fonseca Amaral, Glória de Sant'Ana, Gouvêa Lemos,
Gualter Soares, Guilherme de Melo, Ilídio Rocha, José Craveirinha, Jorge Villa,
Kalungano, Manuel Filipe de Moura Coutinho, Noémia de Sousa, Nuno
Bermudes, Orlande de Albuquerque, Orlando Mendes, Reinaldo Ferreira, Rui
Knopfli, Rui Nogar, Rui de Noronha, Sérgio Vieira and Vítor Matos e Sá, as well
as a few pages on Chope poetry. A three-part interview with Margarido ('Africa?
Pois . . . ' ['Africa? Well, yes . . . '], *Tempo* no. 806 [23 March 1986], p. 48–52;
'Literariamente não são moçambicanos autores não-africanos nascidos em
Moçambique' [Non-African writers born in Mozambique aren't Mozambican, in
literary terms], *Tempo* no. 807 [30 March 1986], p. 46–49; and 'A língua
portuguesa não tem proprietários mas utentes' [We don't own Portuguese we use
it], *Tempo* no. 808 [6 April 1986], p. 44–46), provoked a tart response from
Manuela Sousa Lobo in the same magazine (no. 814 [18 May 1986], p. 45–47) on
the CEI's role, the paternalism of much Portuguese literary criticism on African
writers, the definitions of 'national literature' and 'literary nationality', and on the
role of Portugal in promoting Portuguese in its former colonies. The cover title is
Poetas de Moçambique.

627 **As faces visitadas.** (Faces seen.)
Orlando Mendes. Maputo: Associação dos Escritores
Moçambicanos, 1985. 56p. (Colecção 'Timbila', no. 4).

Orlando Mendes was nearly seventy years old when this collection of poetry
appeared, and was maintaining his place as one of the most prolific of
Mozambique's literary figures. He was born in 1916 on Mozambique Island, and
later went to Portugal to study, obtaining a Master's degree in biology from the
prestigious University of Coimbra, where he later taught. He returned to
Mozambique at the age of thirty-five, becoming a plant pathologist. His literary
output has been published in periodicals in Portugal, Brazil and Mozambique,
and includes poetry, drama, fiction and literary criticism, as well as a book on
medicinal plants.

628 **Lume florindo na forja.** (Light flowering in the furnace.)
Orlando Mendes. Maputo: Instituto Nacional do Livro e do
Disco; Lisbon: Edições 70, 1980. 126p. (Colecção 'Autores
Moçambicanos', no. 3).

Written after independence in 1975, this collection of poems provides, at times, a
disturbing close-up of the struggles around the building of a new Mozambique –

254

Literature. In Portuguese

at other times it is more like, in the words of the critic Guilherme Ismael, 'prose, a press report, or sloganeering'. But Mendes has a strong vision of the poet's role – 'I repeat verses. I insist/on words. Our light/flickers in the furnace./This must be told, not summarised.' In another short poem with the title 'Minimal introduction' Mendes writes that 'History/told in poetry/is the memory of the people/recreated in words./Words/in the struggle which the exploited wage/are the means to cultivate/with more daring and strength.'

629 **País emerso** (Emerging country.)
Orlando Mendes. Lourenço Marques, Mozambique: Empresa Moderna, Edição do Autor, 1975–76. 2 vols.
The first volume includes poetry, drama and stories; the second poetry only. This collection, published at the time of Mozambican independence, marked a sharp break with Mendes' earlier style; on the nature of this break see the review by Sara Abdul Satar in *África: literatura, arte e cultura* no. 4 (1979), p. 482–83, Mendes' reply in no. 6 (1979), p. 105–07, and Russell Hamilton's comments in his *Literatura africana, literatura necessaria* vol. 2 (q.v.). Among Mendes' many literary publications, see also *Trajectórias* [Trajectories] (Coimbra, Portugal: Atlântida, 1940); *Clima* [Climate] (Coimbra, Portugal: Atlântida, 1959. 70p.); *Carta do capataz da estrada* [Letter from the road-works' foreman] (Sá da Bandeira, Angola: Imbondeiro, 1960); *Depois do sétimo dia* [After the seventh day] (Lourenço Marques, Mozambique: Edições Tribuna, 1963. 157p. [Colecção 'Cancioneiro de Moçambique']); *Portanto eu vos escrevo* [And so I'm writing to you] (Viseu, Portugal: Tip. Guerra, 1964. 71p.); *Vespera confiada* [Fresh evening] (Lourenço Marques, Mozambique: Académica, 1968. 106p.); *Um minuto de silêncio* [A minute of silence] (Beira, Mozambique: Notícias da Beira, 1970. 263p. [Colecção 'Prosadores de Moçambique', no. 7]); *Adeus de Gutucúmbui* [Gutucúmbui farewell] (Lourenço Marques, Mozambique: Académica, 1971. 108p. [Colecção 'O Som e o Sentido'. no. 3]); *A fome das lavras* [The hunger of cultivation] (Lourenço Marques, Mozambique: Académica, 1975. 58p. [Colecção 'O Som e o Sentido' no. 6]).

630 **Portagem.** (Toll.)
Orlando Mendes. Maputo: Instituto Nacional do Livro e do Disco; Lisbon: Edições 70, 1981. 2nd ed. 163p. (Colecção 'Autores Mocambiçanos', no. 8).
A novel about a young *mestiço*, João Xilim ('John Shilling') and his migration from country to city. Born in the rural areas, João Xilim discovers that his father was a Portuguese mine-owner, and flees in confusion and disgust from his mother. He moves to the city, but cannot survive, and is compelled to seek work in the mines in South Africa. He returns to Mozambique, but as a *mestiço* can only just get by economically, and spends time in prison. The novel is at times heavily symbolic: the old peasant woman Alima, for example, cannot speak Portuguese and rejects the modern world – 'Coal is black, but it's not for the Blacks.' Mendes writes about his novel that it deals with 'a time when we could not bear to think about our lives, even to ourselves'. Written in the 1950s, the first edition of *Portagem* was published in Beira (Mozambique) by Notícias da Beira in 1965 in the series 'Prosadores de Moçambique', no. 6, 277p., and has also come out in a Brazilian edition from Editora Ática in São Paulo.

255

Literature. In Portuguese

631 **Produção com que aprendo: poesia e pequenas histórias.**
(Production which I learn with: poetry and short stores.)
Orlando Mendes. Maputo: Instituto Nacional do Livro e do
Disco, 1978. 110p. (Publicações 'Notícias').

Another collection by the prolific Orlando Mendes, including the four stories
'Lado a lado para avançar' [Side by side in order to go forward]; 'E um segundo
fósforo se acendeu' [And a second match flared]; 'Entreajuda' [Mutual
assistance]; and 'Tempo de reformado' [Time of retirement].

632 **Eu, o povo.** (I, the people.)
Mutimati Barnabé João (pseudonym). [Lourenço Marques,
Mozambique]: FRELIMO, 1975. [32]p.

Mutimati Barnabé João, as the dedication to this excellent short collection states
'is the individual voice which incorporates the voice of the collective. *I, the people*
now belongs to Mozambique. The Mozambican people are the author'. These
revolutionary FRELIMO poems, in the words of Mário de Andrade, are 'an
attempt by a Mozambican poet to interpret the personal lives of soldiers at war,
recreating, remaking, reconstituting in poetry some of the stages of FRELIMO's
history of struggle'. The poems themselves are good: well crafted and charged
with an authentic feeling for guerrilla warfare. Finding an abandoned Portuguese
encampment, the author fashions a poem from empty beer-cans, scraps of
newspaper used as toilet paper, and cigarette ends: 'He gives me a lot of
information, this enemy/I know that three months ago it was cold in Lisbon,
Portugal . . . ' In a recent issue of *Tempo* (no. 814 [18 May 1986], p. 47) Manuela
Sousa Lobo, following the Portuguese literary review *Colóquio-Letras*, identified
Mutimati Barnabé João in print as António Quadros, who had also published
poetry in colonial times under the pseudonym Grabato Dias.

633 **Silêncio escancarado.** (A public silence.)
Rui Nogar. Maputo: Instituto Nacional do Livro e do Disco;
Lisbon: Edições 70, 1982. 94p. (Colecção 'Autores
Moçambicanos', no. 7).

A FRELIMO poet, and yet a poet of the colonial experience, Rui Nogar has only
published this one collection, a book which deals principally with the traumatic
experience of arrest by PIDE and imprisonment. Nogar was born in Lourenço
Marques in 1932, and joined FRELIMO in 1964. He writes in one poem of the
need to write, to speak out: 'Ah, the silence, the silence/the damned colonial
silence/burying us one by one/under the debris of Portugal.' Nogar is now General
Secretary of the Association of Mozambican Writers, founded in 1982, which has
only recently begun to produce volumes in the series 'Início' and 'Timbila'. Nogar
has said of his own writing that 'the scars of the past have not yet healed', and
that he has 'many things about the past which I haven't passed on yet'.

634 **A inadiável viagem.** (The journey which couldn't be postponed.)
Luís Carlos Patraquim. Maputo: Associação dos Escritores
Moçambicanos, 1985. 71p. (Colecção 'Timbila', no. 5).

Asked in an interview in the Lisbon cultural paper *Jornal de Letras* about the title
of this second collection of poetry, Luís Carlos Patraquim replied that the journey

256

referred to was '. . . towards everything. The journey which cannot be postponed is, really, the urgent need to know things. It is a permanent state of discovery. That is where I am – discovering. To sum it up, I'm in a particular state of remembering childhood, of discovering and living it – it's a certain innocence, which I'm demanding here in Mozambique. Because, as we know, the nation, politics, they have all the arguments.' Patraquim works for Mozambican television, and is the editor of the cultural section in the weekly *Tempo*.

635 **Monção.** (Monsoon.)
     Luís Carlos Patraquim.   Maputo: Instituto Nacional do Livro e do Disco; Lisbon: Edições 70, 1980. 60p. (Colecção 'Autores Moçambicanos', no. 2).
Patraquim was born in Lourenço Marques in 1953, and *Monção* (which also means 'discovery') was his first published collection. It aroused some controversy in Mozambique, with one local critic demanding to know 'Who is Luís Carlos Patraquim writing for?' The same writer accused Patraquim of being out of touch with the masses, and of writing poetry which, while admittedly intimate, individual, and even beautiful, lacked any idea of 'collectivity'. The author replied that he was no élitist, but felt that in the first flush of victory after independence, the individual had been forgotten in favour of the collective. As for poetry, 'people are alienated . . . It is urgently necessary, in this country, to write about love'. The poet is not in himself different from other people, but every individual is different from everybody else.

636 **Poesia de Combate.** (Fighting poetry.)
     [N.p.]: FRELIMO, Departamento de Educação e Cultura; Maputo: FRELIMO, [1971–   .]. irregular.
Poesia de Combate first appeared in November 1971, during the armed struggle, as a publication by FRELIMO's Department of Education and Culture, in order to allow the voices of the guerrillas and militants to be heard through poetry. The first issue contained poems by ordinary fighters, often on political themes, and sometimes achieving some poetic immediacy. The introduction asserted quite reasonably that the struggle was being fought against élitism, against the idea that 'The peasant, the worker . . . cannot feel or understand poetry, even less express himself in poetic forms.' The anthology made its point. The second issue, published after independence but consisting largely of poems written during the war, included work not only by ordinary militants, but also by such eminent figures as Armando Guebuza, Fernando Ganhão, Jorge Rebelo, Josina Machel, Marcelino dos Santos, Rui Nogar and even the much-printed elegy 'Josina, tu nao morreste' [Josina, you have not died] by Samora Machel. In summary, issues so far have been: no. 1 (Nov. 1971. 28p.); no. 2 (Dec. 1977. 128p.); no. 1, 2nd ed. (Feb. 1979. 36p.); and no. 3 (May 1980. 80p.).

Literature. In Portuguese

637 **The saga of a cotton *capulana* (História de uma capulana de algodão).**
Luís Polanah, translated by Tamara L. Bender, with an historical introduction and notes by Allen Isaacman. Madison, Wisconsin: African Studies Center, University of Wisconsin, 1981. 90p. (Occasional paper).

This fascinating novella was first published as a serial in the newspaper *O Brado Africano* (q.v.) in 1958. The narrative is presented in the first person, as told by a cotton *capulana* (or wrap) itself, and focuses on the injustices of forced cotton-cultivation, as well as on other aspects of colonialism in southern Mozambique. Although the narrative device frequently drops away from the voice of the story-teller, this text is still one of the best examples of Mozambican literary prose. Unfortunately, it is not yet available in a Portuguese edition. Polanah now teaches anthropology at a Portuguese university.

638 **The sunflower of hope: poems from the Mozambican revolution.**
Compiled by Chris Searle. London, New York: Allison & Busby, 1982. 148p.

An anthology of poetry by, amongst others, José Craveirinha, Noémia de Sousa, Kalungano, Armando Guebuza, Fernando Ganhão, Jorge Rebelo, Rui Nogar and Sérgio Vieira. All poems are translated by Chris Searle, a teacher who has worked in Mozambique, except for one or two pieces taken from Margaret Dickinson's *When bullets begin to flower* (q.v.). Mutimati Barnabé João's *I, the people* sequence (q.v.) is translated in its entirety. The translations are sometimes erratic, changing the tenses of the original Portuguese for no good reason, for example. In the poem 'We're decolonising the Land Rover', p. 131, Searle translates the lines 'essas mãos inglesas que a criam/Um dia saberão que ajudaram a fazer a revolução', as 'These English hands which forged you/Know that one day they'll help to make their own revolution', rather than 'Will one day know that they helped to make the revolution', a fairly serious and perhaps wilful misunderstanding of the Portuguese tenses, and thus meaning. He is also careless with his references, writing that this poem was published in *Tempo* no. 360 (28 August 1977); the correct source reference is no. 355 (24 July 1977), p. 3. There is a five-page introduction, in which Searle discusses the relationship between poetry and revolutionary politics in a romantic fashion, and biographical and textual notes.

639 **Testamento – 1.** (Testament, part 1.)
Clotilde Silva. Maputo: Associação dos Escritores Moçambicanos, 1985. 109p. (Colecção 'Timbila', no. 3).

A book of poems in Portuguese, written from the 1940s onwards, and organized under such headings as 'O Real Absoluto' or 'Esteta' (Odes to beauty and love.) The introduction is by Moura Vitória. Clotilde Silva was born in Lourenço Marques, in 1925, and has published poetry in newspapers such as *Notícias*, *A Voz de Moçambique* and *Domingo*; in magazines (*Tempo* and *Itinerário*), and in the Orlando Mendes miscellany *Sobre literatura moçambicana* (q.v.). She has been active in poetry readings in Mozambique for many years, and recorded some poems by Miguel Torga; in 1964 she won second prize in the Rui de Noronha literary competition. This is her first published collection.

640 **O núcleo tenaz.** (The still centre.)
Jorge Viegas. Maputo: Instituto Nacional do Livro e do Disco;
Lisbon: Edições 70, 1981. 82p. (Colecção 'Autores
Moçambicanos', no. 10).

A collection of rather wordy poems by Jorge Viegas, who at the time of
publication was director of finances for the city of Nampula. He was born in
Quelimane in 1947, and has published verse in the review *Caliban*, as well as an
earlier book of poetry *Os milagres: poemas* [The miracles: poems] (Quelimane,
Mozambique: Sociedade Gráfica Transmontana, 1966).

In national languages

641 Vutlhari bya vatsonga (machangana). The wisdom of the Tsonga-
Shangana people.
Henri Philippe Junod. Braamfontein, South Africa: Sasavona,
1978. 3rd rev. ed. 353p.

A collection of 1,671 Shangaan proverbs, printed in the original language with an
English translation on the facing page. The proverbs are organized into two
groups according to their ostensible subject-matter – proverbs connected with
animals (further subdivided into wild animals, domestic animals, birds, fish,
insects, and so on), and with people (subdivided into ten topics such as food,
work and warfare). In many cases the proverbs are explained, both in Shangaan
and in English. There is an index of Shangaan words. The first edition, published
in 1936, included 892 proverbs, and some riddles which have been omitted in the
latest edition. There are some other useful collections of the folk-tales and folk
wisdom of the Mozambican people. See also Armando Ribeiro's *601 provérbios
changana* [Six hundred and one Shangaan proverbs] (Lourenço Marques,
Mozambique: Brado Africano, 1971. 121p.); E. J. M. Baumbach and C. T. D.
Marivate's *Swihitani swa xironga* [Ronga folk-tales] (Pretoria: University of South
Africa, 1973. 199p.), which includes some historical traditions collected during a
visit to Lourenço Marques; Elia Ciscato's *Mashiposhipo: proverbi delli espressioni
idiomatiche del popolo lomwe* [Mashiposhipo: Lomwe popular proverbs of
common speech] (Milan: n.p., n.d., mimeo, 2 vols.); and Alexandre Valente de
Matos's massive *Provérbios macuas: cultura moçambicana* [Makua proverbs,
Mozambican culture] (Lisbon: Instituto de Investigação Científica Tropical, 1982.
376p.).

642 **Muambi wa vubumabumeri.** (The narrator of praises.)
Gabriel Makavi. Braamfontein, South Africa: Sasavona, 1980.
93p.

Gabriel Makavi (1897–1982) was considered one of the great stylists of the literary
Tsonga or Shangaan language. He was also well-versed in the traditions of his
area, and his poetry is nowadays considered quite difficult for the modern reader
because of the old-fashioned but beautiful language. Thoroughly Mozambican, he
belonged to a literary community which straddles southern Mozambique and parts

Literature. In national languages

of South Africa and Zimbabwe. In his foreword to this volume of poetry he cites a number of people who influenced him, including Swiss missionaries, and even more interestingly, the present Chief Minister of the Gazankulu bantustan, Hudson Ntsan'wisi. Certainly, Ntsan'wisi has been an important Shangaan literary figure, although his political status in South Africa as a servant of the apartheid régime is, to put it delicately, ambiguous. Despite the title, the content of the collection is a mixture: praise-poems such as 'Malangatana Valente Ngwenya' (p. 45–49), about the painter, or 'I mani Chivambu Eduardo Mondlane?' [Who is Eduardo Chivambo Mondlane?] (p. 76–88), are presented alongside the highly critical 'Ndlala ya ka n'wantsimba-ku-lalela!' [The famine which-stopped-people-having-their-supper] (p. 9–12), about a period early in the century when food was so scarce that those who had some could not eat it without being interrupted by those who had none. Some families were even reduced to selling their girl-children. Makavi also wrote for the Swiss Mission-published newspaper *Mahlahle* (Morning Star). See the interview with him (in Portuguese) in the Maputo weekly *Domingo* (19 September 1982), p. 18–19, with a translation of the Malangatana poem; and the obituary in *Notícias* (13 October 1982).

643 **Utenzi wa vita vya uhuru wa Msumbiji.** (Epic of the liberation war of Mozambique.)
J. M. M. Mayoka. Arusha, Tanzania: Eastern Africa Publications, 1978. 98p.

The *utenzi* is a classical Swahili poetic form, with strict prosodic rules. Swahili is spoken in Mozambique as far south as Quelimane, and the Swahili literary community stretches northwards through Tanzania and Kenya as far as southern Somalia, and includes the islands of Zanzibar and the Comoros. Thus, although this is a Swahili epic poem by a Tanzanian writer, telling in 1000 verses the story of FRELIMO's national liberation struggle, it certainly belongs in this bibliography. With an introduction by Hashim Mbita, the secretary of the Organization of African Unity's Liberation Committee, based in Dar es Salaam.

644 **Musongi.** (Musongi.)
Bento Sitoe. Maputo: Associação dos Escritores Moçambicanos, 1985. 71p. (Colecção 'Início', no. 3).

Musongi is engaged to be married to Benjamim, and the couple are very much in love. But their planned wedding causes all kinds of conflicts between the two families, one lot from an *assimilado* background, the others country folk who want to invite all their relatives to the feast. But in true African style, all the fights can only take place through emissaries. In the end the wedding is called off and Musongi and Benjamim run away; they emerge from hiding to organize their marriage unceremoniously at the local civil registry. Sitoe was born in the Maputo suburb of Mafalala, and is currently teaching the first course in Shangaan (the language of this short novel) to be offered in independent Mozambique, at Eduardo Mondlane University, where he is a lecturer in Modern Literature. He has also conducted linguistic research in Tsonga or Shangaan. The novel shows Sitoe to be a didactic, indeed moralistic writer with strong religious views, but he uses language with humour and with an awareness of the dialectic of folk-wisdom (proverbs, for example). He has observed life in Mafalala carefully, and this carries over to his characters. For Sitoe's views on literature in African languages, see his 'E porquê em Changana?' [And why in Shangaan?], *Tempo* no. 784

(20 October 1985), p. 48–49; and a reply by Almiro Lobo in the same review no. 788 (17 November), p. 49–50.

645 **Zabela.** (Zabela.)
Bento Sitoe. Maputo: Cadernos Tempo, 1983. 62p. (Colecção 'Gostar de Ler', no. 7).

A short novella in Shangaan, spoken in southern Mozambique, and the first literary work in an African language to be published in the country since independence. Sitoe, in an interview published in the Mozambican weekly *Domingo* on 4 December 1983, commented that '*Zabela* is also a challenge, to create a taste for reading in other languages [than Portuguese]. I write fiction in Shangaan so that people can read something other than the Bible, the prayer book and the hymn book, because we have those in all the African languages . . . [*Zabela*] is a Mozambican story. It's about the problem of young people running away from the countryside to the city. 'Zabela' is also the name of the main character; it's the conflict of a young girl who runs away to Lourenço Marques, as it was then, looking for a better life, and ends up in a prostitution ring . . . I wrote it a long time ago.'

The Arts

General

646 The role of culture in the liberation of Mozambique.
Edward A. Alpers. *Ufahamu* vol. 12, no. 3 (1983), p. 143–89.
The question of the role played by cultural expression (poetry, music, drama and the plastic arts) in the development both of opposition to the colonial state and of nationalism in Mozambique – and the two are not the same thing although are often confused – has attracted a lot of attention. Alpers writes informatively and perceptively, showing that cultural expression served the function, *inter alia*, 'of asserting the values of specific African cultures against the dehumanization of colonialism, which either attempted to reduce Africans to nameless and faceless units of labor or relegate them to obscurity'. He ranges over such topics as the Chope *timbila* orchestras, Makonde wood carvings, the *mapico* and *nyau* dance-theatre, proverbs, Zambezian songs, the poetry of Craveirinha and Noémia de Sousa, and the paintings of Malangatana and Virgílio Massingue.

647 Arte viva em Moçambique. (Live art in Mozambique.)
Cadernos do Terceiro Mundo no. 74 (Feb. 1985), p. 87–94.
A special feature consisting of three articles: Mário Trindade's 'Um modo de estar no mundo' (A way of being in the world) on the general characteristics of African art (p. 88–89); Sol Carvalho's 'Psikhelekedana, o artesanato do sul' (*Psikhelekedana*, the handicraft of the south), on the southern Mozambican wood-carving style whose name derives from a corruption of the English word 'crocodile', a common theme (p. 90–92); and 'Os murais da revolução' (The murals of the revolution), by Albie Sachs and Sol Carvalho (p. 93–94).

648   **O combate cultural no nosso país.** (The fight over culture in our
country.)
Samora Machel.   *África: literatura, arte e cultura* no. 5 (July–Sept.
1979), p. 554–58.

A thematic extract from a much longer interview, entitled 'A cultura é a questão
central da revolução', first published in *Tempo* no. 431 (7 January 1979) as a pull-
out supplement (p. 1–16), which, despite the title, covered a wide range of other
topics. The text is of interest as a statement of Samora's views on cultural
questions in the late 1970s: he returned to the attack on foreign cultural influences
in a speech on 1 May of the same year. Here the President expresses disapproval
of such manifestations of Western influence as blue-jeans and long hair, but
points out that 'For the Mozambican people in general, one cannot pose the
problem of breaking with bourgeois imperialist culture, because they are simply
unaware of its existence.'

649   **Tradizione e rivoluzione culturale in Mozambico.** (Tradition and
cultural revolution in Mozambique.)
Guiseppe Morosini.   *Africa* [Rome] vol. 35, no. 1 (March 1980),
p. 43–84.

In this Italian article, published in the journal of the main African research
institute in Rome, Morosini analyses the Frelimo Party's cultural policy in the
period after independence, within an anthropological framework. Basing his
argument on two years of fieldwork in Mozambique, he identifies the 'traditional
cultures' of the pre-colonial 'ethnic groups' in Mozambique, and describes the
changes brought about by the ten-year liberation war against the Portuguese.
Present policy consists of a struggle against 'westernization' on the one hand, and
against 'traditionalism' on the other, a process which Morosini sees as a dialectic
between cultural pluralism and cultural unity. Frelimo posits instead the need for
a synthesis of the positive elements of both. Morosini refers to the cultural
revolutions of such countries as China and Vietnam, as well as to the experience
of the other Portuguese-speaking countries of Africa. Important theoretical
contributions have been made by such outstanding figures as Eduardo Mondlane
and Amílcar Cabral.

'Banda desenhada'

650   *Akapwitchi akaporo:* **armas e escravos.** (*Akapwitchi akaporo*: arms
and slaves.)
João Paulo Borges Coelho.   Maputo: Instituto Nacional do Livro
e do Disco, 1981. 60p. (Banda Desenhada, no. 1).

João Paulo's first album of drawings is set at the end of the 19th century on the
northern coast, where the Portuguese, the Swahili-speaking sheikhs and the
Makuas struggled to abolish on the one hand, or to control on the other, the
profitable trade in slaves, which were exchanged for modern rifles. The 'Marave'

(Suali bin Ali Ibrahimu) was an important leader of this early resistance to colonial penetration, but in defence of his own interests. João Paulo's graphic style in this black-and-white album conveys the drama and excitement, but in general the drawing is not as satisfactory as in his second work *No tempo de Farelahi* (q.v.).

651 **No tempo do Farelahi.** (In Farelahi's times.)
João Paulo [Borges Coelho]. Maputo: Instituto Nacional do Livro e do Disco, 1984. 90p. (Banda Desenhada, no. 4).

Although he works in black-and-white because of the lack of processing facilities for colour in Maputo, and not from choice, João Paulo's style is well adapted to the medium. In this album we can see some of the influence of Hugo Pratt, whose hero Corto Maltese has had some success in French- and Portuguese-speaking countries. The book tells the story of Farelahi and his loose alliance of slave-traders (the 'men with hats'), Swahili sheikhs, and Makua chiefdoms, and of their resistance against the Portuguese under Mouzinho de Albuquerque (q.v.) in the last years of the 19th century in Nampula Province. The album is much more ambitious than João Paulo's earlier *Akapwitchi akaporo* (q.v.), both in terms of graphics and of narrative, and represents a new kind of popular history in Mozambique. For background information on this period, see Malyn Newitt's 'The early history of the Sultanate of Angoche', *Journal of African History* vol. 13, no. 3 (1972), p. 397–406.

652 **Moçambique por Eduardo Mondlane.** (Mozambique, by Eduardo Mondlane.)
Helena Motta. Maputo: Instituto Nacional do Livro e do Disco, 1984. 86p. (Banda Desenhada, no. 3).

Many English readers will perhaps be familiar by now with the 'Cuba for beginners' and 'Marx for beginners' albums, which have spawned a whole series of limitations. This is a brilliantly successful adaptation of Eduardo Mondlane's *Struggle for Mozambique* to the medium by a young Mozambican artist with considerable graphic and narrative skills. Working in black-and-white, and using several different graphic styles, Helena Motta brings alive for us the characterization of Portuguese colonialism in Mondlane's work; the section on education is both enlightening and amusing. Mozambique is a society in which even the few who are literate often have only a shaky grasp of their new skill. The serious application of the 'banda desenhada' as a tool of mobilization and education is therefore important pedagogically and politically; the works of Helena Motta and João Paulo augur well for the future.

653 **Xiconhoca o inimigo.** (Chico Nhoca the enemy.)
Maputo: Departamento do Trabalho Ideológico do Partido Frelimo, 1979. 1 vol. [not paginated].

A highly recommended volume of the popular political cartoons built around the character Xiconhoca, who represents everything which Mozambicans consider politically and socially undesirable. The name (pronounced Shi-ko-nyo-ka) derives from two sources: Xico is a familiar form of Francisco, and in this case refers to the hated PIDE interrogator Francisco Langa, one of a handful of

Mozambicans who worked enthusiastically for the Portuguese secret police. *Nhoca* means 'snake' in virtually all the Mozambican African languages; a somewhat colourless translation might, therefore, be something like 'Frank the Snake', but this conveys little of the odium which the term carries in Portuguese.

Music

654 **Hinos da revolução.** (Songs of the revolution.)
Frente de Libertação de Moçambique (FRELIMO). Lourenço Marques, Mozambique: Imprensa Nacional, 1975. 4th ed. 58p.

Contains the words but not the music of over fifty well-known and well-loved FRELIMO songs. It is alleged that a FRELIMO leader once remarked that 'to sing badly is a political error', and indeed there can be few countries where the collective singing of political songs makes up an essential part of such dignified state occasions as the opening of the National Assembly. These songs are in Portuguese, Nyanja, Swahili and other languages (although for some bizarre reason the Swahili is transcribed as if it were Portuguese: thus 'FRELIMO haina mwisho' – FRELIMO has no end – comes out as *FRELIMO ayi na muixo!*) Listen also to the double album *Hinos revolucionários de Moçambique* by the army choir (Maputo: Teal records, 2 12-inch long-playing records).

655 **A select bibliography of music in Africa, compiled at the International African Institute.**
L. J. P. Gaskin. London: International African Institute, 1965. Reprinted, 1971. 83p. (Africa Bibliography, series B).

An extensive bibliography of 3,040 numbered and indexed references, many of which are analytical citations of musical information on specific pages in more general works. The focus is on 'traditional' rather than modern music. On Mozambican music generally, see entries 1081–1112; on Mozambican musical instruments, entries 1902–1904a; and on Mozambican dance (the *mapico*, the *merombo* and the *nyau*), entries 2667b–2670. There is considerable overlap for the earlier material with Douglas H. Varley's bibliography on African music (q.v.).

656 **Grandes sucessos.** (Greatest hits.)
Alexandre Langa, Xidimingwana. Maputo: Instituto Nacional do Livro e do Disco, 1981. 12-inch long-playing record (no. Ngoma 0056).

Mozambique has a strong tradition of popular music in African languages, and has its own record industry, producing albums such as this one. Alexandre Langa is one of the country's most popular musicians; he was born in Chibuto in Gaza Province in 1943, and started off playing with the legendary Fany Mpfumo. He composes his own material, and his seven songs on this album include the catchy *Meticais*, celebrating the introduction of a national currency in 1980, and *Xitimela xa Manhiça* (Steamer from Manhiça). The album also includes five songs from the older performer Domingos Mantiane Honwana (1936– .), known as Xidimingwana, who also comes from Gaza Province.

657 **Música tradicional em Moçambique.** (Traditional music in Mozambique.)
Co-ordinated by Paulo Soares. Maputo: Gabinete de Organização do Festival da Canção e Música Tradicional, 1980. 72p. maps.

Published by the Ministry of Education and Culture, this illustrated booklet includes the following essays: 'Appreciating traditional music and song', by Paulo Soares (a Mozambican historian working in the National Directorate for Culture); 'Musical traditions in Mozambique', by the late John Marney, an English musician and teacher; 'Arab influence on traditional music', by Martinho Lutero and Carlos Martins Pereira (see also their 'A musica tradicional em Moçambique' [Traditional music in Mozambique], *África: literatura, arte e cultura* no. 11 [Jan.–June 1981] p. 79–88.); 'The relationship between music and dance in southern Mozambique', by Marney; 'The *timbilas* (wooden xylophones)' by Lutero; 'Musical bows of Mozambique', by Maria da Luz Teixeira Duarte, also a historian; and finally Lutero and Martins' '*Nyanga*, the flute dance'.

658 **Catálogo do instrumentos musicais de Moçambique.** (Catalogue of musical instruments of Mozambique.)
Co-ordinated by Maria da Luz Teixeira Duarte. Maputo: Gabinete Central de Organização do Festival da Canção e Música Tradicional, 1980. 31p.

A short, illustrated catalogue prepared by the Central Organizer's Office of the Festival of Traditional Music and Song in 1980. The instruments are listed in alphabetical order by their local African names. For example, *mbila*, a type of wooden xylophone, or *tambore*, a drum. There are maps showing the distribution of each instrument within the country.

659 **Chopi musicians: their music, poetry and instruments.**
Hugh Tracey. London: Oxford University Press for the International African Institute, 1948. 180p. maps.

The Chope-speaking people of Zavala and Inharrime, to the east of the mouth of the Limpopo River, are famous in southern Africa for their xylophone orchestras, which play sophisticated and complex compositions, and for the *msaho* dance. Tracey's book remains the most exhaustive treatment of their musical traditions, dealing with composers, lyrics and 'poetic justice', dancers and the dances, music and the masters, Chope musicians on the Rand, the xylophones themselves (known locally as *timbila*), and techniques for making them. He also prints some appendixes, including letters of Father Andre Fernandes, the first missionary to the area in 1526, a glossary of Chope musical terminology, a list of Chope orchestras on the Rand in 1944, and an analysis of an orchestral piece. The work was also published in Portuguese as *Gentes afortunadas: a música chope*, translated by M. H. Barradas, appearing first in *Moçambique: documentário trimestral* nos 46–55 (April–June 1946 to July–Sept. 1948), and later as a separate volume (Lourenço Marques, Mozambique: Imprensa Nacional, 1949. 273p.). A later work in Italian by a Mozambican researcher benefited from Tracey's advice; see Amándio Dide Mungwambe's 'La musica dei chopi' [The music of the Chope] (Licenciatura dissertation, Pontificio Instituto di Musica Sacra, Rome, 1972. 203p. appendix).

660 **Forms of resistance: songs and perceptions of power in colonial Mozambique.**
Leroy Vail, Landeg White. *American Historical Review* vol. 88, no. 4 (Oct. 1983), p. 883–919.

A comparative article by a historian and a literary critic, based on two collections of songs, the first made in the 1940s among the Chope-speakers of Zavala, in Inhambane, by Hugh Tracey (q.v.), the second among the Sena- and Lomwe-Chuabo-speakers in and around Quelimane in 1975–77 by the authors themselves. In general terms, the songs in Sena express the hope that a 'just lord' will come to right the wrongs done to the people; the songs in Lomwe, however, do not refer to or accept authority, but simply express a desire to be left alone. By contrast, the older songs collected by Tracey in the south refer to local traditions and express a kind of ethnic nationalism. Vail and White conclude that responses to colonial rule varied over space and time, and that generalization is risky. See also Vail and White's *Capitalism and colonialism in Mozambique* (q.v.), which also makes use of song material as historical evidence.

661 **African native music: an annotated bibliography.**
Douglas H. Varley. Folkestone; London: Dawsons of Pall Mall. Reprinted, 1970. 116p.

First published in 1936, this is the basic, although now outdated, bibliography for 'traditional' music; it still has some utility as a guide to the classic literature. The entries are not numbered, there is an author index only and references are arranged geographically. For Mozambique, see under Portuguese East Africa, section 25, p. 68–69. The section has the character of an analytical index to the musical information (a description of some musical event or instrument) in various ethnographic classics – Salt's *Voyage to Abyssinia* (1814), which, surprisingly, has material on Makua music, Henri Junod's *Les Ba-Ronga* (1898), or R. C. F. Maugham's *Portuguese East Africa* (London, 1906). Citations are in chronological order up to 1936, and there are extremely brief indicative annotations.

662 **Que venham!** (Let them come!)
Yana. Maputo: Instituto Nacional do Livro e do Disco, 1981. 12-inch long-playing record (no. Ngoma 0078).

One of Mozambique's finest moments of defiance in the early 1980s was encapsulated in Samora Machel's speech on 14 February 1981, after the South African attack on Matola on 30 January, in which twelve exiles lost their lives. Yana (whose real name is Samuel Munguambe, Jr.) took the slogan *Que venham!* from the President's speech, and used it as the refrain to the slow, sad, yet powerful title-song in this album, with its list of petty consumer goods in exchange for which Mozambican traitors were prepared to sell their country. Yana's style is folksy, consisting of a simple acoustic guitar accompaniment which allows the listener to concentrate on the words of his often highly political songs. He now runs a small music school for children in the capital.

663 **Yuphuro.** (Yuphuro.)
    Yuphuro. Maputo: Instituto Nacional do Livro e do Disco, 1984.
    12-inch long-playing record. (no. Ngoma 0131).

Yuphuro, who have recently taken to spelling their collective name Eyuphuro, are one of the best of the Mozambican musical groups, and what is more, come from the north, from Nampula. Their music is firmly rooted in the local traditions of their area both melodically and linguistically. It should be noted that Mozambican popular music has been dominated for many years by southern singers and groups, especially Chope- and Shangaan-speakers. Yuphuro consists of six members, including Zena Bakar, the female lead singer. They have toured in Western Europe with some success, and have also visited the socialist countries. For more details, see the article 'Para promover a música de Nampula' (Plugging the music of Nampula) by Lourenço Jossias, in the weekly *Domingo* (17 November 1985), p. 5.

Paintings, murals and photography

664 **Malangatana.** (Malangatana.)
    Julian Beinart. *Black Orpheus* (Ibadan, Nigeria) no. 10 [196?], p. 22–29.

An early article which includes Malangatana's own brief account of his life, explaining how he was 'discovered' by the architect Miranda Guedes in late 1959, and how Guedes encouraged him, paying him a monthly allowance and setting him up in a studio. It also contains some reproductions.

665 **Muipiti: Ilha de Moçambique.** (Muipiti: Mozambique Island.)
    Photographs by Moira Forjaz and text by Amélia Muge. Lisbon: Imprensa Nacional-Casa da Moeda, 1983. [not paginated]. maps. (Colecção 'Presenças da Imagem').

Muipiti is the Makua name for Mozambique Island. Moira Forjaz is a talented Zimbabwean photographer and film-maker, who also took the photographs for the Ruth First book *Black gold* (q.v.). This highly recommended volume of well-printed and evocative black-and-white pictures portrays the people and buildings of the island in such a way that even if you cannot understand Amélia Muge's Portuguese notes, the photographs can speak for themselves.

The Arts. Paintings, murals and photography

666 **FRELIMO: terceiro congresso.** (FRELIMO: the third congress.)
Maputo: Instituto Nacional do Livro e do Disco, 1978. [not
paginated].

A highly recommended and lavishly illustrated album of photographs, published
to celebrate the III Congress, held in February 1977. The book includes a detailed
chronology of Mozambican history, and includes some details of party history not
readily available elsewhere. The pictures are on all aspects of the social, economic
and political life of the Mozambican people, before and after independence.

667 **Moçambique: a terra e os homens.** (Mozambique: the country and
the people.)
[Maputo]: Associação Moçambicana de Fotografia, 1982. 159p.

An album of photographs of modern Mozambique, by well-known professional
photographers, such as Kok Nam, Moira Forjaz and Ricardo Rangel. Also
included is work by amateurs, including José Capão (a documentalist and
historian working in the Secretariat for Culture) and António Matonse, a
diplomat. Somewhere in between comes the writer (and now Minister of Culture)
Luís Bernardo Honwana. The introduction, in Portuguese, English, French and
Italian, is by José Luís Cabaço. See also a similar compilation from colonial times:
Moçambique: a preto e branco [Mozambique in black-and-white] (Lourenço
Marques, Mozambique: CODAM, 1972. 80p.).

668 **Grito de Paz.** (Cry of peace.)
Naguib. Maputo: Horizonte Arte Difusão, 1986. 12p.

A catalogue of an exhibition by the young Mozambican painter Naguib, who was
born in Tete in 1955. There is an introduction by Malangatana, and a biographical
note on Naguib by Luís Carlos Patraquim. There are eight full-colour
reproductions and a photograph of Naguib busily painting.

669 **FRELIMO vencerá. FRELIMO will win.**
Tadahiro Ogawa. *The Sun* [Tokyo] no. 124 (Aug. 1973); Tokyo:
Japan Anti-Apartheid Committee, Youth Section, 1973. 1 vol. [not
paginated, with separate booklet].

Ogawa is a Japanese photographer of some talent who visited the liberated zones
in Cabo Delgado between 22 April and 5 May 1973. His photographs, with an
accompanying text in Japanese, occupied the whole of the special August issue of
the Tokyo monthly *The Sun*, which was subsequently reissued with a special dust-
jacket in English, an accompanying booklet in English, and an enclosed booklet
with English and Portuguese translations of the text and picture captions.
Recommended.

670 **Imagens de uma revolução.** (Images of a revolution.)
Albie Sachs. Maputo: Partido Frelimo, 1984. [not paginated].

Magnificent full-colour and detailed reproductions, with a commentary by Albie
Sachs, of seven of the large painted murals which adorn various public sites in
Maputo. These, often highly political, works are by such painters as Malagatana,
or by collectives of artists. An English edition was published by the Zimbabwe

The Arts. Theatre and film

Publishing House in Harare in 1984, but the quality of the paper, and hence the colour plates, was not so high. Also on mural paintings, see the article by Etevaldo Hipólito about Mankew Valente Muhumana, 'Muralistas descem às minas de carvão', (Mural painters go down the coal mines) *Cadernos do Terceiro Mundo* no. 59/60 (Dec. 1983), p. 87–88.

671 **Malangatana of Mozambique.**
Betty Schneider. *African Arts* vol. 5, no. 2 (Winter 1972),
p. 40–45.

Malangatana Valente Ngwenya, usually known simply as Malangatana, is undoubtedly Mozambique's best-known painter, and has been for several years. Schneider's impressionistic and chatty article quotes some of his poetry, and reproduces some early drawings and paintings. On 6 June 1986 Malangatana celebrated his fiftieth birthday and held a major retrospective in Maputo. There was extensive coverage of this and associated events in Maputo's *Notícias* and *Tempo*. See also Rui Mário Gonçalves' 'Um olhar sobre Malangatana: traços biográficos e a obra do pintor moçambicano na opinião de um crítico de arte' (A look at Malangatana: biographical details and the works of the Mozambican painter, from an art critic's point of view), *Cadernos do Terceiro Mundo* no. 58 (Nov. 1983), p. 77–78. On another Mozambican painter of interest, see *Le temps de la passion au Mozambique: six oeuvres de Shikhani* [The time of the passion in Mozambique: six works by Shikhani] (Lausanne, Switzerland: Éditions du Sol, [1974?]. 6p.).

Theatre and film

672 **A Comuna.** (The commune.)
Colectivo de trabalho, trabalhadores dos Caminhos de Ferro de Moçambique, e estudantes da Universidade Eduardo Mondlane.
Maputo: Instituto Nacional do Livro e do Disco, 1979. 93p.
(Colecção 'Teatro', no. 1).

This workshop presentation of the events of the Paris Commune of 1870 was developed by a collective consisting of workers from CFM, the Mozambican national railways, and students from Eduardo Mondlane University, at the height of enthusiasm for political theatre in Mozambique in the late 1970s. Despite considerable difficulties, groups such as Xuva Xita Duma continue to present plays, at least in Maputo, where the Angolan playwright Pepetela's piece 'The revolt in the house of the idols' was given its world première in the mid-1980s, for example.

673 **Pesquisas para um teatro popular em Moçambique.** (Researches towards a people's theatre in Mozambique.)
Anna Fresu, Mendes de Oliveira. Maputo: Tempográfica, 1982.
132p. (Cadernos Tempo. Colecção 'Temas Culturais', no. 1).

This book is the result of over four years of research and experience in popular cinema and theatre in Mozambique. Fresu and Oliveira produced a series of short epic and didactic plays at the Centre for Cultural Studies, as well as puppet shows, shadow plays and audio-visual happenings. At a communal village in Cabo Delgado, they mounted a production which showed the history of the village, whose inhabitants were *regressados* (refugees who had come back from Tanzania after the war). This book includes chapters on people's theatre in Mozambique, with sections on the *nyau* of Tete and the *mapico* of Cabo Delgado; a description of the theatre arts course at the Centre for Cultural Studies; a chapter on drama in the school, the communal village and the psychiatric hospital; and a final section on the production of a series of pieces of different types, including puppet and shadow plays. Much of this material was previously published in *Tempo*.

674 **A sagrada família, ou, a Crítica da crítica do javali, do camaleão, e do Xiconhoca.** (The Holy Family, or, The critique of the critique of the boar, the chameleon and Xiconhoca.)
Grupo Cénico das Forças Populares de Libertação de Moçambique. Maputo: Instituto Nacional do Livro e do Disco, 1980. 51p. (Colecção 'Teatro', no. 3).

The Theatre Group of the People's Forces for the Liberation of Mozambique was formed at Nachingwea camp in southern Tanzania during the armed struggle for independence. In this highly political piece the boar represents greed – his nose always in the trough; the chameleon represents opportunism – he always changes colour; and Xiconhoca (roughly, 'Frank the snake') is a universally accepted and understood figure representing treacherous collaboration with the enemy.

675 *Maputo Mulher*: **um filme polémico.** (*Woman of Maputo*: a polemical film.)
Etevaldo Hipólito. *Cadernos do Terceiro Mundo* no. 80 (Aug. 1985), p. 88–92.

Maputo Mulher was a film produced jointly by the Mozambican National Cinema Institute (INC), and the Kanemo Company, and was made in connection with the OMM's Extraordinary Conference, held in February 1984. The journalist Calane da Silva co-ordinated the producers' ideas with research by the OMM on women's problems. The film was directed by the Brazilian Mário Borgnet, and stars one of Mozambique's top actresses, Ana Magaia, as the progressive 'new woman' Rita, whose opinions clash with the traditional and often reactionary views of Auntie Zavela, played by Lina Magaia, a well-known political figure in Frelimo and the OMM. The article includes an inverview with Lina Magaia. On Mozambican women, see also in the same magazine the interview with Anabel Rodrigues of the OMM Information Department entitled 'A nova mulher moçambicana' [The new Mozambican woman] no. 25 (July 1980), p. 91–95; and the discussion with Sabina Santos and Gertrudes Vitorino, 'Um grande esforço' [A big effort] no. 79 (July 1985), p. 40–42. Of some interest on Mozambican film and film-makers, are

The Arts. Wood carvings

two catalogues published by the National Cinema Institute: see *Retrospectiva do cinema moçambicano* [Retrospective of the Mozambican cinema] (Maputo: Instituto Nacional do Cinema, 1982. 22p.), which includes a brief introduction on the history of film in Mozambique, and catalogues and summarizes twenty-one films; and *Primeiro festival do cinema moçambicano* [First Mozambican film festival] (Maputo: Instituto Nacional do Cinema, n.d. 19p.), which catalogues and summarizes twenty-eight films with biographies of the directors. Miguel Alencar and others have written an account of the experiences and difficulties of training technicians and making eight political shorts and other films in their *Histoire de seize films réalisés de juin à septembre 1978 dans le cadre des ateliers 'Super 8' de l'Université de Maputo au Mozambique* [The story of sixteen films made between June and September 1978 in the Super-8 studios at Maputo University in Mozambique] (Paris: n.p., 1979. 44p.).

Wood carvings

676 **An annotated bibliography of the visual arts of East Africa.**
Eugene C. Burt. Bloomington, Indiana: Indiana University Press, 1980. 371p. (Traditional Arts of Africa).

Despite the title, which appears to limit the interest of the contents to the three countries of East Africa, this bibliography is important for at least one aspect of Mozambican art as well. Burt's work is a professional bibliography of a high standard, listing over 2,000 items on the visual arts; he covers Makonde art in a special section, justifying this by the fact that it is partially Mozambican, as well as Tanzanian. The section includes 140 references (p. 237–258, items 1518–1658). There are author, subject and 'culture' indexes.

677 **Modern Makonde sculpture.**
Aidron Duckworth. [Syracuse, New York: Syracuse University, n.d.]. 105p.

The exhibition catalogue of the first show of Makonde carvings ever to be held in the United States. The show was based on works selected from the private collections of J. Anthony Stout (q.v.), Lewis H. Weinstein, Brack Brown and Susan Stein. The catalogue is of interest primarily for the plentiful black-and-white photographs; Duckworth's text is of little use to anyone who wishes to understand the carvings in anything other than romantic terms. He represents the carvers as a 'proud independent people' living in 'isolation for centuries', and now subject to 'the debasing effects of foreign commercial pressures' upon their work. We arrive at something perilously close to the colonial characterization of the Makonde-speakers as a fierce warrior 'tribe' with facial tattoos who make fine carvers; thus, for instance, did the Portuguese attempt to explain their adherence to FRELIMO, rather than in terms of their concrete experience of colonial exploitation. Duckworth was head of the sculpture section at the Syracuse School of Art.

272

The Arts. Wood carvings

678 **Wood sculptures of the Maconde people: album.**
Introduction and photographs by Manuel Manarte. Lourenço
Marques, Mozambique: Instituto de Investigação Científica de
Moçambique, 1963. [not paginated].

This small album of photographs from colonial times includes a five-page
introduction which argues along diffusionist lines that Makonde carving
'shows . . . a marked influence of the art of the people of the Nile Valley and, in
particular, of those from Upper Egypt'. The Portuguese were, seemingly, unable
to believe that a sub-Saharan African people might be able to develop such an
art-form by themselves. The album was published in two editions, the other being
in Portuguese. There is an extensive literature on Makonde carvings, distinguished
principally by the quality of the illustrations; see, for example, Maria L. Franz'
'Traditional masks and figures of the Makonde', *African Arts* (Autumn 1969),
p. 42–45; and the glossy *Modern Makonde art* by Jörn Korn, with photographs by
Jesper Kirknaes (London: Hamlyn, 1974. 95p.).

679 **Art in East Africa: a contemporary guide to East African art.**
Judith von der Miller. London: Muller, 1975. 132p.

Although this well-illustrated guide concentrates on the art of the three East
African countries, Miller does devote some space (p. 31–37) to Makonde
carvings. She attributes them to migrant workers from Mozambique in southern
Tanzania and in Dar es Salaam. She also identifies three main stylistic innovations
which released Makonde carvers from the formalism of traditional concepts.
These are the introduction, by the carver known as Samaki, of the *shetani*, or
'spirit' as a subject, which allowed for flights of the imagination; the 'tree-of-life'
style, in which dozens of human or animal figures are interlaced in a kind of
totem; and the introduction of modern objects such as telephones, cars, or even
FRELIMO guerrillas, expressing the real world in which the carvers lived. For
the beginnings of an account of the influence of art on nationalist ideas, see the
unpublished but widely distributed seminar paper, presented to the History
Workshop at the Centro de Estudos Africanos by Paulo Soares, an historian,
documentalist and cultural worker, together with the painter Malangatana
Ngwenya, 'Artes plásticas e movimento nacionalista: contribuição para uma
reflexão dos anos 50 e 60 em Moçambique' [The plastic arts and the nationalist
movement: a contribution towards a reflection on the 'fifties and 'sixties in
Mozambique] ([Maputo], mimeo, 1982. 35 leaves).

680 **Modern Makonde sculpture.**
J. Anthony Stout. London: Kegan Paul; Nairobi: Kibo Art
Gallery, 1966. 125p.

Stout, an American art connoisseur and collector, argues that the meeting
between the artistic styles of the Makonde-speaking people of northern
Mozambique and southern Tanzania, and modern urban values, has resulted in
the emergence of a new type of sculpture. The animal, spirit and human figures of
Makonde wood carvings are quite different in subject-matter, style and intention
from the older ritual masks. Certainly, in the 1960s, when this book was
published, the Makonde carvers were seen as constituting the vanguard of a
future renaissance of the fine arts in south-eastern Africa, without resorting to
European models or influence. However, since then, the commercialization of the

carvings for the tourist trade has resulted in a drop in artistic quality. Stout's argument is scrappily presented and does not make enough of the social and political influences at work in the creation of the carvings – for instance, the impact of Portuguese 'pacification' on the Makonde-speakers south of the Ruvuma River. The book remains valuable, however, because of the plentiful illustrations, chosen at a time when the sculptors were at their peak in terms of imagination, freshness, eroticism and vigour.

Museums and Archives

681 **Inventário do fundo do seculo XVIII.** (Inventory of 18th-century materials.)
Arquivo Histórico de Moçambique. Lourenço Marques, Mozambique: Imprensa Nacional, 1958. 357p.

Originally printed in the review *Moçambique* nos. 72–92, this inventory gives detailed descriptions of 266 documents, with textual transcriptions or summaries. The work was done when Caetano Montez was Curator of the Historical Archive. The materials are divided up by the following provenances: India, Portuguese shipping, the Captaincy-General of Mozambique, the Plantation of Mozambique, the Royal Hospital of Mozambique, the Auditor-General of Mozambique, miscellaneous, Cabo Delgado, Sofala, Inhambane, the Rios de Sena, the Lacerda e Almeida expedition, the Fair of Dambarare, and the chiefs of the Rios de Sena. See also the more general works by Fernando de Carvalho Dias: 'Notícias dos documentos da Secção dos Reservados, Fundo Geral da Biblioteca Nacional de Lisboa, respeitantes às provincias ultramarinas de Angola, Cabo Verde, Guiné, Macau, Moçambique, S. Tomé e Principe e Timor' [Report on the documents in the Reserved Section of the General Collection of the National Library at Lisbon, on the overseas provinces of Angola, Cape Verde, Guinea-Bissau, Macau, Mozambique, São Tomé and Principe, and Timor] *Garcia de Orta* vol. 5, no. 2/3, (1957); and 'Ultramar português e a expansão na África e no Oriente: breve notícia dos documentos manuscritos de Fundo Geral da Biblioteca Nacional de Lisboa: extracto do ficheiro geral' [Overseas Portugal and the expansion into Africa and the East: a short report on the manuscripts in the General Collection of the National Library at Lisbon; extracts from the general card catalogue] *Garcia de Orta* vol. 3, no. 3/4 (1955); vol. 4, no. 1/4 (1956).

682 **Boletim do Museu de Nampula (Museu Regional 'Comandante Ferreira de Almeida').** (Bulletin of the Nampula Museum (the Major Ferreira de Almeida Regional Museum).)
Nampula, Mozambique: 1960–61. nos 1–2.

This is really an ethnographic scholarly journal; the first issue (of two published) includes an extremely brief (two-and-a-half-page) guide to the Museum itself. Otherwise, the contents consist of articles dealing with a wide range of topics – the Makua language, the *mapico* dance of Cabo Delgado, a medical study of a rare bone disease, pottery in northern Mozambique, and so on. A substantial proportion of the authors appear to be missionaries or priests. The Nampula Museum is closed at present and will eventually become the National Museum of Ethnography.

683 **Documentação histórica moçambicana.** (Mozambican historical documents.)
Maria de Lourdes Esteves dos Santos de Freitas Ferraz. Lisbon: Junta de Investigações do Ultramar, 1973– .

Summarizes the contents of a series of 529 individual documents, dating from between 1608 and 1753, from Boxes 1, 2 and 3 in the Mozambican section of the Arquivo Histórico Ultramarino in Lisbon. The documents are cited in chronological order, with name, place and subject indexes, and a short introduction. Also on the Mozambican contents of the AHU, see Francisco Santana's massive three-volume guide, *Documentação avulsa moçambicana do Arquivo Histórico Ultramarino* [Unbound Mozambican documents in the Overseas Historical Archive] (Lisbon: Centro de Estudos Históricos Ultramarinos, 1964–74), which contains 3,789 pages and is staggeringly detailed.

684 **A luta armada de libertação nacional através do Museu da Revolução: um guia.** (The armed struggle for national liberation through the Museum of the Revolution.)
Julieta Marta Álvaro Massimbe. Trabalho de diploma for the Licenciatura, Arquivo Histórico de Moçambique, Universidade Eduardo Mondlane, 1985. 120p.

This thesis consists of a model guide to the Museum of the Revolution, which was founded on 25 June 1978 at Alta-Maé. The Museum is the responsibility of Frelimo's Department of Ideological Work. The guide follows the physical (and chronological) organization of the Museum itself, presenting the history of the Mozambican revolution, as conceived here: essentially the history of the liberation war, with lots of maps, and photographs of objects and documents on display in the Museum. The final section consists of official biographies of the heroes of the armed struggle, including Eduardo Mondlane and Josina Machel.

685 **Monografia dos principais edifícios e monumentos da Ilha de Moçambique.** (The principal buildings and monuments of Mozambique Island.)
[Maputo: [n.p.], 1981]. [16]p.

Prepared at the time of Portuguese President Ramalho Eanes' state visit to Mozambique, this is a useful little guidebook to the Island, which is virtually an entire museum in itself. It describes twenty-three monuments: the St. Sebastian Fortress; the Chapel of Our Lady of Baluarte; the All Souls Monument and St. Gabriel's Field; the monument to the dead of the First World War; the Convent of St. Dominic; the Palace of St. Paul; the Chapel of St. Paul; the Church of Mercy; the Museum of Sacred Art; the Bishop's residence; the Jesuit Hostel; the bandstand; the Bridge of Customs and Excise; the Customs House; Rickshaw Plaza; the Chapel of St. Francis Xavier; the Church and *fortim* (fortress) of St. Anthony; the *fortim* of St. Lawrence; the central Mosque; the Hindu temple; the Bridge to the Continent; the Church of Health; and the hospital. A much more detailed and ambitious guidebook was prepared over forty years ago by the historian Alexandre Lobato; see his *A Ilha de Moçambique: monografia* [Mozambique Island: a monograph] (Lourenço Marques, Mozambique: Imprensa Nacional, 1945. 156p.), which consists of a brief history followed by a guide to the city and its buildings, with some statistical tables. See also Lobato's later illustrated work *Ilha de Moçambique: panorama histórico* [Mozambique Island: an historical panaorama] (Lisbon: Agência Geral do Ultramar, 1967. unpaginated).

686 **Museu Histórico-Militar do colonialismo em Moçambique.** (Military History Museum of colonialism in Mozambique.)
Tempo no. 307 (22 August 1976), p. 18–26.

This critical article is divided into three sections, the first on the Museum itself, the second devoted to a vigorous attack on the Museum's contents and organization, and the third on the Fortress of Our Lady of the Conception in Maputo, which housed the Museum. Some of the objects were later removed to the Museum of the Revolution, and the Museum was reorganized and reopened as a museum of colonial history; it now houses, among other objects, the large equestrian statue of Mouzinho de Albuquerque which used to stand beside the cathedral in Maputo's main plaza. See also, on the Fortress of Our Lady, Octávio Roza de Oliveira's lengthy 'Breve notícia sobre a história de Fortaleza de Nossa Senhora da Conceição, de Lourenço Marques, onde se encontra instalado o Museu Histórico-Militar de Moçambique', [A short note on the history of the Fortress of Our Lady of the Conception in Lourenço Marques, which houses the Military History Museum of Mozambique] *Boletim da Sociedade de Estudos de Moçambique* vol. 35, no. 144/145 (July–Dec. 1965), p. 189–234.

687 **O guia do Museum.** (Guide to the Museum.)
Museu Nacional da Moeda. [Maputo]: Edições IV Congresso do Partido Frelimo, 1983. 51p.

The National Money Museum opened in June 1981 during the first anniversary celebrations for the introduction of the metical, the national currency. This illustrated guide takes us through the three rooms dedicated to Mozambican currency of various periods and authorities (including the pound sterling used by

Museums and Archives

the Banco da Beira during the time of the Mozambique Concessionary
Company). Rooms 4 and 5 are devoted to African countries, Room 6 to the rest
of the world and Room 7 to medallions. The guide includes a glossary of
numismatic terms.

688 **Relatórios da Curadoria dos Negócios Indígenas existentes no
Arquivo Histórico de Moçambique, 1902–1960: inventário.** (Reports
of the Native Affairs Agency in the Historical Archive of
Mozambique, 1902–60: inventory.)
Calisto Pacheleke. Trabalho de diploma for the Licenciatura,
Arquivo Histórico de Moçambique, Universidade Eduardo
Mondlane, 1985. 215p.

The Native Affairs Agency was responsible, above all else, for the flow of African
labour to the mines, and to the plantations inside the country. This is an inventory
of 749 reports produced by the Agent-General, the branches in South Africa and
Southern Rhodesia, the National Union of Commercial and Industrial Employees,
WENELA and the Zambezian agencies. Each citation includes the title, date,
pagination and a reference to the box number in the Historical Archive of
Mozambique. There are detailed subject and author indexes.

689 **Museu de Arte Sacra, anexo à Igreja da Misericórdia, Ilha de
Moçambique.** (Museum of Sacred Art, belonging to the Church of
Mercy, Mozambique Island.)
[Alberto Feliciano Marques Pereira]. [N.p.]: Comissão Provincial
das Comemorações Centenária de Vasco da Gama e Luís de
Camões, 1969. [15]p.

The Museum of Sacred Art was housed in the former hospital wing of the Holy
House of Mercy, a mediaeval Portuguese colonial institution which was closed
down only in 1915. The collection was based on the old treasury of the House of
Mercy, including vestments, paintings, images, pilasters, crucifixes and other
religious objects. This pamphlet was issued to commemorate the opening of the
Museum, and includes a general account of its origins and several illustrations of
objects from the collections. Both the text and the captions are given in English as
well as Portuguese. This Museum is one of three on the island, the other two
being the Museum of the Navy, and the Palace-Museum of St. Paul, the former
official residence of the Capitães-Gerais, or governors, which contains excellent
examples of furniture in the Indo-Portuguese style. Neither of these museums
has published a guide. For Mozambique Island itself, see Moira Forjaz's excellent
book of photographs *Muipiti* (q.v.).

690 **Museu Municipal da Beira.** (Beira Municipal Museum.)
Octávio Roza de Oliveira. Beira, Mozambique: Comissão
Regional de Turismo, 1975. 39p.

This odd little publication describes a project for a museum which was, in Roza
de Oliveira's own words 'closed to the public, while awaiting permanent quarters
in the mezzanine of the Library' (p. 3). It describes future sections on
Archaeology (subdivided into Prehistory, Rock Art, Protohistory and the

278

Zimbabwe Culture, Protohistory and the Iron Age); Palaeontology; Mineralogy; Ethnology; Ethnography (subdivided into the Bushmen [sic] and Tongas); Numismatics; Sea-shells; and, almost literally, Odds and Ends from the Colonial Period. There are a few paragraphs in English on p. 39, which describe the plans for the future museum; it should be noted that this guide was published in 1975, which was, as the cover reminds us, 'The Year of Independence', when many ambitious plans were made. The plates include photographs of various objects from the museum, and a view of Beira at the end of the 19th century, looking like a Wild West town. (All the captions to the plates are printed both in Portuguese and in English.) Although the collections still exist at the time of writing (mid-1986), it appears that the project for the Museum has now effectively been abandoned.

691 **Produção agrícola e mão-de-obra, 1941–1960: repertório de documentos do arquivo do Posto Administrativo de Ocua.**
(Agricultural production and labour, 1941–60: guide to documents from the archive of the Administrative Post of Ocua.)
Paulo Ricardo Ribeiro Soares. Trabalho de diploma for the Licenciatura, Arquivo Histórico de Moçambique, Universidade Eduardo Mondlane, 1985. 112p.

Portuguese local administrators in colonial times were responsible for all aspects of the life of their districts – administration, 'native' affairs, development, colonization, budget, personnel, traditional law courts, and so on. Soares organized the papers from the Administrative Post of Ocua, in southern Cabo Delgado, according to the old administrative classification in the various 'processes' or dossiers, and selected those related to agricultural production and labour over two decades, for inclusion in this guide. The result is a detailed microstudy of the kind of source material produced by the Portuguese colonial state. There is a detailed subject index, produced by computer, a chronology and an index to the official Portuguese administrative classification for documents.

692 **Fundo do Governo Geral: inventário dos relatórios, 1906–1960.**
(The archive of the Governor-General: an inventory of the reports, 1906–60.)
Maria da Luz Prata Dias Teixeira Duarte. Trabalho de diploma for the Licenciatura, Arquivo Histórico de Moçambique, Universidade Eduardo Mondlane, 1985. 115p.

A carefully prepared inventory of the report series of the Mozambican Governor-General's secretariat from 1906–1960, now in the collections of the Historical Archive of Mozambique (AHM). The inventory stops in 1960, because of a change in filing and numbering procedures introduced in that year, although the series continues up to 1975. These are reports *filed* in the secretariat, but not necessarily *produced* there; they therefore cover almost all imaginable topics. Each entry includes the title of the report, its date, author, the organization which produced it, pagination, and an indication as to whether the copy is an original or a carbon. There are 550 entries, although the numbers go up to 769; many reports are missing or are duplicated. Teixeira Duarte includes essential and well-prepared indexe: of authors and subjects. Her introduction discusses some of the institutions which produced the reports – public works, ports and railways, the Portuguese bureaux of native affairs in both South Africa and Southern Rhodesia, the Inspectorate of Administrative Services and Native Affairs, and ecclesiastical institutions.

693 **Museu de História Natural: o que é o como visitá-lo.** (The Museum of Natural History: what it is and how to visit it.) [J. A. Travessos Santos Dias, Maria Leonor Correia de Matos, Augusto Júlio Pereira Cabral]. Maputo: Universidade Eduardo Mondlane, 1979. 3rd rev. ed. 88p.

The first edition of this guide to Maputo's Museum of Natural History (and, in fact, ethnography) was published in 1977, and the second was simply a reprint. However, two new rooms were opened to the public in 1978, for Reptiles and for Invertebrates, and so an entirely new edition became necessary. The museum consists of rooms for birds, terrestrial mammals, an ethnographic gallery, reptiles and invertebrates, and a so-called 'transitional area', or garden, with life-size models of prehistoric animals. The guide is simply and accessibly organized, with a brief introduction, a section on 'How to visit the Museum', and descriptions of the exhibition rooms. The foyer is dominated by a large panel on animal evolution, the skeleton of a hippopotamus, and another, smaller, panel on human evolution. The 'Birds' salon is not restricted to species permanently resident in Mozambique, and includes over forty cases. The guide also presents a lengthy explanation of the materials in the ethnographic gallery. It has black-and-white illustrations, but no floor-plan of the museum, no telephone numbers or addresses, and no simple explanation of how to get there! This museum, unlike some others in Mozambique, is still functioning, and has recently published a more detailed guide to the *Galeria de Etnografia* [The Ethnography Room] (Maputo: Museu de História Natural, n.d. 29p.).

Mass Media

Newspapers

694 **O Brado Africano.** (The African Cry.)
Lourenço Marques, Mozambique: Grémio [Associação] Africano
de Lourenço Marques, 24 December 1918 to 23 November 1974.
nos.1–2544. weekly.

This newspaper, founded by the *mestiço* brothers João and José Albasini, is a
vitally important source for the history of anti-colonial and Africanist feeling in
the south. Several generations of black and *mestiço* intellectuals and writers were
associated with the paper, which was continually in trouble, changing its title
often (to such variants as *O Clamor Africano*). The paper published material in
Shangaan as well as Portuguese. The American historian Jeanne Penvenne has
made telling use of *O Brado* in her doctoral dissertation (q.v.); the Mozambican
researcher Paulo Soares has prepared an anthology of writing from the
newspaper, which is currently awaiting publication. Luís Polanah's story *The saga
of a cotton capulana* (q.v.) was first published in Portuguese in this paper. For
a brief summary of the history of *O Brado*, see António Sopa's catalogue of
Mozambican periodicals (q.v.). The Albasini family have played an important
part in southern Mozambique's political, cultural and even sporting history. For
one aspect, see Jacobus B. de Vaal's 'Vise-konsul João Albasini (1813–1888): die
rol wat hy in die geskiedenis van noordostlike Transvaal gespeel het en sy aandeel
aan die ekonomiese en politieke betrekkings tussen die Portugese en die regering
van die Zuid-Afrikaanse Republiek' [Vice-consul João Albasini (1813–88): his
role in the history of the north-east Transvaal and his place in economic and
political developments between the Portuguese and the government of the South
African Republic] (DLitt dissertation, University of the Orange Free State,
1948.). This was later published as 'Die rol van João Albasini in die geskiedenis
van die Transvaal', *Archives Yearbook for South African History* vol. 16, part 1
(1953).

Mass Media. Newspapers

695   **O Campo.** (The Countryside.)
Maputo (CP 2546, Avenida Amílcar Cabral no. 214); Gabinete de Comunicação Social, 29 June 1984– . monthly.
This monthly newspaper is put together from reports sent in by 240 part-time, amateur journalists – by the peasants, in short. It contains local, rural news items and 'how-to' stories about undisciplined soldiers, building houses, new crops, literacy campaigns, bandit attacks, constructing water filters, village football teams and all the other aspects of country life in Mozambique. The paper is actually printed and published by the Office of Mass Communications (Gabinete de Comunicação Social) in Maputo, and has a tiny print-run of ony 5,000 copies, although clearly demand must exceed this. The GCS also put out radio and television programmes based on information from the network of 'people's correspondents' in co-operatives and communal villages all over the country. *O Campo* is unique, not only in Mozambique, but probably in the whole of Africa. See also the commentary by Albino Magaia in *Tempo* no. 788 (17 November 1985), p. 24–25.

696   **Combate: órgão de informação das Forças Armadas de Moçambique (FPLM).** (Combat: newspaper of the Mozambican armed forces (FPLM).)
Maputo: Comissariado Político Nacional das FPLM, 25 September 1981– . weekly.
This newspaper was launched in 1981 as part of a general reorganization of the Mozambican press, and to begin with was on sale to the general public. It was quite popular since it often contained news about the war with the armed bandits, for example, not published in *Notícias*. It is unclear whether it is still being published or not.

697   **Diário de Moçambique.** (Mozambique Daily.)
Beira, Mozambique (Rua D. João de Mascarenhas, CP 81): 25 September 1981– . daily.
Mozambique's second Portuguese-language daily, this paper should not be confused with the *other* Beira paper, also daily and also called *Diário de Moçambique*, which was published by the Bishop of Beira between 24 December 1950 and 15 March 1971; however, the title of the second *is* a tribute to the quite progressive line followed by the first, according to the Minister of Information. This paper, which usually goes on sale in Maputo about mid-afternoon, has much better coverage than *Notícias* of events in the northern and to some extent central provinces, as one might expect.

698   **Domingo.** (Sunday.)
Maputo: Notícias, 27 September 1981– . weekly.
Mozambique's Sunday newspaper was edited, from its foundation until 18 September 1983, by the photographer and jazz-buff Ricardo Rangel, who turned the two-sectioned paper into a kind of extended review magazine, with long articles on music and literature and plenty of photographs. After his departure, the second 'caderno' (section) became much more newsy, and editorial responsibility was effectively consolidated with that of the daily *Notícias*. The first

282

section has by-and-large retained its character as recreational reading. Until *Domingo* was founded, *Notícias* had appeared seven days a week.

699 **Notícias.** (News.)
Maputo: Sociedade de Notícias, 15 April 1926– . daily.

This is Mozambique's main daily newspaper, with a current print-run of around 40,000. It was founded as a semi-legal opposition paper in 1926; in 1974 it was the centre of a struggle for a progressive line in journalism (see Guilherme de Melo's *A sombra dos dias* (In the shadow of the days) [Lisbon: Bertrand, 1981] for an account of this). In recent years the paper has faced increasingly severe technical problems (such as old press machines and paper shortages), and the quality of the journalism is variable. Nevertheless, since *Notícias* prints many political speeches, communiqués, parliamentary papers, laws and official documents in their entirety, it is also a journal of record, and hence important on that account.

700 **Notícias da Beira.** (Beira News.)
Beira, Mozambique: Notícias da Beira, 1951 to 16 September 1981. nos 1–11,568. daily (from 20 August 1966).

This was the industrialist Jorge Jardim's newspaper, and at one time was run for him by the PIDE agent Evo Fernandes, its subdirector. (Fernandes, a Portuguese citizen, later achieved a certain notoriety as the Lisbon spokesman for the armed bandits, but fell out of favour with his South African masters.) In 1974 the paper was the scene of a fierce conflict between the reactionary management and progressive journalists and workers, which was resolved only by a direct FRELIMO intervention in October of that year. The paper was eventually closed down by the government in 1981, as part of a general press reorganization, and was replaced by the *Diário de Moçambique* (q.v.).

701 **A Tribuna.** (The Tribune.)
Lourenço Marques, Mozambique: Publicações Tribuna, 7 October 1962 to 12 November 1975. nos 1–3140. Periodicity varied.

Founded by António de Gouveia Lemos, Ilídio Rocha and João Reis, *A Tribuna* started off as a morning paper, and later briefly became a weekly, disappeared, and re-emerged as an evening paper. Soon after its foundation it was taken over by the Banco Nacional Ultramarino (the National Colonial Bank). In 1963 publication of the paper was suspended by the government for ten days for offences against the censorship regulations. In May 1975 it again became a weekly, but did not survive the departure of its editor, Fernando Magalhães, for Portugal.

702 **Voz Africana.** [African Voice].
Beira, Mozambique: Centro Africano de Manica e Sofala, 1932 to 15 February 1975. nos 1–556[?].

Mozambique's 'other' African newspaper, after the *Brado*, this journal had a chequered history, ending up in the hands of the industrialist Jorge Jardim. For some time the paper was run for him by the FRELIMO deserter Miguel Murupa. The paper, together with *Notícias da Beira*, entered a crisis in August 1974 from which it never really recovered, and it closed down before independence. A recent study by Lourenço de Rosário, 'A oralidade através da escrita na *Voz Africana*' [Spoken language in writing in the *African Voice*] was published in the review *Angolê* no. 6, (July–Sep. 1987) p. 14–15; the review is produced by the Angolan Embassy in Lisbon.

General periodicals

703 **Boletim da Sociedade de Estudos [da Colónia] de Moçambique.**
(Bulletin of the Society for the Study (of the Colony) of Mozambique.)
Lourenço Marques, Mozambique: Dec. 1931–Dec. 1974.
nos 1–176. quarterly.

The Society for the Study of Mozambique was founded in the early 1930s by the engineer Joaquim de Freitas and a group of friends. Most countries in Africa have a journal of this character; a local outlet for dilettante administrators or amateur scholars to try their hand at some ethnographic, botanical or linguistic research, and these periodicals always contain something of permanent value, as well as large quantities of dross. The *Boletim* was the dominant journal on Mozambique until the early 1960s, when the best writing began to be published in more specialized reviews published by the various research departments, and it was reduced to printing the texts of lectures or conference papers delivered to the Society. The phrase 'of the Colony' was dropped from the title in 1951; the *Boletim* did not survive past independence. An as-yet-unpublished index has been prepared by António Sopa of the Historical Archive in Maputo. Other general periodicals of interest to students of Mozambique, although dealing with all Portuguese colonies, include *Studia* (Lisbon: Centro de Estudos Históricos Ultramarinos, 1958–74. no. 1–38, 2 issues per year), especially for historical articles; and *Garcia de Orta* named after a well-known Portuguese botanist (Lisbon: Junta de Investigações do Ultramar, 1953– . 4 issues per year; later divided into 7 series, 1972– .), mainly for long articles on the natural and human sciences.

704 **Moçambique: documentário trimestral.** (Mozambique: a quarterly documentary.)
Lourenço Marques, Mozambique: Repartição Técnica de Estatistíca; Centro de Informação e Turismo, Jan./March 1935 to July 1961. nos 1–105.

Jointly published, in an odd collaboration, by the Central Statistical Bureau and the Centre for Information and Tourism, this expensive-looking magazine, on heavy high-quality paper, with huge margins, fancy type-fonts, and glossy plates, was an apparent mixture of propaganda and science which the Portuguese seemingly hoped would get them a hearing all over the world. Many prestigious works first appeared in its pages, together with, it must be pointed out, much that was of no real value. The magazine covered history, ethnography and folklore, the economy, and social and scientific subjects.

705 **Não vamos esquecer! Boletim informativo do Oficina de História.** [We shall not forget! Information bulletin of the History Workshop.] Maputo: Centro de Estudos Africanos, Universidade Eduardo Mondlane, February 1983– . irregular.

This journal was originally founded with the objective of bringing articles and source materials about the armed struggle to as wide an audience as possible within Mozambique. The first issue, in which all material was published anonymously under collective editorial responsibility, included an article on the Liguilanilu co-operatives in Cabo Delgado in the late 1950s, and a bibliographical guide to Cabo Delgado Province, as well as interview material on the life of Paulo Samuel Kankhomba, an early FRELIMO commander who was assassinated during factional struggles in the late 1960s. The second issue (no. 2/3 [December 1983]) included interviews with Maputo workers, and a signed article by Judith Head on Sena Sugar Estates. Subsequent issues have been delayed by technical problems with printers. Incidentally, the title is a phrase from a FRELIMO song much liked by the late President Samora Machel, the tenor of which is that we must not, and indeed cannot, forget the past if we are to understand the present.

706 **Tempo.** (Time.) Lourenço Marques, Maputo: Tempográfica, 20 September 1970– . weekly.

A popular weekly news-magazine which was launched in the late colonial period. From mid-1974 until about 1976 *Tempo* published important articles and textual materials which are unavailable elsewhere; unfortunately issues from those years are now difficult to obtain. Since then, the content has tended to be drier, although the magazine has carried some excellent reports on the war against the armed bandits, for example. The book reviews are occasionally acid, and a recent (1986) exchange between Alfredo Margarido and Manuela Sousa Lobo on Mozambican literary history was enjoyably ferocious. Best of all, however, in the *Tempo* of the 1980s, are the letters pages, a fascinating sociological guide to the day-to-day preoccupations and discontents of the average Mozambican citizen. Special numbers appear for events such as FACIM (the annual trade fair) or for state visits. On the occasion of Samora Machel's visit to Japan in 1986, a special number came out in English for the first time.

Directories and Current Reference Sources

707 **Africa Research Bulletin.**
Exeter, England: Africa Research, 1964– . monthly.

A digest of African events, with regular coverage of Mozambique and the region. It is issued in two series: one political and the other economic, and is based on a wide range of Western and African press sources which are summarized, synthesized and cross-referenced. It is especially useful for summary accounts of the meetings of such regional organizations as SADCC (the Southern Africa Development Coordination Conference) or the 'Cinco' (the five Portuguese-speaking countries in Africa – Mozambique, Angola, Guinea, São Tomé, and Cape Verde), and on inter-state relations. The economic series frequently carries items such as budget résumés, as well as news on different crops and commodities. See also the weekly *African Economic Digest* (London, 1980– .) for fast and regular information on the Mozambican and other regional economies. Both these journals are, of course, only as good as their sources.

708 **AIM Information Bulletin.**
Maputo: Agência de Informação de Moçambique, 1976–
monthly.

This invaluable (and now computer-produced) news summary also comes out in French, but ironically has appeared only a couple of times in Portuguese, and is written by Mozambican and foreign journalists. No index has ever been published, unfortunately. AIM also publishes features and provides a photograph service. Its address is Caixa Postal 896, Maputo, Mozambique. There is a very similar news review entitled *Mozambique Information Office News Review*, which is published by the Mozambique Information Office (MIO) in London and which is probably easier for European subscribers to obtain. An American bulletin, less oriented towards hard news, is produced by the Mozambique Resource Centre in New York under the title *Mozambican Notes*.

286

709 **Anuário Católico de Moçambique.** (Mozambique Catholic Annual.)
Lourenço Marques, Mozambique: Conferência Episcopal de
Moçambique, 1961–74. 4 vols. irregular.
A strange publication, which despite its title was published only in 1961, 1966,
1971 and 1974. The first issue was not produced by the Episcopal Conference, but
by Father Francisco Maria Pinheiro. Given the church's ideological role in
colonial Mozambique, this is an important, if dubious, source of information.

710 **Anuário de Moçambique.** (Mozambique Annual.)
Lourenço Marques, Mozambique: Bayly, 1914–[1979]. annual.
The main Portuguese-language commercial directory. Title changes were
as follows: *Anuário de Lourenço Marques* [Lourenço Marques Annual]
(1914–47); *Anuário da Colónia de Moçambique* [Colony of Mozambique Annual]
(1948–50/51); *Anuário da Província de Moçambique* [Province of Mozambique
Annual] (1951/52–1970/71); *Anuário do Estado de Moçambique* [Mozambique
State Annual] (1972/73), and lastly the title as given above. It appears that the
last edition was for 1979. The work includes commercial listings by towns and
provinces, seating plans for cinemas, names and addresses of various officials, and
lots of other miscellaneous information.

711 **Facts and Reports: Press Cuttings on Southern Africa.**
Amsterdam, The Netherlands: Holland Committee on Southern
Africa (Angola Comité), November 1970– . biweekly.
An absolutely essential and readily available source of up-to-date information on
the southern African region in general and on Mozambique in particular. The
bulletin consists of photographic reproductions of the actual press clippings from a
wide range of international and local newspapers in English (Portuguese and
Afrikaans material is omitted). Radio reports from the BBC's *Summary of World
Broadcasts* are also included. The items are arranged in categories by country and
Mozambique normally covers two or three pages. Each issue carries an index to
clippings in the previous issue on the back page. Other press-clipping services on
the region, or on Africa as a whole (none as useful for Mozambique as *Facts and
Reports* but all with some coverage), include the *ANC Weekly News Briefing*,
principally on South Africa; *AF Press Clips*, from the State Department in
Washington, DC, and mainly taken from US newspapers; and the Hamburg
Aktueller Informationsdienst Afrika, from the Institut für Afrika-Kunde, which,
despite its title, is mainly in English, since its clips are taken exclusively from
African newspapers.

712 **Africa Contemporary Record: Annual Survey and Documents.**
Edited by Colin Legum. New York, London: Africana,
1968/69– . annual.
This is a standard reference work which includes a summary of the year's events
for each African country, as well as a series of formulaic essays on topics such as
the relations between the USSR and Africa. Mozambique is covered from the
beginning of the series and early volumes contain fair summaries of the progress
of the liberation war. Where possible the country articles include statistical tables
from such sources as the United Nations Economic Commission for Africa. For a
similar, highly respected general source, see the *Africa Research Bulletin*.

Directories and Current Reference Sources

713   **Missões Diplomáticas, Consulares e Representações de Organizações
Internacionais.** (Diplomatic and Consular Missions, and
Representatives of International Organizations.)
Ministério de Negócios Estrangeiros, Direcção Nacional do
Protocolo. [Ministry of Foreign Affairs, National Directorate of
Protocol].   Maputo: Imprensa Nacional, 1985. 192p. annual.

This handy diplomatic directory is a useful current reference work in a country
where even a telephone book can sometimes be hard to come by. The 1985
edition included a list of all the diplomatic missions in Mozambique, in
(Portuguese) alphabetical order, consulates, representatives of such international
organizations as the OAU (Organization of African Unity), UNDP (United
Nations Development Programme) and WHO (World Health Organization) (in
their Portuguese-language manifestations the OUA, PNUD and OMS respectively), military attachés, member states of the United Nations, and the names of
members of such Mozambican Party and State bodies as the Politburo, the
Secretariat of the Central Committee, the Permanent Commission of the People's
Assembly, and the Council of Ministers.

714   **Moçambique Directory.**
Lourenço Marques, Mozambique: Bayly, 1899–1952. annual.

Bayly's English-language commercial annual began life as the *Delagoa Directory*
in 1899, and probably continued under that title until 1929; in 1930 it reappeared
as the *Lourenço Marques Directory*, which continued until 1947. The third and
final title is given above.

Bibliographies

Africa and the Portuguese Empire

715 **Bibliografia Científica da Junta de Investigações do Ultramar.**
(Scientific Bibliography of the Research Board for the Overseas
Territories.)
Lisbon: Centro de Documentação Científica Ultramarina, 1960– .
annual.

With entries classified by the Universal Decimal Classification, this is a major
source for all types of Portuguese colonial publication. It includes many analytical
entries, especially for articles from the important journal *Garcia de Orta*. Earlier
volumes are especially strong in the natural sciences, but the series also covers
social science, geography and applied sciences. Published by the Centre for
Scientific Overseas Documentation of the Board for Overseas Research (now the
Institute for Tropical Research), the first volume covers the period 1936 to 1958,
and includes 1,697 citations from the Centre's catalogue; subsequent annual
volumes were much smaller. In volume 23, published in 1981 in mimeographed
format, we are promised a cumulation by 1983, but this does not yet seem to be
available. There are geographical and author indexes.

716 **Cumulative bibliography of African studies.**
International African Institute.   Boston, Massachusetts:
G. K. Hall, 1973. 5 vols.

A cumulative card index containing all the titles of books, and more importantly,
articles, published in the bibliographical section of the quarterly journal *Africa*
from 1929 to 1970, and in the *International African Bibliography* (q.v.) for
1971–72. The card index was retrospectively supplemented by cards that refer to
items missed at the time that the regular bibliographies went to press. In
particular, every article indexed in *African Abstracts* (about 16,500 items between
1940 and 1971) is included, with a reference to the abstract. Mozambican

289

Bibliographies. Africa and the Portuguese Empire

references appear in vol. 3, p. 342–57. The classification within countries or geographical zones is by broad topic, such as education, archaeology, anthropology and so on. Within anthropology, items are arranged by 'tribe'. The catalogue as a whole has an index to subject headings used, and to ethnic groups and languages. It is continued in the *International African Bibliography* (q.v.).

717 **Africa Index to Current Periodical Literature.**
Edited by Colin Darch, Alice Nkhoma-Wamunza. Oxford: Hans Zell; Munich: K. G. Saur, 1977– . annual.
Includes only items from journals published in Africa, including some coverage of Mozambique, Angola and Guinea-Bissau. The latest issue to appear was no. 6, indexing articles published in 1981; it listed nearly 1,500 items from 150 serials. Mozambican publications are regularly indexed: *Construir, Justiça Popular, Tempo*, and *Estudos Moçambicanos* are systematically included. Entries are classified by broad subject group, with author and detailed subject indexes, geographical reference codes and a list of publishers' addresses.

718 **Bibliografia das publicações sobre a África de língua oficial portuguesa entre Janeiro de 1975 e Janeiro de 1983.** [Bibliography of publications on Portuguese-speaking Africa, January 1975 to January 1983].
Jill R. Dias.   *Revista Internacional de Estudos Africanos* [Lisbon] no. 1 (Jan.–June 1984), p. 243–303: *continued as* 'Bibliografia das publicações recentes sobre a África de língua oficial portuguesa' no. 2 (June–Dec. 1984), p. 201–27; no. 3 (Jan.–Dec. 1985), p. 241–61.
A useful current bibliography of books and articles on Portuguese-speaking Africa, arranged in broad subject categories (e.g., history and anthropology, languages, literature and culture) under geographical areas and countries. The first issue included items 754 to 1031 on Mozambique; the second, items 268 to 362; and the third, items 213 to 267. The listing is especially useful for material published in Portugal and in Mozambique, often overlooked in current English-language bibliographical sources.

719 **Portuguese Africa: a guide to official publications.**
Mary Jane Gibson.   Washington, DC: Library of Congress, 1967. 217p.
This indispensable, but now outdated, work follows the usual Library of Congress style, and achieves the usual Library of Congress standard of excellence. It is organized by country of publication of the government document in question; hence Mozambique has its own section, but there is plenty of material on Mozambique in the Portugal section as well. This problem is overcome by the provision of a detailed index. Gibson's work includes 2,831 citations. The bibliography is extremely useful for checking errors in Mário Costa's work (q.v.), which is often careless about details of official publications.

720 **Obras em língua alemã sobre a África de expressão oficial**
portuguesa: a colheita dos primeiros anos oitenta. (Works in
German on Portuguese-speaking Africa: the harvest of the early
1980s.)
Franz-Wilhelm Heimer. *Revista Internacional de Estudos*
Africanos no. 2 (June–Dec. 1984), p. 177–99.

A useful literature survey by a West German Angola-specialist living in Lisbon,
with quite a lengthy discussion of the works mentioned. On Mozambique Heimer
refers to the writings of Martin Schaedel (q.v.) on African labour, Michael
van Lay on religion, Herbert Schröer, Wolfgang Schoeller on economic relations,
and Bernhard Weimer, the only non-Portuguese-speaker, on foreign relations, as
well as to the works of Peter Meyns. Among German scholars who have also
published in English, Portuguese or French on Mozambique, he mentions Kurt
Habermeier (q.v.), Ursula Semin-Panzer and the veteran historian Gerhard
Liesegang (q.v.).

721 **International African Bibliography: Current Books, Articles and**
Papers in African Studies.
London: Mansell for the School of Oriental and African Studies,
1973– . quarterly.

This is a current general social sciences bibliography on Africa, which goes back
in various forms to 1929, when the International African Institute began to issue a
quarterly bibliography of current literature in its journal *Africa*. In 1973
responsibility was passed over to the SOAS. Issues are arranged thematically and
then by country; each number normally has about a dozen references on
Mozambique. A five-year cumulation for 1973–78 was published by Mansell in
1981 (368p., nearly 20,000 references). For other sources of current information
on Mozambique-related articles and books, see also Chris Allen's increasingly
irregular 'Current Africana' in the *Review of African Political Economy* and
Recently Published Articles (q.v.).

722 **Africa south of the Sahara: index to periodical literature, 1900–** .
Library of Congress, African Section.   Boston, Massachusetts:
G. K. Hall; Washington, DC: Library of Congress, 1971–85.
4 vols, 3 supplements.

This work in its original form consolidated the card services of the African studies
research centres CARDAN, CIDESA and others, and supplemented them with
Library of Congress's own entries. Many of the cards reproduced include
abstracts. The main work, published by Hall in 1971, covered 1900–70; the first
supplement, covering 1971–72, published in 1973, indexed 960 serials; the second
supplement, covering 1973–76, came out in 1982. The supplement for 1977, the
first to be published by Library of Congress itself, appeared in 1985 in a smaller
format, and does not reproduce cards. It also adopted a new six-part thematic
division (anthropology, languages and the arts; education, health, social
conditions; geography, history and religion; economic development; politics and
government; and international relations). It is, therefore, necessary to look in six
places for Mozambican material. However, Mozambican coverage in this last
issue is scant, comprising a few *Tempo* and South African articles. Nevertheless,

this work, which has now been suspended, together with the *Cumulative bibliography of African studies* (q.v.) and its successors, constitute essential entry points for access to the extensive periodical literature on Mozambique. Also of great importance is J. O. Asamani's massive *Index Africanus* (Stanford, California: Hoover Institution Press, 1975. 452p. [Hoover Institution Bibliographic Series, no. 53]), which indexes over 200 Africanist serials, 20 Festschriften and 60 conference proceedings, to produce over 25,000 references to articles published between 1885 and 1965.

723 **Africana: bibliographies sur l'Afrique luso-hispanophone, 1800–1980.** [Africana: bibliographies on Portuguese- and Spanish-speaking Africa, 1800–1980].
René Pélissier. Orgeval, France: Éditions Pélissier, 1981. 205p.

A collection of seven survey articles originally published between 1965 and 1979 by the iconoclastic French Africanist. There is an index of titles, organized by country. The pieces are, with their original places of publication, as follows: 'Eléments de bibliographie: l'Afrique portugaise dans les publications de la Junta de Investigações do Ultramar (Lisbonne)' [Bibliographic sketch: Portuguese Africa through the publications of the Overseas Research Board, Lisbon], first published in *Genève-Afrique* vol. 4, no. 2 (1965); 'État de la littérature militaire relative à l'Afrique australe portugaise' [The state of the military literature on Portuguese southern Africa], from the *Revue Française d'Études Politiques Africaines* (hereafter *RFEPA*) no. 74 (Feb. 1972); 'Sur la guérrilla en Afrique portugaise' [On the guerrilla war in Portuguese Africa], *RFEPA* no. 100 (April 1974); 'Décolonisation de la littérature consacrée à l'Afrique des Ibériques' [Decolonization of writings about Portuguese and Spanish Africa], *RFEPA* no. 122 (Feb. 1976); 'Miscellanées, 1964–78' [Miscellany, 1964–1978], a collection of short reviews published in *RFEPA* between the dates indicated. Mozambique is covered in items no. 155–64; '"Re-impressions" d'Afrique' [Africana reprints], a useful guide to 19th-century travel literature. Mozambique is covered on p. 178–84. *RFEPA* no. 156 (Dec. 1978); 'L'Ibéro-Africa par les textes' [Portuguese- and Spanish-speaking Africa through the texts), *RFEPA* no. 159 (March 1979). Mozambique is covered on p. 192–95.

724 **Bibliographies for African Studies 1970/75– .**
Yvette Scheven. Waltham, Massachusetts: Crossroads Press; Munich; Oxford: Hans Zell, K. G. Saur, 1977–

Yvette Scheven's regular five-year bibliographies of bibliographies have many virtues; they are well organized under topical sections (thirty-one rubrics) for subject bibliographies, and by country for geographical ones (see under Portuguese-speaking Africa as well as under Mozambique). They include articles and monographs. From the third volume onwards, publication has been taken over by Hans Zell, an imprint of K. G. Saur, and the physical size of the book has become more manageable. See also *A world bibliography of African bibliographies* by Theodore Besterman, revised by J. D. Pearson (Totowa, New Jersey: Rowman & Littlefield, 1975. 241 columns), which covers the period to the end of 1973 but only includes monographs; and the now very outdated *A bibliography of African bibliographies covering territories south of the Sahara* (Cape Town: South African Public Library, 1961. 4th ed. 79p. [Grey Bibliographies, no. 7]). A Mozambican bibliography of bibliographies has been prepared by Maria da Luz Teixeira Duarte, and will be published by the Historical Archive of Mozambique.

Mozambique

725 **Mozambique since 1920: a select bibliography.**
Chris Allen. In: *Mozambique: proceedings of a seminar held in the Centre of African Studies, University of Edinburgh, 1st and 2nd December 1978.* Edinburgh: Centre of African Studies, 1979. p. 178–204.

Together with the Enevoldsen (q.v.) and Stage (q.v.) compilations, this 509-item checklist is one of the most useful bibliographies on Mozambique, despite its self-imposed limits of chronology and language, and a few other faults. Portuguese-language material is excluded, as are ephemera (i.e., liberation movement press releases, etc.) and technical items. The main sections, which are further subdivided, deal with Portuguese colonialism, colonial Mozambique, and Mozambique during the Transitional Government and after independence. There are no annotations, no contents list, and no indexes. The work is also available as an offprint.

726 **Catálogo de impressos, mapas e publicações.** (Catalogue of printed works, maps and publications.)
[Lourenço Marques, Mozambique]: Depósito de Impressos e Publicações, Imprensa Nacional de Moçambique, 1960–76. nos 1–9. irregular.

An irregular sales catalogue of government and official publications from colonial and immediately post-colonial times. From no. 4 (1966) onwards, the word *mapas* was dropped from the title, and the last issue (no. 9 [1976]), was called *Catálogo de impressos e livros* [Catalogue of printed works and books]. Earlier catalogues also exist: *Catálogo das publicações e impressos a venda na Imprensa Nacional de Moçambique, referente a Outubro 1955* [Catalogue of publications and printed works for sale at the National Press of Mozambique, Oct. 1955] (Lourenço Marques: Imprensa Nacional, 1955); and *Catálogo de publicações, impressos, cartas, mapas, e plantas a venda na Imprensa Nacional de Moçambique, relativo a Julho de 1959* [Catalogue of publications, printed works, maps, charts and plans for sale at the National Press of Mozambique, July 1959] (Lourenço Marques: Imprensa National, 1959). Large quantities of legislative and administrative material are listed, but some monographs are also included on such subjects as history. Prices and order numbers are given, but are of academic interest only. These catalogues supplement to some extent the bibliography on government publications by Mary Jane Gibson (q.v.).

727 **Catálogo dos livros com interesse para o estudo de Moçambique.**
(Catalogue of books relevant to the study of Mozambique.)
Maputo: CEDIMO, 1978. 194p. (Documento de Trabalho,
no. 15).

This 'working paper' from CEDIMO is an author catalogue of the Mozambique
collection which was inherited from the old colonial Documentation Centre of the
National Overseas Bank, when it was transformed into the National Centre for
Documentation and Information. The catalogue includes 3,355 meticulously
catalogued references, in alphabetical author order, but with no indexes of any
kind, and no introductory apparatus worth mentioning. It was rumoured that a
subject index had been prepared, but this has never appeared. The citations
include CEDIMO call numbers, which are now of academic interest since the
collection itself has been dispersed, many items ending up in the Historical
Archive. Despite its limitations, this is a general bibliographical source of
considerable importance for Mozambican studies.

728 **Bibliografia nacional moçambicana, 1975–1984: contribuição e
mostragem.** (Mozambican National Bibliography, 1975–84:
contribution and model.)
Joaquim Chigogoro Mussassa. Trabalho de diploma for the
Licenciatura, Arquivo Histórico de Moçambique, Universidade
Eduardo Mondlane, 1985. 183p.

In 1979 the Instituto Nacional do Livro e do Disco (a Mozambican state
publishing house) produced two million school textbooks and published fifty-six
other titles in print-runs totalling over 750,000 copies. All of this activity is outside
bibliographical control. This thesis, prepared under the supervision of Colin
Darch, is an attempt to list all the post-independence monographic publications
produced in Mozambique, up to the end of 1984. Excluded are items of
Mozambican interest published outside the country, periodicals and analytical
entries. In fact, the work includes all identifiable 1975 publications, as there is
usually no way of knowing whether they came out before or after independence
day (25 June). Chigogoro Mussassa inspected all the items included; the citations
are arranged by the Universal Decimal Classification, and the compiler provides
full cataloguing in the style of the International Standard Bibliographic
Description (Monographs) and the Regras Portuguesas de Catalogação (1984).
The work lists 704 items (but goes up to no. 707 with a couple of jumps), with
author and title indexes, a list of publishers and their addresses (where possible)
and a glossary. There is an explanatory introduction, and a short bibliography on
the question of national bibliography and its role. Plans have been made to
publish the work in a revised and augmented edition.

729 **Bibliografia geral de Moçambique.** [General bibliography of
Mozambique.]
Mário Costa. Lisbon: Agência Geral do Ultramar.

Costa's classic bibliography is the starting point for all subsequent efforts in
Mozambican bibliography, despite its manifest defects. Entries are arranged in
topical chapters, but they are not numbered; nor is the bibliographic description
rigorous. It is sometimes extremely difficult to identify a publication from Costa's
citations – the census publications are especially irritating in this regard. Despite

these criticisms, an essential work. See also the supplement by Filipe Gastao Almeida de Eça.

730 **Writing and research on Mozambique, 1975–1980.**
Colin Darch. *Mozambican Studies* no. 1 (1980), p. 103–12.
A short and selective survey of social science research and writing in the first five years of independence with the emphasis on work done at the CEA or at Eduardo Mondlane University. Thirty-three items are listed, and some unpublished papers and projects are mentioned in the text. The article is divided into sections on bibliographical sources, economic studies, historical studies and current research.

731 **Portuguese-speaking Africa, 1900–1979: a select bibliography.**
Volume 2: Mozambique.
Susan Jean Gowan. Braamfontein, South Africa: South African Institute of International Affairs, 1982. 281p. map. (South African Institute of International Affairs. Bibliographical series, no. 10).
A highly professional 2,077-item bibliography on 20th-century Mozambique, covering politics and government, foreign relations, and economics and development. Included are author and subject indexes, and a list of journals cited. The compilation is extremely useful for the important body of South African-published material on Mozambique, much of which is not easily available from other bibliographical sources. Gowan scrupulously indicates items which she was not able to inspect. On the negative side, however, some ephemeral material is included. There is a short introduction on work method and the scope of the volume.

732 **The People's Republic of Mozambique.**
IDOC Bulletin [Rome], new series, no. 2–3 (Feb.–March 1978), p. 1–28.
A special issue of the bulletin of the International Documentation and Communication Centre (Via S. Maria dell'Anima 30, 00186-Rome, Italy), a left-wing Christian research institution more widely known simply as IDOC. The bulletin includes a general text on Frelimo taken from the Fall 1977 issue of *LSM News*; a translation of the Council of Ministers' text 'How the Enemy Acts' (July 1977); and a piece entitled 'Mozambican Christians today' from the National Pastoral Assembly held in Beira in September 1977 and first published in *Libertar* [Lisbon] in January 1978. Most important of all, however, is a rag-tag bibliography on p. 17–28, which includes all kinds of ephemeral material, much of it from Europe, on history, Samora Machel, reconstruction, the economy, educational policy, reconstruction aid, international relations, the 1977 general elections, and the churches; all these items are cited with their IDOC call numbers.

733 **1º. catálogo bibliográfico de Moçambique.** (First bibliographical catalogue of Mozambique.)
Lourenço Marques, Mozambique: Imprensa Nacional, 1932. 24p.
It is unclear whether this early publication is a bibliography or a catalogue of publications. Each unnumbered entry consists simply of the title, the author and

Bibliographies. Mozambique

the date, and the work is organized around the following subjects, some with further subdivisions: literature and travel; history; local geography; administration; economy, colonization and regional studies; the natives; missions and religious activity; soils and climate; hydrography, lighthouses, the sea, fisheries; agriculture; animal husbandry; health and hygiene; education; ports and railways; surveying; statistics; publicity; and, inevitably, miscellaneous.

734 **Relatórios e artigos sobre Moçambique nas colecções do Centro de Estudos Africanos.** (Reports and articles about Mozambique in the collections of the Centre of African Studies.)
Maputo: Centro de Estudos Africanos, 1980. 18p. (Boletim bibliográfico, no. 1).

This, the first and, at the time of writing, the last, bibliographical bulletin of the Centre of African Studies (CEA) includes 140 references, organized in a broad subject classification, with no indexes. On the publications of the CEA, see the evaluative note by Michel Cahen 'Publications du Centro de Estudos Africanos de l'Université Eduardo Mondlane, Maputo, Mozambique' *Politique Africaine* no. 5 (1982), p. 113–15; Cahen also makes some comments on the CEA's documentation activities, as well as on other Mozambican libraries and centres in his 'Portuguese colonialism in Mozambique – Le colonialisme portugais au Mozambique' *Bulletin de Liaison du CREDU* [Nairobi] no. 9 (Dec. 1981), p. 40–47, published in parallel English/French texts.

735 **Catálogo dos periódicos moçambicanos precedido de uma pequena notícia histórica: 1854–1984.** (Catalogue of Mozambican periodicals, preceded by a short historical note: 1854–1984.)
António Jorge Diniz Sopa. Trabalho de diploma for the Licenciatura, Arquivo Histórico de Moçambique, Universidade Eduardo Mondlane, 1985. 327p.

This computer-compiled catalogue is a major contribution to Mozambican critical and historical bibliography, by the librarian in charge of the book and periodical collections at the Historical Archive. The most comprehensive work in its field, this catalogue will, when published, certainly replace Ilídio Rocha's *Catálogo dos periódicos e principais seriados de Moçambique* [Catalogue of the periodicals and principal serial publications of Mozambique] (Lisbon: Edições 70, 1985). Sopa includes 1,306 entries, as against Rocha's 1,000, but the difference is certainly even greater since Sopa does not cite variations in serial title (as opposed to changes of title) under separate entries. Sopa's indexes cover names of persons, and of titles in chronological order and under place of publication. These last two indexes allow for the reconstruction of historical and geographical patterns in periodical publishing in Mozambique. Entries are as complete as possible, and are based on autopsies of the serials themselves, thus correcting many of Rocha's errors. Sopa also includes long annotations on the character, politics and history of each serial. The catalogue was consulted during the compilation of this bibliography and proved invaluable.

Index

The index is a single alphabetical sequence of authors (personal and corporate), titles of publications and subjects. Index entries refer both to the main items and to other works mentioned in the notes to each item. Title entries are in italics. Numeration refers to the items as numbered.

African Abstracts 716
African Affairs 188, 439
African Arts 678
African Association see Associação Africana
African Concord 24
African Economic Digest 707
African Guild see Grémio Africano
African insect life 78
African international relations: an annotated bibliography 412
African Journal of Political Economy 357
African liberation reader 174, 186
African native music: an annotated bibliography 655, 661
African Research and Documentation 288
African societies in Southern Africa: historical studies 460
African Studies 266
African Studies Review 185
Africana: bibliographies sur l'Afrique luso-hispanophone, 1800–1980 35, 723
Os Africanos de Lourenço Marques 558
Afrique-Asie 395
Afro-Asian Writers 6th Conference, Luanda (1979) 606
Age structure in urban Africans in Lourenço Marques 558
Agitators 201
Agnation, alternative structures and the individual in Chopi society 523
Die agrargeographische Struktur von Mittel-Moçambique: nahr- und sozialräumliche Grundlagen der Bantulandschaft 46
A agricultura tradicional de Moçambique. 1. Distribuiçâo geográfica das culturas e sua relação com o meio 476
Agricultural cooperatives 185, 472–504
Agricultural marketing in District of Alto Molócue, Zambézia Province 459
Agricultural pricing policy in Mozambique, Tanzania, Zambia and Zimbabwe: study commissioned by the Nordic aid agencies 479

Agricultural production 53, 492, 691
  FRELIMO policy 195, 491
Agriculture 2, 5, 11–12, 25, 57, 348, 356–357, 398, 472–504, 543, 553, 599, 733
  colonial policy 579
  cooperative 185, 451
  development 485
  18th century 153
  family sector 476, 491–492, 497–498
  Goa 142
  Inhambane 164
  Iron Age 85
  mechanization 20, 482, 490, 504
  peasant 476, 491–492, 497, 512
  planning 444
  plantation 30, 495, 500
  Ronga people 226
  Shona people 136
  statistics 473, 486, 536, 545
  Tete 42
  waste residues 464
  Yao 221
Agro-Industrial Complex of the Limpopo – CAIL 484, 486
Agro-industry 530 see also Sugar
Agronomia Moçambicana 472
Agrupamento e caracterização étnica dos indígenas de Moçambique 235
Aid agreements 464
AIM – Mozambique Information Agency 377, 615
  Information Bulletin 345, 708
Akapwitchi akaporo: armas e escravos 650–651
Aktueller Informationsdienst Afrika 711
Alba, S. 611, 616
Albasini, João 694
Albasini, José 694
Alberto, M.S. 235
Albuquerque, O. de 626
Alcohol 530
Alcoholism 561
Alegre, Costa 610
Alencar, M. 675
Alentejo
  aristocrat 26
Alexandre, V. 107, 143
Alexandre Dáskalos Prize (1962) 626
Algae 552

298

301

B

303

Birds 61, 72–73, 77, 83, 548, 693
  mangrove swamps 547
Birds of the southern third of Africa 72,
  83
Birmingham, D. 104, 158, 163, 362,
  456
Bishop of Beira 697
Bishop of Zanzibar 265
Bissio, B. 173
Bithrey, W. B. 249
*Black gold: the Mozambican miner,
  proletarian and peasant* 151, 155,
  511–512, 514, 522, 665
Blacks 207
Bleek, W. J. H. 242
Blum, J. M. 462
Board for Overseas Research
  Centre for Scientific Overseas
    Documentation 715
Board for Overseas Studies
  Centre for Cultural Anthropology
    223
Board of Settlement 493
Bodleian Library, Oxford 288
Boeder, R. B. 249
Boletim Agrícola e Pecuário 545
Boletim da República 365
*Boletim da Sociedade de Estudos [da
  colónia] de Moçambique* 45, 97,
  287, 703
Boletim das Alfândegas 542
Boletim de Informaçao 406
*Boletim do Museu de Nampula (Museu
  Regional 'Commandante Ferreira
  de Almeida')* 682
Boletim Económico e Estatístico 208,
  539
Boletim Geral do Ultramar 232
*Boletim mensal da Direcção Provincial
  dos Serviços de Estatística Geral*
  539
Boletim Mensal de Estatística 539
Boletim mensal estatístico 539
Boletim Municipal 193
Boletim Nacional 406
Boletim Oficial 365, 565
Boletim: a saúde em Moçambique 317
Boletim trimestral 508
Boletim Trimestral de Estatística 539
Bolton, P. 20
Bonner, P. L. 458, 523
Boormans, Father Daniel 275, 282

Border disputes *see* Frontiers
Borges Coelho, J. P. 141, 149, 189,
  194, 650–651
Borgnet, Mário 675
Bossen, G. D. 433
Boston, T. D. 132
Bostrychidae 66
Botany
  medicinal plants 309, 316
  Tchiri Valley 36
  tea 495
  Zambezi 36
  see also Flora
Botelho, S. X. 6
Botswana 65, 76
Bourdillon, M. F. C. 227
Bowen, M. 498
Boxer, C. R. 112–114, 168, 290
O Brado Africano 138, 619, 623, 625,
  637, 694, 702
Bragança, A. de 174, 186, 357, 395,
  592
Brandberg, B. 559
Bravo, N. S. 474
Brazil 29, 109, 128, 367, 601, 624, 627,
  630
  relations with Mozambique 425
*Breve estudo sobre a Ilha de
  Moçambique acompanhada d'um
  pequeno vecabulário
  portuguez-macua* 242
Breyer-Brandwijk, M. G. 316
Brezhnev, Leonid 431
Bribery 178
brigadas 391
Brighton
  seminar (1979) 363
Bristle-worms 63
Britain 33, 56, 149, 167, 170, 312, 350,
  394, 521
  ally of Portugal 159
  exploration 9, 32–34, 36, 38
  quarrel with Portugal (1886–90)
    118, 429, 453
  relations with Mozambique 414, 421,
    425
  research libraries 288
British Broadcasting
  Corporation – BBC 11, 445, 711
*British Central Africa: an attempt to
  give some account of a portion of
  the territories under British*

Child mortality 301
Child-rearing 139
Children 299–302
    abandoned 336
Chimoio 418
China 12, 175, 357, 415, 431, 517, 649
Chinde 51, 255
Chinese agitators 201
Chinese people 209
Chinese porcelain 89
Chinyanja basic course 249
Chipanga mission 250
Chissano, Joaquim 423
Chisumphi religion 286
Chitlangou, son of a chief 291
Chittick, N. 104
Chokwe 348, 479, 501
Cholera 317
Choncol, M.-E. 549, 555
Chongoene 321
Chope chiefdoms 126
Chope language 88, 235, 238, 270–272
Chope people 232, 234
    music 646, 659–660, 663
    poetry 626
    women 340
*Chopi musicians: their music, poetry
    and instruments* 659
Christian Democrats 428
Christian Science Monitor 422
Christianity 128
    spread 284
Christians
    left-wing 732
Christie, I. 191, 399
Chronica do Rei Dom Emanuel 168
Chuabo language 88, 235–236, 240,
    264, 268, 660
Church 220, 709, 732
    18th century 153
Church and State 278
*Church in Mozambique: the colonial
    inheritance. Minutes of a
    discussion between the Roman
    Catholic bishops and the govern-
    ment of Mozambique* 278
CIDESA card service 722
Ciência e tecnologia 593
CIFEL steel works 469
Cinco 707
cipaio 18
circunscrição 43

Ciscato, E. 641
Cities
    'Portuguese' 59
Citizenship 25
Citrus fruits 489
Civil liberties 19
Civil servants 52, 384
O Clamor Africano 694
Clancey, P. A. 61
Clans 7
    Makua 230
    Ronga 226
Clarence-Smith, W. G. 107, 118–119,
    355
Clark, J. D. 104
Class struggle 10, 364, 405, 525, 529
Class system
    Nguni 160
*A classe trabalhadora deve conquistar
    e exercer o poder na frente da
    ciência e da cultura* 576
Clemency 373
Clerc, A. D. 291
Cliff, J. L. 304, 324
Clima 629
Climate 2, 39, 52–53, 57, 473, 476, 487,
    548, 553, 557, 733
Clough, M. 419
Clyde Mitchell, J. 218
CMEA – Comecon 430
Coal 41, 51, 464
Coastal dunes 548
Coastal shipping 506
    statistics 542
Coconut 21, 478, 489
Coelho, C. A. F. de C. 383
Coetzee, C. 70
Coger, D. M. 35
Cohen, S. 587
COI – Congress of Industrial
    Organizations 354
Coimbra, R. D. H. 292, 558
Coimbra University 212, 627
*Colectânea de Estudos do Gabinete de
    Estudos Técnicos* 465
Colectivo de trabalho, trabalhadores
    dos Caminhos de Ferro de
    Moçambique, e estudantes da
    Universidade Eduardo Mondlane
    672
Collections for a handbook of Makua
    246

308

309

Cotton production in Mozambique: a
    survey 494
Cotton-ginning mills 481, 494
Cotton-seed oil 478
Council of Ministers 374, 713, 732
Courtois, V. J. 264
Coutinho, A. R. 426
Couto, D. de 168
Couto, F. 626
Couto, M. 17, 615
Covane, L. A. 436
Cozinha moçambicana 3
Cozinha moçambicana: uma questão
    cultural 21
Craveirinha, Grabato Dias, Rui
    Knopfli 619
Craveirinha, José 606, 611–613,
    617–619, 621, 626, 638, 646
Credentials Commission 401
Credit 393, 536
O crescimento da cidade colonial de
    Lourenço Marques 47
A criação de alfândega da ilha do Ibo e
    a contribuição das ilhas para o
    comércio e a vida de Moçambique
    no século XVIII 156
Crime 368, 377
    statistics 544
Criminal justice 368
Crise e ressurgimento: o corpo policial
    de Lourenço Marques na
    sublevação do distrito em
    1894–1895 137
Critical perspectives on Lusophone
    literature from Africa 605
Crónica dos anos da peste 619
Crop protection 490
Crowder, M. 104, 110
Crown lands see prazos
Croyance du peuple shangane et
    christianisme 283
Crustaceans 552
A cruz e a espada 278
Cruz, M. J. da 141, 525
Cruz e Silva, T. 86, 96, 141
Cuba 12, 175
    people's courts 373
Cuba for beginners 652
Cuenod, R. 258–259
Cuidados de saúde primários em
    Moçambique: outros níveis de
    atenção de saúde 305

Cuisine 3, 21
A cultura algodoeira na economia do
    norte de Moçambique 474
A cultura é a questão central da
    revolução 648
Cultural exchanges 427
Culture 15, 197, 400, 561, 606, 649,
    718
Cumulative bibliography of African
    studies 716, 722
Cunene River 70
Cunha, A. R. da 217–218, 221
Cunha, J. da Luz 183
Cunha, S. 585
Cunha Jardim, A. P. da 589
Cunnison, I. 228
Cuppen, G. M. M. 283
Currency
    dual 530
    museum 687
    national 434, 656
Customs, local 383
Customs and excise 153, 156, 384
    statistics 538, 542
Cyclones 491

D

Da Asia 168
Da população de Moçambique:
    achegas para a estatística da
    Colónia 212
Dados estatísticos de base 536
Dagnino, F. 369
Dahomey 602
Daily News 191
Daily Telegraph 1, 188
Dairy farming 497
    see also Cattle
Dale, D. 256
Dambukashamba 294
Dams 25, 102, 466
Dance 646, 655, 657
    mapico 646, 655, 673, 682
    merombo 655
    msaho 659
    nyau 646, 655, 673
Dandelot, A. 64
Danes 28

315

External traders in the hinterland of
    Sofala, 1810–1889 455
Eyuphuro see Yuphuro

F

As faces visitadas 627
FACIM 706
Facts and Reports: Press Cuttings on
    Southern Africa 11, 711
Fagan, B. 95, 104
Fage, J. D. 104
Fair of Dambarare 681
A familia e a sociedade 336
Family Health Care, Africare 307
Family life 561
    diversity 369
    Yao 218, 221
Family planning 299, 307
Famine 328, 330, 333, 491
FAO – Food and Agriculture
    Organization 68, 79, 490, 492
FAO species identification sheets for
    fishery purposes: eastern Indian
    Ocean (Fishing Area 57) and
    western Central Pacific (Fishing
    Area 71) 68, 79
Farelahi, Sultan 149, 651
Faria e Sousa, M. de 168
Farm-tool industry 470
Fascism
    Portuguese 117, 341, 381
Fauna 2, 57, 82, 548, 552, 553, 556–557
    birds 61, 72–73, 77, 83, 547–548
    butterflies 84
    insects 66, 78, 548, 557
    mammals 64
    mangrove 547
    marine life 60, 62–63, 68, 79, 80–81
    sea shells 70–71
    snakes 67
Fauvet, P. 345
Federal Republic of Germany – FRG
    see West Germany
Fernandes, A. 65, 74
Fernandes, António 145
Fernandes, E. 700
Fernandes, Father Andre 659
Fernandes, R. S. de M. 392
Fernandes dos Santos, P. 426
Ferrão, V. C. 622

Ferraz, M. de L. E. dos S. de F. 683
Ferreira, C. 52
Ferreira, G. da V. 66
Ferreira, M. 601, 604–605, 608, 623
Ferreira, M. C. 66
Ferreira, P. 494
Ferreira, R. 626
Ferreira da Costa, J. G. 55
Festival of Traditional Music and Song
    Central Organizer's Office (1980)
    658
Feudalism 132
Field guide to the birds of east and
    central Africa 73, 83
Field guide to the birds of southern
    Africa 73
Field guide to the butterflies of Africa
    84
Field guide to the coral reef fishes of the
    Indian and West Pacific oceans 60
Field guide to the larger mammals of
    Africa 64
Field guide to the national parks of East
    Africa 83
Field-guide to the reef-building corals
    of the Indo-Pacific 551
Field guide to the snakes of southern
    Africa 67
Field guide to the trees of southern
    Africa 76
Figueiredo, L. 134
Figuring African Trade 457
Films 665, 673, 675
Finance 19, 127, 398, 444–451, 480,
    503
    accord 418
    statistics 536, 544
Findlay, F. R. N. 22
Fine arts 601
Finland
    PHC 322
First contribution to the knowledge of
    the Massingir Stone Age artefacts
    102
First look at the import and export
    trade of Mozambique, 1800–1914
    457
First National Seminar on Mathematics
    Teaching 596
First Plan (1953–58) 444
First, R. 155, 184, 512, 514, 522, 592,
    665

Freyre, G. 109
Friedland, E. A. 138, 293, 346
Frontier agreements
(1891) 56
(1954) 56
Frontiers 19, 111, 166, 202, 389–390,
438
Tete-Malawi 56
with Natal 548
Nyasaland 56
Fuelwood 464
Fuller, C. E. 224, 234
Fundo de Fomento Algodoeiro 477
*Fundo do Governo Geral: inventário
dos relatórios, 1906–1960* 692
FUNIPAMO – United African
People's Anti-Imperialist Front of
Mozambique 177

G

Gabinete de Communicação Social –
GCS 695
Galeria de Etnografia 693
Galha, H. T. 513
Galvão, D. 626
Galvão da Silva, M. 134
Gambe 89
Gamitto, A. C. P. 228
Ganhão Fernando 567, 612, 626, 636,
638
interviewed 576
Gann, L. H. 103, 188
Garcia, A. 507
Garcia, D. 385
Garcia, J. G. 65
Garcia, R. 99
Garcia de Orta 65, 703, 715
Gardinier, D. E. 105
Garlake, P. 89–92, 95–96
Gas 51, 464
Gaskin, L. J. P. 655
Gasperini, L. 568–570
Gaza Empire 154, 233
Gaza Kingdom 104, 126, 137, 160, 277,
387
Gaza Province 10, 23, 34, 86, 111, 152,
166, 301, 334, 348, 455, 479, 501,
656
census data 216
drought 330

Eduardo Mondlane cooperative 483
health workshop (1981) 321
Gazankulu 642
GCS – Gabinete de Communicação
Social 695
General history of Africa 104, 106
General Security Directorate 178
General Students Union of Black
Africa – UGEAN 186
Genetics
and drugs 318
Genève-Afrique 10, 226, 723
Gentes afortunadas: a música chope
659
Gentili, A. M. 185
*Geografia física de Moçambique:
esboço geográfico* 39
Geographia 52
Geographical Society of Lisbon 384,
387
Geography 2, 5, 19, 39–59, 555, 715,
722, 733
physical 36, 53–55
Tchiri Valley 36
Zambezi 36
*Geologia da bacia do rio Zambeze,
Moçambique: características
geologico-mineiras da bacio do rio
Zambeze, em território
moçambicano* 51
*A geologia e o desenvolvimento
económico e social de
Moçambique* 44
Geology 44, 53–54, 57, 487, 548, 557,
562
bibliographies 41–42, 44
economic, 44, 599
Geothermal energy 464
Gerdes, P. 596
Geresdorff, R. von 480
German colonial interests 36, 118, 202,
305, 394
German Democratic Republic – GDR
see East Germany
German invasion 144
Ghana 620
Gibson, M. J. 719, 726
Gifford, T. 368
GNP – Gross national product 553
Goa 290, 602, 604
archives 112, 135
Catholics 142

320

323

statistics 536, 546
(1806) 537
Infant mortality 310, 317
infiltrados 404
A influência da língua portuguesa sobre a suahíli e quatro línguas de Moçambique 268
Informação económica 342
Informação estatística 1975–1984 342, 541
Information services 19
Ingwane, J. P. S. 297
Ingwavuma 548
Inhaca Island 94, 159, 547, 551–552
Inhambane 63, 70, 96, 139, 152, 262, 480, 512, 518, 660, 681
  census data 216
  health workshop (1985) 321
  land tenure 164
  malnutrition 330
  trade 171
Inhambane: Kulturgeographie einer Küstenlandschaft in Südmoçambique 46
Inharrime 270, 659
Inharrime River 224
Inhassume River 224
Initiation rites 334, 336
INLD – Instituto Nacional do Livro e do Disco 617, 624, 728
Inquérito agrícola de 1937–1938 e 1938–1939 545
Insects 78, 548, 557
  xylophagous 66
Inspecção de Instrução Pública 572
Inspecção Superior do Plano de Fomento 444, 446
Institut für Afrika-Kunde 711
Institute for Tropical Research 715
Institute of Current World Affairs 422
Institute of Social Studies 470
Instituto de Estudios Políticos para América Latina y Africa – IEPALA 278
Instituto de Investigação Agronómica de Moçambique 477
Instituto de Investigação Científica de Moçambique 595
  Secção de Arqueologia 92
Instituto do Algodão de Moçambique 477
Instituto Nacional de Estatística 543

Instituto Nacional do Livro e do Disco – INLD 617, 624, 728
Instituto Superior de Ciências Sociais e Política Ultramarina – ISCSPU 19, 52, 384
A instrução pública em Moçambique: sua evolução 582
Insurance 398
Inter-Territorial Language Committee for the East African Dependencies 265
INTERMACOM 461
Intermediate Development Plan (1965–67) 448
INTERMETAL 461
Internal war in Mozambique: a socio-psychological analysis of a nationalist revolution 197
International Affairs 355
International African Bibliography: current books, articles and papers in African Studies 721
International African Institute 716, 721
International Defence and Aid Fund – IDAF 184, 199
International Documentation and Communication Centre, Rome – IDOC 732
International issues 1
International Journal of African Historical Studies 189, 267, 355
International Journal of Health Services 319
International Labour Organization – ILO 511, 532
International Monetary Fund – IMF 324
International Police for the Defence of the State – PIDE 18, 117, 633, 653, 700
International relations 412, 419–421, 722, 732
  see also Treaties
International relations on the south-east coast of Africa, 1796–1856 421
International Standard Bibliographic Description (Monographs) 728
Internationalism 298, 400, 413
  proletarian 409
INTERQUIMICA 461
Intervenções dos delegados [ao quarto Congresso] 404

Introduction to Chinyanja 249
Introductory handbook and vocabulary
    of the Yao language 269, 274
Inventário do fundo do seculo XVIII
    681
Inventory of select documents from the
    Immanuel Wallerstein collection of
    political ephemera of the liberation
    movements of Lusophone Africa
    and Anglophone southern Africa
    (1958–1975) on microfilm 186
Investigation of Manekweni,
    Mozambique 89, 92, 96
Investment 388, 394, 536
    state farms 451, 491, 497
Iron 51, 456
    production 496
Iron Age 85–86, 95, 163
Iron Age research in Mozambique:
    collected preliminary reports 86
Irrigation 490, 493, 553
Isaac, G. 104
Isaacman, A. 15–16, 106, 110, 112,
    143, 155, 185, 225, 281, 294,
    370–371, 474, 526, 637
Isaacman, B. 16, 110, 143, 155, 339,
    370–371
ISCSPU – Instituto Superior de
    Ciências Sociais e Política
    Ultramarina 19, 52, 384
Ishemo, S. 20
Islam 287
    expansion 275, 452
Islam in sub-Saharan Africa 287
Islamic Associations 282
Islamic settlements 93
Ismael, G. 616, 628
Ismaili Shi'ias 287
Issue 412, 415
Italy 619
Itinerário 639
Ivens, R. 31
Ivory 145, 455
Ivory and slaves in east central Africa:
    changing patterns of international
    trade to the late nineteenth century
    37, 125

J

Jackson, M. V. see Jackson Haight

Jackson, R. 249
Jackson Haight, M. V. 421
Jansen, P. C. M. 309
Japan 113, 706
Jardim, J. 343, 700, 702
Jeeves, A. H. 517
Jelley, D. 300, 310, 550, 554
Jesus Gouveia, M. de 384
Jigger flea 362
Jinadu, L. A. 597
João Belo 49
    see also Chai Chai
Johannesburg
    railway to Maputo 434
John Paul 20
John, H. T. 4
Johnsen, V. 344, 360
Johnson, H. 155, 295
Johnson, P. 349, 425, 440
Johnston, A. 573
Johnston, Sir Harry H. 33, 36, 236, 241
Jonsson, L. 94
III. Jornadas de Saúde, Chongoene, 9 a
    13 de Novembro de 1981 321
Jornal d'Agricultura da Companhia de
    Moçambique 545
Jornal de Letras 634
Jornal do Professor 574
José, A. 29
Jossias, L. 663
Jourdan, P. 463
Journal of African History 9, 95, 107,
    131, 139, 142, 286, 507, 526
Journal of Ecology 551
Journal of Epidemiology and
    Community Health 310
Journal of Southern African Studies
    118, 125, 150, 169, 197, 226, 355,
    437, 458
Journals 703–706
    ethnography 682
Journey of the pombeiros 29
Judite, F. 575
Júnior, J. R. 610
Junod, H. A. 220, 223, 226, 234, 257,
    277, 334, 661
Junod H.-P. 232, 641
Junta das Missões Geográficas e
    Investigações do Ultramar 49
Junta de Exportação do Algodão 477
Junta de Investigacões do Ultramar 99
juntas 381, 391

327

Land use 39
   and abuse 550
   planning 490
Land-holdings
   19th century 204
Lands of Cazembe: Lacerda's journey
   to Cazembe in 1798 29, 228
Langa clan 334
Langa, A. 656
Langa, Francisco 18, 653
Language groups 57, 88, 235
   see also Gwambe; Makonde;
      Makua; Nyanja-Sena; Ronga;
      Shona; Tsonga; Yao
Languages 235–241, 718, 722
   Makua-Lomwe 242–246
   minor 263–274
   Nyanja-Sena 247–255
   Shona 256
   Tsonga 257–262
The languages of Mosamibique [sic]:
   vocabularies of the dialects of
   Lourenço Marques, Imhambane,
   Sofala, Tette, Sena, Quellimane,
   Mosambique, Cape Delgado,
   Anjoane, the Maravi, Mudsau,
   etc., drawn up from the mss. of W.
   Peters and from other materials
   242
Lanham, L. W. 266
Lappé, F. M. 468
Last to leave. Portuguese colonialism in
   Africa: and introductory outline
   120
Later prehistory of eastern and
   southern Africa 98
Lavén, N. 559
Lay, M. van 720
Leaders, nationalist 14, 177
Leadership 191, 358
   crisis (1968–70) 14
   Frelimo 584
Leakey, R. E. 96, 99
Lebombo mountains 548
Ledger, J. 78
Legislação aplicável ao ensino
   particular: Diplomas Legislativas
   nos. 58/71 de 5 de Junho e 49/73 de
   7 de Julho 572
Legislação aplicável aos serviços de
   educação e ensino que se ministra
   em Moçambique 565

Legislação sobre o ensino 572
Legislação sobre ensino liceal: reforma,
   estatuto e programas para
   1947–1948 572
Legislation 365, 368, 370–371, 374,
   382, 386, 463, 726
   colonial 375, 380
   constitutional 373
   cotton 477
   education 565, 572, 575
   family 369, 371
   labour 116, 377, 522, 525, 532
   land tenure 367, 376
   mission activity 284
   nationality law 366
Legitimacy 422, 439
Legum, C. 712
Lei de terras 376
Leigh, N. 308
Lemos, A. S. G. 619
Lemos, G. 626
Lendas da Índia 168
Leo Milas affair 123
Lepidopterists *see* Butterflies
Lesotho 76
Let's build agricultural producer
   cooperatives: socialist agricultural
   development strategy in
   Mozambique, 1975–1983 498
Lettow-Vorbeck, P. E. von 144
Levy, S. 422
Liberated zones 173, 179, 358–359,
   368, 395, 416, 491, 669
   education 567–570, 596
   legal system 371, 377
   people's courts 373
Liberation movements 123, 424
   publications 406
   Soviet support 431
   see also FNLA; FRELIMO; MNR;
      ZANU
Liberation struggles 1, 8, 10, 12, 14,
   24, 53, 104, 112, 119–120, 138,
   158, 311, 325, 416, 420, 643, 649,
   712
Libertar 732
Libraries 535, 734
Library of Congress 719
   African Section 722
O Liceu Salazar de Lourenço Marques
   589
Lições de missionologia 590

328

Mali
  PHC 322
Malnutrition 308, 329–330
  protein-caloric 302
Maltese, C. 651
Mammals 64, 548, 693
Manarte, M. 678
O mancebo e trovador Campos
  Oliveira 604
Mandala, E. 526
Mandela, E. 136
mandioca 332
Manekweni 85, 90–92, 96, 101, 126
  excavations (1975) 89
Mang'anja people 286, 526
Manghezi, Alpheus 295, 328, 502, 512,
  519, 527
Mangoche, M. V. B. 248–249
Mangroves 63, 547
Manhiça 270
Manhunts 527
Manica 41, 111, 118, 127, 207–208,
  281, 418, 429, 496, 525
Manifesto 626
Manjacaze 334
Manpower 510–523
  see also Labour
MANU – Mozambique African
  National Union 175–176, 180, 186,
  223, 275, 282
Manual of Portuguese East Africa 2
Manuel II, King of Portugal 148
Manyika language 238, 240, 256
Manyikeni, a zimbabwe in southern
  Mozambique 92, 96
A mão-de-obra portuguesa e a indústria
  mineira da África do Sul 507
Maoism 12
Mapa cor-de-rosa 31
Mapa das povoações criadas até 31 de
  Dezembro de (1959–) e sua
  situação legal 43
Mapa rodoviário de Moçambique 505
Mapas 43
mapico dance-theatre 646
Mapondera 294
Maposse, D. 613
Maps 52, 59, 141
  agricultural 473
  frontier 56
  language areas 88, 245
  mangroves 547

musical instruments 658
  ornithological 61
Maputaland 548
Maputo 50, 74, 152, 418, 498, 502
  Central Hospital 308, 327
  speech by Machel 324
  guide-book 27
  health centres 300
  infant mortality 317
  Maxaquena suburb 560
  2nd OMM conference (1976) 336
  port 434
  railway to Johannesburg 434
  see also CEA; Eduardo Mondlane
    University; Lourenço Marques
Maputo Bay 159, 547–548, 552
Maputo Province 47, 382
Maputo antes da independência 48, 558
Marasinghe, M. L. 376
Maravi Empire 134, 650
Maravi people 125, 228, 232
Marcum, J. A. 424
Margarido, A. 579, 619, 626, 706
Maria, C. 626
Marine biology 60, 62–63, 68, 79–80,
  551–552
Marine fish resources of Mozambique
  80
Mário, T. 17
Marital problems 220
Marivate, C. T. D. 641
Marketing 473, 504
  grain 459
  maize 479
Marks, S. 104
Marney, J. 657
Marques, Álvaro 17
Marques, António 392
Marques, G. B. 426
Marques de Almeida, A. A. 579
Marquette University, Milwaukee 105
Marracuene 50
  see also Vila Louisa
Marriage 336, 369
  inter-racial 561
Marsh, J. 440
Marshall, J. 357
Martelli, G. 1
Martin, D. 349, 425, 440
Martin, P. M. 158, 163, 362
Martinho, F. 605
Martins, D. de C. 302

Martins, H. 311–312, 319
Martins, J. F. 373
Martins, J. S. 147, 524
 see also Capela, J. [pseudonym]
Martins Pereira, C. 657
Marwick, M. G. 29, 228
Marx for beginners 652
Marxism 12, 222, 395, 598
 and historiography 103, 107, 141
Marxism-Leninism 172, 335, 398
O marxismo-leninismo no contexto
 moçambicano 598
Marzagão, C. 313, 319
Mashiposhipo: proverbi delli
 espressioni idiomatiche del popolo
 lomwe 641
Mashonaland 429
Masks 678, 680
Mass media
 newspapers 694–702
 periodicals 682, 703–706, 717,
  722
 see also Films; Radio; Television
Massacres
 Mueda (1960) 14
 Tete (1972) 115
 Wiriyamu (1972) 187–188, 199
Massangano 187
Massimbe, J. M. A. 47, 159, 684
Massingir 30, 86, 102
Massingira, J. 24
Massingue, V. 646
Matabele 233
Match that lights the flame: education
 policy in the People's Republic of
 Mozambique 566
Maternity cases 310
Matola 92, 94, 662
 Iron Age research 86, 96
Matonse, A. 667
Matos, O. de 426
Matos e Sá, V. 626
Mau Mau 158
Maugham, R. F. 661
Mauritius 550
Mavia language 236, 240, 273
May, J. M. 329
Mayoka, J. M. M. 643
Mbaga Bady, A. 138
mbila 658
M'Bona cult 286
Mbwiliza, J. F. 350, 457

McCracken, J. 125
McLachlan, G. R. 73
McLellan, D. L. 329
McLeod, L. 37
McMartin, A. 38
McMurdo territorial concession 118
Mdzonga, O. 158
Measles 308
Mechanization
 agricultural 20, 482, 490, 504
 state farms 482
Medeiros, E. de C. 141, 147, 203,
  229–230
Media
 US 420
 Western 333, 349
 see also Mass media
Medical care in Portuguese Africa,
 1885–1974 554
Medicinal and poisonous plants of
 southern and eastern Africa: being
 an account of their medicinal and
 other uses, chemical composition,
 pharmacological effects and
 toxicology in man and animal 316
Medicine
 herbal 306, 309, 316, 627
 traditional 306
 see also Drugs policy; Preventive
  medicine
MEDIMOC 461
Meeuws, R. 553
Meine Erinnerungen aus Ostafrika 144
Meinhof noun classification 258
Melamed, A. 326
Mello e Castro 134
Mello Machado, A. J. de 230–231
Melo, A. 426
Melo, G. de 193, 610, 626, 699
Memoirs of East Africa 134
Memória estatística sobre os domínios
 portuguezes na África Oriental 6
Memórias da costa d'África oriental
 127
Memórias do Instituto de Investigação
 Científica de Moçambique 97
Mendes, E. J. 65
Mendes, M. C. 48, 558
Mendes, O. 309, 602, 607, 621,
  626–631, 639
Mendonça, F. A. 65
Mendonça, G. 314

332

Mora, D. 613
Morais, J. M. 86, 96–97, 101–102
Morality
    Ronga 226
Morbidity patterns 307, 330
Moreira, A. 250
Moreira, C. 579
Moreira, E. 284
Moreira, J. 141
Moreira de Almeida, L. 582
Moreira Júnior, M. A. 380
Moreira Lopes, M. E. 102
Morocco 312, 408
Morosini, G. 649
Morrumbene 270
Mortality
    child 301
    infant 310, 317
    mining 517
    patterns 307, 330
Mosambik 28
Moser, G. M. 605, 608–609
Moslems *see* Muslims
Mossuril, Camisão 242
Mota, F. de 616
Mota Lopes, J. 354
Motta, H. 652
Mountains 57
Moura, J. V.–B. C. 148
Moura Coutinho, M. P. de 626
Moure, J. 583
Mousinho de Albuquerque 387
Mouzinho de Albuquerque, J. A. 52,
    124, 137, 147, 275, 380, 384–385,
    387, 390, 650, 686
*O movimento migratório de
    trabalhadores entre Moçambique e
    a África do Sul* 522
*O movimento operário em Lourenço
    Marques, 1898–1927* 524
Movimento Popular de Libertação de
    Angola – MPLA 612
*Mozambican development: a
    bibliography covering social
    science literature with emphasis on
    the period after 1965* 360, 725
Mozambican History Workshop 173,
    185, 189
Mozambican Institute of Scientific
    Research – IICM 41–42, 218
    Memórias 61
Mozambican Nordic Agricultural

Programme – MONAP 591
Mozambican Notes 708
Mozambican Party 339
Mozambican Studies 510
Mozambican Women's
    Organization – OMM 21, 299,
    335, 337, 578
    Extraordinary Conference (1985)
    336–337, 675
    health care 306
*Die mozambiquanische Aussenpolitik,
    1975–1982: Merkmale, Probleme,
    Dynamik* 417
Mozambique African National
    Union – MANU 175–176, 180,
    186, 223, 275, 282
*Mozambique: the Africanization of a
    European institution: the Zambesi
    prazos 1750–1902* 225
*Mozambique and Angola: reconstruc-
    tion in the social sciences* 595
Mozambique and South Africa 507
Mozambique Channel 79
Mozambique Chartered Company 20,
    151, 207–208, 210, 251, 284, 362,
    394, 525, 687
    wound up (1942) 211
Mozambique: a country study 5
*Mozambique: dream the size of
    freedom* 14, 407
*Mozambique economy with special
    reference to its interdependence
    with South Africa* 507
*Mozambique: food and agriculture
    sector, preliminary study* 489
*Mozambique: from colonialism to
    revolution, 1900–1982* 16, 155, 370
Mozambique: a history 140
*Mozambique in the twentieth century:
    from colonialism to independence*
    24
Mozambique Information
    Agency – AIM 377, 615
    Information Bulletin 345, 708
Mozambique Information Office,
    London – MIO 368
    News Review 708
Mozambique Institute, Tanzania 198
*Mozambique: an interpretation of the
    nature, causes and outcomes of the
    pre-colonial stages of African
    economic development* 132

335

Mussa Quanto, Sultan 149
Musti, B. 492
Mutemba, A. S. 50
Mutimati Barnabé João 612–613, 623, 632, 638
Mwari religion 286
Mwata Cazembe IV Keleka Maya 29, 228
Myre, M. 74
Mzila, King of Gaza 34

N

Nachake, J. 613
Nachingwea training-camp 373, 674
Naguib 668
Nairobi
  Coryndon Museum 83
Naissance de Mozambique: résistance et révoltes anticoloniales, 1854–1918 154
Naissance et évolution d'un état par la lutte de libération nationale: Mozambique 138
Nam, Kok 667
Namaacha 321
Namarroi 495
Namibia 76, 174
  Soviet role in development 431
Nampula Museum 682
Nampula Province 33, 152, 183, 296, 332, 385, 457, 473, 481, 494, 586, 640, 651, 663
  Erati District 243
  health workshop (1976) 321
  Prisoner's Centre 368
Nangololo 275
Não vamos esquecer! Boletim informativo do Oficina de História 185, 705
Nascimento, E. 569, 584
Nasi Pereira, E. A. 230
Näslund, R. 559
Natal 34, 69, 139, 458, 460, 530, 548, 552
  labour shortage 159
National Antiquities and Museums Service 94
National Assembly 411, 444, 654
  see also People's Assembly

National Centre for Documentation and Information 727
National Cinema Institute – INC 675
National Coal Directorate 464
National Colonial Bank 701
National Colonial Congress (1901) 380
National Commission for Natural Disasters 330
National decision-making for primary health care: a study 322
National Democratic Union of Mozambique – UDENAMO 172, 175–177, 180, 186
National Director of Information 354
National Directorate for Culture 657
National Front for the Liberation of Angola – FNLA 174
National Geographic 51
National Housing Directorate 560
National Institute for Books and Records – INLD 617, 624, 728
National Journalists' Organization 607
National Library, Lisbon 137, 681
National Money Museum 687
National Museum of Ethnography 682
National Overseas Bank Documentation Centre 727
National Pastoral Assembly (1977) 732
National Planning Commission 216, 599–600
National research councils in developing countries: SAREC seminar with collaborating agencies, Stockholm, Tammsvik, 16–21 January 1983 600
National security 4–5
National System of Education – SNE 573, 588, 596
National tuberculosis control programme in the People's Republic of Mozambique 554
National Union for the Complete Independence of Angola – UNITA 174
National Union of Commercial and Industrial Employees 688
National Union of Teachers – ONP 39
Nationalism 1, 12, 14, 106, 117, 138, 140, 177, 182, 185, 197, 202, 438, 612, 679
  economic 364
Nationality law 366

337

Nationalization 423, 434
  banks in Tanzania 352
Native Affairs Agency 688
Native Statute (1954) 575
  abolished (1961) 209, 216
    impact 381, 383
NATO – North Atlantic Treaty
  Organization 24, 184, 190
Natural disasters 23, 361, 491
*Natural history of Inhaca Island,
  Mozambique* 552
Natural resources *see* Resources
Natural sciences 715
Navigators
  Portuguese 54, 113
  see also Explorers
Ndanga, O.T. 438
Ndau language 88, 240
Ndau people 227, 285
Negrão, J. G. 141, 189, 194, 600
Negritude 298
Negrophile Institute 13
Neil-Tomlinson, B. 20, 388
Nelson, H. O. 5
NESAM – Nucleus of African
  Secondary-School Students of
  Mozambique 623, 625
Netia 481
Neto, Agostinho 433
*New England merchants and mission-
  aries in coastal nineteenth-century
  Portuguese East Africa* 171
New Scientist 84
New York 708
Newitt, M. D. D. 20, 119, 149–150,
  651
Newspapers 694–702, 711
Ngoni people 36, 233, 367
Ngungunyane 137, 170, 277, 387, 429
Nguni outburst 104
Nguni people 139, 160, 228, 232, 285,
  525
  migrations 233
  trade 455, 458, 460
Ngwenya, M. 679
*O nhamussoro e as outras funções
  mágico-religiosas* 285
nhemba 3
Niassa 30, 33, 152, 183, 193, 208,
  326–327, 388, 521
  liberated zone 173, 491
Niassa Company 362, 388, 394

Night-clubs 26
Nijmegen University 283
Nile Valley 678
Nimpuno, K. 559
Nkavandame, L. 373, 408
Nkhoma-Wamunza, A. 717
Nkomati Accord (1984) 433–435, 439,
  443
Nkomati contacts
  with South Africa (1983–84) 345, 357
Nkomati River 32, 74
Nkomati states 160
Nkosi, L. 624
Nkosi, Z. 507
*No reino de Caliban III: antologia
  panorâmica da poesia africana de
  expressão portuguesa. Vol. 3:
  Moçambique* 601, 623
No tempo do Farelahi 149, 650–651
*Noções elementares da geografia de
  Moçambique* 39
Noções gramaticais da língua chisena
  247
Nogar, Rui 606, 618, 626, 632, 636,
  638
Nogueira da Costa, A. M. de C. S
  132, 151, 157, 294
A noite dividida 611
Nordic aid agencies 348, 479
Nordin, L. 559
Norgaard, O. 360
Noronha, Rui de 601, 607, 610, 612,
  621, 623, 626, 639
Norte 622
North Africa 36
North Atlantic Treaty Organization –
  NATO 24, 184, 190
Norwegian Institute of International
  Affairs – NUPI 494
Norwegians 28, 80
Nós matamos o cão tinhoso 624
A nossa luta 191
As nossas receitas 21
*Notas sobre fontes estatísticas oficiais
  referentes à economia colonial
  moçambicana* 203, 213, 534
Notes on Tshopi origins 234
Notícias 193, 216, 337, 404, 411, 590,
  619–620, 639, 642, 671, 696–699
Notícias da Beira 240, 630, 700, 702
*Notícias dos domínios portugueses na
  costa de África oriental* 127

338

Novas bases para o ensino de adaptação: Portaria no. 15:971 de 31 de Março de 1962 572
Novels 630
Novo regime de ensino e programas da instrução primária geral da Província de Moçambique 581
N'qaba 233
Ntsan'wisi, H. 642
O núcleo tenaz 640
Nucleus of Secondary-School Students of Mozambique – NESAM 623, 625
Numismatics 687, 690
NUPI – Norwegian Institute of International Affairs 494
Nurse, D. 267
Nurses 300
  paediatric 301
  training 326
A nutrição no Ultramar português subsídios para uma bibliografia 329
Nutritional levels 302, 307, 310, 561
Nwafor, A. 400
Nyaggah, M. 563
Nyanja people 228, 235
  cults 286
  songs 654
Nyanja-Sena languages 236, 238, 240, 247–255
Nyasaland 111, 217
  frontier agreement (1954) 56
  see also Malawi
nyau dance-theatre 646, 673
Nyungwe language 264

O

OAU – Organization of African Unity 24, 713
  Liberation Committee 643
A obra hidroagrícola do Baixo Limpopo: medidas a adoptar para o seu desenvolvimento 493
Oceanography 80, 548
Ocua 691
Office of Mass Communications *see* GCS
Ogawa, T. 669
Ogot, B. A. 96, 99

Oil, 51, 464
  pollution 550
O'Keefe, P. 310, 550
O'Laughlin, B. 492, 592
Olifants' River 102
Oliveira, E. V. de 223
Oliveira, Mário de 448
Oliveira, Mendes de 673
Oliveira, O. R. de 686
Oliveira, T. M. A. dos S. 152
Oliveira Boleo, J. de 39
Oliveira Figueiredo, R. O. de 507
Oliveira Martins, J. P. 30
Oliveira Torres, F. 554
Olivença 183
Oliver, R. 104
Ollivier, C. 466
O'Meara, D. 437
O'Meara, P. M. 408
Omenana 400
Omer-Cooper, J. D. 104, 160
OMM – Mozambican Women's Organization 21, 299, 335–337, 578
  Extraordinary Conference (1985) 336–337, 675
  health care 306
OMS *see* WHO
One hundred years of Chewa in writing: a select bibliography 249
ONP – National Union of Teachers 39
Opello, W. C., Jr 197–198
Open University 295, 325
Operation Gordian Knot 189
Opium Company 30
Oporto University
  Faculty of Medicine 554
Oral sources 152, 158, 185, 281, 294–295, 526–527
Organic Charter and Overseas Administrative Reform (1836) 162
Organization of African Unity – OAU 24, 713
  Liberation Committee 643
Organization of Mozambican Workers – OTM 533
O oriente africano português: síntese cronológica da história de Moçambique 162
Origens do colonialismo português moderno 107

339

Origins of migrant labour from Mozambique to South Africa, with special reference to the Delagoa Bay hinterland, ca. 1860–1897 513
Ornelas, A. de 380
Ornithology *see* Birds
Oslo 494
OTM – Organization of Mozambican Workers 533
OUA *see* OAU
Out of underdevelopment to socialism: report of the Central Committee 405
Outline of Mahiva grammar 273
Outline of Makua grammar 246
Ouwehand, M. 260
Overseas Council 448
Overseas Historical Archive 153, 683
Owen, Captain William 159, 168, 421

P

Pacheleke, C. 128, 688
Pacific Ocean 551
'Pacification' campaigns 390
Paediatrics 301
PAFMECA – Pan-African Movement for East and Central Africa 180
Painting 646, 664, 668, 671
País emerso 629
Paiva, F. M. F. de 493
Paixão, B. 581
Paixão, E. 616
Palace-Museum of St. Paul 689
Palaeontology 548
Paleoclimatic significance of petrografic [sic] composition of Olifants' river terraces coarse deposits in Massingir 102
Palgrave, K. C. 75
Palm oil 478
palmatória 18
Palmer, E. 76
Palmer, R. 340
Pammenter, N. W. 547
Pan-African Movement for East and Central Africa – PAFMECA 180
Panorama de educação em Moçambique, 1973 579
Panorama do ensino na Província de Moçambique 579

Papagno, G. 150
Papua New Guinea
    PHC 322
Para a história da arte militar moçambicana, 1505–1920 161
Para uma caracterização da linguagem poética de José Craveirinha 618
Parágrafos de literatura ultramarina 602
Paralelo 20 623
Paramedical training 308, 310
Parasites 308
Pardal, J. da C. 22
Paris 157, 305
    UNESCO (1969) 106
Parreira, A. A. 251
Parsons, N. 340
Parsons, Talcott 197
Partido Frelimo *see* Frelimo Party
Party School 359
Pastoralism 91
Paternalism 626
Paton, A. 291
Patraquim, L. C. 17, 615, 634–635, 668
Paula e Silva, R. de 80
Pearson, J. D. 724
Peasant consciousness and guerrilla war in Zimbabwe: a comparative study 158
Peasantry 20, 295, 391–392, 476, 498, 525, 527, 530
    female 335
    imported 379
    Inhambane 164
Peasants and rural economy in Mozambique 503
Pegado e Silva, J. R. de O. 153
Peires, J. B. 139
Pélissier, R. 35, 106, 119, 154, 723
Pemba 59
    see also Porto Amélia
Pena, A. 17
Penetração e impacto do capital mercantil português em Moçambique nos séculos XVI e XVII: o caso de Muenemutapa 132, 151, 157
Penvenne, J. M. 16, 155, 189, 338, 355, 520, 528–530, 694
People 2, 733
    reed-townships 292
People's Assembly 298, 366, 374, 400,

340

341

346

351

353

354

W

Wallerstein, I. 163, 186
Wallerstein collection
  FRELIMO documents 186
Wallis, J. P. R. 38
Wallwork, J. F. 165
Walt, G. 324–326
Wardman, A. 501
Warhurst, P. R. 429
Warsaw University 240
Washington, DC 307, 418, 711
Wasteland in Mashonaland 22
Water resources 553
  Zambezi 20
Water supply 393, 487, 513
  Beira 292
  and health 310
Watts, G. 311, 327
We killed mangy-dog, and other stories
  624
We're building the new school: diary of
  a teacher in Mozambique 586
Wealth 126
Webb, C. 326
Weber, P. 46
Webster, D. J. 523
Weimer, B. 417, 720
Weinstein, L. H. 677
Welch, Revd S. R. 114
WENELA – Witwatersrand Native
  Labour Association 521, 688
Werger, M. J. A. 557
West Germany 312, 417, 430
  relations with Mozambique 425
West Indies 296
Western Europe 118, 663
Western media 333, 349
Western Sahara 408
Westman, B. 28
What to do when the doctors leave 311,
  327
Wheeler, D. L. 160, 170
When bullets begin to flower: poems of
  resistance from Angola,
  Mozambique and Guiné 621, 638
Whitaker, P. M. 123
White, C. B. 171
White, C. P. 502
White, Eduardo 603
White, L. 119, 169, 355, 500, 660
Whiteley, W. H. 274

Whites 207, 209
WHO – World Health Organization
  322
  Bulletin 332
Whooping cough 308
Wieland, T. K. 4
Wield, D. 20, 325, 363, 462, 599
Wild animals 57
Wildlife 489, 552
  conservation 550
Wilkinson, A. R. 182
Williams, J. G. 73, 83–84
Williams, R. 326
Wilson, R. L. 262
Wine 384
  trade 453
Wiriyamu 187–188
Wiriyamu massacre (1972) 187–188,
  199
Wisner, B. 335
Witchcraft 496
Witwatersrand Native Labour
  Association – WENELA 521, 688
Witwatersrand University,
  Johannesburg 266, 353, 558
  Zoology Department 552
Wolfers, M. 399
Women 10–11, 17, 126, 334–340, 357,
  399–400, 500, 502, 527
  education 578
  peasant 295, 335
    and family planning 299
  as producers 335
  release from agricultural labour 139
Women in transition: southern
  Mozambique, 1975–6: reflections
  on colonialism, aspirations for
  independence 340
Women's liberation 15
Wood sculptures of the Maconde
  people: album 678
Woodcarving 646–647, 676–680
Woodward, H. W. 246
Word variation in Makua: a phrase
  structure grammar analysis 244
Work songs 295, 519
Worker-peasant alliance 11, 335, 400
Workers of African trade 526
Working class 528–529
  emergence 525
Working papers in southern African
  studies 523

World Bank
Berg Report (1981) 479
World bibliography of African biblio-
graphies 724
World Health 313
World Health Forum 313
World Health Organization – WHO
322
Bulletin 332
World Today 105
World War I 121, 148, 158, 226, 388,
530
German invasion of Mozambique
144
World War II 181, 425
Writings and research on Mozambique,
1975–1980 344
Wuyts, D. 364, 451, 503–504
Wuyts, M. 294, 501

X

Xai-Xai *see* Chai Chai
Xavier, I. C. 127, 134
xibalo see Labour, forced
Xiconhoca 674
Xiconhoca o inimigo 18, 653
Xidimingwana *see* Honwana, D. M.
Xigubo 619, 626
Xitimela 508
Xuva Xita Duma 672
Xylophagous insects 66
Xylophone *see mbila, timbila*

Y

Yale University 123
Wallerstein collection 186
Yana 662
Yao grammar 274
Yao language 236, 238, 240, 264, 267,
269, 274
Yao people 36, 125, 217–218, 221, 232,
235, 367, 452
Yao village: a study in the social
structure of a Nyasaland tribe 218
Os Yaos 217
Yaos. Chiikala cha wayao 217

Yô Mabalane! 18, 625
Yonge, M. 552
Young, S. J. 340
Youth, 19, 399
Yugoslavia 181
Yuphuro 663
Yusufu 87

Z

Zabela 645
Zaire 222, 557
Zambesi prazos *in the 18th century* 150
Zambesi salient: conflict in southern
Africa 201
Zambezi basin 20
Zambezi Development and Settlement
Commission 467
Zambezi expedition of David
Livingstone, 1858–1863 38
Zambezi Mission Inc. 241, 255
Zambezi River 36, 38, 51, 75, 168, 228,
250, 286, 390, 466, 526
water resources 20
Zambezi Valley 30–31, 142–143, 225,
294, 432, 500, 516, 526
flora 65
lingua franca 250
white settlers 467
see also prazos
A Zambézia 30
Zambézia Province 30, 33, 111, 119,
136, 183, 193, 473, 481, 494–495,
688
marketing problems 348
maize 479
Zambia 29, 36, 65, 123, 144, 158, 194,
248, 362, 456, 512
relations with Mozambique 399, 417
Zambia's relations with Malawi,
Botswana, Mozambique,
Zimbabwe and South Africa: an
analysis within the context of
southern Africa 438
ZANU – Zimbabwe African National
Union 196, 297
Zanzibar 263, 643
Zavala 270, 659–660
cooperatives 480, 496
Zezeru 256
zimbabwe 85, 89–92, 95–96

Map of Mozambique

This map shows the more important towns and other features.

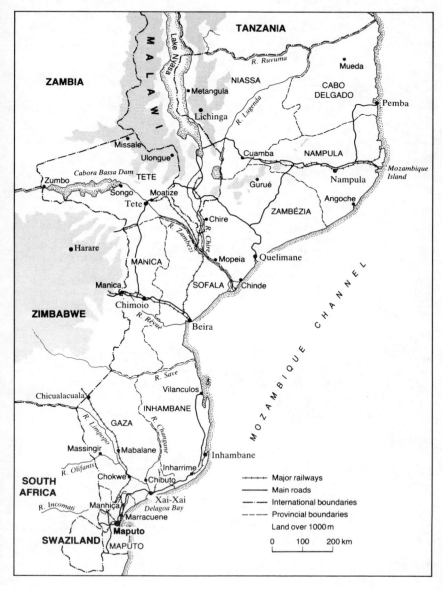